CHELTENHAM:
A NEW HISTORY

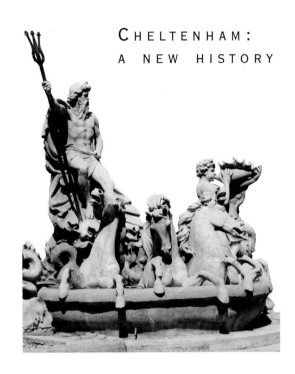

CHELTENHAM
a new history

ANTHEA JONES

CARNEGIE

FOR PETER AND OSCAR,

AND IN MEMORY OF JONATHAN

© Anthea Jones, 2010

First edition

First published in 2010 by Carnegie Publishing Ltd,
Carnegie House,
Chatsworth Road,
Lancaster LA1 4SL
www.carnegiepublishing.com

British Library Cataloguing-in-Publication data
A catalogue record for this book is available from the British Library

ISBN 978-1-85936-154-2   *hardback*

Designed, typeset and originated by Carnegie Publishing
Printed and bound by Butler, Tanner & Dennis, Frome

FRONTISPIECE

View of Cheltenham
from Leckhampton
Court.
PHOTOGRAPH: AUTHOR,
2010

Contents

PREFACE

I N A T O W N of the size and character of Cheltenham, there are many printed accounts of different aspects of its history, buildings and institutions. There have been two substantial histories. In 1868 John Goding published *Norman's History of Cheltenham*. George Norman had been the printer and publisher of the *Cheltenham Examiner*, and it seems that Goding entirely rewrote, rearranged and enlarged an earlier publication, as well as adding eighty-three views in lithography or woodcuts. He wrote of the particular value of a history reviewing 'extraordinary development in the present century'. This was a somewhat disorganised collection of valuable material. Goding lived in the town and knew it well. He was part of the tradition of nineteenth-century town historians such as James Bennett of Tewkesbury, whose *History* of that town was published in 1830, in transcribing and printing documents verbatim to the enormous advantage of anyone following in their footsteps. Goding preserved some sources which appear now to be lost.

Gwen Hart's *History of Cheltenham* in 1965 acknowledged that Goding's book had been a quarry of information for her. Her own book, as well as being better organised and indexed, can be put beside Goding as a major published source of information. She was particularly concerned to trace the history of the government of the town from the manor through the Commissioners appointed under specific Acts of Parliament to the chartered Borough Council, and her book effectively ends when that milestone was passed in 1876.

Each book published on Cheltenham contributes to understanding. Sue Rowbotham and Jill Waller, Steven Blake, former Museum and Collections Manager of Cheltenham Art Gallery and Museum, Robin Brooks, and the Cheltenham Local History Society which commenced publication of a journal in 1983, have added particularly to the published history of the town, and so, too, has Mary Paget to the history of Charlton Kings. Both Charlton Kings and Leckhampton publish local history journals.

This book approaches the history of Cheltenham from a different standpoint. It attempts to unravel the factors that underlie the topography and street plan of the present town. It focuses particularly on questions of land ownership and social and economic structure, comparing these with other Gloucestershire towns, and reveals some unappreciated aspects of this town's history.

INTRODUCTION

ANY VISITOR to Cheltenham appreciates immediately the impression of light which the streets of Regency or early Victorian terraces create, with their facings in white or light-coloured stucco, and the unusual number of well-tended, colourful gardens and parks running through the town which open up long vistas between the buildings towards the hills. Public buildings and institutions also impress. The visitor might be less aware of the narrower streets of later nineteenth-century artisan houses, which were in their way smaller versions of many of the Regency terraces, and might pass through the twentieth-century council developments and the industrial and trading estates around the older core without comment, though these are a significant part of the modern town.

The more energetic explorer will find old village centres on the edge of the suburbs: Charlton Kings, Leckhampton, Prestbury and Swindon, which are separate parishes, and for their inhabitants have distinct identities. Smaller settlements now long subsumed within the borough have left traces in the place-names of the town: Arle, Alstone, Naunton, Sandford and Westal in the historic Cheltenham parish, Bafford and Ham in Charlton Kings, Broadwell in Leckhampton. Behind most viewpoints is the backdrop of the Cotswold escarpment, rising within a few miles to its highest point, 1,000 feet, at Cleeve Hill. Cheltenham farmers had only a narrow neck of land giving them access to Cotswold hill pasture and woodland, and the town is almost entirely in the wide valley of the Severn; its easiest communications were northwards to Tewkesbury and westwards to Gloucester. Cheltenham could not become 'the gateway to the Cotswolds' until the road improvements by turnpike commissioners in the eighteenth and early nineteenth century made the ways onto the hills less difficult.

There have been three or perhaps four phases in Cheltenham's history. What came before William the Conqueror's great survey of his new kingdom in 1086 is not known, but at that time Cheltenham was like thousands of other places throughout the country – a settlement of people cultivating the land. The history of medieval manors may not appear relevant to the modern, busy town, but the topography of development was shaped and moulded by patterns of land ownership established long before the modern town began to grow.

The first major change in Cheltenham's fortunes was the creation there of a market town, possibly in the early thirteenth century, which for hundreds of years gave it a distinctive

1

character in addition to essential agricultural activity. This development has been unjustly neglected, for it has had an important long-term influence on the shape of Cheltenham today. The visit of George III in 1788 to drink the waters, and the dramatic pace of development in the early nineteenth century, have tended to obscure the earlier nature of the town, and to overshadow what had gone before. Cheltenham ranked among the larger market towns in Gloucestershire during the seventeenth century, only the city of Gloucester and the parliamentary boroughs of Cirencester and Tewkesbury being larger and more varied in economic structure.

A significant development was under way before the king's visit. For perhaps a hundred years or more, Cheltenham was acquiring something of the character of a residential centre for the more affluent. Captain Skillicorne, who effectively inaugurated the spa, and is the subject of possibly the longest church monumental inscription in the country, built on this feature of the small town. People came to Cheltenham to enjoy country life combined with an urban environment, and to escape London in the summer with its notorious unhealthiness. Some came to live there permanently. It became notably attractive to single women of means. Though not yet overtaking Gloucester or Tewkesbury, the foundations of a town with a difference were laid.

The population of England and Wales grew at an unprecedented rate in the late eighteenth and early nineteenth centuries, and Cheltenham faster than most. The increasing number of affluent people wanted houses, lodging houses for the summer, servants, and services. Cheltenham flourished on this basis. The female population outweighed the male by a considerable factor. In the short space of fifty years, from the end of the eighteenth century, Cheltenham changed from a market town serving an extensive agricultural manor and parish and its hinterland to a large residential spa. In 1801 the population of Cheltenham parish was 3,076, and of the four surrounding parishes another 1,556; by 1851, Cheltenham had grown to 35,051, and the four other parishes to 6,858. Cheltenham had increased ten-fold, while the population of England and Wales had only doubled in the same period.

During the next hundred years, Cheltenham's rate of growth slowed; in 1891 the borough's population had reached 42,914 and the surrounding parishes, which might by then be termed suburbs, 9,223. From this time the borough boundaries were gradually enlarged to take in parts of surrounding parishes, as suburban development gathered pace and the built-up area spread outwards. In 1931 the population of Cheltenham Borough was 49,418, but thereafter diversification of the economy brought with it renewed rapid expansion. At the 2001 census Cheltenham Borough had 110,000 people, making it the equal of Gloucester as by far the largest urban areas in present-day Gloucestershire.

The last stage in the history of Cheltenham has been a change of focus in the twentieth century. The old lifestyle of the affluent largely collapsed after the First World War, there was much unemployment in Cheltenham, and the borough council, which in 1876 had acquired the status given by a royal charter, worked hard to attract industry, and to raise the standard of housing in the borough. A number of firms found Cheltenham a convenient and suitable place for their headquarters and offices. The establishment of GCHQ in the town solidified this trend.

There are many well-worked images of Cheltenham. In the twenty-first century the name may resonate with the Gold Cup, the Festivals: Literature, Music, Science, Jazz; with GCHQ or with Cheltenham Ladies' College, which is notable not only for girls' education but not least because it occupies the site of the first Royal Well, where George III drank the waters in his fruitless search for health. As a conservation area, it is 'Regency Cheltenham' that provides a potent image, and for the holiday-maker it is 'the gateway to the Cotswolds'. All these are valid images, but there is much more to the variety and vibrancy of the town's economic life, and to the story of its centuries of development.

From many angles the former Eagle Star tower (*right*) is a focal point in the view of Cheltenham. When it was first built it was considered intrusive, but it does blend Cotswold stone colouring with simple lines, and was symbolic of the revitalisation of the town's economy after the Second World War. Cheltenham College chapel (*left*) is a more traditional landmark, built at the end of the nineteenth century in an architectural style redolent of the late medieval Perpendicular, emulating the older universities, just as St Paul's Training College had done earlier. This very successful school was founded in 1840, and established on its present site in Sandford three years later. The school is fortunate in a substantial endowment of playing fields, including this splendid cricket ground used annually for the Gloucestershire Cricket Festival, which started in 1872.

PHOTOGRAPH: AUTHOR, 2009

This mid-nineteenth-century painting by an unknown artist shows the commanding view of Cheltenham from
Leckhampton hill and also the small size of the settlement at that time. The Cheltenham hundred boundaries
were probably decided upon from such vantage points. Leckhampton Hill was appreciated greatly by the town's
inhabitants, as well as being used by visitors for recreation.

CHAPTER ONE

TERRITORY

C HELTENHAM was more than just a village even in the early medieval period. There are two pointers to its being of more than average importance. It was the subject of the first entry in the Gloucestershire section of Domesday Book, compiled in 1086, under the heading *Terra Regis*, land of the king, which in each county followed a description of the shire town. In Gloucestershire, the county town was described first in some detail, and then briefly a number of royal holdings in Wales and Monmouthshire, followed by the borough of Winchcombe, which had once been the capital of a small shire but had been amalgamated with Gloucestershire before the Norman Conquest. Cheltenham was therefore an important manor. It was also the centre of a Domesday 'hundred'. At the same time it was the name of a small unit within the hundred called a vill, or township. Throughout his kingdom the king's authority was exercised through the sheriff of each county, who had authority over each hundred, and within a hundred over individual communities through the reeve of each vill. The reeve, the priest and six men from each vill provided or checked the information which was to be entered in Domesday Book. Finally, Cheltenham was the name of a parish. The areas of these administrative units overlapped, but their boundaries were very different.

THE CHELTENHAM HUNDRED

The hundreds were the administrative areas, beneath the level of the counties, into which most of the different kingdoms of England were organised by the time that they were forged into one state in the tenth century. Once established, the geography of the hundreds endured with few modifications into the nineteenth century.[1] The system was probably introduced as early as the eighth century in Wessex but in the mid-tenth century in the Midland shires. Each hundred originally contained 100 units which, as Domesday Book shows, over the southern counties were called 'hides' but in the former Danelaw counties, 'carucates' or ploughlands. The system of Midland shires, each based on one defended town, was organised in the early years of the eleventh century, and Gloucestershire was defined at this time, although it was enlarged about 1017 by the addition of Winchcombeshire. The Domesday survey suggests those shires had been assessed at round numbers of hides, which were then divided between the constituent settlements of the hundred. In the south, the units were less regular. Hides and carucates were both measures of tax liability and did not describe exact amounts of land, though each may have approximated to 120 acres of arable or ploughed land (in other words, an area which could, or did, support an extended 'family'). The hide was divided into four quarters, called in Latin 'virgates' or in English 'yardlands'. A newer assessment, the 'plough', was also being used by Domesday commissioners. Normally there were more ploughs than hides or carucates in Domesday's accounts.

In Domesday Book, Cheltenham hundred was assessed at 30 hides; estates of similar size occur quite frequently during the Anglo-Saxon period.[2] The hundred comprised Cheltenham itself and the named settlements of Prestbury, Leckhampton and Swindon. To the north was a second 30-hide unit, named Cleeve, later Bishops Cleeve, attached to which were Southam, Gotherington and Stoke (now Stoke Orchard) and 'Sapleton' or Sapperton, a place-name which is now lost but was in the parish of Bishops Cleeve. This manor belonged to the bishop

At the time of the Domesday Book survey in 1086, and for some 150 years after, Cheltenham hundred was a fairly regular oblong of territory, before Prestbury was transferred to Deerhurst hundred. The Anglo-Saxons, or possibly those from an even earlier period, showed an impressive ability to define such territories without the benefit of maps. They made use of natural features where possible, and of field boundaries and old roads. Here, they might well have stood on the top of the Cotswold scarp to gain an impression of the land below. It is interesting that so many of the churches are dedicated to St Mary, and perhaps all were made parish churches at the same time, whereas Leckhampton's church, dedicated to St Peter, might make a claim to have been the original 'chief' church of the manor.

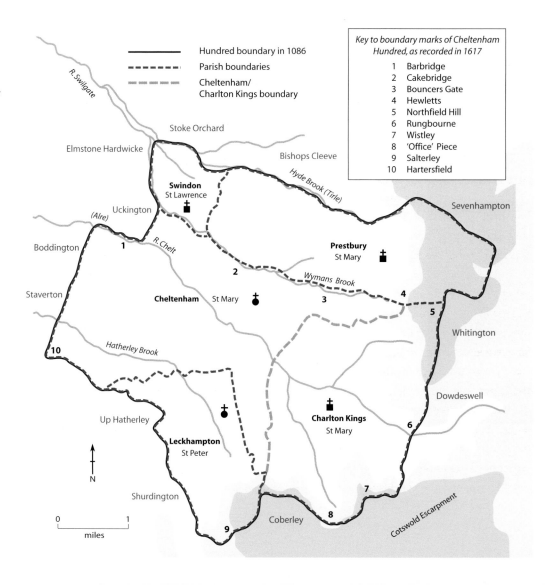

Key to boundary marks of Cheltenham
Hundred, as recorded in 1617

1   Barbridge
2   Cakebridge
3   Bouncers Gate
4   Hewletts
5   Northfield Hill
6   Rungbourne
7   Wistley
8   'Office' Piece
9   Salterley
10 Hartersfield

of Worcester, and was in Tibblestone hundred, named from the marker for the outdoor meeting place of the men of the hundred. Another 30-hide unit in Gloucestershire was the manor of Westbury, also belonging to the king. To judge from how central Cheltenham is within its hundred, and the comparatively simple line of its boundary, this 30-hide unit had coherence and possibly predated the creation of the hundred itself. In other words, it might represent a much older territorial unit adapted in the pre-Conquest period for administrative purposes.[3]

It was not unusual for a man's land to be identified by reference to the hundred in which it lay, rather than to a place-name pinpointing it more exactly. In Dorset a nice example concerns the manors in the Piddle or Puddle valley, where no fewer than thirteen were called 'Puddle' in Domesday Book, though a variety of alternative place-names might have been used. A similar method of identifying an estate could have been used at a meeting of bishops at *Clofesho* in 803, in discussing a dispute between the bishops of Hereford and of Worcester. Gloucestershire was in the diocese of Worcester until the Reformation. It was recorded that the two monasteries of Beckford and Cheltenham had been given to the bishop of Hereford, but the bishop of Worcester claimed that they ought still to pay some tax to him, their share of his *refectum* or cost of his daily living. The archbishop of Canterbury asked Deneberht, bishop of Worcester, to give up half – in other words, to share it equally with Hereford – and he agreed; each church would pay him the due amount every other year.[4] This record is the reason for the suggestion that there was a 'monastery' in Cheltenham, long before the Domesday reference to a church there and priests with their two ploughs.

The word *monasterium* as used in the ninth century is best translated as 'minster', because that word gives less of an impression of an enclosed community of monks on the pattern of later monasteries. A 'minster' was a collegiate church, rather than a monastery. It would have had a number of priests and deacons ministering to a large parish and evangelising the surrounding area – the term 'mother church' is often used to describe this role. As Cheltenham was the name of the hundred, was the monastery referred to actually in Cheltenham township or in Cheltenham hundred? Could the monastery have been at Prestbury which, as its name informs us, was a 'priest's manor'? Prestbury manor and church at the time of Domesday and for five centuries afterwards belonged to the bishop of Hereford, one of the parties to the dispute at *Clofesho*.[5] If Prestbury were at first the church for the 30-hide estate of Cheltenham, its position would have been comparable with another Prestbury, the one in Cheshire which was the parish church for the town and borough of Macclesfield and its ancient hundred.[6] On the other hand it was the regular practice for a minster church to be sited in or near each of the king's hundredal manors.[7] Political considerations often underlay gifts of land to churches in the Anglo-Saxon period, and the organisation of dioceses and of hundreds. The gift of the priests' manor of Prestbury to Hereford could have been made to compensate for some aspect of diocesan organisation. What is known about Cheltenham church in the early twelfth century supports the conclusion that it was the minster church.

Prestbury was later transferred from Cheltenham hundred to Deerhurst hundred. In 1247, the administration and revenues of Cheltenham hundred were given by the king to the Norman monastery of Fécamp, on the Channel coast north of Le Havre. This move may have prompted the bishop of Hereford to negotiate the separation of his Prestbury manor from Cheltenham hundred,[8] because no bishop would want his estates under the control of another ecclesiastical institution. The bishop was able to attach Prestbury to a hundred which was close to his other estates (though not contiguous). Other examples show how an important man, with royal permission, could form a hundred to bring scattered estates under his own control; an excellent example is provided by the bishops of Worcester, with the constituents of their hundred scattered through Worcestershire and Gloucestershire. To more logical nineteenth-century eyes, these seemed irrational arrangements, and they were gradually reformed. But Prestbury remained part of Deerhurst hundred, even as the hundreds themselves became obsolete in the nineteenth century.

TITHING AND TOWNSHIP

The hundred had a number of functions. The free men of the area met for a hundred court held every four weeks, dealing with justice and disputes between members, with thieves and petty offenders and, especially, with taxation. For the purposes of exercising justice, the hundred was divided into small groups of men who were made responsible for each other's good behaviour. Nominally there were ten or twelve men in each group, which was known as a 'tithing' (from the Anglo-Saxon word for 'ten'). As early as the mid-tenth century the 'man over the tithing' was responsible for checking on possible thefts, and as the system developed the tithing became a geographical area – a sub-division of the hundred. By the early twelfth century each tithing was reviewed by the sheriff twice a year to confirm that it was 'full', at meetings known as 'view of frankpledge'. Frankpledge means 'free pledge', which is explained as 'free engagement of neighbour for neighbour' (instead of the lord or the kindred being responsible for dealing with criminal behaviour). In theory every man over the age of 12 years who had been resident for a year and a day should have attended, though there were certain exceptions such as knights, clergy and servants; in practice often only the headmen of the tithings attended. The custom of the area and of the hundred was always respected, and could vary substantially from place to place.[9]

Fines for misdemeanours, and a customary payment from each tithing called *cert money* or *tithing penny*, meant that control of the hundred had financial benefits. The king sometimes chose to grant a hundred to a favoured courtier or to a church. Possession of Cheltenham hundred was customarily attached to the manor of Cheltenham. As a consequence, the manor court which met every three weeks also acted intermittently as the hundred court, and both were granted to the abbey of Fécamp in 1247. The functions of tithings in administering justice within the hundred declined with the gradual introduction of itinerant judges, and the steady increase in the powers of royal courts of law and county justices. Nonetheless,

for centuries hundred courts continued to be held in the name of successive manorial lords, and they collected the money paid by the tithings. From at least the early fourteenth century, when the first manor court records are extant, there were ten tithings in Cheltenham hundred represented at the view of frankpledge: Cheltenham vill and the bailiff of the borough, Alstone, Arle, Westal with Naunton and Sandford, Ashley, Bafford, Charlton, Broadwell, Leckhampton and Swindon.[10]

Tithings continued in use into the seventeenth century for taxation purposes, and into the nineteenth century as practical sub-divisions for the everyday administration of a large parish. Thus, until the early nineteenth century, five churchwardens were customarily chosen in Cheltenham: two for Cheltenham township, one for each for Alstone and Arle, and one for Westal, Naunton and Sandford combined.[11] Even later in the nineteenth century the tithings were still in use in the administration of the poor law.

'Township' was an Anglo-Saxon term; its Latin equivalent was 'vill'. Many were of ancient origin and formed largely self-sufficient agricultural territories. They reflected early division of the countryside, to provide groups of farmers with a fair share of the variety of natural resources of the area: arable land (both good and bad), pasture, meadow and wood. In Gloucestershire, the system of agriculture was not generally based on dispersed and separate farms but, over large areas, was the communal or cooperative one of common arable fields split into numerous long narrow strips, where each holding was allocated land dispersed through the township. The easily worked and fertile sandy soil of Cheltenham township was bordered by low-lying meadow in some directions and by hill pasture on the Cotswolds, so over the estate as a whole there was a good variety of soil and situation. The sandy soil,

As its name probably indicates, Cheltenham was notable for the water meadow or *hamm*. The Chelt rarely covers the old flood plain, thanks to canalising, culverting, and other large flood defence works, but in 2007 the river rose suddenly and dramatically, and flooded this Sandford Park area and much else of Cheltenham, too. Sandford tithing was named from the crossing point of this normally modest river, and Sandford mill is just a short distance upstream from here.
© MARY NELSON, 2007

though a relatively small patch, was some of the county's best agricultural land: regrettably, in some ways, most was lost in the nineteenth and twentieth centuries to the onwards march of bricks and mortar.[12]

Townships were often, but not always, coincident with tithings. Sometimes they were too small for the purposes of frankpledge or of raising and collecting taxes. In such instances two or more townships were combined to form a tithing or vill, and the individual townships were then designated 'hamlets'. For this reason, in Cheltenham hundred there were more townships than the tithings named in the view of frankpledge. For example, in a taxation list for 1327 Ham and Northfield were also named as vills, but were combined with Charlton township in a tithing.

Cheltenham might possibly have been termed a *villa regalis*, that is a vill which provided the framework for royal administration. There is no record of any Anglo-Saxon king summoning his lords to a meeting in Cheltenham, or of a royal palace there; probably there was no need for one so close to Gloucester, where the first two Norman kings built a castle to replace the palace at Kingsholm and spent Christmas on at least five occasions.[13] Cheltenham is not included in the list of Anglo-Saxon royal vills which was compiled by Peter Sawyer,[14] but there is good circumstantial evidence for thinking that it might have had that status before the time of Edward the Confessor.

It is very significant that, in Domesday, Cheltenham matched Cirencester in the payments that it was obliged to make to the king, and also the manor of Barton Regis which was absorbed into Bristol.[15] Cirencester was clearly established as a royal vill: it was the capital of a small kingdom in 577 and its capture was important in the early history of the Anglo-Saxon conquests. It was the scene of another battle in 628, also recorded in the *Anglo-Saxon Chronicle*, and assemblies were held there on three occasions in the tenth century, and again in 1020. The renders (money due to the king) from both Cheltenham and Cirencester in the time of Edward the Confessor consisted of £9 6s. in money and 30 loaves of bread for dogs; in addition Cirencester provided some wheat, malt and honey. In both places the provision of loaves for dogs had been commuted to a payment of 16s. by 1086, when both places paid King William £20 (with an extra 5s. from Cirencester) and 20 cows and 20 pigs. Cheltenham did not develop as a thriving urban centre as rapidly as Cirencester, which perhaps reflected the encouraging presence from 1133 of an Augustinian abbey at the latter. But its equivalent status at the time of the Conquest is surely revealed by the remarkable similarity of the payments due.

One or more townships, or even just a part of a township, might constitute a manor and also a parish. Although the parish was given additional administrative tasks, especially from the mid-sixteenth century onwards, the ancient townships continued to be relevant to the operation of open-field systems and for the collection of the tithes due to the church. Over the centuries, as different forms of local organisation were imposed on the countryside, the relationships between parish, manor, tithing and township became very complicated, a process well demonstrated in Cheltenham hundred.

Manors

To identify geographical location the Domesday commissioners used vills, or townships, but in describing legal status and landholding they thought in terms of manors. A manor was a territory under the ownership, general supervision and control of a lord, often an absentee. Some manors were tiny, formed of a single small independent estate; others, like Cheltenham, were very large and comprised aggregations of several vills. Their origins are still the subject of considerable debate among historians, but it is clear that in southern and midland England they may have been developing two or three centuries before the Norman Conquest. Thus, Danegeld, a national tax probably first imposed by Ethelred II in 991 to buy off the Danish raiders, was paid at the manor, though it was collected by the reeve of each vill.[16] In 1086 Cheltenham hundred was divided into five manors: Cheltenham, Prestbury, Swindon, and two manors in Leckhampton (though by 1086 two manors which had existed there twenty years earlier had been combined).

The lord of the manor normally had his own land in the manor, called his demesne or home farm (and later categorised as 'freehold'). However, most of the land of the manor was held from the lord by tenants, including those who held freely (that is, without having obligations to work for the lord on his demesne). Freeholdings were not very numerous in Gloucestershire in the eleventh century; in Cheltenham hundred there were just three: two belonged to the church, one in Cheltenham and one in Prestbury, and there was a second small freehold in Prestbury. Most inhabitants of the manor were *villeins* or *bordars*, most easily translated as villagers and smallholders. They had to work for the lord for a certain amount of time each year, providing him with a labour force. Their independence was limited by the custom of the manor, and though their legal status gradually became more clearly defined over the ensuing three centuries, it also tended to become less favourable. Cheltenham was classed as 'ancient demesne', that is a manor belonging to the king in 1066, and here, as in other such instances, the villeins probably acquired a more favourable legal position than those in ordinary manors. There were also slaves in early Norman England, although even at the time of the Conquest their status was gradually being changed from slavery to that of tightly controlled tenants (or bondsmen) working small plots of land. Domesday records that this had happened at nearby Hailes before 1086.

The Domesday survey was undertaken primarily to confirm who were the landholders in the kingdom, twenty years after the Conquest. However, it also facilitated more efficient tax collection, with the introduction of an up-to-date method of assessment using cultivated land or 'ploughs' instead of hides. In the whole hundred of Cheltenham there were 89 landholders, excluding lords of the manor, and 29 slaves. The number of ploughs, 54, was nearly double the number of hides, suggesting that a great deal more land was under cultivation than had been the case at an earlier time when hides were assessed (and when, as a rule of thumb, there was one plough per hide). The statistics for each manor are given in the table below:

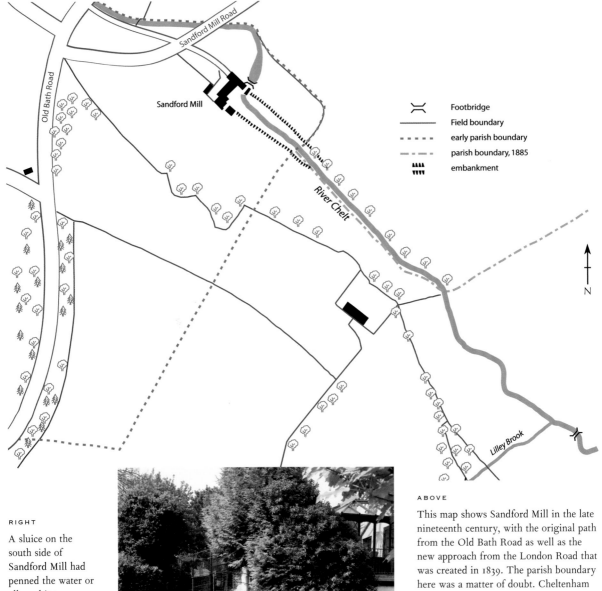

Footbridge
Field boundary
early parish boundary
parish boundary, 1885
embankment

Sandford Mill

Old Bath Road

Sandford Mill Road

River Chelt

Lilley Brook

N

A sluice on the south side of Sandford Mill had penned the water or allowed it to pass over several small waterfalls and along a short channel back to the river's natural course. By the early twentieth century the pond had been drained and the water canalised so that it all ran through the sluice and over the series of rapids to continue along its old course.

PHOTOGRAPH: AUTHOR, 2009

This map shows Sandford Mill in the late nineteenth century, with the original path from the Old Bath Road as well as the new approach from the London Road that was created in 1839. The parish boundary here was a matter of doubt. Cheltenham Vestry in 1823 concluded that it left the Old Bath Road to go round the mill, but Charlton Kings Vestry in 1831 sent walkers through the mill itself; probably they assumed that the mill pond and tail race constituted the river Chelt, and so formed part of the boundary. However, the meanders of the river had been bypassed to supply the mill, and the water was confined between substantial banks to create a pond. The Ordnance Survey plotted the parish boundary along a ditch north of the mill, approximating to the river's earlier course, but later the boundary was moved to accommodate the new Holy Apostles' church in Charlton Kings.

Cheltenham hundred in Domesday Book

Manor	Hides	Ploughs	Tenants	Slaves
Cheltenham	10	24	36	7
Leckhampton	7	7	19	7
Prestbury	10	14	25	11
Swindon	3	9	9	4
Totals	30	54	89	29

In the manor of Cheltenham 22 of the ploughs were on the 8½ hides belonging to the king – 3 were on his own land, the royal demesne, 18 on the holdings of 36 villagers and smallholders, and 2 on the holdings of the 'priests'. The church in Cheltenham had 1½ hides, held by Regenbald, one of the king's important clerical servants. There were seven slaves and five mills. The land must surely have been cultivated by labourers about whom Domesday Book is silent. King William's reeve held the manor of Cheltenham, which he had enlarged

In June 1824 the *Gentleman's Magazine* published an engraving of Prestbury church in order to encourage 'the wealthy and the gay' from the Metropolis – who at that time of year were coming to the fashionable town of Cheltenham – to visit Prestbury. The correspondent, E.J.S., wrote of the 'unrivalled prospect' the church commanded, 'embosomed in orchards'. He commented that it was a 'low building', though with an interesting tower. The lower two stages of the tower are thirteenth-century, and there is no obviously earlier fabric. A major restoration was carried out by G. E. Street between 1864 and 1868, substantially altering the appearance of this south side. The Priory is shown on the left-hand side.

BY COURTESY OF ERIC MILLER

by adding another plough, two small-holders, four villagers and three mills (two were the king's and one the reeve's) which indicates his power to alter administrative boundaries. He had either reorganised the holdings or he had taken more land into cultivation. It shows the reeve's power and his personal status.[17] A mill was often the reeve's responsibility. It is notable that the king's reeve in King's Barton had added two mills to that manor, and in Thornbury, Old Sodbury, Avening and Tockington the reeves had added one mill. There seems to be some Norman initiative involved.

There is no indication in the Domesday account of Cheltenham of a nascent town, unless the ten smallholders were the forerunners of those traders who became established on Cheltenham market in the thirteenth century, a process which has been identified in other emergent towns after the Conquest.[18] No reference is made to freehold plots, to burgages (the distinctive form of landholding in urban areas), or to a market. Winchcombe, a few miles away, was termed a borough (a fairly uncommon designation in Domesday Book) and a survey by Evesham Abbey at about the same date recorded 151 burgages there.[19] Tewkesbury and Cirencester were not called boroughs, but in both places Domesday noted the existence of a market. These three places were already much more obviously urban communities than Cheltenham and would remain so for several centuries.

Prestbury and Swindon were ecclesiastical manors, which meant that with Regenbald's land in Cheltenham manor the church held just over half the hides in the hundred. Prestbury was held by the bishop of Hereford, and was linked with Sevenhampton which stretched eastwards from Cleeve hill as Prestbury stretched westwards. Its ten hides were cultivated by 23 tenants and two freeholders (one of whom was the priest) with 14 ploughs between them; the bishop had 11 slaves. There was a large tract of woodland here, for the Cotswold scarp was still substantially tree-covered at this date. Swindon was held by Archbishop Thomas of York as tenant of the church of St Oswald in Gloucester. Two of the nine ploughs were on the lord's demesne; nine villagers and smallholders were the tenants of the manor; and there were four slaves.

The seven hides in Leckhampton were divided into two manors, later called the manors of Leckhampton and Broadwell, which remained distinct until the sixteenth century. The nineteen tenants in 1086 had between them seven ploughs and seven slaves. There was a small amount of woodland here, almost certainly on the slopes of the hill. The possible existence of a third Leckhampton manor in Domesday has been much discussed. However, its name was spelled *Lechetone*, quite different from *Lechantone* and *Lechametone* which can unquestionably be identified with modern Leckhampton. Records of early forms of the name do not support the identification of *Lechetone* with Leckhampton, while Domesday arithmetic of the total hides in each place, as well as the form of the name, suggest in fact this entry refers to Latton near Cricklade, which is now in Wiltshire.[20] The freehold estates in Leckhampton were further divided after 1086, giving rise to several independent substantial landholders,[21] and some of the demesne land of the royal manor of Cheltenham was in fact in Leckhampton.

There is no mention in Domesday Book, or in any surviving Anglo-Saxon source, of Charlton Kings, which was a major subdivision of Cheltenham manor and also became a parish. There is no record of the name earlier than 1187, but it is an Anglo-Saxon name and refers to a settlement of *ceorls*. *Ceorl*, or churl, has since acquired the sense of 'rough', but in the Anglo-Saxon period it was a legal term referring to all those below noble rank and above that of slave – though its usual implication is that of the lowest rank of freeholder, someone of moderate status. If he had a hide of land he was nearer to the later yeoman than to a crofter;[22] with less land he would be a villein or villager, tied to his landholding under a lord, but not a slave. Later he might be called a husbandman.

Significantly, the word *ceorl* does not occur in place-names with the suffix 'ham', which normally marked a prestigious and ancient manor. H.P.R. Finberg carried out a study of the 56 places called Charlton (including variations in spelling and pronunciation) which are named in Domesday Book or earlier documents.[23] It was striking that many appeared as 'satellites' of other manors and, in a good proportion of these cases, of a royal manor. He discussed Charlton Kings as one of ten similar post-Domesday names and concluded that the Charltons were settlements of the lord's own husbandmen, near the administrative centre of his estate where his hall would have been. Finberg specifically used Cheltenham as his example of the process he envisaged: a gradual granting away of estates or manors from a larger original unit, as happened with Leckhampton, Prestbury and Swindon, while the king kept Charlton longest in his lordship. 'Kings' was a later suffix to distinguish it from Charlton Abbots, another good example of Finberg's argument; Charlton Abbots was a satellite of the king's manor and borough of Winchcombe. Looking at the entry for Cheltenham, therefore, it seems certain that some of the 24 villagers noted were resident in Charlton Kings.

Charlton Kings fits into the pattern of a multiple estate, a large unit of landholding which embraced a variety of different smaller units, each with a specialised or distinct role. Thus, in the multiple estate of Cheltenham in the eleventh century, Leckhampton was the 'place where leeks (or garlic or herbs) were cultivated', and hence was the manor's 'kitchen garden';[24] Prestbury was 'the priests' place'; and Swindon, the 'swine pasture' (the 'don' or hill, being slightly higher ground in an otherwise well-watered and low-lying tract of land).

PARISHES

In contrast to the hundreds, the pattern of parishes was not imposed from above in a relatively uniform manner but instead emerged haphazardly. In the earliest period of the conversion of the Anglo-Saxons to Christianity, the diocese of each bishop was roughly that of a separate kingdom. Thus, the bishop of the Hwicce, based in Worcester, had responsibility for the territory which later became Worcestershire and Gloucestershire, and a part of Warwickshire. The origins of the people called the Hwicce are obscure. The lack of early Anglo-Saxon burials in their area could indicate that they were Christian and were not immediately overrun by

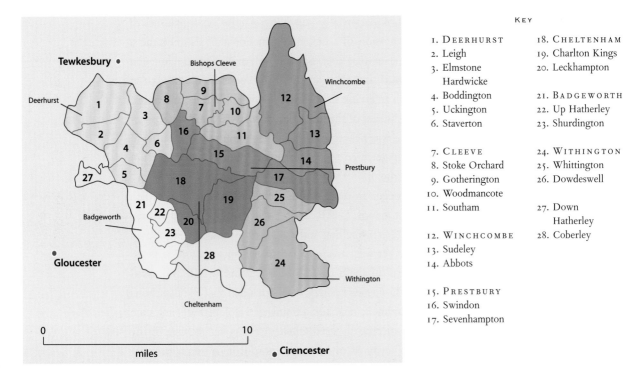

KEY

1. DEERHURST	18. CHELTENHAM
2. Leigh	19. Charlton Kings
3. Elmstone	20. Leckhampton
Hardwicke	
4. Boddington	21. BADGEWORTH
5. Uckington	22. Up Hatherley
6. Staverton	23. Shurdington
7. CLEEVE	24. WITHINGTON
8. Stoke Orchard	25. Whittington
9. Gotherington	26. Dowdeswell
10. Woodmancote	
11. Southam	27. Down
	Hatherley
12. WINCHCOMBE	28. Coberley
13. Sudeley	
14. Abbots	
15. PRESTBURY	
16. Swindon	
17. Sevenhampton	

As the Christian religion was adopted by Anglo-Saxon kings, it is probable that a pattern of 'minster' parishes was established. A minster provided the nucleus for the further conversion and consolidation of the church within a large area, and was staffed by a small community of priests. A minster often had subordinate churches or chapels serving smaller groups of inhabitants. There is evidence in Anglo-Saxon charters, or in later territorial or ecclesiastical relationships, of minster churches at Bishops Cleeve, Deerhurst, Cheltenham (more likely than at Prestbury), Winchcombe and Withington, while Badgeworth church had at least two dependent chapelries and was an estate held by St Peter's, Gloucester, in the ninth century. Only the unusually large parishes of Cheltenham and Winchcombe in later periods reflect the churches' earlier significance; elsewhere smaller parishes were created within the old minster areas.

the invading and pagan Anglo-Saxons. The diocese was created in 679 or 680 and probably preserved the boundaries of the kingdom of the Hwicce until the Reformation, although the kingdom itself disappeared in the eighth century. Winchcombe had been of importance in this kingdom, which explains the brief existence of Winchcombshire.[25]

Each bishop was provided with estates which supported him to a standard comparable with the king's chief ministers, the earls. The Church was closely associated with royal authority and supplied kings with literate administrators. The king, in return, enforced the payment to the church of tithe, a tenth of the produce of fields and gardens, and also the payments from each householder or communicant. For most churches, tithe was a larger source of income than land, and this helps to account for the substantial differences in income between individual churches. The details of which produce paid tithes varied from parish to parish, and over the centuries there were many adjustments. In many Gloucestershire parishes tithes were abolished in the later eighteenth or early nineteenth century, when the land was enclosed by Acts of

The lowest stage of the tower of Cheltenham parish church, St Mary's, is one of the earliest parts of the church, built during the twelfth century. Typical of Norman church design, it separated the nave and the chancel; possibly there were no transepts, although the tower was later pierced with large arches when transepts were either added or enlarged. The tower stairs opened into the church; the blocked-up doorway was in the south-east angle. This suggests its original function may have been defensive.

PHOTOGRAPH: CARNEGIE, 2009

Parliament, and tithe-owners were handsomely compensated. This was to be of considerable importance in Cheltenham.

Gradually local churches were built to serve individual vills or groups of communities, with the duty of converting and baptising the inhabitants, the primary task of the Christian church. Although the foundation dates of many remain completely obscure, or are only known with uncertainty, it is clear that by 1086 churches were very numerous – not least, it was possible to require the priest of each vill to provide information to the Domesday commissioners. These village churches collected some or all local tithes and land was provided for the priest. But once established, a church was likely to be reluctant to lose any area subject to its authority, as this implied also loss of some of the regular payments by parishioners. As further churches were founded, existing ones sought to safeguard their interests. Older parish churches might therefore establish superiority over other churches in their area, denying subordinate churches full parochial status so that they were regarded as chapels and were served by chaplains or curates, paid a stipend and denied the independence of a rector. Such tensions can readily be observed in the Cheltenham area.

Manors and vills were the basis of the emerging parish structure. Powerful lords in the tenth century wished to have their own church and priest and to control payments of tithes. The bishop of Hereford, for example, was well placed to make Prestbury a separate parish at an early date, and similarly the archbishop of Canterbury, who held the manor of Swindon in 1066, could secure its separation as a parish in its own right. Indeed, Swindon parish had possibly been separated from Prestbury, rather than from the king's manor of Cheltenham. In about 900 the bishop of Worcester leased three of the five hides at Elmstone Hardwicke, stating that the other two hides 'shall belong to Prestbury',[26] suggesting that Elmstone Hardwicke then adjoined Prestbury rather than, as it did later on, Swindon. Furthermore, at a later date the bishop of Hereford, lord of Prestbury, held land in Swindon.[27] Between Swindon and Prestbury the boundary skirted around fields, and seems to have cut through land belonging to the original Hyde Farm: two Swindon fields had the name 'Hyde' attached them and a field called 'Stapling' matches two on the Prestbury side of the boundary called 'Stapleton'.[28] A 'staple' was a post, often a boundary post. The bishop of Hereford probably created Hyde Farm after the boundary was fixed, as parishes usually respected the administrative arrangements of territory current when they were defined.

Domesday Book offers only occasional information on ecclesiastical arrangements and geography, but it recorded that Cheltenham church was endowed with 1½ hides of land, and was held by Regenbald, a man described as 'the first great pluralist'. His name is also written as Reginbald or Reinbald, which suggests that he was not an Anglo-Saxon. He was, though, an important figure at court, witnessing a number of Edward the Confessor's charters – the written documents confirming land grants or transfers – and clearly helping to run Edward's administration (though he was not a 'chancellor', as is sometimes suggested) Neither was he a bishop, although Edward specifically conferred on him that *status* but without the title or duties, calling him 'my priest'. Possibly there was a canonical obstacle to him becoming a bishop. After the Norman Conquest, Regenbald quickly offered his support to William and almost at once, in 1067, was confirmed in all his estates. He may briefly have served William as chancellor. He owned the church at Bray in Berkshire and, like another of its vicars many centuries later, no matter which king reigned he retained his position.[29] He was important enough for other men to be identified in Domesday as his relations: his brother held land near Cirencester from Gloucester Abbey, and his son, who also held land in the county, was one of the king's thanes or ministers. He may therefore have settled locally; one Domesday entry calls him 'Regenbald of Cirencester'.

Regenbald's property consisted primarily of nineteen churches, which meant that he was the rector of each, collecting tithes from the parishes and the profits from the lands attached to those churches. As well as Cheltenham and Cirencester, Regenbald held four urban churches, all associated with royal demesne – Frome and Milborne Port in Somerset, and Cookham and Bray in Berkshire. Domesday notes that at Cookham and at Cirencester a market had recently been founded, indicating considerable economic expansion of the estate. At Cirencester, Regenbald either founded a collegiate church with a number of canons, or left his estates after his death for such a foundation. No hint of a collegiate church appears in Domesday but in 1133, when Henry I substituted regular Augustinian canons for secular canons at Cirencester, he endowed them with Regenbald's widespread estates.[30] The original charter of Henry I was lost, in all probability in 1142 when Cirencester castle was burned during the civil wars between Stephen and Matilda. Successive rewritings of the charter later added to the story, giving rise to a number of misconceptions about the antiquity of the collegiate church and the course of events.[31]

EASTERN ARCH UNDER THE TOWER.

In July 1843 the *Gentleman's Magazine* published several architectural drawings of Swindon church prior to the drastic 'restoration' that was being planned, in order to record it before much was swept away. One drawing shows the serious crack in the western face of the tower, and another the Norman eastern archway joining tower and nave. The plan demonstrates that the sides of the tower on the north-west and south-west are longer than on the north-east and south-east. It is also curious to find the entrance to the church through the north-east side of the tower, where it remains. Happily the tower was not seriously altered during the Victorian restorations.

AUTHOR COLLECTION

The basis of the nave and chancel of Swindon church are Norman and the very unusual tower, with its eccentric shape, is also Norman. It almost appears that the builders lost confidence – or lacked the resources – to complete it and closed it as economically as possible, with five unevenly sized walls creating a hexagon smaller than the intended building. The rather drastic restoration of Swindon church took place a little earlier than the other old churches in the area, and was the work of Thomas Fulljames in 1844–46. Massive internal Norman walls and piers were demolished, and much other fabric removed. Fortunately the plan to disguise the shape of the tower by adding a vestry on the south side was not implemented.

PHOTOGRAPH: CARNEGIE, 2010

As one of Regenbald's estates, in 1133 the lands and revenues of the church in Cheltenham passed to Cirencester Abbey, which became the rector of the parish and responsible for appointing priests to serve its inhabitants. The endowment was described in successive charters as the church of the vill and its land, one mill, chapels, and all other things pertaining to a church.[32] Regenbald was not an entrepreneur in Cheltenham's history, as others who owned the rectory were to be. This was to have some importance in the subsequent development of the town, both in respect of the position of the curate of the church, and in the areas of land first available for building development as the Spa began to draw people to the town.

As well as Cheltenham and Prestbury, the parishes of Leckhampton and Swindon in Cheltenham hundred were probably formed around the time of the Norman Conquest. The architecture of the buildings themselves shows that both were stone buildings of the Norman period, and could have replaced older wooden churches. At Leckhampton there is a Norman font, which demonstrates that the church was parochial and had the right to baptise, and the Norman south arcade of the nave survived until its unfortunate destruction in about 1830. At Swindon there is an unusual hexagonal Norman tower and here the massive internal Norman walls and pillars remained until their removal about 1845.

Part of Leckhampton continued to be within the parish of Cheltenham. The church is first documented between 1162 and 1164 in an agreement set out in the Cirencester cartulary (a collection of charters and other documents about rights and title to property).[33] The archbishop of Canterbury adjudicated in a dispute between the abbey and Henry, priest of Leckhampton. The canons claimed Leckhampton church was at law merely a chapel of Cheltenham. Henry accepted this, and agreed to pay the canons 2s. a year for the chapel and for tithes from land held by Geoffrey Cook and Oliver de la Mare which belonged to Cheltenham church. The payment of this sum to Cirencester Abbey was duly noted in the 1291 *Taxatio* of Pope Nicholas, a comprehensive survey of church incomes, but Leckhampton was not designated a chapel. The dispute flared up again in 1303 (or perhaps a monk with an antiquarian turn of mind went through the records and discovered the earlier agreement) and the commissary of the bishop of Worcester, repeating the earlier decision, ruled against John Gamage, rector of Leckhampton, who had claimed independence from Cheltenham. The status of the rector and the parish were not challenged again, but some land in Leckhampton continued to pay tithes to Cirencester.

This Norman-period font at Leckhampton (*left*) is evidence of a parish church here in the late tenth or early eleventh century. A piece of masonry with a consecration cross incised on it has been placed beneath a window, and another with a medieval mass dial (*right*) was incorporated into a buttress on the south side. Mass dials are found on churches dating from the thirteenth to the fifteenth centuries.

PHOTOGRAPHS: CARNEGIE, 2010

George Rowe's drawing of Leckhampton St Peter shows the church before the building work of 1865–66, which involved the removal of much of the fabric, enlargement of the church to the north and west, and rebuilding and resiting of the north porch. John Middleton was the architect, said to be portrayed on a carving in the porch (*opposite page*). The only substantial ancient fabric which then remained was the central tower and spire and the chancel. Prominent in the drawing is the south aisle, which apart from its east wall was completely replaced. Middleton also secured the removal from the churchyard of an ancient stone tomb and was alert to preserving odd items of interest but not in their original context.

BY COURTESY OF ERIC MILLER

These two cases, and the territorial arrangements in Leckhampton, reveal much about the way manor, vill and parish were inter-related, and illustrate the technical importance of the terms 'chapel' and 'church'. An undated note in the Cirencester cartulary details a ploughland in Leckhampton, formerly of John Giffard and said to be 220 acres in extent, which had paid tithes to Cheltenham church and so after Regenbald's bequest, to Cirencester Abbey. The Giffard family were patrons of Leckhampton church and held the chief manor, so had this land been part of Cheltenham manor demesne? It was in two furlongs, named in the cartulary as *Wollfynchewell* [perhaps *Goldfynchewell*] and *Merestowe* [probably Merestone], and in a field towards Moorend and Westal. It therefore abutted the Cheltenham parish boundary. At some time merestones, or boundary stones, had been set out to divide an arable field, the line zigzagging round strips of land. The field-name 'Merestone' has persisted on both sides of the boundary and is still in use in road names.[34]

It is no surprise that Cheltenham parish once had Leckhampton within its territory nor that the king's demesne included land in Leckhampton. But in what circumstances would part of Leckhampton pay tithes to, and be recognised as in, Cheltenham parish, a situation that existed until 1778 when the remaining common fields were enclosed by Act of Parliament? A possible sequence of events would be: first, the division of the existing open fields to create a new vill or township of Leckhampton, allocating to it some land on the hill and some in the valley; second, the creation of manors, each holding land scattered in the common fields; and third, the creation of a parish of Leckhampton at the behest of one or more lords. The church at Leckhampton is placed midway between two probable manor house sites, Leckhampton Court and the moated site which it is supposed may have been associated with Broadwell manor. The parish served those living in the township, but a full ploughland, the substantial holding of one man, had not been included in the new parish, though the land was intermingled with others paying tithes to Leckhampton.

A case has been made that Hatherley and Badgeworth churches were also subject originally to Cheltenham, but this seems much less clear.[35] In 1291 payment of 1s. to Cirencester Abbey is noted from Up Hatherley, a chapel in the parish of Badgeworth. This may be linked with documents in the Cirencester cartulary relating to the difficulty the abbey had in collecting tithes from a particular piece of land in Hatherley. The origin of the dispute seems to lie in a clearing or 'assart' in a wood. Sometime between 1148 and 1167 Osbert, clerk of Hatherley, confessed to Godfrey, archdeacon of Gloucester, that tithes were owed to Cheltenham from this assart. In compensation, he agreed to give two pounds of incense to the abbot of Cirencester, as rector of Cheltenham church. This seems to confirm some sort of early link with Cheltenham. A hundred years later, Llanthony Priory disputed with Cirencester about tithes of calves born while pastured on land said to be in the parish of Cheltenham but belonging to Down Hatherley. In 1279 during another dispute Llanthony claimed to have a manor in Down Hatherley and to pasture sheep between Michaelmas and Easter in 'a wood called Dunhatherley'.[36] A payment of 5 shillings was agreed 'without prejudice'.

At no time was it asserted that Hatherley *church* was subject to Cheltenham – rather, that a certain piece of land was in Cheltenham parish. This may refer to an extensive wood on the western edge of Cheltenham, about 2 miles by 1½ miles across, which Domesday Book described in the entry for Badgeworth. The shape of the boundaries of Up Hatherley show clearly that it was once within Badgeworth, and this large area of woodland was therefore on the boundary between Cheltenham and Badgeworth (and hence, subsequently, of Up Hatherley). The implication is that it was common woodland, shared between the parishes

This carving which can be, seen inside the porch of Leckhampton church, is said to be a depiction of John Middleton, the church's mid-nineteenth-century architect.
PHOTOGRAPH: CARNEGIE, 2010

and townships, and that Cheltenham manor had rights within it. Before boundaries became rigid, rights of pasture in an area like this were often shared among different communities. Subsequently, the wood was cleared and first a farmstead and later a manor established. The name Hatherley itself indicates 'a clearing or enclosure hedged with thorn' and is recorded early in the eleventh century, when it was associated with Badgeworth in a land grant.[37] Hatherley Lane is an ancient road linking Cheltenham with Up Hatherley, its antiquity apparent from the fact that it formed part of the boundary between two tithings in Cheltenham parish. A very small manor of Hatherley was listed in Domesday Book, in the king's hands – it was associated with Sandhurst and can be identified as Down Hatherley. Once again the tenacity of the medieval church in maintaining ancient rights and traditions opens a small window onto very much earlier territorial arrangements.

One other parish in the area of Cheltenham hundred remained legally a chapelry of Cheltenham until after the Reformation, and the rector of Cheltenham and his lay successor collected the tithes. Charlton Kings had a chapel from at least 1187, when the Cirencester cartulary records its consecration by the bishop of Hereford; each week divine service was to be celebrated on Sunday, Monday, Wednesday and Friday, and on festival days. It is important that there was no manor of Charlton in Domesday Book, and that the area was an integral part of Cheltenham manor. Although parish boundaries were eventually established, based on those of the agricultural townships which existed from a much earlier date, the church at Charlton Kings had no local revenues as of right. It had to rely on private enterprise to supply the income for a chantry priest if Cirencester Abbey failed to recognise its obligation to supply a chaplain for the parishioners.

The tithing of Arle in Cheltenham might also have become a parish, as there was a chapel with a cemetery (which is normally a sign of parochial rights) but without the right to baptise. The Cirencester cartulary preserved the deed of Walter de Brussels, who gave a yardland to Cheltenham church between 1143 and 1150 in order to secure services three times a week in his chapel and the cemetery in Arle which the bishop of Worcester had consecrated. A confirmation of a gift at the same date by one Butler, to secure service in his chapel in Cheltenham, could have referred to this private chapel.[38] After the Reformation the chapel, like many others, fell into disuse, but Dr Parsons, chancellor of the diocese of Gloucester, observed about 1700 that

> Arle is a little village seated about a mile from Cheltenham, where is an ancient court house now belonging to Sir Fleetwood Dormer, which came by his wife that was a Lygon, with a pretty chapel in it.

This was not the medieval chapel but was in the house itself. Alas, Arle Court was demolished in 1881.[39]

Thus, when the first surviving list of parish churches was made in 1291, there were just four

Like the other old churches in the area, St Mary's Charlton Kings underwent drastic restoration, in this case in 1877–78. Without Victorian restoration, it is possible that all the old churches in the area would have fallen down, but the loss of much ancient detail is marked. George Rowe produced lithographs about 1840 of all the local churches here. Here, the transepts may be fourteenth-century, and the tower early fifteenth-century; it is an impressive demonstration of Charlton Kings' sense of independence and importance, even though technically still a chapel to Cheltenham church and without either a local rector or vicar. At the time the tower was built the Grevil family were substantial landowners in the parish, and it would be reasonable to suppose that they were instrumental in glorifying the church.

parishes in the hundred of Cheltenham. In order to encourage a crusade by Edward I, Pope Nicholas allowed the English king to collect, for six years, the tax normally paid to the papacy. The surviving list was made to ensure that the king collected all he was entitled to – which he did, though he failed to go on the crusade! Cheltenham had the largest income of the four, which reflected the fact that the parish covered a larger area from which tithes were paid.

The resources of the churches in Cheltenham hundred in 1291

Cheltenham	£24 0s. 0d.
Leckhampton	£6 0s. 10d.
Prestbury	£14 6s. 8d.
Swindon	£4 6s. 8d.

BOUNDARIES

Boundaries were of crucial importance, as the foregoing discussion demonstrates, but they were not rigidly defined. The ability of people, centuries before they acquired maps or surveying equipment, to plot the layout of estates should be saluted. It was not even necessary to rely on hedges or fences to mark a continuous boundary. Descriptions attached to charters note salient points, often natural features such as watercourses, ponds or trees, but where boundaries were unclear or there was no obvious line on the ground, stones or crosses might be placed as markers.

The comparatively simple boundary of Cheltenham hundred, when compared with the more complicated parish boundaries within its limits, supports the antiquity of this ancient 30-hide unit. Barbara Rawes studied the earliest description of the boundary, given in 1617 to John Norden when he was surveying the manor of Cheltenham for Prince Charles, later Charles I.[40] It then excluded Prestbury, but otherwise had probably not changed materially in the centuries since 1086. From a viewpoint on the edge of the Cotswold scarp, a rough square of territory stretched north-westwards. Streams rising on the higher ground flow westwards towards the Severn, and only on the north could the Hyde Brook provide a clear natural boundary with Bishop's Cleeve – the stream was called the Tirle in an eleventh-century copy of a late eighth-century charter for Bishops Cleeve, and this word meant simply 'stream'.[41] Separating Cheltenham from Prestbury for some distance there is a parallel stream, Wyman's Brook, which was the hundred boundary in 1617, and can be presumed to have been so since 1247 when it is likely that Prestbury was taken into Deerhurst hundred. To the west, an ancient road called the Greenway probably formed the boundary for some distance and then

A perambulation of Cheltenham parish boundary was made on 21 and 22 May 1823, and a map was prepared to show the details of the route. A cartouche on the map shows the procession headed by Mr W. Buckle, the head constable. It does not show the children of the National School and of the Lancasterian Establishment who followed the leaders, as reported by the *Bath and Cheltenham Gazette* of 27 May 1823. Young people were always included in a perambulation; before detailed printed maps became common, knowledge of the exact line of a boundary had to be learned and passed on to the next generation.

GLOUCESTERSHIRE ARCHIVES D2216/2

The western section of Cheltenham parish boundary follows Wymans Brook, but there are some small deviations, showing that the meanders of the brook had shifted but the parish boundary had not been altered to match them. The pond belonging to Robert Capper of Marle Hill is the basis for the Pittville boating lake. In origin it was a mill pond, and its banks were man-made. It was assumed that the parish boundary went through the centre of the pond, and a rowing boat with adults and children apparently established this section of the boundary.

GLOUCESTERSHIRE
ARCHIVES D2216/2

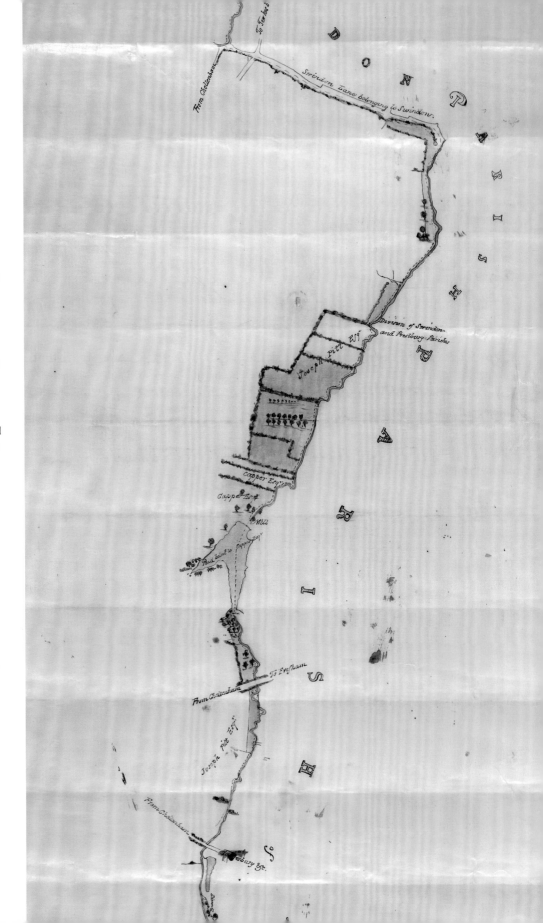

Wyman's Brook (at this point skirting round Swindon, where it was called 'Swyndon Brook'). To the south of the Greenway, the boundary was in part at least a division between arable fields and pastures.

Along the higher ground on the south side of the hundred, there were boundary markers such as woodland, stones on Northfield Hill, and a noticeable 'edge' called *Office piece*, its name derived from the Anglo-Saxon *offes* meaning edge. From the old London to Gloucester road where it runs close to the edge at Pegglesworth, there can be a magical view on a misty morning of Cheltenham's white stucco houses clustered round St Mary's church spire, shining in the first rays of sunshine. It is impossible to catch with a camera, only a painter could do justice to the view. The Rungbourne or Rindburne (*rinde* was an Anglo-Saxon word for hill or edge and *bourne* was a river) was another boundary mark of the hundred and was the name for the upper part of the Chelt. Two meadows, north and south of the Chelt at Dowdeswell End, were called 'The Rungbournes' in the seventeenth century, confirming the identification of the Rungbourne with the upper Chelt.[42] The same name also occurs in a charter for a property called *Onnanforda*, gifted to a church in Withington in 759, which comprised the modern Andoversford, Upper Dowdeswell and Pegglesworth; Dowdeswell parish boundary follows this upper part of the river. Wistley was also named both in the 759 charter and in the 1617 account of Cheltenham hundred.[43]

These specific examples are telling evidence for the antiquity of the 1617 Cheltenham hundred boundary. More generally, there are other indications that it goes back at least to the Anglo-Saxon period. Part of the north-west boundary of the Withington estate, as set out in an early eleventh-century hand in Hemming's cartulary (which contains copies of early charters relating to Worcester cathedral estates) appears to match the Cheltenham hundred boundary, though the markers are differently described. In the Gloucester cartulary there is a list of donations to the abbey in Abbess Eafe's time, between 735 and 767; Arle is named, and also Pinswell, acquired by Eafe 'for leading her sheep there'. Finberg noted the Greenway as linking Badgeworth with Pinswell near Upper Coberley, and it can be continued beyond Badgeworth to Arle, and thence to a point north of Elmstone Hardwicke where it joins an old road from Gloucester to Evesham.[44] Arle is the one vill in Cheltenham hundred which was recorded before the twelfth century – in other words, its boundaries are very early. All these are tantalising glimpses of the antiquity of the territorial arrangements of the area.

Within the hundred, parish boundaries are much less simple, zig-zagging across arable fields, and taking in odd pieces of land to suit manorial arrangements: Cheltenham, Leckhampton and Prestbury all had access to hill pasture and wood, and all had some valley land and meadow. Without maps to describe parish boundaries, these irregularities would not have appeared as odd as they do to modern eyes. For example, Cheltenham parish had two projecting fingers of land, one towards Hewletts incorporating hill pasture and wood, the other extending, or intruding, between Charlton Kings and Leckhampton. As Charlton Kings parish was defined later than the other four parishes in the hundred, this complication was deliberate, and must

This early nineteenth-century engraving of Marle Hill, published by S. Y. Griffith & Co., shows very clearly the lake that formed part of the parish boundary of Cheltenham and Prestbury. Marle Hill estate was owned privately until 1931, when the house and its remaining land were purchased by Cheltenham Corporation. These were subsequently sold for housing development in 1964, and the house itself demolished. But in 1892 the Corporation had purchased the whole of the lake and a small strip of land on its north side, at the same time as it had bought other land to extend the Recreation Ground west of the Evesham Road.

represent a determination on the part of Cheltenham to retain particular areas of land. It had the most intricate bounds, with several short sections of brook and road and in one place an 'old hedge'.

One method of establishing boundaries was by walking or perambulating along them. Parish boundaries were customarily perambulated on Rogation Day. A perambulation of Cheltenham parish boundary was made on Tuesday and Wednesday, 21 and 22 May 1823, and afterwards a map was drawn showing it in detail; a second map was later produced with corrections.[45] These give a clear picture of the boundary just before the nineteenth-century changes. The boundary was marked on the map on the Cheltenham side of rivers, roads and hedges, or along the middle of such features, and the cartographer noted the names of the adjacent parishes. To judge from the drawing in the cartouche of the map, a very respectable company of gentlemen set out from the church. The *Bath and Cheltenham Gazette* reported, probably with excited exaggeration, that nearly a thousand inhabitants accompanied the procession, headed by local officials and followed by 'town children of the National School and

Lancasterian Establishment'. The young were necessarily involved so that they could report on the bounds in the future – oral testimony for later generations.

Where on the boundary did the walkers begin? Possibly they went first to Barbridge, where the old hundred perambulation began and, if they followed the usual Anglo-Saxon practice, went clockwise. They walked along Swindon Lane, now in part Kingsditch Lane; fields on each side of Swindon Lane were called Kingsditch, suggesting how the boundary between the Chelt and Wyman's Brook had been defined across otherwise unmarked land, at first perhaps to separate the bishop's land of Prestbury from the king's land of Cheltenham. Further on, the Cheltenham party, or a token crew, is shown in a little sketch rowing across the middle of a pond belonging to Robert Capper of Marle Hill House. His fishpond was noted on the 1885 Ordnance Survey map, then it became Marle Hill Lake, and now it is the Pittville boating lake. When the walkers reached Hewletts, there was confusion about the proper course; the amended map corrected the short cut across the fields which appears on the earlier one. A similar confusion arose at Sandford mill, where the walkers followed the Old Bath Road past the mill, placing the mill in Charlton Kings, but on the second map the mill was included in Cheltenham.

A few years later, on Monday 12 September 1831, the parishioners of Charlton Kings perambulated *their* parish boundary; 'George Bond, Robert Cleevely, passed (with Mr Watling *et al.*) through the Mill at Sandford and waded along the stream at Mill Tail', making clear the division of the mill between the two parishes. This group marked various boundary points by digging crosses in the ground. Leckhampton parishioners perambulated their bounds on Monday 19 October 1835.[46] All these perambulations contributed to the mapping of the area, which was of relevance to the definition of the new parliamentary borough of Cheltenham.

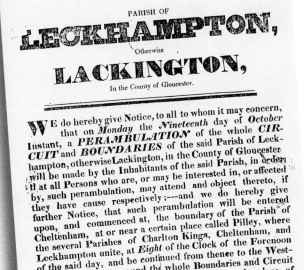

This poster advertising the perambulation of Leckhampton on 19 October 1835 draws attention to the existence of disputes about the boundary, which possibly stimulated the perambulation. Parish rates were probably higher in one parish than another, hence likely objections to a house being included on the 'wrong' side of the line. Paint was carried and used to mark appropriate boundary points. The inhabitants began from the point where three parishes intersected and walked in a clockwise direction, as had been customary from as far back as Anglo-Saxon descriptions of boundaries. Leckhampton churchwardens gave both forms of the name; they obviously did not want to be accused of improper notification of the event.

These very worn and large effigies, which may now be found beside Leckhampton church porch, date from the fourteenth century. They might represent members of the Giffard family, lords of the manor of Leckhampton; their feet are resting on dogs. The effigies are not in their original position, which would probably have been in the chancel of the church.

PHOTOGRAPH: CARNEGIE, 2010

The acreage of parishes was recorded in the 1831 census, after much accurate information had been collected in connection with assessing local taxes, and before the widespread alterations made later in the century.[47] In Cheltenham hundred, in order of size, they were as follows:

Parish areas in the former Cheltenham hundred returned in 1831

Parish	Acres
Cheltenham	4,301
Charlton Kings	3,499
Leckhampton	1,614
Prestbury	3,054
Swindon	730

Most of the old Cheltenham parish boundary is now enveloped in building development, but interesting reminders of the former fields often remain in the alignments of roads and lanes and in their names.

CHAPTER TWO

STRUCTURES

TITHINGS, MANORS AND PARISHES were the framework for the daily lives of medieval people, but they were not static. Tithings were adjusted; new manors and parishes were established, in response to political circumstances; and in the thirteenth century burgage plots and a market introduced a different structure in Cheltenham. Agriculture, however, was much the most important occupation of the inhabitants in the century following the Norman Conquest. Each township had its own field system, and husbandmen worked within the constraints of the open fields in each. Township boundaries, however, are less well documented than parish boundaries, because their relevance largely disappeared following the enclosure of open fields. Over the centuries that process so eroded the old field system that by the time the Ordnance Survey maps were being prepared, from the beginning of the nineteenth century, the landscape had been transformed. Moreover, nineteenth- and twentieth-century building has obliterated hedgerow alignments that might have given clues to older boundaries. Nonetheless, enclosure maps and awards in the eighteenth and nineteenth centuries, and tithe maps and apportionments made after the Tithes Commutation Act of 1836, can reveal much about townships and their boundaries. They can also reveal the existence of hitherto unsuspected townships. As many sources as possible have been collated by Barbara Rawes to reconstruct township and tithing boundaries for Cheltenham hundred as it was from the mid-thirteenth century.[1]

TOWNSHIPS AND COMMON FIELDS

Manors and parishes did not alter the lay-out of township fields. Domesday Book made no mention of the vills or townships in Cheltenham, and only Arle was recorded in the Anglo-Saxon period, but like Charlton, the other vills appear to have Anglo-Saxon names, which implies that they existed before 1066. Thus, Alstone means 'Aelf's ton' or settlement; Naunton, the 'new settlement'; and Westal, the west *halh* or nook of land, all of them coined in the Anglo-Saxon language.[2] There was a great deal of low-lying land in the parish, near the Chelt and Wyman's Brook, and the name Cheltenham itself is in part a reflection of this. 'Ham' is a common suffix to a place-name, but can derive from two similar-sounding but quite different words, *ham*, meaning 'manor' and *hamm* meaning 'water meadow'. In this case, 'water meadow' appears to have been the origin. The meadow in question could have been the meeting place of the men of the hundred. Ham in Charlton Kings is considered to have a similar derivation; although close to the Cotswold scarp, its name suited meadows beside the brook which flows into the Chelt. Leckhampton, on the other hand, is a 'ham', a manor. This place-name element often indicates an important manor, and was typical of an early phase of Anglo-Saxon naming.

The first part of the name Cheltenham, on the other hand, has proved to be difficult to interpret and has puzzled commentators who have considered it at least since the eighteenth century. Smith's discussion in *The Place-Names of Gloucestershire* proposed no firm conclusion, suggesting that the river name Chelt may have been an early river name of unknown meaning, or a back formation from the place-name (that is, the river took its name from the place on its banks), which still leaves its meaning a puzzle. It does appear that an earlier name might have been 'Arle'. A fourteenth-century manuscript, the so-called 'Westminster Domesday', transcribing Edward the Confessor's writ concerning Pershore and Deerhurst, gives a description in Anglo-Saxon of the boundaries of the territory.[3] Several of the boundary marks mention 'Arle', which was clearly a river – the phrase 'along Arle' is used. By following through the boundary marks it becomes apparent that this was a section of what we now know as the River Chelt. As with the name Rungbourne, which was preserved as a field name, a meadow in Boddington was called Arle meadow in 1464 and was still so known in the nineteenth century. Smith suggested that the word 'Arle' meant 'alder'.

Cheltenham township was the core of Cheltenham manor. A rectangle of land running approximately east and west, it was bounded southwards for much of the distance by the River Chelt, and northwards by Wyman's Brook, though the township took in a small amount of ground south of the river Chelt to include Sandford mill. As noted in the previous chapter, a

The river Chelt is normally little more than a stream rising in the Cotswold hills behind the town, and sunk in a deep channel. But its descent is fairly short and rapid, and its course is relatively confined once it reaches the built-up area of Charlton Kings and Cheltenham, particularly since much of it has been canalised to supply the mills along its course, or culverted when Cheltenham was being developed. Here near the centre of Cheltenham it is a surprisingly rural scene as it runs along the edge of Sandford Park.

PHOTOGRAPH: AUTHOR, 2009

Floods are not new in Cheltenham. In 1855, for example, a flood destroyed Jessop's Nursery. More recently, on 20 July 2007, after an exceptionally heavy and long-lasting downpour, the Chelt had collected a huge amount of water running off the hills, and flooded a substantial area of the town. New flood defences failed to collect the torrent. The Promenade – which was once a marshy field – was under water (*left*), as was the Bath Road and Bath Parade. The Playhouse, with its banners advertising the Music Festival, and once a health spa, suffered considerable damage.

© MARY NELSON, 2007

narrow eastwards projection reached Hewletts. The medieval town of Cheltenham developed along a street parallel with, and close to, the Chelt. The Upper and Lower (or East and West) Fields, and Whaddon Field occupied the tract of sandy soils north of the street. The detailed work by Barbara Rawes demonstrates the careful allocation of open fields to soil type. The sands run out close to the Charlton Kings parish boundary, and become shallower towards Wyman's Brook, where 'The Marsh' was situated, its name graphically illustrating its tendency to become waterlogged. In the early medieval period, alone of the townships in the manor, Cheltenham appears to have had a nucleated centre of settlement, later subsumed into the burgages of the market town.

South of the Chelt were two townships, Arle and Alstone, each with a separate field system. The townships, of which Arle was the more northerly, were largely bounded by the Chelt while including a small amount of land north of the river, and reached south-west to Hatherley Lane. Both were fairly regular rectangles of territory. Though the original charter is lost, Gloucester Abbey preserved in its records a list of donations made to the abbey between 735 and 757, among which was 20 hides in *Alre* (*Ahie* is an alternative reading) [4] which was a territory based on the river. Rawes commented on what appeared to be a regular rectangular layout of Arle's fields, which she considered was possibly as ancient as the eighth century. Arle Court was a large and important house close to the Chelt and to the boundary with Alstone. It could well have been the chief house for both townships, perhaps even of the manor of Cheltenham itself.

Rawes also noted that in origin Arle and Alstone were probably one land unit, subsequently divided as cultivation of the area became more intensive with progressive clearing of the woodland, of which there was a great deal in the early medieval period. The boundary between the respective fields of Arle and Alstone was described as 'the grand meare' in a survey of 1635 (a 'mere' was a boundary), showing the division of a once-larger territory.

The name Alstone is not recorded until as late as 1389, but within its area some of the most significant elements in Cheltenham's eighteenth-century expansion took place. Now it is more densely developed than Arle. The township included Bayshill and Benhall, both names recorded in the fifteenth century, 'Bays' deriving from a personal name, Benhall from a personal name and 'nook of land' (*halh*). Other Alstone field names perpetuated in street names in the twenty-first century included Sandfield, Rowenfield (deriving from *rewayn* meaning 'aftermath' of mowing), and Granley (originally a green lane). There were two mills on the Alstone section of the Chelt. Soil types and fields were particularly well matched in

Charlton township contrasts with Cheltenham because it did not have a highly organised and unified open-field system with a village settlement as its nucleus. Anglo-Saxon *ceorls*, or free farmers, may have been given the task of opening up and settling previously uncultivated areas. Like Collum End in Leckhampton, the 'Ends' are evidence of this process, each a small and distinct group of farms. The church, often the natural focus of a settlement, itself gave a name to one small settlement, 'Church End', later 'Horsefair'. In a land tax list for 1715, entries were grouped under Ham, Churchend, Moorend, East End, Bafford and Cudnell, showing that at least three of the Ends were clearly defined areas.

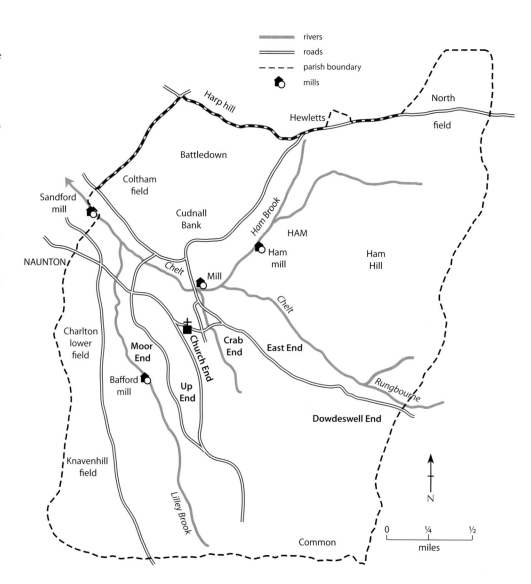

RIGHT

Collum End Farm, Leckhampton, was built in the sixteenth and early seventeenth centuries, but the timber framing at ground-floor level has been largely replaced with stone, and the house reconstructed. Some early timber framing survives at the west end (right-hand side). In 1881 William Hicks was the farmer at Collum End, occupying 208 acres. Collum End Farm, with its farmyard and buildings, survived as a farmhouse until 1960.

PHOTOGRAPH: AUTHOR, 2009

BELOW

Collum End was probably won from a wooded area – the first part of the name might be derived from 'coal' or charcoal – the second from *hamm* meaning meadow. The first record of the name is in 1570. Collum End was planned with long tofts on the south side of the modern Church Road running back towards Leckhampton Court, whose owners probably set it out. The arable Collum field reached to the parish boundary, and is bisected by Leckhampton Road. Listed simply as 'Leckhampton village' in the 1851 census, Collum End was the main settlement in Leckhampton until nineteenth-century building along the Bath Road.

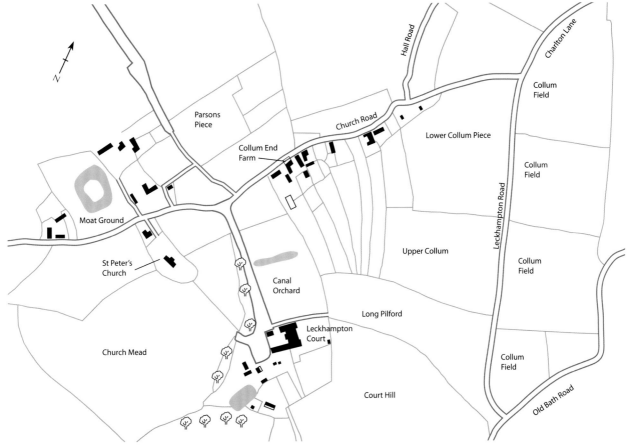

this township. Sandfield occupied an area of sands defined by the Chelt and a small tributary stream; there was later a concentration of market gardening here. Rowanfield was largely clay. Alstone tenants had pieces of land in each field, thus having a share of two sharply contrasting soil types. In the southern corner of the township, fields called Benhall Wood, Wood Ground, Oak Ground, and Wood Brooks, all point to the one-time wooded nature of the area. South of the Hatherley Brook was Redgrove, on stiff blue lias clay, which became a separate manor granted to Llanthony Priory in the mid-twelfth century.

Even where a township consisted largely of common fields, there was usually at least some land held by individual owners and not part of the common field system. In particular, this might include lands belonging to the lord of the manor, or described as held 'in severalty' (that is, not in common but separately), and land which had been cleared and settled in the medieval period and thus not incorporated into an earlier and well-established open-field system. A local example is Fiddlers Green, in the township of Arle but not included in its common field system.

While Cheltenham, Arle and Alstone appear to have approximated to classic open field townships, Westal, Sandford, Naunton and Charlton Kings do not; there are indications in all these townships of clearance and settlement at a date significantly later than the creation of open fields. Charlton Kings, in particular, is made up of a number of small and dispersed settlements, several of which are significantly named 'End': thus, Church End, Moor End and East End were areas differentiated in later tax records, and Crab End, Up End and Dowdeswell End were also distinct. In the Midland counties the place-name element 'end' almost always refers to land which was colonised, at a comparatively late stage, by carving out new fields from the marginal areas – either on the edge of the territory, or on the poorer quality ground, or both. It is likely that as each 'End' was cleared, a small group of husbandmen shared the newly created arable, so that Charlton became a patchwork of small communities. It is logical to assume that the clearing and settling of the Ends came after a larger-scale organisation of common fields had taken place in Cheltenham, Arle and Alstone. If it had been earlier, the various Ends would have been drawn into a common unit – but they were not.

The ability of land-owners in the sixteenth and seventeenth centuries to enclose some land subject to common rights points to the limited numbers of people involved in each 'End'. It was not difficult for one energetic and ambitious owner to buy out a handful of neighbours. The actions of John Prinn give a particularly well-documented local example. From 1696 he was buying properties containing scattered strips of land which would eventually make up the consolidated Charlton Park estate.[5] The creation of Charlton Kings parish brought these dispersed farmsteads within one administrative unit which had not previously existed. The boundary between Cheltenham and Charlton Kings, with its zigzag pattern, shows it was defined between pre-existing sections or furlongs in much older arable fields. Charlton Kings was given a long eastern section, Charlton Lower Field, which provided the early husbandmen with their arable, and was among the last fields in the parish still to be cultivated in strips.[6]

Were the *ceorls* or husbandmen of the period before 1066 made responsible for pushing settlement and cultivation eastwards to the lower slopes of the Cotswolds? Charlton Kings is a large parish, but there is much land on the scarp slope and the Cotswold hills within its bounds. It is impossible to know how many *ceorls* there were to give Charlton its name – perhaps very few. The same would be true of Charlton Abbots near Winchcombe, where Domesday Book records just four villagers, two smallholders and six slaves.

The three townships of Westal, Naunton and Sandford were combined for purposes of national taxation, and the fields of each are not easily distinguished. However, their inhabitants could still be counted separately in the nineteenth century and therefore the houses in each township were recognised even if their fields were not clearly separated. Furthermore, certain holdings had lands both in the township of Naunton and also in Charlton Kings parish, in effect ignoring that boundary.[7] For example, when the Cheltenham church lands were itemised in 1632 there was a distinct unit called 'Naunton Meese' ('meese' means a 'messuage' or site for a dwelling house) which included land in Benbridge and Knavenhill fields in Charlton Kings, in the field shared by Westal and Naunton townships, and in Oldmeade field in Naunton.[8] It is possible that the four villagers and two smallholders who Domesday Book stated had been added to Cheltenham by the reeve were resident in Naunton. The boundary of Charlton Kings would have appeared more logical if it had abutted directly onto Leckhampton instead of going round Naunton, suggesting that this little township was also a late creation.

Westal, always listed first of the three, was already a distinct unit in the twelfth century and might be termed a sub-manor. The existence in the eighteenth century of fields named Westal Court ground, Westal furlong and Westal orchard points to there being an earlier enclosed area round a minor manor house.[9] Beyond were several fields called Merestones, named with reference to the parish and township boundary. Westal Green is now a large roundabout at the junction of Lansdown and Andover roads, occupied by a garage, and Westal Court was near by. There was probably a significant wooded area in Westal, adjoining Redgrove, which might have been royal demesne, devoted to the keeping of deer. The name Lyppiatts, perpetuated in several Cheltenham street names, derives from a gate in an enclosure fence which deer could leap but which prevented the passage of other animals, and one of the tax-collectors in Cheltenham in 1327 was Simon the forester. This may, therefore, have been a royal deer park in the early medieval period.

To the east of Westal was the new settlement of Naunton, in the long peninsula of Cheltenham parish which intruded between Charlton Kings to the east and Leckhampton to the west. To the north, Naunton had a field which it shared with Westal and Sandford. Naunton township itself was on sandy soil, and its field was eventually split into a large number of very small strips. The third township, Sandford, was clearly named for the nature of its river crossing. The modern Promenade and Montpellier Walk follow the boundary of the township and mark the edge of the clay soil to the north, although Sandford mill was also on a clay patch. Although there may once have been common rights over the fields of these three townships, all were extinguished at a relatively early date and without an Enclosure Act. As a result, 600 acres were still subject to tithe payments in 1849. In these townships consolidation of the fields partly took place through the Delabere family of Prestbury and Southam, who in the eighteenth century progressively bought out other owners.

The open field or common field system had two defining characteristics. The first was that each large arable field was divided among a number of houses or messuages, each being allocated a set of long, narrow strips which were approximately a furlong in length; this was a convenient distance for oxen to pull a plough without resting. Each strip was of several plough widths, and approximated to an acre. Every second or third year a field was left uncultivated or fallow, in order that its fertility could recover. The second characteristic was that while a field was fallow, or between harvesting a crop and ploughing and seeding the next, animals could be put there to graze, which helped to fertilise the land. As there were no fences or hedges between the strips – they were not enclosed – animals of different owners mingled indiscriminately. These were the commonable or open fields referred to in Enclosure

Acts of the eighteenth and nineteenth centuries. Such a system depended totally on effective cooperation, and the system worked best within a manorial context, where the lord's court made decisions and passed regulations about procedures each year and disciplined, by means of fines, those who offended against the common weal.

The arrangement is outlined in the manor court book for 1557 relating to Charlton Kings, where a three-field system operated.[10]

> Commons in Charlton
> It is reported that all the grounds in Charlton Kings (besides homesteads) did heretofore lie in common without stint or number, some as Lammas grounds, and the rest from the end of harvest until Candlemas for two years and the third year by the whole year'.

The farming year was punctuated by religious festivals which marked each stage of the work: thus, Lammas Day was 1 August and Candlemas was 2 February. The entry suggests that in earlier centuries it had not apparently been necessary to limit ('stint') the number of sheep or cattle put into the fields. Each husbandman would keep as many as was needed to plough his land, maintain its fertility and supply produce, and the larger graziers or sheep-masters had not pushed against the relative equality of the system. In the mid-sixteenth century, though, this communal balance had begun to break down. The decision quoted above might imply that the whole parish operated as one unit, but in fact further decisions confirm that there were several small field systems in Charlton Kings: Howbeach field in the east, and Bafford, Cudnell and Up End, located in the west, north and south of the parish.

The decisions of the manor court were recorded on strips of parchment, sewn together into a continuous sheet and then rolled up, hence their name 'manor court rolls'. They contain many orders concerning agricultural practices. Later court books for Cheltenham manor make it clear that each of the tithings had a separate open field system, even though in practice the farms crossed township boundaries. Goding quoted orders of the court in 1710 that 'no sheep [or pigs] shall be kept in Cheltenham fields until harvest be ended in all the said fields' and 'no man shall keep more than two sheep per acre of land in Cheltenham fields'; 'no cattle shall be kept in Alstone fields until the fields be clearly rid' (that is, harvested); and 'no man shall keep any cattle in Arle fields until rid'.[11] Infringement of the orders was punished with a fine of 39 shillings (nearly £2), a heavy penalty which perhaps indicates that it was becoming harder by this date to secure compliance.

LEFT

A fall of snow often reveals the patterns of ridge and furrow in a field, the snow lying thicker in the ancient furrows than on the ridges. The purpose of ploughing to form ridges was sometimes to assist in drainage on a clay soil, providing not only channels to draw the water off, but also dry ridges for the sheep to stand on in wet weather. It also facilitated the division of open fields into strips, four ridges making an acre. The curving reverse-S shape of the furrows was caused by the cumbersome ox plough swinging out wide before turning at the end of the furrow. This photograph is of Court Hill, Leckhampton.

© ERIC MILLER

LORDS OF THE MANOR

Gloucestershire in 1086 was divided into many manors, with much land shared in common fields and few 'free' holdings. The structure of manors and of common fields shows the power of the lord to divide and allocate, and debates among historians about the antiquity of common field agriculture are closely linked to others about how and when the manorial system came into being. The oldest manors, which probably predated the Norman Conquest by a considerable period, seem to have had the tightest and most comprehensive structures. Those instituted later were less coherent, with looser structures.[12]

Medieval lords of the manor of Cheltenham were probably distant figures, not only when the manor was in royal ownership, but also when the king granted the estate to a monastery. There was an ecclesiastical lord of Cheltenham for three centuries, until the dissolution of the monasteries at the end of the 1530s. However, there were also periods when the manor was granted to laymen, who may have been closer to, and taken more personal interest in, its affairs. Cheltenham acknowledged the authority of successive lords of the manor through the stewards or bailiffs appointed to run the estate, and later through the lessees or 'farmers' who held leases of the manor. The stewards organised and presided over the three-weekly court which regulated the agricultural practices in the open fields of all constituent townships, and punished minor offences with fines. To them, also, fell the twice-yearly task of summoning all the tithings in the hundred to the view of frankpledge. The first surviving manor court rolls which record these proceedings date from 1327.[13] But there were also several independent or semi–independent manors within the boundaries of Cheltenham manor. While the regulation of the Cheltenham common fields concerned these other manorial lords if their lands were intermingled with those of Cheltenham manor tenants, they also held their own courts. Surveys of Cheltenham manor generally did not include these areas. The oldest was the rectory manor. In the twelfth century, two more manors, Charlton (Ashley) and Redgrove, were separated from Cheltenham.

CHELTENHAM MANOR

As a result of the civil war between Stephen and Matilda in the twelfth century, Miles, earl of Hereford, and then his son Earl Roger, became the lord of Cheltenham manor. Each created a small but separate manor within the estate; Miles created Charlton (Ashley) and then Roger created Redgrove. Miles was constable to Henry I, succeeding his father, Walter, as sheriff of Gloucestershire and constable of Gloucester castle. For these services he was given a Welsh estate based on Brecknock. His superior lord was Earl Robert, one of the illegitimate sons of Henry I, but it has been said that after Earl Robert 'he was the most powerful baron of the West Country'. Henry I died in 1135 and his nephew Stephen, Count of Mortain and Boulogne, made himself king, pushing aside the claim of Henry's daughter Matilda, the king's nominated successor. The new king confirmed Miles in his honours of Brecknock and Gloucester. Miles received Stephen at Gloucester in 1138, but as soon as the Empress Matilda (with her half-brother, Earl Robert) arrived in England to fight for her crown, he renounced his allegiance to Stephen and joined her party, going to Bristol to declare his fealty. He accompanied her from Bristol to Gloucester, which was her headquarters for the next two years. There she was more secure than anywhere else, with Miles and Robert of Gloucester her strongest supporters. It was said that Miles 'behaved to her like a father in deed and counsel'.[14] Matilda speedily rewarded him, granting the castle of St Briavel's, Newnham, and the Forest of Dean; confirmation of the grant shows that this estate included Cheltenham. In 1141, as her power increased, she made him earl of Hereford.[15] He was her ablest commander, but he died in a hunting accident at Christmas 1143.

Miles's son, Roger, inherited the earldom and land, and in 1154, when Matilda's son became king as Henry II, he confirmed Roger in the estates which had belonged to his father, except for St Briavels and the Forest of Dean which he reclaimed.[16] However, Roger's loyalty was in doubt – he rebelled against the king in 1155 – and none of his sons was made earl of Hereford, though it appears that they retained his lands.[17] In 1200 King John revived the title of earl of Hereford for Miles's grandson, Humphrey de Bohun, but required him to relinquish his claim not only to the land between Severn and Wye but also, east of the Severn, to Cheltenham. Thereby Cheltenham returned to royal control, an estate sufficiently valuable for the king to want it back as part of the 'demesne of the kings of England'.[18] The concept of the royal demesne as the inalienable endowment of the English kings from the time of Edward the Confessor was developing at this time.[19]

A generation later, Cheltenham became a pawn in the struggle against France. In 1247 the Norman abbey of Fécamp surrendered to the king the valuable Cinque ports of Rye and Winchelsea in exchange for the manor and hundred of Cheltenham, together with some other estates. Fécamp, an important port, had a major Benedictine abbey founded in 1003 by Duke Robert of Normandy; unfortunately there is no history of its English possessions.[20] The background to the 'exchange' was England's loss of most of its French possessions. Shortly after the failure of his military expedition to Poitou in 1242, Henry III seized lands in England which were still held by Norman lords, including monastic houses. The abbot of Fécamp had little choice and no doubt accepted reluctantly the loss of Rye and Winchelsea in return for other less strategic estates. At the time, the bishop of Hereford held Cheltenham on a five-year lease from the Crown. He was assured that he could remain in possession, and two years later the bailiff of Fécamp was told not to prevent the bishop harvesting his fruit which he had planted.

From this time, Cheltenham nominally had a monastic lord of the manor until the Dissolution. French monasteries often kept only a single monk in England, to administer their estates and remit the profits to the parent monastery. These men, much disliked, lived like laymen and were seen to be draining money away to France. The estates were known as 'alien priories', though technically this term applied only to those small monasteries still controlled by overseas houses. Occasionally, kings would confiscate property from alien priories to replenish the royal treasury. Where there was a resident monastic community, as at Deerhurst, it was usually excepted from parliament's censure and the king's seizures, because no more than a small token rent went to the superior foreign monastery and religious life in England was served. But Cheltenham was a purely temporal possession, its management handled by the bailiff of Warminghurst near Steyning in Sussex,[21] a major Fécamp church and manor.

When war with France resumed in 1295 Edward I, desperate for financial resources, took the estates of French priories into his hands, having the previous year surveyed all their estates, including Cheltenham.[22] There was suspicion that French monks or priors acted as spies, exacerbating the dislike of money draining away from the country, and confiscation made it more difficult for the monasteries concerned to support the war against the English. The war increased English hostility towards French landlords, so confiscating these properties was popular. Englishmen could lease the affected estates on favourable terms. From this time onwards alien possessions were never secure – but neither was the position of the English lessees. The estates might be restored to the French house for short periods, and then again taken into the king's hands. On each such 'restoration', the king received a large fine for the privilege of returning the lands, and the priories also had to pay an annual rent, making them effectively tenants of their own property.

In the 1340s, when the English estates of Fécamp were in the king's hands, Cheltenham was leased to Thomas of Bradeston. In 1345 he was granted the full right to hold the courts previously enjoyed by the abbot. He paid the king a large rent, though in return was spared the heavy tax on the wool output from his estates. Thomas of Bradeston died in 1360. In 1374, Simon of Burley was given custody of Cheltenham manor,[23] and nine years later, during the schism of the Church between rival popes, a grant to him specifically stated that the property was in the king's hands because of the French war. He was also guaranteed a pension and an alternative endowment if the estate were restored to the abbot, a provision that had become essential if Englishmen were to take on the tenancy of alien estates. Records of Cheltenham courts have been found from the period when he was the lessee. As more laymen took the risks involved, they became more determined that the estates should not be restored to the French abbots. Members of the Commons petitioned the king in this sense on a number of occasions, and from 1414 all the lands of alien priories were confiscated permanently and transferred to English ownership. Unlike the dissolution of the monasteries four generations later, the suppression of alien priories involved the transfer of most of the property not to the Crown but to the Church.

A great deal was granted to English monasteries and later to Eton College and King's College, Cambridge. Henry V founded two new religious houses which benefited – a Carthusian house at Sheen in 1414 and, in 1415, the year of Agincourt, a house for the fourteenth-century Swedish order of Bridgettine nuns. This was established in the king's warren at Twickenham, and named Syon after Mount Zion in Palestine. Among its many other endowments it received the bailiwick of Warminghurst, and thus the manor, church and hundred of Cheltenham.[24] This unique English Bridgettine house was a double monastery, for a prioress and 59 nuns, 17 priests or deacons and eight lay brothers.[25] Over a decade earlier Henry, Lord FitzHugh, constable of England, had tried with little success to bring the Swedish order to England, but the personal support of Henry V was crucial, and perhaps also that of his sister who was married to the king of Sweden. In 1426 work started on new buildings north of the village of Isleworth and in 1431 the community moved there. The immense church, as

The ancient custom of the parish of Swindon with respect to tithe payments was recorded in 1704 in response to the request by the diocese for a 'terrier' or list of the rights of the church. The tithes probably were ancient, as the churchwardens and rector state. Rules governing tithe were localised and often complex. The spelling might not be very modern, but the list of what Swindon's rector had customarily collected is clear. A tenth of corn and hay was the most substantial payment. Some tithes were paid in money, for example for every person over 16 years, and for gardens. People occupying land in the parish but not living in it paid a rate described as 'vicarage tithe'. Calves, sheep, lambs, fleeces, pigs, apples and pears, and eggs all attracted tithe. The rector had to keep a bull and a cow for the use of the parish.

GLOUCESTERSHIRE ARCHIVES 297 T6

Aprill the 27th 1704

The ancient custom of the p[ar]ish of Swindon for ye payment of tythes and other dewes belonging to the minister of the said p[ar]ish.

I[m]pr[imi]s wee pay for offerings two pence a person att above sixteen years of age

wee pay for Corne & hay the tenth cock & sheff

wee pay for vikedg tythe one shilling Eight pen a pound

for all that live out of the p[ar]ish

wee pay for milch cows wee sumer a peny a cow

wee pay the tenth calf at fourteene days ould but if not tenn

hee may tythe at ye seavent and he that have not a tyth calfe

for the calfe he seleth to pay oone peny out of a shilling and for the

calfes that you wene a peny a calf or if a calfe be killed the minister to have the left shoulder

wee pay the tenth lame but if seaven there is one due

and tythable one the third day of may

wee pay the tenth pigg but if seaven there is one due and tythable att two weeks old

wee pay for sheep we shere the tenth fliss if cept in thr p[ar]ish

all the year if sumerd out of the p[ar]ish wee pay but halfe tythe

wee pay for sheepe that are sould before the third day of May wee pay a halfpence

a sheep and after the third of may wee pay a peny untill they are shere

hee that have not a tythe lame if hee sels any Ewes & lams before the third of

may for to pay a peny and if after wards three halfpence

wee pay for tyth apples & pares the tenth & at the time of gathering

wee pay a peny a garden

The minister is to keep a bull and a Cow for the use of the p[ar]ish

wee pay for Eggs at Ester two for a hen & three for a cock

Tho. Morgan Rect[o]r   John Sturmy   } Church
John Surman   Thomas Hortton   } wardens

large as Salisbury cathedral, was not finished until 1488; the present Syon House is built over its west end and around the cloister garden.

Syon was one of the wealthiest religious houses in England in 1535.[26] It was given the property of five French monasteries, among them Fécamp, although initially this estate had been given to Sheen. There was confusion over royal grants on more than one occasion, particularly when Henry VI looked for gaps in titles to find funds for Eton and his new college at Cambridge. The prioress of Syon enquired into all the titles and in 1443 obtained letters patent from Henry VI confirming the property in Sussex and Gloucestershire. This was reiterated in 1461, on the accession of Edward IV. The manor of Cheltenham was an important endowment, with its extensive demesne lands in Cheltenham itself, and 160 acres in Leckhampton – although the Sussex estates were more than three times as valuable when surveyed in 1492.[27] But it was some time before Syon gained the advantage of the Cheltenham estate because an English farmer (or lessee) was already in possession. Sir John Cornwall (or Cornewaill) and his wife, Elizabeth of Huntingdon, had been granted Cheltenham for their lifetimes.

Sir John was an interesting character, the first lay lord of the manor, apart from the king, of whom much is known. He was born about 1364, reputedly on board ship near St Michael's Mount,[28] and was a man of great physical strength, noted for his skill in tournaments as well as his valour in war. He collected large sums of money in ransoms for French prisoners – in 1412 he received 21,375 crowns after the success of the expedition to Aquitaine,[29] and three years later fought in the vanguard with the duke of York at Agincourt. John Leland, the king's antiquary who travelled the country 100 years after Cornwall's death, noted 'A man of great renowne in the raigns of Henry V and Henry the syxte', who built part of the castle of Ampthill (Bedfordshire) 'of such spoiles as it is saide that he wanne in France', and that he was 'a man of greate fame in owtewarde warres, and very riche'.[30] Sir John married an heiress, the daughter of Sir Edmund de Arundel, and after her death performed, it was said, so well in a tournament in York in 1400 that he won an even wealthier wife, Elizabeth daughter of John of Gaunt. She was known as Elizabeth of Huntingdon, because of her own second marriage to a half-brother of Richard II, John Holland, duke of Exeter and earl of Huntingdon, who was executed in January 1400 after conspiring against Henry IV.

In 1403 Henry IV, his brother-in-law, granted Sir John a lease of Fécamp properties jointly with the bailiff of Fécamp Abbey. This was a recognised method by which a monastic estate was in effect taken over by an English farmer. It was granted free of taxes, ensuring that the status of 'ancient royal demesne' was not lost while in another's hands. After the deaths of Sir John and his wife the estate would have reverted to the king, had he not already granted it away to Syon. The bailiff died in 1409. Cornwall wrote to the abbot of Fécamp from Lille, where he was expecting to take part in a tournament, suggesting it would be to abbey's advantage to grant him, his wife and son a lease for 100 or 120 years, because he would be an assured remitter of money to the abbot. He pointed out that, because of the war with France, they had been granted the abbey's properties by king, council and parliament, and he drew attention to the great profit that had accrued to Fécamp Abbey during the last forty or fifty years. The abbot refused the offer.

Sir John was not in Cheltenham very often, for it was but one among many properties, and he was often abroad, but from time to time he certainly attended sessions of the court, and he and his wife asked for lampreys, of which they were very fond, to be sent to Cheltenham.[31] Where did they stay when they came? The courthouse, where the business of the manor was transacted, was next to the churchyard, and does not appear to have been a very impressive building. There is no indication of a large medieval house in Cheltenham apart from Arle Court, which is poorly documented before the sixteenth century, but is perhaps where they were accommodated.

Elizabeth died in 1425. In 1433 Sir John Cornwall was created Baron Fanhope (taking his title from his manor of Fownhope in Herefordshire), and Baron Millbrooke, after a manor in Bedfordshire which he had recently purchased, shortly before his death. Nearby was Ampthill and its castle, where he died in 1443 aged about 80 years. Neither title continued, because his only son had been killed fighting in France. Towards the end of his life Sir John had endowed a chantry in the Blackfriars chapel in London, and there he was buried. On his death Syon Abbey applied for confirmation of its title to the lands, and made a survey or extent of the property, the first detailed information about Cheltenham since the Domesday survey. From this date onwards, the people, the town and the countryside are revealed in gradually increasing detail. Syon's effective tenure of the manor of Cheltenham lasted for a little less than a hundred years. For the inhabitants, the change of lord probably made little immediate difference, but while the monasteries seem to have held strongly to traditional forms, their dissolution stimulated change. When Syon was dissolved in 1539, Cheltenham returned to royal lordship.

RECTORY MANORS

The greatest lord in Cheltenham was of course the king, whose overall authority could hardly be challenged, but from at least the reign of Edward the Confessor his immediate authority did not extend over the land of the church in Cheltenham. This was the rectory manor, held by Regenbald the priest. Land belonging to a rectory or vicarage, known as 'glebeland' (from the Latin *gleba*, 'soil'), was free of obligations in money or services to the lord of the manor, though if it included scattered strips of arable in the common fields, it was subject to the practices and regulations governing those fields. Only a substantial amount of land, such as the 1½ hides in Cheltenham, would constitute a manor, with a manorial court for villagers or customary tenants. The lands of the rectory manor were intermingled in the open fields with those of other tenants of Cheltenham manor, but it had its own court. In Prestbury, though not recorded until after Domesday, the church also had a small manor of one carucate or ploughland. Both these churches and manors, and their endowments, were given to monasteries.

LEFT

The three steps, the base and the shaft of the cross in the churchyard of the parish church of St Mary in Cheltenham are probably fourteenth-century in date. In the later nineteenth century it was topped by four 'meaningless gablets' in place of the sundial that used to be there and which was drawn by George Rowe in his *Guide* of 1845. The original head was perhaps destroyed during the Reformation or by Puritans during the Commonwealth. The churchyard cross was important in the processions which involved an illiterate congregation in the services, particularly on Palm Sunday, and it may also have served as the focus of the market. Could it also have served to assert the abbot of Cirencester's authority *vis à vis* the monastic lord of the manor?

PHOTOGRAPH: CARNEGIE, 2009

RIGHT

There is a fourteenth-century cross in the churchyard of St Mary's, Charlton Kings. It was restored in 1913, and a replacement head was designed reflecting fifteenth-century patterns. It is striking that Cheltenham and Charlton Kings both have churchyard crosses of the same period. This suggests an initiative by Cirencester Abbey. On the outside of the south wall there is a medieval mass dial, similar to the one in Leckhampton (*see* page 21).

PHOTOGRAPH: AUTHOR, 2009

The rector of a church had authority in his particular parish, and the land with which that church was endowed was his for life or until he resigned from the living. So also were the tithes of produce, the offerings of parishioners, fees for their baptisms, and for their burials if they were prosperous, and any donations made to the church. The details varied from parish to parish, and were not invariable from century to century, but they were always to a great extent determined by what was accepted as the custom of the parish. The whole bundle of these rights was called the *rectory* (which was not the residence of the rector, as in modern usage). Usually an endowment of land implied also that there *was* a house, but this was not always so. Regenbald could be termed the rector of Cheltenham at the time of Domesday, because he held the Church and enjoyed its rights and incomes, though he probably never lived in the parish. After Henry I gave Cheltenham church to his new foundation of Augustinian canons in Cirencester, the canons corporately became the rector and lord of the rectory manor. Augustinian canons were not monks, but priests who lived according to a monastic rule; they could go into the community, and could serve the church of Cheltenham themselves and collect its revenues. The abbey held separate courts for its tenants and also claimed view of frankpledge.[32] The Cheltenham estates were extended by purchasing more land, and through receiving property as gifts; for example, there were gifts from Walter of Brussels for the service of his chapel at Arle and another by Butler for his chapel. Land acquired in these ways was not part of the rectory manor, and when towards the end of the thirteenth century the jurors of Cheltenham manor court suggested that the abbot was evading his service to the Cheltenham courts, it was presumably in respect of lands such as these.

But Cirencester was apparently not able to secure total control of the rectory for nearly a hundred years after Henry I's charter, because there were disputes about its legal rights. A *vicar* stood in place of a rector, as *vice*-rector. He was appointed by the rector, and his endowment, usually only a part of the total rectory, was his by right and not by favour. Moreover, at his death the rector was legally obliged to appoint another man to the vicarage. In contrast, a *chaplain* was a curate, a priest able to fulfil the duties of the care or 'cure' of souls, but without independent status; he was dependent on a wage or stipend paid by the rector and he served in what might be regarded as a chapel associated with the mother church. Some time before 1180, at the latest, a priest called Reginald claimed himself to be properly the vicar of Cheltenham. The abbot and canons, on the other hand, chose to call him a chaplain. Reginald embarked on a long and apparently bitter dispute with them over his proper status, in a series of public arguments before 'no less than four popes, two archbishops, and several bishops, abbots and priors', whose judgements were carefully preserved in Cirencester Abbey's records.[33]

The first indication of the dispute is a puzzling decision that Randulf the priest, a canon of Cirencester, would renounce *his* claim to the vicarage if Reginald agreed to pay him four marks (£2 13s. 4d.), a sum comparable with the customary annual stipend of a curate. Randulf thus seems to have had a rival claim to the same vicarage. It emerged that Reginald's father, Lambert, had held land to which Reginald was required to surrender his claim, hinting that

Lambert may also have been vicar of Cheltenham. If that was so, it perhaps reflects the traditional position of the hereditary priest. The Norman Church was not in favour of this Anglo-Saxon practice (not least because it maintained an Anglo-Saxon man of authority who might counteract the position of the Norman lord). As early as 1102 a council at Westminster agreed that sons of priests should not be heirs of their fathers' churches, and this was repeated in 1175, exactly the time when Reginald's claims were in dispute.[34] A monastery was in a stronger position to challenge a hereditary incumbent than was a layman, and this may sometimes have been the motive behind a gift of a church to a monastery.

Reginald agreed that his father had held the land only for life, and that he in turn would hold it for life, paying 10s. a year for the land and £1 a year for the vicarage. But then a new abbot, Richard, seems to have secured Reginald's renunciation of the vicarage, Reginald being paid eight marks (£5 6s. 8d.) if he stopped his harassment of the abbey. A letter written between 1187 and 1194 to the abbot and canons of Cirencester stated that the dispute concerned a quarter-portion of Cheltenham church. Minster churches not uncommonly had several priests who shared their endowments and were known as 'portioners'. Possibly, three of the portions been made over to Cirencester but a fourth been retained by the hereditary vicar.

Finally, in 1195, the pope confirmed that on Reginald's death the church of Cheltenham and the chapel of Charlton, together with Reginald's fourth portion, should be transferred to the abbey, provided that the income was used for hospitable purposes. This was termed 'appropriation', whereby revenues were taken from the church for other purposes – in this case, to the abbey's own use. When the bishop of Worcester confirmed the appropriation in 1216–17 (perhaps on the death of Reginald) he required the abbey to support two chaplains to serve the church of Cheltenham, but the appropriation of the revenues seems to have been secured, for in 1535, almost 350 years later, a large part of the income from Cheltenham rectory was indeed passed to the abbey's cook.

Yet control over Cheltenham church by Cirencester Abbey was still not complete. The archdeacon of Gloucester claimed that his predecessors had received three 'procurations' (payments made on the occasion of a visitation, originally of food) because the church had been divided into those three parts and, further, that a fourth payment was made in respect of Charlton chapel, making up the four portions into which it appears from the letter quoted above that the control of the church had been divided. This gives further support to the status of Cheltenham church as an Anglo-Saxon minster. In a judgment dated 20 March 1230 the chancellor and dean of Oxford University set aside the archdeacon's claims,[35] and the abbot of Cirencester was finally master of Cheltenham church.

It had not been unprincipled to assign all the tithes for the support of another church, and better-endowed parish churches such as Cheltenham and Prestbury were valuable additions to the income of a monastery. But after Henry VIII's dissolution of the religious houses, those revenues which had been redirected to them from parish churches were taken by the king and most were subsequently lost to the church. They frequently passed to laymen, as was the case in Cheltenham, with long-term effects on the development of the town. Another implication, which might be more immediately relevant, was that for centuries the parishioners of Cheltenham had a poorly paid curate. Attempts by private individuals and families to remedy the deficiency, by endowing chantries, were frustrated by Edward VI's closure and seizure of those endowments.

The history of Prestbury rectory has a number of similarities to that of Cheltenham.[36] The bishop of Hereford was the lord of Prestbury manor at the time of the Norman Conquest, and possibly long before. In 1136, a new monastery, called Llanthony Secunda, was founded at Gloucester for the canons of the existing house of Llanthony Prima near Abergavenny. That same year Robert de Bethune, bishop of Hereford, granted Prestbury church ('under the hills') with its chapel at Sevenhampton ('upon the hills') to Llanthony because the latter's possessions had been 'greatly diminished by reason of the ravages of war' – in other words, the serious attacks by the Welsh.[37] Bishop Robert, who had himself been prior of Llanthony Prima, requested Miles the constable (he who was soon to be made earl of Hereford) to provide a new site for the canons at Gloucester. Miles was persuaded to help them because his father was buried in Llanthony Prima, and his ancestors had been benefactors to the priory. He gave a site, consisting of a hide of land near Gloucester together with the church of St Owen, to establish Llanthony Secunda, and most of the canons moved there.

His grant at Prestbury was of the rectory land and the tithes of the villagers' land, but not the two-thirds portion of tithes of grain from his demesne which was in the possession of the dean and precentor of Hereford, nor the

Although the dovecote near the Priory in Prestbury is a seventeenth- or early eighteenth-century building, it might well have replaced an earlier structure, possibly after the rectory was sold to the Baghot family. At the end of the thirteenth century the bishop of Hereford had a dovecote in Prestbury worth 5s. a year; this may have been near his manor house, now gone, or near the rectory which the bishop granted to Llanthony Priory in the twelfth century. It was a privilege of a lord of the manor or a rector to have one: the doves ate valuable corn, and so the farmers of the manor were not allowed to keep them. The Prestbury dovecote has now been converted to a house, but in this old photograph it appears to have been a coach house.

COURTESY OF MR AND MRS B. MORRIS

Llanthony Priory became rector of Prestbury after 1136, through the grant by the bishop of Hereford. The Priory collected the rector's tithes and farmed his land-holding. Other lands were given to the Priory, and the estate was known as both rectory and manor. The house called the Priory was built at several different dates, mainly since it passed into secular hands, but there are traces of a fourteenth-century timber hall of four bays open to the roof, built while Llanthony held the estate. The Crown held the house from the dissolution until 1608. Between 1608 and 1622 it was owned by the Earl of Pembroke, and it seems likely that he or his lessee added the two bays of two storeys at each end of the hall. The external stone casing is eighteenth-century, and there have been further substantial additions.

PHOTOGRAPH: AUTHOR, 2009

tithes of his park. In other words, the diocese of Hereford retained its own valuable assets. The bishop's policy of keeping his park free of tithe probably encouraged the preservation of its boundaries, distinguishing it from the surrounding lands. This contributed surprisingly, and unexpectedly, to Cheltenham's future prosperity, because this convenient, compact and flat area from the 1830s was used for the racecourse. Llanthony Secunda appropriated Prestbury rectory just as Cirencester appropriated Cheltenham, but the parishioners of Prestbury had the advantage of a vicar. Some thirty years later, another Bishop Robert of Hereford enlarged the grant to Llanthony by adding to it the small tithes of lambs, wool, swine and cheese from the demesne.

About this time the vicar was endowed with half a yardland, half a house and some tithes. Although the priory was later licensed to appropriate the vicarage, in fact vicars continued to be appointed. In 1294 it was reported that Llanthony's land comprised one carucate or ploughland, while the bishop of Hereford held seven carucates in Prestbury and Sevenhampton. But though small, the Llanthony estate in Prestbury was called a manor and in 1365 it had nine tenants, while the house near the church (later the Priory) was described as the manor or rectory house. After the dissolution, the rectory estate was sold to a layman, as was Cheltenham rectory. Moreover, Elizabeth I took possession of the bishop of Hereford's Prestbury estate. Thus, with the exception of the vicar's share, all the church land at Prestbury ultimately passed into lay hands.

THE MANOR OF CHARLTON OR ASHLEY

In the twelfth century two more small manors were defined within Cheltenham's boundaries which, like the rectory manor, were independent and held their own courts, but were not, however, discrete territories. The more important was the sub-manor of Charlton, which remained a 'member' (a sort of subsidiary) of Cheltenham manor; it was later known as the manor of Ashley.[38] In a list compiled between 1211 and 1213, the grant which created the manor is said to have been made by Miles, earl of Hereford, who had been lord of Cheltenham; he had become an earl in 1141 and died in 1143, giving an approximate date to the event (although in 1246 it was said that the grant had been made by Henry II, who succeeded to the throne in 1154). It was confirmed to Walter of *Esselega* in 1159–60 by Matilda's son, Henry II, when it consisted of land valued at £10. At this time the estate was identified simply as being in Cheltenham, but some years later, in 1190–91 when Walter of Ashley paid Richard I to confirm his title, it was identified specifically as in Charlton.

In 1235–36, on the marriage of the king's sister, a later Walter de Ashley paid an aid (a compulsory levy) for his holding of half a knight's fee, one of the taxes based on feudal obligations, and at his death in 1246 the manor consisted of one virgate or yardland in demesne and nine yardlands in villeinage, suggesting that the land had been cleared and settled. There was no mention of a manor house, and Walter probably never lived on his Charlton manor.

This postcard of Cudnall Street, formerly the road to London, shows it early in the twentieth century; postcards had only been accepted by the Post Office since 1894, and after 1902 the picture occupied one side, as here, with message and address sharing the other side. Cudnall was the nucleus of one of Charlton Kings' farming communities. The new manor of Walter of Ashley was allocated every other croft on the south side of Cudnall Street, and arable land would have alternated similarly with that of holdings remaining in the king's hands. The turnpike road bypassed Cudnall Street, which retains a quiet country atmosphere, with its mixture of interesting brick and stone walls, and houses of all periods and sizes, a number of which are listed. Hetton Lawn was the home of Revd Henry and Mrs Liddell, grandparents of Alice, and Lewis Carroll visited here in 1863.

© CHELTENHAM ART GALLERY AND MUSEUM

He held several estates elsewhere, and is a good example of an emerging 'middle class' of small landowner. His 'home farm' or demesne probably served as the holding of the bailiff of his manor. Later records show that the land belonging to the manor was scattered through the area. The arable was mainly in Castlefield and Middle field. Of the houses or tenements, one was in Moorend, one in Up End and four in Cudnall, where every other holding on the south side of the street had been allocated to the manor. It also included waste land east of the Hearne Brook, and probably the development of East End followed. The pound for keeping stray cattle was here, and one more house, which served as the courthouse for the manor until the later nineteenth century.

The name 'Ashley' later came to be applied to this manor in Charlton because the first holders were identified by their main estate at Ashley, near Tetbury on the border between Gloucestershire and Wiltshire. The name 'Ashley manor' is first recorded in 1625, to distinguish this sub-manor from the rest of Charlton township. It became a convenient division or tithing in the parish of Charlton Kings. Eventually this estate provided the nucleus of Charlton Park, though the house known by this name since 1784 was not Ashley manor house but was called The Forden.[39]

THE MANOR OF REDGROVE

Redgrove in Arle, a second, smaller manor created by Walter the constable between 1155 and 1160, also became independent of the manor of Cheltenham.[40] Like the manor of Charlton, it offered opportunity for development. Walter was the son of Miles, earl of Hereford, but did not succeed to the earldom on the death of his older brother, Roger, because of the latter's rebellion against Henry II in 1155. In his foundation charter Walter granted land at 'Hatherley' to Llanthony Secunda, the Augustinian priory at Gloucester founded by his father.[41] The land was described as an assart, which indicated a newly cleared area of land in a forest, and this small estate was later identified as 'Redgrove'. It is so described in 1535 in the *Valor Ecclesiasticus* and in 1616 when James I granted it to Gloucester Corporation. Walter's gift included an assart in Oakley wood which was in Prestbury, Ham and Charlton; furthermore, Walter allowed or encouraged two of his own knights to give more land in the area to Llanthony Secunda.

Redgrove was situated at the south-western edge of the hundred and parish of Cheltenham, and was probably largely wooded, the soil south of the Hatherley Brook being the difficult stiff blue lias clay.[42] In 1294, Llanthony's estate here was described as two carucates (or eight yardlands). The assart in Prestbury, Ham and Charlton was one carucate, and there was also a dovecote.[43] By 1535 Llanthony had free and customary tenants in Redgrove. The monastery was dissolved in 1539 and a survey of 1540 mentioned lands and tenements in Redgrove, rents at Canehill in the parish of Staverton, and in Harthurste:[44] Harthurstfield was in Cheltenham manor, and it appears in the definition of the boundaries of Cheltenham manor and hundred in 1617, but Harthurst (deer wood) was another boundary settlement like Up Hatherley, and was

Although long after the creation of Redgrove manor, field names on an exceptionally clear enclosure map of Arle and Alstone of 1835 give a good indication of where it was on the western edge of Cheltenham parish and manor. Numbers 258, 261, 262 and 264 were called Redgrove, and numbers 260, 275 and 277 were Grove field. Number 265 was the mansion house and pleasure grounds where the new Arle Court was to be built. Hatherley Road defined much of the township's boundary, but a large field on the south-east side of the road was in Arle, showing how tenurial relationships governed land boundaries.

in several parishes.[45] After the dissolution of Llanthony the history of Redgrove is complicated and confusing, as the priory's manor was broken up. Thereafter the name Redgrove might refer to a field, a settlement, or a manor.

LORDS AND VILLS IN 1316

In 1316 parliament agreed that one man should be sent from each vill 'not being a city borough or royal demesne' to serve for sixty days in the king's army against the Scots,[46] and in each county the sheriff was asked to return the names of the lords of each vill. The *Nomina Villarum* gives a simplified picture of the situation in Cheltenham, simply stating that the hundred belonged to the abbot of Fécamp who was the lord of the vill. The status of ancient demesne meant that no mention was made of subordinate vills or manors such as Charlton and Redgrove. Prestbury was included in Deerhurst hundred, which belonged to the prior of Deerhurst. The lord of Prestbury manor was the bishop of Hereford. Leckhampton and Swindon were not ancient demesne. There were four lords in Leckhampton: John Lovell, Walter de Bradwell, John de Bradenstocke and John de Monmouth;[47] three separate free landholdings had been recorded in Domesday, though in the hands of two lords, and a fourth landholding had been part of the king's Cheltenham manor demesne, and this had probably been granted away to create the fourth freehold. The lord of Swindon was Robert Moryn.

Further subdivision of these freehold estates was likely as the fortunes of particular families waxed and waned.

Villagers

The manor was of great importance to all inhabitants. Its boundaries set the limits of the area within which they worked and the manor court maintained discipline within the common fields, regulating what could be grown and where animals could be pastured. Villagers who were tenants of the manor were fined at the court for transgressing these rules. The cultivators of the soil could not easily leave their land and move elsewhere and their marriages were subject to supervision because this affected who would be the future occupiers of the land through inheritance. The social structure of the manors in Cheltenham hundred was dominated by the villeins or villagers. They were the husbandmen of later centuries, who cultivated the land and

Leckhampton Court, through recent extensive restoration, survives as an important medieval house. The battlemented central block contains the early fourteenth-century house, but it is partly masked by the lower line of battlements above a later linking corridor. Like the Priory in Prestbury, the oldest part of the Court is the great hall, which is to the left of the porch, a very lofty room with large traceried windows; it is now a chapel. The other rooms of the same period have been altered substantially. The central porch is also fourteenth-century. The house was possibly built about 1320–30 for Sir John Giffard. The family also became lords of the second manor in Leckhampton and patrons of the church and at a later period rectors of the parish, absorbing some of the church's endowment.
PHOTOGRAPH: AUTHOR, 2009

The two carved stone effigies in the south-west corner of Leckhampton church are thought to be of Sir John Giffard, who died in about 1330, lord of the principal manor in Leckhampton and his lady. The effigies have been moved several times in rearrangements or restorations of the church. In the most recent removal Sir John and his lady have been transposed; Samuel Lysons, in his *A Collection of Gloucestershire Antiquities* (1804) shows them the other way round.

PHOTOGRAPH: CARNEGIE, 2010

provided the lord of the manor with a workforce for his demesne – though being required to work on the lord's own land was a burden which was particularly resented.

At the time of the Norman Conquest, villagers or villeins were not as tightly constrained within the manor as they later became, through legal definition of their position as 'unfree'.[48] However, by the thirteenth century on royal demesne manors such as Cheltenham, the villeins had more independence of the lord than elsewhere. The king could not personally supervise his manors and so use was made of a special legal procedure or writ, which ensured that his lands were protected from possible embezzlement by those who farmed or leased the manors or attempted to change the customs. This gave villeins some protection, whereas those in other manors generally had little defence against a lord's encroachments.

Manorial custom was the principle on which decisions about entitlement to land were made.[49] Villein holdings were described in terms of the 'virgate' or yardland, which represented an early and simple assessment of comparative size, rather than an accurate measurement, so that tax and services could be allocated among them. A yardland consisted primarily of arable land, together with a share of pasture in rough grassland on the downs or hills, and of grazing on the arable fields between harvest and ploughing or while lying fallow for a year. Meadow was particularly valuable as the hay provided winter fodder; each holding probably had some access to meadow, but in Cheltenham details of individual holdings are not available until the mid-fifteenth century.

An extent or survey of Cheltenham manor was made in 1294, in anticipation of the king's confiscation of alien priories. By this date the manor had been reduced by the small manors of Charlton (Ashley) and Redgrove.[50] The lord's demesne consisted of 149 acres of arable land, 30 acres of meadow, and some pasture and wood. The number of villein holdings was 127, and it seems there were 126 villagers, so that only one man had two holdings. Over the following years, this neat pattern became distorted as successful husbandmen took on more land from the less successful. There was a detailed schedule of the work that each villager had to do for the lord during the year. Seventy holdings had onerous services, including ploughing, weeding, mowing, reaping and carting. Another 47 helped with haymaking, harvest and carting, and ten paid nominal rents of two hens and one cock each. In practice, though, all these 'works' had been converted to money rents.

FREE HOLDINGS

Lords of the manor who held land directly from the king were responsible for paying the tax for which the manor was assessed, and for supplying men for the army. They passed on some of their burden of military service and taxation to one or more manorial tenants, in return for giving them land free of most manorial obligations, thus making them 'free men' and their land 'freehold'. Free men did not fit comfortably into the manorial structure, but if their landholdings were within the common fields they could not easily convert them into fully independent units. Freeholders often sought to buy out other occupiers whose lands intermingled with theirs, in order to consolidate their land, or to exchange strips in order to achieve the same goal.

In Domesday Book no free men were noted in Cheltenham other than the church, and just two in Prestbury; one of the Prestbury freemen was called a *radknight*, a 'riding man' whose duties probably were to carry letters for the king. A survey of a much later date, about 1450, records the freeholding in Alstone of a toft and half a hide (two yardlands) in the hands of Thomas Anford and his associates, formerly of Henry Best and associates and before that again of Matilda Bayse, noting the obligation attaching to this holding: that the holder 'should carry letters as by ancient custom'. This duty reflects the type of freehold noted in Domesday in Prestbury and elsewhere, and 'ancient custom' was an accurate description of an archaic form of land tenure; it offers a hint that the Domesday survey may have omitted small freeholds of this type in Cheltenham. Matilda Bayse's estate was to be of exceptional importance in the development of Cheltenham: she held land on the hill close to the river Chelt which became known as Bayshill, and later ownership of Bayshill opened the door to the construction of the first Cheltenham spa and the house of Lord Fauconberg, memorably occupied by George III and his family in 1788.

Other small freeholds are documented in the twelfth-century records of Cirencester Abbey.[51] For example, the yardland in Arle that Walter of Brussels 'held freely' and gave, sometime between 1143 and 1150, to pay for services in his chapel. Three copies of mid-thirteenth century charters from Walter Hawlf were conveyances of small parcels of arable to the abbey. Two of these, 2 acres in Alstone and an assart of 6 acres in Gravendon furlong, had been purchased from Ralph Russell and Mabel, his wife. Walter Hawlf had paid them 40 shillings (£2) and a further half mark (6s. 8d.) to Mabel individually. The name Gravendon, 'wood hill', emphasises the relatively recent clearance or assarting of this land for arable cultivation. Walter also gave the abbey three parcels amounting to 2 acres and another assart, in 'Rodeway', which he had acquired from William de Fonte for which the canons had to pay

4d. to the king as William de Fonte had paid. The conveyances refer to strips in the common fields, described as one acre or half an acre. These transactions of such small amounts of land may suggest that Cirencester was attempting to consolidate its holdings, and the charters perhaps represent one half of an exchange of strips in the common fields. A wish to improve the estate is evident in the transactions which allowed the abbey to stop up a lane between its mills, later known as Cambray mill, and its 'court', the Rectory or Parsonage house.[52]

These documents, and others of the thirteenth century dealing with equally small parcels of land,[53] show that there were a number of small freeholders in Cheltenham, and the names of witnesses to the charters indicate others able to attest to the transactions. Rodney Hilton observed of the West Midlands at the end of the thirteenth century that even without lists of freeholders on their estates, 'the great number of free charter witnesses in the monastic cartularies would emphasise their presence'.[54] The witnesses to Walter Hawlf's charters included William Franklin of Cheltenham, in one case named as William Freeman; his name points to his distinct status. Later documents were witnessed by his son and by Walter, Adam and Simon of Naunton. Roger of Hamme, Reginald of Alstone and John of Arle were witnesses appearing in company with William the Franklin, Simon Moryn, lord of Swindon, and various clerics.[55] Confirmation that there was a significant number of freeholders is found in the survey of the alien priories which the king ordered in 1294; some 23 free tenants were noted. How many had holdings as ancient as Prestbury's *radknight* or Matilda Bayse's letter-carrying freehold it is impossible to say, but there is an intriguing coincidence between the 23 and the 24 villein holdings of Domesday Book. Perhaps the Domesday villeins established their position as freeholders, rather than merging with a large number of unfree manorial tenants. Freeholds also originated from the clearance or assarting of former wooded areas, and through the lord creating holdings owing military service in order to meet his obligation to supply so many soldiers for the king's army. Prestbury manor also experienced an apparent increase in free tenants, from one *radknight* and a priest in 1086 to 24 about 1280, mostly from the process of assarting but in three instances linked with military service.[56]

BURGAGES

Before 1294 another important group of holdings was established in Cheltenham, the burgages set out along the High Street. Burgage tenure was a distinctively urban form of landholding, approximating to freehold, and burgages (or burgage plots) were the regularly sized units of land subject to this tenure. Typically, they would be created by the lord for occupation and purchase by merchants and craftsmen. In some cases burgages were integral to the creation of a new town, in others they followed the existence of a market and a concentration of merchants and craftsmen which already in effect constituted a town. In 1294 there were 52 burgages in Cheltenham.[57] In neighbouring Prestbury the bishop of Hereford had also created burgages by this date, and about 1280 there were thirty.[58] No more information is available for Cheltenham until the mid-fifteenth century but clearly its commercial development had begun.

By 1806, the date of Cheltenham township enclosure map (*below*), the High Street burgage plots had mostly been subdivided into halves, quarters, or even smaller fractions. Nonetheless, the map gives an impression of how they had been laid out, with a concentration on the north side of the street, and with a back lane giving access to the plots from the rear, particularly necessary after the frontages had been developed into a continuous line of buildings. Around the church and the former court or manor house there was some open space. East of Greyhound Lane, which was later widened and became North Street, the shorter plots suggest that burgages were laid out here after the initial foundation of the market. Further east, there appear to have been no burgages on the south side of the street, but a row of small houses suggests speculative development on church land.

GLOUCESTERSHIRE ARCHIVES, D2025

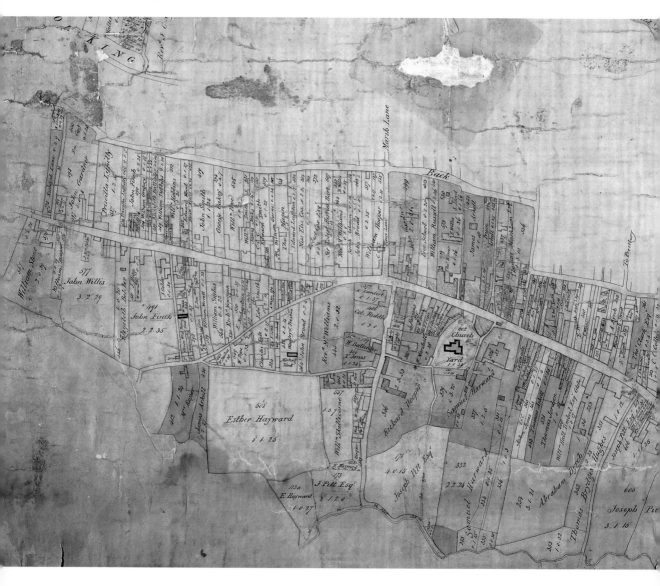

CHAPTER THREE

GROWTH

THE ECONOMIC PROGRESS of Cheltenham from the thirteenth century, and its increasing visibility as a town, can be traced from surviving national records of taxation, and from two surveys of the manor on the occasions when there was a change of monastic ownership. The two surveys, of 1294 and 1453, also point to changes in the land-holding structure. Unlike the Domesday survey, the later ones did not cover the entire area which had been within Cheltenham hundred in 1086, because of the existence of independent manors, but they nonetheless give valuable insight into the development of both the town and its surrounding rural hinterland.

Some towns appear to be ancient and natural meeting places, situated at the crossing of several routeways or tracks where traders met to exchange goods, but whose precise origins cannot be documented. They have been categorised by Everitt as 'primary towns'.[1] Winchcombe, a borough second in importance only to Gloucester in Domesday Book, may be an example. Other towns were 'planted' by medieval lords of the manor as speculative ventures. A lord would lay out a series of rectangular plots (known as burgage plots) along one or both sides of a roadway and, at that time or later, formalise the trading functions of the new town by obtaining the right to hold a market. Apart from their regularity, the distinguishing characteristic of the burgage plot was that it did not carry any obligation of work for the lord of the manor, though its owner still had to pay a small or nominal rent to acknowledge the residual interest of the lord. In later terminology, it was freehold.

The word 'burgage' derives from the same root as 'borough', which for the Anglo-Saxons meant a fortified town. To them a 'port' was a market town, but that term dropped out of use and by the twelfth century the word 'borough' was generally used of all towns. But that term also acquired a more restricted legal meaning, indicating a town separate from the manor in which it was situated, having a royal charter, and – later – the right to self-government by a town council. The phrase 'market town' was then used either as an all-purpose description, or for places with less prestige.[2]

Although Cheltenham was termed a borough on one occasion in the early fourteenth century, it had no charter – not even a market charter – and its status as a borough is therefore perhaps questionable. However, there were burgages in Cheltenham, and the presence of such tenure is generally regarded as one of the indicators of borough status. The picture is therefore confused. The holders of burgages in Cheltenham did not completely free themselves from manorial control until 1717,[3] and the town did not acquire the status of a chartered borough until 1876, although it had become a parliamentary borough in 1832.

There is no indication, either from archaeological or documentary source, that Cheltenham had begun to develop urban functions and attributes by 1086, unless it is the mention of ten smallholders in Domesday Book. Dyer has shown how such smallholders were often recorded living close to recognised towns, or in places where a town would soon develop. In Tewkesbury, for example, 'sixteen smallholders round the hall' in 1066 may have been the nucleus of the later town; Domesday Book notes that William the Conqueror's queen, Matilda, had founded a market there before 1086, possibly exploiting a development already under way.

A town supplied goods to, and exchanged produce from, the surrounding rural area. Smaller market towns had a hinterland covering the villages and hamlets in approximately a six-mile radius.[4] It is quite likely that in Cheltenham, as in hundreds of other emergent towns, a market already existed well before there was any written record of its presence. Cheltenham was the focus of a large agricultural estate with several townships, and the centre of a hundred. There was often a market in a hundredal manor – it followed naturally from the collection of taxes paid to the lord and to the king, which tenants funded by selling goods. By 1294, for example, the labour services which the tenants of the manor owed to Cheltenham's lord were all 'sold', which meant that the lord collected money instead of requiring actual work on his demesne, and this implied that they sold their produce for cash in a local market.

Ancient markets existed by prescription (that is, without a charter), but that meant that they were outside the direct control of any individual.[5] Manorial lords were rarely content with such an arrangement, because it denied them potential revenue. Selling goods became a source of income to the lord of the manor when he obtained a charter, and could be an advantage to the townsmen: goods brought to market from outside paid a toll to the lord, but townspeople were exempt. The king's right to license the holding of markets was steadily asserted,[6] and as a result, from the mid-twelfth century, it was standard practice for a manorial lord to obtain a charter from the Crown, allowing him to hold a market in his manor.

There was certainly a market in Cheltenham in 1226, but the date of its foundation is unknown. It was apparently customary and prescriptive, not chartered. Neither is it clear whether the 52 burgage plots which are recorded in 1294 had been deliberately laid out on a new site, or whether an unofficial market became successful and the burgages followed. It is clear, though, that in 1226 Cheltenham was not simply a rural village. In that year the king granted a lease of the manor to 'the men of Cheltenham' for four years at a rent of £64 a year. The writ to the sheriff of Gloucestershire goes on to say that the men of the manor should have a market on a Thursday and a three-day fair starting on St James's day, 25 July.[7]

The grant implies that there was already some body able to administer the market, and the date is within what Finberg called the 'golden age of borough-making' between 1200 and

1350. Some 21 new Gloucestershire boroughs existed by 1334, not all of them established by charter, but because much more written evidence survives from this period than from earlier periods that may give a false impression.[8] It seems unlikely that the men of the manor could pay a sizeable rent and hold a weekly market if there were not already traders living there and, perhaps significantly, one man who witnessed a charter granting land in Cheltenham to Cirencester Abbey in the mid-thirteenth century was called John Merchant.[9] The burgage plots were laid out at a time when the king was lord of the manor; there was little need of a charter in these circumstances, although the men of Cheltenham would later assert, when setting out their rights to John Norden who was surveying the manor for the future Charles I in 1617, that there had been a charter 'but how ancient they know not'.[10]

Markets flourished where there was good road or river communication, which was not obviously the case in Cheltenham, although its location resembled that of several new Gloucestershire towns of the early Middle Ages.[11] The market at Cheltenham was sited at the foot of the Cotswold hills, at a point where a track linked the Severn valley with the upland, although the route eastwards climbing the Cotswold scarp was steep. Successful markets often had access to different types of agricultural land, which encouraged the sale of a diversity of products, and that was certainly the case here. Broadway, where the abbot of Pershore was granted a market charter by Richard I between 1196 and 1198, was comparably sited,[12] and the 'way' which climbs the scarp there is also very steep.

Much closer, and representing real competition, was Prestbury, where in 1249, 23 years after the king's grant of the manor and hundred to the men of Cheltenham, the bishop of Hereford was licensed by Henry III to have a market on Tuesdays. It was probably held in the wide and stylish street called The Burgage, which had been newly laid out. The main routeway from Gloucester and Cheltenham to Winchcombe went through Prestbury but did not pass along The Burgage. It climbed the scarp onto the Cotswolds and from thence a branch went to the bishop of Hereford's other manor of Sevenhampton. Forty years later Prestbury was called a 'borough', and about that date there were thirty burgage plots in the street.[13] No doubt the bishop of Hereford wished to compete with Cheltenham market a few miles away, but Prestbury market was not so successful; not only was Cheltenham's market better established, but the later a market was instituted the smaller were its chances of flourishing.[14] It dwindled, though shifted to Mondays in 1394. In the 1520s, according to Leland, it was revived, but had faded away by the middle of the seventeenth century.[15]

The immediate competitors to Cheltenham's market were those of Gloucester and Tewkesbury, both of which were readily accessible and drew on the fertile land of the Severn plain; Cleeve Hill interposed a significant barrier to travel to Winchcombe. It was important in their development that Cheltenham, Tewkesbury and Winchcombe were all centres for unusually large manors, and this no doubt helped to establish the links for the farmers with their own market. Gloucester as the county town was naturally the centre for many more services than the other towns.

Paying a fixed rent or 'farm' for a manor for a certain number of years, as the men of Cheltenham did, was not unusual. It is found at all periods, including before the Norman Conquest, but was particularly frequent in the late twelfth and early thirteenth centuries. For example, at this time two-thirds of manors belonging to Worcester Priory were farmed.[16] For the lord, farming the manor meant an income that did not fluctuate with the price of produce or the size of the harvest. For the tenants, they assessed and raised the money for the farm among themselves but had no other payments to make. The farm also enabled them, especially where the demesne arable was in strips intermixed with their own land, to divide the demesne conveniently between themselves and so to cultivate larger blocks of land. Furthermore, the farm included the king's pastures, which enabled villagers to keep more sheep, so increasing the fertility of the land because a larger number could be folded on the arable fields at night, and increasing the production of wool which was the most rewarding cash crop at the time.

For the men of Cheltenham, independence lasted only a few years. The initial grant was renewed in 1230 for ten years, the writ repeating that the men shall have the 'due customs pertaining to the hundred, with a weekly market on Thursday and a yearly fair'. But in 1236 Cheltenham was one of the estates granted by Henry III to Queen Eleanor for her dowry, and not long afterwards, in 1247, the manor and hundred were granted to Fécamp Abbey. Whether thereafter the townsmen attempted to win independence or not, monastic lords were reluctant to encourage the process, and Cheltenham borough was not formally separated from the rural manor.[17]

The borough was not strikingly ambitious. In 1294 there were fewer than half the number of burgages as at Chipping Campden or Tewkesbury, and a tenth of the number at Gloucester.[18] Nonetheless the commercial functions of Cheltenham were of some importance. There was

There are no reliable pictures of Cheltenham High Street earlier than the nineteenth century, but this postcard with a wagon, postmarked 30 October 1906, is a reminder of how transport was horse-drawn, and that farmers and small-holders brought their produce to market each week on foot or by horse and cart. Before the spa development, High Street contained farmhouses as well as craftsmen's shops and gentlemen's residences.

© CHELTENHAM ART GALLERY AND MUSEUM

High Street, Cheltenham.

little overlap between the burgage-holders and the agricultural tenants; the burgesses were a separate community of tradesmen, not smallholders with farming interests, though the two groups lived side by side in the same street. It was said later that the borough had no fixed boundaries 'because other lands lie dispersedly and intermixed with the Burgage tenements of which the Borough consisted, but … in their lists of Borough tenants it may be seen how far the burgage extendeth.'[19]

CHELTENHAM IN 1294

Twelve free men were required to give evidence for the 'extent' or survey of Cheltenham manor in 1294, which was undertaken in anticipation of the confiscation of alien priories. Fécamp's manor did not include the rectory lands held by Cirencester Abbey, nor the manors of Ashley and of Redgrove which had been granted away more than a hundred years before, but nonetheless it comprised most of Cheltenham and Charlton Kings. The survey reveals that 23 freeholds had been created since 1086, a trend similarly evident in Prestbury manor.[20] The most striking change in Cheltenham, however, was the increase in the number of those holding land. In 1086 there had been 36 villeins or villagers and seven slaves, but in 1294 the total of land-holders, 201, had almost quintupled – 23 freeholders, 52 burgesses and 126 villagers. Moreover, as indicated in 1246, there were another eighteen half-yardlands in Ashley manor.[21] The 1294 survey suggests a recent and tidy allocation of land; only one man had two holdings. But over the following years the picture was increasingly complicated by successful husbandmen taking on others' land and building up their holdings. The survey unfortunately gives no indication of the structure of the different townships.

The Promenade is a comparatively new street, but it is now the scene of a regular farmers' market, and before Christmas for several weeks there are stalls or booths not unlike the medieval markets. The regular weekly market is still held in Cheltenham, but after several moves over the last 200 years, it has been put out of sight in an area off the High Street which on the other six days of the week is a car park.

PHOTOGRAPH: CARNEGIE, 2009

The royal demesne had been substantially reduced since 1086 when it was four carucates. In 1294 it consisted of 149 acres of arable land, 30 acres of meadow, and some pasture and wood, together described as one carucate in the *Taxatio* of Pope Nicholas in 1291. An *inquisition post mortem* of Adam le Despenser, four years later, stated that he held a carucate of 160 acres in Leckhampton. The demesne of the Cheltenham manor was a relatively small proportion of the total area. For comparison, about one-fifth of the acreage of the bishopric of Worcester's manors was demesne land, but in Cheltenham it was a sixth in 1086 and by 1294 was much smaller still.[22] When the manor was again surveyed in 1453 the demesne was said to be 1½ carucates; possibly the extra half-carucate was the result of increasing the amount of arable cultivated each year, by adopting a three-year rotation leaving one-third of the fields fallow instead of half.

Cheltenham manor yielded the king a considerable income for a few years after 1294, a little over £82 a year if it could all be collected.[23] The villagers provided just over half this amount, nearly £42. Fifty-two burgesses paid fixed and largely nominal rents for their plots and in addition twelvepence each for their gardens.[24] Together with the dues paid by 23 free tenants, these contributions amounted to nearly £14. The rent of the demesne was £5 12s. 8d. There were some other small sources of income.

For nearly fifty years, since Fécamp abbey had been granted the manor in 1247, Cheltenham had contributed to the rebuilding of a very large and beautiful Gothic church in Fécamp, though it may be doubted whether many Cheltenham citizens ever saw it. In Cheltenham, the church of St Mary was rebuilt in the early fourteenth century; the nave, aisles, and rose window in the north transept are all of this period, and so is the spire, leaving few traces of the earlier, Norman church. The chancel was also extended, but this was the responsibility of the rector, Cirencester Abbey. How far responsibility for the rebuilding was shared between Fécamp abbey, Cirencester Abbey, or the inhabitants of the town cannot be known.

RELATIVE PROSPERITY IN THE FOURTEENTH CENTURY

Taxation records surviving from the early fourteenth century are a valuable source for estimating the relative prosperity of different places. The main method of taxation was the 'lay subsidy', so called because the clergy were taxed separately. At the end of the thirteenth century, a determined attempt was made to increase the yields of the subsidy, which was levied on the assessed value of personal property or 'moveables'. Unusually, in the 1327 lay subsidy roll for Minety, then in Gloucestershire but now in Wiltshire, 'moveable property' was itemised, from which it seems that it mainly comprised animals and corn.[25] The tax was not intended to be imposed on goods for domestic use but on produce offered for sale. It was not an income tax, and fell more heavily on producers than on those drawing rent from land; it may even have encouraged the leasing of demesnes as a way of avoiding tax.

It was usual to impose a higher rate on urban communities than on rural, but the 1327 lay subsidy was paid uniformly at the rate of one twentieth of the valuations. In 1332 a fresh national assessment was made: in rural areas one-fifteenth of the value of personal property, in boroughs, towns and ancient demesnes one-tenth, and these became the standard rates from 1334. A new method for raising the tax was introduced that year: the amount to be contributed by each place was negotiated with the local community by two royal commissioners for each county, and only totals were recorded nationally. Each place used its own local rating list to collect its allocated amount.[26] Records survive of the individual assessments in 1327, and the total assessment for each place in 1334.

The instructions concerning rates of taxation were not very precise. Sometimes a higher rate was to be paid by men in 'cities, boroughs, and market towns', but in 1294 it was 'cities, boroughs and royal demesne'. The tax officials in the county decided into which category each place came. Many of the so-called boroughs listed in one year might appear with the description 'royal demesne' in others. After noting that the taxers and the sheriff had local knowledge to help them, Willard observed that 'communities not classed locally as boroughs would strongly object to being selected for taxation at the higher rate'.[27] On just one occasion, in 1313, Cheltenham was styled a borough. But in 1307 no places at all in Gloucestershire were stated to be boroughs and in most years, Gloucester and Bristol were the only two places in the county so described.[28]

Number of occasions when Gloucestershire taxation boroughs were recorded, 1294–1336

Bristol	11
Cheltenham	1
Cirencester	6
Gloucester	11
Minety	1
Newent	1
Newnham	1
Winchcombe	2

In 1327, when Bristol, Gloucester, Cirencester, Tewkesbury and Winchcombe were all labelled 'villa' (or town), Cheltenham and Swindon were 'villata', little town. On the other hand, Cheltenham, and with it Charlton Kings, could hardly challenge the description 'royal demesne', which similarly led to a higher rate of tax. Winchcombe town, too, was ancient demesne, but the rural tithings in that parish were not, nor were Leckhampton, Swindon and Prestbury.

Nor was Cheltenham regarded as important enough to warrant sending a representative of its burgesses to parliament. The pressing need for money, in particular to finance wars in France, forced Edward III, who came to the throne in 1327, to call parliaments at which he could obtain the agreement of representatives of the people who paid the taxes; the cooperation of wealthy merchants had always been essential. Subsidies were agreed by borough representatives, the burgesses, as well as county representatives, the knights of the shire.[29] The boroughs of Bristol and Gloucester were invariably represented in parliament, and in 1337 a burgess was sent to parliament from Cirencester, but not from Cheltenham.

The names of individual taxpayers and the amount of their assessments in the surviving 1327 Gloucestershire lay subsidy roll offer some insights into Cheltenham and other market towns; the assessments in Arle, however, are largely illegible, and so are the names of some taxpayers.[30] The sums paid were mainly between one shilling and two shillings, meaning that the assessments were between £1 and £2; goods valued at less than ten shillings were not usually taxed. The sub-taxers, who were local men, may have under-assessed their neighbours; in Cheltenham they were John of Arle, Walter Sturmy and Simon the Forester. They were taxed separately by the chief taxers for the county at a standard one shilling, although they could not be poor men as they were effectively bankers; the process of handling money also gave them opportunity to enrich themselves.[31] They are not included in the table below.

The hundred of Cheltenham was made smaller some time after 1086 when Prestbury was detached, perhaps about 1247. Within the hundred, the head men of tithings, which in some cases corresponded with manors, were obliged to attend the hundred court. The boundaries of the newer manors were not defined geographically, as seems natural to generations used to precise Ordnance Survey maps, but were nonetheless clearly understood as covering particular crofts and tofts and their allotments of arable strips and pasture rights. Although the manor court was entwined with the hundred court, Cheltenham manor was distinct from the hundred and did not include those tithings that were also manors.

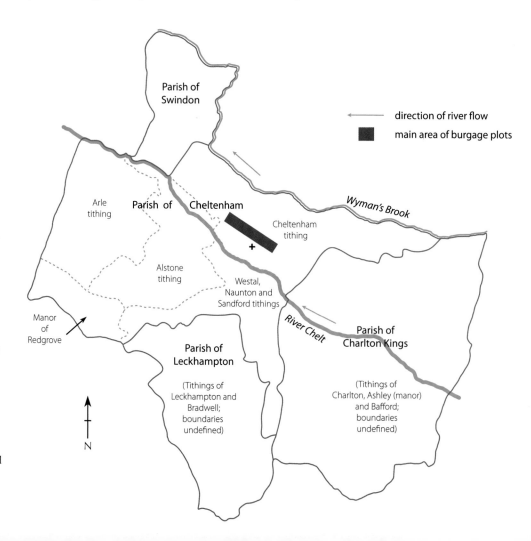

The carved heads
on the capital on
the eastern arch of
the tower crossing
at St Mary's
parish church,
Cheltenham,
are evidence of
structural work to
widen the arch,
perhaps in the
fourteenth century
at the same time
as the elaborate
covered piscina (*see*
page 71) was placed
in the chancel;
they would have
been seen by the
priest, not the
congregation. While
the two upper heads
are refined, the
lower one is less so,
and may have been
a portrait of the
stonemason.

PHOTOGRAPH: CARNEGIE,
2009

Tax was collected by tithings or vills, not parishes. Four vills in Cheltenham parish were named, but not Naunton and Sandford which were customarily entered under Westal; a mill mentioned in Westal was Sandford mill. Ham and Northfield were named as well as Charlton Kings. Tewkesbury and Winchcombe were similar to Cheltenham, these parishes also containing several agricultural townships as well as an urban community.[32]

Taxpayers in 1327

Vill or tithing	Number whose tax is known	Number paying over 2s.*	Number whose tax is not known
Cheltenham parish	65	25	13
Cheltenham town	*40*	*12*	
Alstone	14	7	
Arle	2	(1)	8
Westal	9	5	5
Charlton Kings, Ham and Northfield	44	18	
Leckhampton	21	6	2
Prestbury	29	15	
Swindon	14	6	
Tewkesbury parish	95	40	
Tewkesbury town	*62*	*33*	
Winchcombe parish	103	14	[c.10]
Winchcombe town	*51*	*4*	*[c. 10]*

* In this analysis, only those paying a penny or more over two shillings are included in the higher-rated group.

There was a larger number of more prosperous inhabitants in the urban part of Cheltenham than in Winchcombe, but Tewkesbury had nearly three times as many. Charlton Kings also had a good number of the more prosperous. A dozen taxpayers in the Cheltenham area had goods worth more than £5, paying 5 shillings or more in tax: one in Cheltenham town, two in Alstone, three in Charlton Kings, four in Prestbury, one in Leckhampton. Alice Moryn of Swindon, a member of the lordly family, was assessed at £15, and paid the most tax in the Cheltenham area. John Tomms in Prestbury was worth £10. Two more women were worth more than £5 – Joan of 'Netfeld' [?Northfield] in Charlton Kings, nearly £9, and Joan of 'Northeye' in Alstone, £5.

By far the highest rated individuals were in Tewkesbury: John Athelam at over £25, and Nicholas de Morton, at over £23, and six people rated at more than £5. This prosperity helps to explain the existence of a number of early and well-built timber-framed houses in that town. Gloucester, however, was in a different league, with 257 taxpayers in the four wards of the 'vill'; here there were twenty people assessed at more than £5 though only one, Robert Pope, reached £20.

At about this time, surnames in England began to be fixed, often based on occupation or place of residence. They are not very informative of occupation in Cheltenham; three men were called 'Dyer', implying a textile industry, and one 'Herringmonger'; Hubert the Marshal was a royal functionary or steward, in the town during one of the periods when the manor had been taken back into the king's hands. Hugh the chaplain lived in Westal. There are more indications of Winchcombe's occupations, with a weaver, tailor, smith, palfreyman, parchment-maker, slater, and miller, and these occupations may have been typical of other towns including Cheltenham. Tewkesbury's longer-standing and more distinctly urban characteristics are illustrated in a much wider range of occupations. Surnames can also reflect the place of residence – for example two men in Charlton Kings were 'de Northfield' – while other people were named because they lived near a local landmark – for example, Thomas atte Mill in Westal; Thomas atte Stile in Alstone; and Robert atte Oke, Thomas atte Well, Hugh Inthehale, and Matilda atte Mill, all in Charlton Kings. Surnames could also reflect a migrant's place of origin if from further afield; examples are Robert de Prestbury and John de Elkeston in Leckhampton, Margery de Upton and John de Stoke in Cheltenham.

An important man who probably took his name from the Cheltenham area was William de Westal, a member of parliament for Gloucestershire in 1343 and 1344, but not a Gloucestershire taxpayer in 1327. Another example is the prosperous de Cheltenham

Although there is evidence of a twelfth-century stone church in Cheltenham, it was extended and reconstructed in the following two centuries. This elaborate canopied piscina is of the fourteenth century. This is where the monk or priest representing the rector, that is Cirencester Abbey, washed his hands, and suggests that the abbey felt the need for a gesture of importance when the townspeople and the lord of the manor, at that time the king or one of his lessees such as Sir Thomas de Bradeston, were rebuilding the nave.

PHOTOGRAPH: CARNEGIE, 2009

family. Between 1325 and 1338 William de Cheltenham represented Gloucestershire in parliament and in 1338 so did John de Cheltenham, who was given a licence in 1339–40 for an oratory in Charlton. Five men with this surname paid tax in Gloucestershire in 1327, but none lived in Cheltenham. Thomas de Cheltenham in Gloucester and John in Winchcombe were not prosperous, and neither was John in Brockworth. But John in Newington Bagpath and Ozleworth, and Walter in Sandhurst, were among the more prosperous, assessed at £20 and £40 respectively. William de Cheltenham was a Gloucester citizen, serving at least seven or eight terms as bailiff of the city (an office which devolved on the wealthiest members of the community) and was one of four men named in the county commission of the peace in 1341. He served as steward of the bishop of Worcester in 1339, and was steward of the Berkeley estate.[33] The family continued to be of importance; a man with this surname served as abbot of Tewkesbury at the end of the fifteenth century and died there in 1509.[34]

It would be interesting and helpful to know how many households were *not* taxed in 1327, but this is difficult to estimate. There is no obvious relationship between either the number of burgages or the numbers of manorial tenants compared with the number paying tax. There were more burgages in Cheltenham when surveyed in 1294 than taxpayers in 1327 and, as might be expected, many more tenants than taxpayers. In Tewkesbury, likewise, there were 114 burgages in the same year, 1327, as the lay subsidy, and only 62 taxpayers in the town. It might be estimated that a quarter of households were taxed and that there were on average three persons in a household, so that the population of Cheltenham town might have been about 500, and of the whole parish perhaps 800. Not until the mid-sixteenth century is there another base for calculations, and the population then was between 700 and 800.

Taxpayers in 1327, burgages and the poll tax

	1327 tax payers	Burgages	Poll tax (1377) numbers
Cheltenham town	40	52	
Cheltenham parish	65	201 tenants	
Gloucester	250	508 (*c.*1100)	2,239
Tewkesbury town	62	114	
Winchcombe town	32	151 (*c.*1100)	203

For Cheltenham no records of the poll tax of 1377 have survived, but it is clear from Gloucester and Winchcombe that calculating population totals there is no less problematic. The poll tax on 'heads' included many wives, sons, daughters, servants and apprentices, but young children and the 'poor' were not included. It also came after the ravages of the Black Death, which caused the deaths of as many as one-third or even half the population, and it is more than likely that Cheltenham experienced the same dramatic number of deaths. At

Gloucester in 1327 the population might have reached 4,000, but the poll tax only recorded 2,239 people.[35]

Following the new method of assessment in 1334, did the same taxpayers find themselves paying, or was the tax spread more widely through the community? Only Gloucester, and Bristol – which by this date was a separate county – were categorised as boroughs; Cheltenham paid the higher rate as ancient demesne.[36]

Amounts raised by lay subsidies in 1327 and 1334 in £ (rounded up)

Town or vill	Tax raised in 1327	Tax raised in 1334	Assessed wealth in 1334
		At rate of one tenth (borough or ancient demesne)	
Cheltenham parish	9	14	141
Cheltenham town	*4*	*7*	*71*
Alstone	2	2	15
Arle	1	3	29
Westal, Naunton and Sandford	2	3	27
Charlton, Ham and Northfield	5	5	51
Winchcombe town	*5*	*11*	*107*
Cirencester borough	13	25	250
Gloucester	28	54	541
		At rate of one fifteenth	
Leckhampton	2	3	41
Prestbury	4	6	86
Swindon	2	3	41
Tewkesbury parish	13	20	301
Tewkesbury town	*10*	*16*	*242*
Winchcombe (excluding town)	4	6	95

Urban areas were undoubtedly being made to contribute substantially more to the king's treasury in 1334 than in 1327, a measure of their increasing commercial activity and relative prosperity, though they were probably still under-assessed because it was more difficult to value shop goods than cattle and barns full of corn. Rural areas had been affected by the Great Famine of 1315–17, and land was already being abandoned even before the Black Death struck in the late 1340s. The tax returns reflected this, although Gloucestershire nonetheless remained one of the wealthiest counties in the country.[37] The 1334 list suggests that Cheltenham lagged behind Winchcombe as a prosperous urban centre, which runs counter to the picture gained from the earlier subsidy.

THE WORK OF THE TOWN

There is only limited evidence for occupations in Cheltenham during the medieval period, and as has been shown, surnames do not give much help. The market certainly continued, and the tolls were farmed, or let out, by the lord. It is likely that there was a special court which could deal immediately with any disputes occurring in the market – at the end of the sixteenth century it was claimed that a court of *Pied Pudre*, or Pie Powder, so named from the 'dusty feet' of market traders who had walked to the market, had met 'by all the time whereof the memory of man is not to the contrary'.[38] There are no records of the court, so how long that span of time had been is unknown.

The general business of law and order in the town itself was not, however, dealt with in a special court (as it would have been in a chartered borough) but in the manor court which, as noted in chapter 1, was also a hundred court. Both Fécamp and later Syon abbeys had a complete 'liberty' in Cheltenham hundred, so that they could deal with all offences, even to hanging a criminal. There are, in consequence, no records of presentments in the county assize rolls. Any borough was jealous of its privileges in this regard; when the Marshalsea Court met in Cheltenham in 1407, Gloucester claimed that it was hearing cases involving the town's burgesses over which it should not have jurisdiction, as that was contrary to the 'liberties of the borough'.[39] This was during the lease of the Fécamp estate to Sir John Cornwall, and the king's steward or marshall held a court to deal with the king's personal interests.

Surviving Cheltenham court rolls date from 1332–33, 1377–78, 1384–85, and some from the early fifteenth century.[40] In the roll for 1421 the salaries of officials of the manor were set out. The most important was the steward, appointed by the lord, and paid 50 shillings. Under him was the high bailiff (responsible for supervising the lord's estate), 40 shillings, a clerk, 20 shillings, an under-bailiff, and a cryer or catchpoll who collected in moneys due, both paid 3s. 4d. Grievances were presented to the court by the borough bailiff, who spoke first, and by the tithingmen, including one for Cheltenham tithing. The rolls contain their names, the sums of money paid at the view of frankpledge, fines for non-attendance at the court (an offence committed more than once by the prior of Llanthony), orders from the royal administration which would normally go to the sheriff of the county, and cases concerning law and order. The offences ranged from assault and battery and instances of raising the hue and cry, to theft, disputes, trespass, failure to pay debts, and enforcement of the assize of ale and bread, which fixed both price, weight or quantity, and quality.[41] Compurgation or 'wager of law' was used, an archaic system of determining whether or not someone was guilty of an offence. The most usual method was trial by 'six hands', in which five people joined the accused in swearing his innocence; occasionally twelve hands were required. Although out of use for two centuries, wager of law was not abolished until 1833, in one of the modernising acts of the Whig government.[42]

The regularity of presentments in the later fourteenth century rolls for breaking the assize of ale suggests that here as elsewhere it was being used as a licensing system to raise income for the lord. In April 1378, for instance, 21 men and one woman in Cheltenham were charged amounts ranging from twopence to sixpence for brewing and breaking the assize, with in addition one each from the tithings of Arle, Alstone, and Westal, three from Bafford and two from Ashley. At that court there were no breakers of the assize in Charlton. On another occasion Robert Owlpenne brewed and sold beer which had not been tasted, so he was ordered to have it tasted. Brewing beer for sale was a small-scale activity; innkeepers brewed for their own establishments and so did keepers of alehouses.

These rolls contain numerous cases of debt and trespass, which sometimes concerned animals allowed to roam onto another's land. Thus, in 1384 Thomas Chaloner's dogs devoured fifteen sheep belonging to another. In 1378 a man unlawfully cut down thorn bushes and trees, probably desperate for firing. A woman was fined for trespass in 1385 and found to be a common scold or brawler. Cases of assault and battery were frequent, where fists or sticks had drawn blood. Millers were accused of charging an excessive toll for grinding. The miller of 'Prestesmull' was most often in trouble, but those from Arle, Alstone, Sandford mill in Westal, and Leckhampton were sometimes fined. The miller of 'wheelmill' was in trouble on at least two occasions; his may have been a horsemill, as most mills were driven by a waterwheel which would not have been a distinguishing characteristic

Among the few transfers of messuages and land registered in these rolls were examples of leasing for three lives, allowing occupation of the holding for as long as any one of the three named was living; of a widow granted her 'freebench' for occupation of a holding while she remained a widow; and of the transfer of 2½ acres of land for the lifetime of one Margery, a widow, and for twelve years after her death, according to the custom of the manor. The custom of the manor allowed property to be bequeathed away from the eventual heir for a period, a matter considered in more detail in the next chapter. A fine was paid for marriage of a daughter without the lord's licence, 'against the custom of the manor'; and another for a man marrying the holder of a messuage and a half yardland, transferring the ownership from his wife to himself. Most transfers were of small amounts of land, specified in acres. Some

George Rowe's *Guide*, first published in 1845, started with a picture of the High Street before the age of the spa. Rowe lived in Cheltenham from 1832 until 1852. This sketch perhaps owed something to his imagination, or perhaps he had seen a drawing, but generally his sketches were based on observation. Rowe was a skilled draughtsman, and his or an accomplice's pen and ink illustrations in the *Guide* are a delight; he also travelled widely, painted, and produced over 650 lithographs. A variation of this sketch was published as a postcard about 1902 by James Anderton, toy dealer in the High Street. Was there a common source, or did Anderton rework Rowe's small romantic sketch?

Rowe's *Guide* includes an illustration of a house at the eastern end of the High Street belonging to Mr Attwood, fishmonger and dealer in game, which, as Rowe observed, was a 'remain of Cheltenham's more primitive domestic architecture'. The right-hand side of the house appears to have been a single-storey open hall, which could well have dated from the fifteenth century; on the left was a two-storey solar wing. Some time in the sixteenth century a chimney had been inserted in the hall, which was then ceiled to give an upper room, lit by a dormer window. Another house of somewhat similar appearance, the ancient basket shop, survived at the other end of the High Street long enough to be photographed, but was demolished in 1967.
AUTHOR COLLECTION

concerned burgages or fractions of a burgage, showing that there was already subdivision, and in one instance a small 'parcel' of a burgage was carefully described and exchanged for another parcel.

A little information on occupations can be found in the court roll of two special sessions of the peace held in Cheltenham in 1422–23, at which attempts were made to control both prices and wages – which were thought to be rising alarmingly – by fining those convicted of overcharging. High prices were possibly the result of a declining population, with a consequent shortage of labour on the farms, or a local harvest-failure; dearth, or near-famine conditions occurred generally in the country over a decade later, in the years 1437–38.[43] Eleven butchers were fined, as well as four bakers, a fishmonger, a labourer selling corn, and three innkeepers for selling both food and fodder for horses at too high a price. A tanner overcharged for leather sold to a shoemaker, who in turn charged too much for sandals, as did two other shoemakers. Nine weavers demanded too much for their work.[44] Although the list is clearly not fully representative, and only gives an insight into a single year, it helps to build up a picture of the economy of Cheltenham – these are all trades which might be expected in a small market town.

CHELTENHAM IN 1453

Just over a hundred years after the survey or extent of Cheltenham manor made for Fécamp, a new monastic owner – the abbey of Syon – was prompted to have the manor surveyed, after it had gained full possession following the death of Sir John Cornwall in 1453. This was a much more complete survey, describing in detail the holdings, their present and previous holders, and the rents each paid. It located the holdings in Cheltenham, Alstone, Arle, Westal and

Sandford tithings (but did not name Naunton); in Bafford and Charlton tithings in Charlton Kings; and in Leckhampton. Over 160 years later the text of the survey was copied into a manorial record book by John Stubbes or his clerk, while he was either under-steward or steward of the manor, perhaps in preparation for the visit of John Norden, the royal surveyor, in 1617.[45]

This lengthy survey shows that by the mid-fifteenth century most of the 52 burgages in the town had been divided into halves, thirds, quarters and even smaller pieces, so that there were now 119 individual burgage plots held by a total of 82 different people. There were, indeed, very few entire burgages; half-burgages were most usual, owing the lord sixpence each year. The list of burgage-holders began with Thomas French, the chaplain of St Mary's, who occupied a whole burgage. The trustees of chantry property held 27 separate properties scattered through the town, originally probably ten whole burgages, but by 1453 some 9½ and a number of smaller pieces. The chantry trustees of Charlton Kings had a half burgage. After the suppression of the chantries a hundred years later, the chantry lands were acquired by Richard Pate for the endowment of the grammar school and almshouse.

The agricultural land in the manor was described in terms either of the yardland or of acres, and most land was categorised as 'base' or 'customary', a traditional form of tenure which later became known as copyhold. The demesne was freehold and leased to tenants, included below under the heading 'leasehold', but otherwise small freehold plots were scattered through the townships.

Tenancies in 1453 (excluding burgages)

Township	Free	Leases	Base	Customary	Totals	No. of tenants
Cheltenham	6		41		47	43
Arle	3	12	16	27	58	47
Alstone	9	2	17		28	23
Sandford			13		13	11
Westal			11		11	10
Charlton	3		18		21	16
Ham demesne		19			19	17
Bafford	7		20		27	17
Totals	28	33	136	27	224	184

Although some people had more than one holding, the process of engrossing (adding to properties by acquiring land belonging to another holding) had not gone very far. The term 'toft' was used of a small close where a house had been allowed to decay, and in the fifteenth century their number was increasing, for example on the bishop of Worcester's estates in the area.[46] Tofts were noted in the Cheltenham survey in all the townships; in Bafford they appear to have been called 'tenements'.

Tofts in the Cheltenham Survey

Township	Tofts	Township	Tofts
Cheltenham	8	Charlton	1
Arle	5	Ham demesne	
Alstone	6	Bafford 'tenements'	5
Sandford	7		
Westal	7		
	33	Totals	6

It does not suggest that there had been a wholesale conversion of arable to pasture, but some holdings certainly had been amalgamated. In Charlton Kings, for example, Margaret Childs owned a freehold messuage and two yardlands, an acre, and two separate half-yardlands, all at one time belonging to different people. Here, too, William Goodridge junior held by base tenure a messuage and a half-yardland, another messuage and six acres, and a toft with five acres, previously held by three other men. By the mid-sixteenth century the Goodridge family had, by this process, become significant landowners.

Charlton tithing was furthest from the traditional pattern of yardland holdings – by 1453 only five half-yardlands remained, and most of its holdings were small and measured in acres. This structure made it easier for tenants in succeeding centuries to consolidate their land without requiring an Act of Parliament to enforce enclosure. Most of Bafford tithing, on the other hand, was still divided into yardlands. Overall, half-yardland holdings predominated throughout Cheltenham manor. Services owed to the lord by yardlanders were specified, as they were in the earlier extent, and then valued in money. The numerous smallholdings in Cheltenham tithing show that if there had once been a regular organisation of yardlands, it had certainly broken down by the mid-fifteenth century. Arle and Alstone were the nearest to a classic open-field structure. Two 6-acre holdings in Sandford were held by millwrights (one of whom was a woman), a form of tenure that could be as old as the Sandford mill.

No details were given of pasture and meadow belonging to the lord of the manor which was leased *en bloc*, but details were given of other demesne land, which was mostly in Ham in Charlton. There is no mention of a house, but it is possible that the king had created a freehold in Ham from a former demesne holding, as may also have happened in Arle. John de Cheltenham has tentatively been associated with Ham Court, on the occasion in the previous century when he was granted a licence to have mass celebrated in his oratory in 'Charlton'.[47] Ham was certainly a freehold held of the king at a later date, by a form of tenure known as free socage,[48] which required the holder to perform some honourable duty but not military

Holdings in 1453

| Township | Numbers described in yardlands | | | | | Numbers in acres |
	½	1	1½	2	Total	
Cheltenham	16	1			17	31
Arle	11	7		1	19	5
Alstone	12	7		2	21	5
Sandford	6	2			8	4
Westal	9				9	2
Charlton	5				5	16
Ham demesne					0	19
Bafford	12		1	3	16	11
Totals	71	17	1	6	95	93

service. William de Cheltenham held 'Lordysmersh', and there was a meadow and a few acres of arable in Arle. A parcel of demesne in Oakley paid no rent 'on account of the density of thorns and undergrowth', a tantalising glimpse into the landscape.

Thomas of Arle was a freeholder of two yardlands and a messuage or house in Arle in 1453 and lessee of 9½ acres of demesne. The later very substantial house called Arle Court was not named in this survey, nor in other medieval sources, though in the mid-twelfth century Walter of Brussels gave land for a chapel in Arle, pointing to the existence of a freehold estate, and John of Arle was a freeholder who witnessed several charters very early in the fourteenth century. The daughter of another John of Arle married Robert Grevill, a descendant of the William Grevill of Chipping Campden who had purchased Ashley manor in 1387, and she had probably inherited the Arle estate.[49] Robert Grevill sold his Arle estate to his brother William, a steward of Cheltenham manor and a notably wealthy man;[50] Robert himself was resident in 1507 in Charlton Kings, and in his will he asked to be buried in the parish church there. William Grevill became a serjeant-at-law in 1504, joining the select group from whom judges were chosen; at this date the serjeants were said to be 'the richest advocates in the whole world' and the admission ceremony required a sumptuous feast where gold rings were distributed to everyone.[51] In 1509 he was made a judge. William lived in Arle. He made his will in October 1512, and died the following year. He was a little afraid that his brother Robert might not accept his will, so he gave him his best horse 'if he be no letter of my will'.

The extent of William Grevill's wealth is revealed in his will.[52] He was a great keeper of sheep, like his more famous namesake (and probable ancestor) of Chipping Campden, 'the flower of wool merchants in all England', who had died in 1401. A thousand sheep in Lemington were to be sold to raise money to improve the highways between Gloucester and Cheltenham; the income for one year from his sheep on the farms of Ditchford, Calcote,

Puckham and Broad Campden was to supply money for building the church at Llanthony; and the next year the money from the wool clip was to be used for building the cloister vault at Winchcombe. There are references to his manor of Dorne, and lands in Hanging Aston in Worcestershire, in Cheltenham, Alstone and Charlton, and to a burgage in Moreton. The manor of Overhampton (Great Hampton near Evesham) was to provide money to build a north aisle and tower in the church at Todenham near Lemington. His wife, Margery, was to enjoy a life interest in the manor of 'Elmstone in Hardwicke' (part of the lost township of Elmstone was in Uckington), and other lands in Gloucestershire. These lands were not necessarily all held outright: some may have been leases with time still to run.

There was no mention in his will of burgages in Cheltenham, though the 'mese' or messuage occupied by John Atwood, nailer, was bequeathed to twelve most honest persons for ever for finding the 'holy loaf'. This was a religious, rather than a charitable, donation. There was a custom that at the end of the parish mass, a loaf of bread was presented by one

Sir William Grevill of Arle Court died 'the ix day of Marche the iiij [4th] yere of the reigne of Henry the viij [VIII]'. His memorial brass in Cheltenham parish church, now very much worn, shows him with the coif of the serjeant-at-law, a black patch worn on top of the wig; it is one of only four brasses in the county showing a judge. Beneath him are the figures of three sons. He and his wife are turned towards each other, and under her are eight daughters. The brass was originally in the chancel, but when Cecil T. Davis wrote *The Monumental Brasses of Gloucestershire* in 1899 it had been moved to the bottom of a step, where it was subjected to heavy wear. Now it is back in the chancel, but on the wall, having been reset in 1920.

PHOTOGRAPH: CARNEGIE, 2009

Elborough Cottage in Charlton Kings was a tenement in the manor of Ashley, and stood on a narrow croft on the south side of Cudnall Street, with 40 acres of land on the north side. Two or three cruck-framed bays are dated to the fifteenth century, one a 'hall' open to the roof (as confirmed by smoke-blackened timbers). A grand stone fireplace and chimney were inserted in the sixteenth century, and the service bay to the right extended and converted to a parlour lit by an oriel window. Three men with the surname Elborough in Charlton Kings were assessed on goods in 1522: John Elborough senior on £4, Thomas on £3 and John junior on £2; Alice Elborough, widow, owned a burgage and a quarter in Cheltenham borough in 1617.

PHOTOGRAPH: AUTHOR, 2009

of the householders, blessed, cut up and distributed to the congregation as a substitute for the reception of holy communion; it was a solemn ritual, performed by each household in turn.[53] Did William Grevill find the Cheltenham householders too poor to provide the loaf each Sunday?

He must have been a devout and rather puritanical man, asking to be buried simply and without an ostentatious memorial, in the church wherever he should happen to die. He entrusted the abbot of Winchcombe with the rent of lands and house in Dorne and Hanging Aston for twenty years, to provide a priest to pray for him, and made large provision for prayers to be said for him, for his family, and for others, probably relatives, including John Arle with wife Alison and daughter Margaret. Nine abbots and no fewer than eighty poor men, given two pence each, were to say prayers in 35 named churches; Cheltenham, Swindon, Leckhampton, Charlton and Prestbury were named first in the list. Near-contemporary examples suggest that these were perhaps the places where he sold wool: John Fortey, a wool merchant of Northleach, asked in 1458 for prayers to be said in 120 churches, and William Midwinter, also of Northleach, whose will was proved in 1501, in 21 churches, while his wife, a year later, specified a more modest ten churches 'where I have been most accustomed to buy wools'.[54]

A brass memorial to William Grevill was placed in front of the altar in Cheltenham church, showing him in his judge's robes, his wife and their seven or eight daughters and three sons kneeling beneath. The brass survives, although very worn and moved from its original site, and is one of only four in Gloucestershire showing judge's robes. Three daughters were living when William died: Alice, wife of Robert Wye; Eleanor, wife of Robert Vampage; and Margaret, wife of Sir Richard Lygon. He left his 'books of law and other subjects' to his three sons-in-law, 'to the entent that they should have corage to lerne the better and to pray for my soule'. He also had numerous brothers, brothers-in-law, nieces and nephews. His clothes at Arle he left to Robert Vampage, and his goods there were to be divided between his wife and two elder daughters. He also had a house at Lemington where his father had lived; clothes there went to Robert Wye and household stuff to his daughter Margaret, but she was given relatively few bequests because it appears that when she married Sir Richard Lygon of Madresfield Court near Malvern, Arle Court was her dowry.

William Grevill's wife, Margery, was still living at Arle Court in 1522, when she was the only one of the five Grevills listed in the military survey to be assessed on goods as well as land; her goods in Arle were valued at £40, a relatively large sum. She also had land in Cheltenham, Alstone, Lemington, Deerhurst and Deerhurst Walton, and Evington in The Leigh. After her death Sir Richard Lygon and his wife may have lived at Arle until *his* mother died, and the couple then presumably moved to Madresfield.[55] Margery's relation, Sir Edward Grevill, was also a major Gloucestershire landowner in 1522; his estates included Charlton Kings (£20), Charingworth (£26), Over Quinton (£12), Welford on Avon (£7 18s. 8d.) and Weston on Avon (£5 6s. 8d.).

THE MILITARY SURVEY OF 1522

The Military Survey made in the summer of 1522 was an ambitious attempt by Henry VIII and his chancellor, Cardinal Wolsey, to raise large sums of money and to recruit an army to renew war with France. Commissioners required township or parish constables to submit two lists: one to record who was the lord of each 'town' and who owned the land, with its value; and a second enumerating the taxable wealth of the inhabitants in 'goods', the able-bodied men between the ages of 16 and 60 years, and the military equipment that was available for use (whether 'harness', that is, suits of armour, or weapons). They were also to include the value of church benefices, and the income of hospitals, chantries and guilds. The Gloucestershire manuscript conflates the two lists, and those for the western half of the county are more informative than for the east.[56] People were taxed on whichever source of wealth would yield most revenue to the king. Assessments were usually in round figures, such as £10 or £20, though some used the mark, the older unit which was two-thirds of a pound (13s. 4d.). Local returns show that constables followed a geographical order round the streets and districts.

The method of compiling the lists was clearly not standardised. In Tewkesbury, for example, large numbers of names were entered with no assessment for land or goods, and these men were 'able' to serve in the army, but Cheltenham appeared to be short of able-bodied men because few names are entered without an assessment. Winchcombe's list was notable for the eleven men noted as 'a Scot', obviously not expected to contribute to an English army. There were twelve sets of harness, or full suits of armour, in Cheltenham, 26 sets in Cirencester and 34 in Tewkesbury, but only four in Winchcombe. The variety of weapons reveals what early

Numbers assessed in the Military Survey, 1522

Parish or tithing	Assessed on lands, salaries and stipends	Assessed only on 'goods'	Total tax-payers	Nil assessments	'Able'
Cheltenham parish	122	40	162	3	14
Cheltenham township	70	25	95	3	10
Alstone	18	8	26		1
Westal, Naunton and Sandford	20	4	24		2
Arle	14		14	3	1
Charlton Kings	6	41	47		3
Leckhampton	3	14	17		1
Prestbury	20	29	49	2	15
Swindon	5	8	13		1
Cirencester	23	67	90	6	14
Tewkesbury parish	76	112	188	111	113
Winchcombe parish	20	87	107	71	106

sixteenth-century warfare might involve. Tewkesbury could offer bows and arrows, bills, axes, swords, and a 'pollaxe' used customarily to slaughter animals, but the Cheltenham constables did not record such everyday implements of husbandry or butchery.

Cheltenham had more taxpayers than Cirencester, and the town considerably outweighed the rural townships. 'Goods' could be personal or commercial stock, and few Cheltenham inhabitants were wealthy in these terms; overall, 7 per cent were assessed with £50 or more in goods. The highest individual assessment among the four towns was that of Christopher Tolle of Cirencester, with £280 in goods, and Tewkesbury had more men than Cheltenham whose goods were valued at £50, though none was as wealthy as Tolle.

Owners, rather than occupiers, were taxed on land – there were relatively few of these assessments – but those who occupied their own land may have been assessed only on their moveable goods, as were those holding land by lease or copy of court roll. Sir Edward Grevill was much the largest landowner in Charlton Kings, assessed at £20, and Henry Knyght in Leckhampton owned the same amount, while his assessment for goods, £200, was the largest in Cheltenham hundred. Margery Grevill in Arle, the widow of the wealthy judge William, had 53s. 4d., in land and £40 in goods. All other land valuations in Cheltenham are below £10, most substantially so. There were many more small landowners here than in either Tewkesbury or Cirencester.

The role of the Church as a landowner stands out. Both Syon abbey and Cirencester

Assessments for goods in the Military Survey, 1522

Parish or tithing	£2–£9	£10–£49	£50–£99	£100 or more	Totals assessed
Cheltenham parish	43	23	4		70
Cheltenham township	30	13	4		47
Alstone	8	4			12
Arle	2	4			6
Westal, Naunton and Sandford	4	2			6
Charlton Kings	28	13	1		42
Leckhampton	8	5	1	1	15
Prestbury	24	5			29
Swindon	7		1		8
Cirencester	38	25	7	4	74
Tewkesbury parish	74	56	10	5	145
Winchcombe parish	73	23			96

Abbey were important absentee landlords in Cheltenham, their estates being valued at £70 each. Tewkesbury and Winchcombe abbeys were also outstanding landowners in their 'home' towns, and the bishop of Hereford in Prestbury. No secular owner's land assessment approached them.

'Home' town estate	Lands		Rectory		
Tewkesbury abbey	£127	3s. 4d.	£36		
Winchcombe abbey	£104		£23	18s.	0d.
Bishop of Hereford in Prestbury	£92	12s. 0d.			

Thirteen years later the valuations of Cheltenham lands in the *Valor Ecclesiasticus*, an enquiry in 1535 into church property, were similar: for Syon £79, and for Cirencester £74 in tithes, rectory land and a mill. Income varied little from year to year. The accounts for Syon's Cheltenham manor in 1540, after it had been taken over by the Crown, itemise almost £56 in rents, and £14 for the 'farm' or lease of the manor and its land. Lord Andrew Wyndsor, the brother of Syon's last prioress, was the farmer. Other sources of income to Syon had been 'tolls of the fairs', a modest 6s. 8d., the traditional payment of 'tithing silver' or 'cert money' of a penny per man in each tithing, totalling £3 8s. 4d., and fees and fines paid in the manor court, £1 17s.[57]

The Knappings was an Ashley manor tenement in Charlton Kings, dating from the fifteenth century or even before; it contains three mighty pairs of crucks, one of which is shown here (*right*). The oldest part of the house is in the centre. There was a two-bay open hall (smoke-blackened timbers testify to a central hearth with no chimney to take away the smoke) and a service bay; possibly there was originally a fourth pair of crucks. A further single bay has been added at each end, and the whole subsequently cased in brick. The mullioned window at the south end may be late sixteenth-century, and the fleur de lys casement fastener. At this time a chimney was inserted in the hall, which was ceiled, and fireplaces built back to back in hall and adjacent room. The Knappings was a high-quality husbandman's house. An informed guess is that in 1557 it belonged to Walter Currer, who was assessed in the Military Survey with goods worth 40 shillings. The parallels with Elborough Cottage suggest that there had been some enfranchisement of Ashley copyholds in the fifteenth century.

PHOTOGRAPH: AUTHOR, 2009

REFORMATION

THE DISSOLUTION OF THE MONASTERIES

The dissolution of the monasteries and, a little later, the suppression of the chantries, had important long-term effects in Cheltenham. Religious institutions were 'perpetual corporations' – that is, they never died and their ownership of land would have continued indefinitely. Often they had properties and estates scattered across England. The dissolution, at a stroke, ended that arrangement, and represented a dramatic shift in landownership. While monastic houses were major business enterprises, by the sixteenth century they perhaps tended to conservatism. Certainly, their dissolution seems to have encouraged agricultural change and, in particular, the process of enclosure which was under way in the mid-century.

The monasteries associated with Cheltenham were among the richest in the country. Syon's gross income in the *Valor Ecclesiasticus* was £1,944, that of Cirencester £1,326 and of Llanthony £849. Tewkesbury, too, was a wealthy abbey, with a gross income of £1,478 while St Peter's, Gloucester, with £1,745, was the wealthiest in the county. Its abbey church became the cathedral for the new diocese of Gloucester, created in 1541. Only 28 monasteries in the whole country had incomes of over £1,000.[58]

As discussed in chapter 2, if a monastery had been granted a rectory – with the intention that part of its income would support a priest while most would fund the functions of the monastery – a vicarage should have been instituted, with an endowment of some land and the church dues paid by parishioners. Bishops (who were responsible for pastoral care within their dioceses) might encourage, but could not enforce, such an arrangement. In many cases the monasteries merely appointed a salaried 'chaplain' or curate, dependent on the monastery and his parishioners' generosity. Thus, at Cheltenham in 1522 Richard Drake was the chaplain, with a stipend of £6 13s. 4d., although the income of the rectory was no less than £70. He was probably the man of that name who in 1540 was parish priest of Tewkesbury, occupying one of the Abbey Cottages.[59] The 1522 Military Survey made no reference to a chaplain at Charlton Kings, but there was a vicarage in Prestbury. Neither Cirencester nor Tewkesbury had instituted a vicarage, while that at Winchcombe had been appropriated as well as the rectory. It would take centuries to provide well-established clergy in these places.[60]

The abbeys of Syon and Cirencester, and Llanthony Priory, were all closed in 1539 and their lands and revenues transferred to the Crown. A special Court of Augmentations was established to deal with the former monastic estates, and to arrange for sales to laymen. As a result much land passed out of ecclesiastical possession and into the hands of ambitious courtiers who were in a good position to identify the best bargains, or was acquired by existing landowners. However, the Crown retained the manor of Cheltenham, including Charlton Kings, and also the rectory, letting both out on leases. They were not sold until the early seventeenth century. In contrast, the small manor of Redgrove was sold immediately following the dissolution of Llanthony Priory.

SUPPRESSION OF THE CHANTRIES

The destruction of the chantry chapels in the reign of Edward VI had a more immediate effect on the inhabitants of Cheltenham. A chantrist was a priest who sang or intoned prayers, and in the previous two or three centuries numerous chantries were founded across England by pious inhabitants. In many instances this was to provide a minister in a local church or chapel where there was no incumbent rector or vicar, as in Cheltenham and Charlton Kings. Others were private chapels, where the priest was dedicated to praying for the souls of the founder and his kin. Chantries might also be founded by the influential citizens of a town to provide their own organisation and communal meeting place where there was no town council or guild.[61] There were guilds in Cirencester and Tewksbury and a Guildhall in Winchcombe, but none in Cheltenham. It was also common for chantry priests to teach boys who might in turn become priests, which seems to have been the case with St Katherine's chantry in Cheltenham.

As with the monasteries, a survey of chantry property was made to ensure the Crown's acquisition of all their assets once suppressed; it was authorised in the last year of Henry VIII, 1546, but was followed by a second assessment in 1548 because there had been suspicions that property was being concealed. The commissioners' reports are known as the 'chantry certificates'. Cheltenham had two chantries, one for a priest to sing prayers at the altar of the Blessed Mary and another at the altar of St Katherine, in memory of the founders and of all Christian souls. Thomas Ball was the priest of one, with an income of £4 13s. 4d., and Edward Grove of the other, earning £4 a year. These were the same amounts listed in the 1522 Military Survey. The chantry founders were

The north porch was the last medieval addition to Cheltenham St Mary's, perhaps about 1500, with a vaulted ceiling with Tudor roses carved in the bosses, supporting an upper room that was reached from the outside by a spiral staircase. This room might have been for a chantry priest who watched at night and had a window into the church to enable him to keep an eye on anyone below, or it might simply have been a muniment room. The ancient parish chest, now in the south aisle, used to be in the porch. Between 1729 and 1847 the upper room housed a Blue Coat school; this had been started in 1713, one of a number founded at that time to spread religious knowledge. A large opening in the wall of the upper room was made in 1890 to turn it into a small gallery. At the same time the porch was converted to a baptistry, and windows were inserted.

PHOTOGRAPH: CARNEGIE, 2009

George Rowe may have romanticised his drawing of Swindon church, but it was made at a time when a drastic restoration of the church was under discussion. This is one in a set of local views advertised in 1840. Rowe shows the simple, cottage-like nave, and the interesting small north aisle, which was actually the seventeenth-century chapel of the lord of the manor. The thatched cottage in the churchyard belonged to the church, and until the nineteenth century there was no wall separating it from the churchyard; otherwise the cottage survives. It might originally have housed a chantry priest.

GLOUCESTERSHIRE ARCHIVES A324/8

unknown, but were said to be 'divers' people at unknown dates. There was also a chantry in Charlton Kings; again the date of the foundation and the names of the founders were not known, but its purpose was the same as in Cheltenham. There William Hall, aged 40 years, received 10s. for serving the altar of Our Lady. In 1548 he had no other church living, but he was possibly the same man who had been a chaplain in Stow-on-the-Wold in 1522, with an income of 30s.[62]

The abolition of the chantries dispossessed many of the priests who had ministered in the churches and chapels. After the second visit by the royal commissioners, it was noted in a memorandum that Edward Grove

was charged by special covenant between the parishioners of the said town of Cheltenham and him, always to teach their children, which town is a market town, and much youth within the same, near whereunto is no school kept. Wherefore it is thought convenient to

signify unto your worships the same to be a meet place to establish some teacher, and erect
a Grammar School so it might stand with the King's Majesty's pleasure.[63]

The school probably met in the chantry chapel of St Katherine in the north transept of the
parish church, where there is a splendid rose window which echoed the wheel upon which the
saint was martyred. For the rest of Edward VI's short reign and into that of Mary Tudor, a
salary of £5 a year was paid to 'the schoolmaster of a certain Grammar School of the foundation
of the Chantry of St Katherine' in Cheltenham.

The flowing cusped tracery of the exceptionally large rose window in the north transept of Cheltenham St Mary's
is early fourteenth-century; the glass is Victorian, donated at the time of the major rescue and restoration of the
church. Windows with a wheel-like shape are thought to have been inspired by the martyrdom of St Katherine,
who was broken on a wheel, and beneath the window there would have been an altar dedicated to the saint. One
of the two chantry foundations in the church was for the service of St Katherine, and the priest would have sung
prayers at the altar. In 1546 St Katherine's chantry priest was Edward Grove, who also taught some of the boys of
the town, probably in the same north transept. This led Richard Pate, a chantry commissioner, to recommend the
establishment of a grammar school in Cheltenham.
PHOTOGRAPH: CARNEGIE, 2009

CHELTENHAM GRAMMAR SCHOOL

The memorandum about the school may have been drafted by Richard Pate, one of the chantry commissioners in Gloucestershire, and a Gloucester lawyer, MP and recorder, who is best-known as the man who founded and endowed Cheltenham grammar school. Several members of his family had land in Cheltenham in the Tudor period, and some were evidently prosperous. Richard Pate himself was probably born in Cheltenham in 1516, almost certainly the son of Walter Pate, a substantial tradesman who was assessed on the considerable sum of £20 of goods in 1522. Walter was a butcher, baker and innkeeper, and in the manor court rolls for 1527–29 was one of two men accused of charging too much for candles.[64] William Pate was assessed on £12 of goods in Charlton Kings in 1522. No other Pates were named in Gloucestershire.

In his will Richard Pate named his brother William, and if this was the same man assessed in 1522 the link with Cheltenham is much strengthened, for William's parents were both buried in the Lady Chapel in the parish church, a position indicating their high status and a connection with the rectory. In several documents Richard Pate named Minsterworth as his residence, rather than either Cheltenham or Matson near Gloucester (an estate which his wife had brought him and where he started to build a sizeable house). In his will he referred to his 'convenient portion' of lands and tenements, and he had clearly amassed considerable property in the Gloucester area, including leases of the rectories of Minsterworth, Norton and Churchdown.

As a Chantry Commissioner, Richard Pate could identify the property with which, together with other lands, he later endowed both the grammar school and almshouses in Cheltenham. He paid for a school to be built in the High Street in 1571 and three years later received a grant from Elizabeth I of the former

Richard Pate is an example of a man made rich by the huge transfers of property at the Reformation. His portrait hangs in Corpus Christi College, Oxford, where he was a student between 1532 and 1536. The college, founded in 1517, encouraged modern humanistic learning, which may have made Pate a keen Protestant, and enabled the college to escape dissolution. In 1544 Pate was appointed under-steward and keeper of the manorial courts pertaining to the former Cirencester Abbey, a significant link with Cheltenham; two years later he became a chantry commissioner in Gloucester and Bristol. He used these positions to financial advantage, and was able to buy jointly with Sir Thomas Chamberlain a large amount of chantry property, some of which was later given for charitable purposes. He had also married a well-endowed widow. He was buried in Gloucester Cathedral.

When Richard Pate Esq. transferred property to Corpus Christi College, Oxford, in 1586 to support a free grammar school and an almshouse in Cheltenham, he employed a scrivener of unusually exuberant style, who put four drawings above the elaborate letters in the first line of the deed. One shows a two-storey school house with a tiled roof, and the second is inside the schoolroom, with six pupils sitting on benches facing each other, a schoolmaster and an usher; in the middle there appears to be a small brazier giving off smoke. The second set shows a larger, tiled two-storey house with three chimneys, and next to it the scene inside: two women praying at the back, three men in the front, and a priest facing his little congregation. The pictures may be notional but were clearly relevant.

Cheltenham chantry lands with which to endow it. In 1585 he transferred these chantry lands, with others which he had purchased, to Corpus Christi, the Oxford college which he had attended, requiring that three-quarters of the income should be devoted to 'the perpetual maintenance and foundation of a free Grammar School at Cheltenham' and a 'Hospital or Almshouse for six old poor people', of whom two were to be women.[65] The master's salary was to be £16 a year, for teaching at least fifty children some Latin and Greek. The transfer was to take effect from Pate's death, which occurred in 1588. The deed recording this was decorated with drawings of a school with its pupils and staff and an almshouse with its inmates. This was the beginning of a long association between the town and Corpus Christi.

A map made in 1787, showing the property owned by the college in Cheltenham and Swindon, identified 34 separate and scattered lots totalling 18 acres, mainly narrow burgage plots, each one given its abutments, and the four largest each of ¾ acre.[66] The schoolhouse was built on one of them; there was a pasture adjoining it, and with it came the right to pasture one cow on the common fields.[67] In 1682 George Townsend, who had himself attended Cheltenham grammar school, gave the school the right to present a scholar to Pembroke College, Oxford, in rotation with the grammar schools at Northleach, Chipping Campden and the Crypt School in Gloucester. He also endowed a small charity school for poor children.

POPULATION IN THE CHANTRY CERTIFICATES

The chantry certificates contain the first accounts of parish populations, described in terms of the number of 'houselinge' people, that is, those who received the bread in the communion service (a 'housel' being a sacrifice). In 1551 Bishop Hooper surveyed his new diocese of Gloucester, again asking for returns of communicants, though in these the numbers returned were modestly qualified by the word 'about'. Twelve years later Bishop Cheyney had to inform the privy council of the number of households in each parish. Taken together, these returns give a good estimate of the number of people in each parish: after careful research John Moore concluded that they are generally reliable.[68]

Parish populations in the mid-sixteenth century

| | Communicants | | Households |
Parish	1548	1551	1563
Cheltenham	500	526	164
Charlton Kings	310	315	103
Leckhampton		102	20
Prestbury		160	54
Swindon		60	16
Cirencester	1,400	1,460	320
Tewkesbury	1,600	2,600	396
Winchcombe	800	700	199

The first chantry certificate for Cheltenham returned 500 communicants, but the second, in 1548, noted 600; the lower and more consistent figure has been used. The population of Cheltenham parish was smaller than that of Winchcombe, while Cirencester and Tewkesbury were significantly larger, a position which remained relatively unchanged throughout the next two centuries.

A bell is standing on the north side of the chancel in the parish church, with the date 1674. It weighs over 100 lbs. Its provenance is unknown, but it seems likely that it was a school bell, used to summon the pupils to a church school in the morning. If so, when new buildings were erected, it would be appropriate to move the bell to the church and so preserve it.

PHOTOGRAPH: CARNEGIE, 2009

Two doorways in the south wall of Prestbury church once gave access to a rood loft, which would have spanned the width of the church, effectively separating the priest's area of the church in the chancel from the congregation in the nave. When Henry VIII and his chief minister, Thomas Cromwell, began the work of reforming the Church of England to make it Protestant, they required what they regarded as superstitious images to be removed, and most rood lofts were torn down. Unusually the stairs as well as the doorways have survived at Prestbury. A similar rood staircase has recently been uncovered at the parish church of South Lopham, Norfolk.

PHOTOGRAPH: CARNEGIE, 2010

In the mid-sixteenth century communion was first taken at the age of ten, so the numbers have to be adjusted to allow for younger children and thereby arrive at an estimate of total population. A quarter of the population may have been under ten, and a multiplier of 1.33 has been applied to give population totals which can then be related to household size in 1563. It seems clear, using this method, that the Tewkesbury return for 1551 should read 1,600, identical to three years earlier.[69]

Population and household size, 1548–63

Parish	Population estimates (× 1.33)		Ratio of population to households	
	1548	1551	1548	1551
Cheltenham	665	700	4.0	4.3
Charlton Kings	412	419	4.0	4.1
Leckhampton		136		6.8
Prestbury		213		3.9
Swindon		80		5.0
Cirencester	1,862	1,942	5.8	6.1
Tewkesbury	2,128	3,458	5.4	8.7
Winchcombe	1,064	931	5.3	4.7

In 1551 there was a widespread outbreak of the 'sweat' which, often accompanied by plague, severely affected Gloucestershire. In consequence, the population may have fallen in some parishes. Between 1556 and 1563 the population of Gloucestershire declined more than the national average, during a period of poor harvests followed by typhus, 'famine fever' and, in 1557–59, an epidemic of influenza. In small parishes such as Leckhampton and Swindon, average household size was influenced by the existence of one or two large households – for example, Leckhampton Court or Swindon Manor – where there were likely to have been several household servants. A national average of 4.75 people per household has been generally accepted, and the local figures are consistent with this, lending credibility to the returns and the picture they give for the mid-sixteenth century.[70]

A 'grammar' school was designed to teach boys enough Latin to enable them to study at a university and become clergymen. The chantry priest of St Katherine in Cheltenham was required to teach, and the school continued certainly into Mary Tudor's reign. When Elizabeth became queen in 1558, the school was probably restarted with a Protestant ethic, and Richard Pate was probably involved. In 1571 he started to build a house 'sufficient for the instruction of boys and for a dwelling for the schoolmaster'. In 1586 school and almshouse were endowed and Corpus Christi agreed to administer the foundations; the school master was to be assisted by an usher. Pate died two years later. Corpus Christi gave up the management of the school in 1881. This photograph was taken in the 1880s.

© CHELTENHAM ART GALLERY AND MUSEUM

CHAPTER FOUR

TRANSITION

T HE NINETY YEARS between the dissolution of the monasteries and the accession
of Charles I in 1625 was a crucial period of transition in Cheltenham. The monasteries
of Syon and Cirencester had had significant influence over landholders who, after the
monasteries' dissolution in 1539, could start a process of economic modernisation. When
new landowners tried to assert their rights, collective action could lead to definitions more
favourable to the manorial tenants. Monastic demesnes were sold either by the Crown directly,
or to speculators who handled the sales, creating freehold estates which could be regarded
as manors although lacking some of the distinctive characteristics of those in earlier periods.
Manorial rights were also sold to individual tenants who could raise the necessary money, so
creating smaller freeholds.

Monastic estates in Cheltenham were only gradually sold by the Crown. The one immediate
transfer was Llanthony Priory's small manor of Redgrove, which was broken up. Its history
is complicated and confusing. Several decades before the dissolution, William Grevill of Arle
Court and his wife had leased Redgrove lands from the priory.[1] After Grevill's death in 1513,
and the expiry of the lease in 1519, his son-in-law, Robert Wye, secured a fresh lease jointly
with his son, but manorial rights and the land called the 'grove' were not included. In 1540,
after the dissolution, Sir Richard Lygon was granted Redgrove manor 'in fee', which meant
that he held it directly from the king and the 'grove' was part of his manorial estate. From
this time the estate was referred to as 'the manor of Redgrove and Arle Court',[2] a connection
reflected in some modern road-names in the area (though not the actual location of Redgrove).
Mrs Eleanor Lygon, whose dower was Arle Court, the house in which she lived after she was
widowed,[3] promoted some enclosure of land in Arle in 1580, and in 1597 Arnold Lygon secured
agreement to enclose 'Grove field'. This formed the basis of a new 'Grovefield' estate where
the present Arle Court was eventually built.[4]

The Crown retained parts of the Redgrove lands until 1617 when James I gave 50 acres and
a tenement there, together with a few houses in the city of Gloucester and some parcels of land
in outlying hamlets, to Gloucester Corporation to support the hospital of St Mary Magdalen.[5]
Although the hospital had not been suppressed, the dissolution of Llanthony Priory left it
poorly endowed; in 1599 Gloucester Corporation agreed to repair the building in return for

Charitable bodies such as Corpus Christi College, St Mary Magdalene Hospital and other church institutions preserved longer than most secular land-owners the early disposition of their land holdings. They were equally conservative about replacing existing buildings. After the relatively late enclosure of Arle and Alstone in 1835, the land held by Gloucester Corporation as the endowment of St Mary Magdalen Hospital was still scattered through the former open fields, and illustrates the nature of the holding which had been granted by James I in 1617.
GLOUCESTERSHIRE ARCHIVES P78/SD1/1 AND 2

being given the patronage of the hospital. The 1617 survey of Cheltenham manor made for Prince Charles, later Charles I, noted that 29 acres in Harthurst field was the endowment of St Mary Magdalen Hospital, described in a lease of 1737 as a yardland; it also recorded John Houldshipp, a yeoman of Cheltenham, with a half-acre freehold close called Redgrove in Arle on which a house was built, together with 8¼ acres of land.[6] The name 'Redgrove' had become ambiguous.

From the early seventeenth century the Gloucester Corporation land is well documented. Part was in strips intermixed with other small freeholdings, as shown in a 1759 map of Hartisfield farm, made for William Ashmead, gentleman.[7] The Charity Commissioners reported on Gloucester charities in 1826 and said that a farm called Redgrove was at 'Heydon' in Cheltenham; Haydon, on the border of Staverton, Boddington and Cheltenham, was divided between the three parishes.[8] A yeoman farmer at Haydon seems to have been the tenant of the hospital's Redgrove lands for a considerable time before 1826, while the farm buildings, situated close to the old Gloucester Road, were in Boddington. The Charity Commissioners noted that the tramway from Gloucester to Cheltenham now ran through the farm, for which compensation had been paid. The older Gloucester to Staverton road follows this route.

THE CHURCH AFTER THE DISSOLUTION

As well as the temporal possessions of the monasteries, such as manors and lands, the Crown also acquired the advowsons, glebeland and tithes of parish churches, some of which had been appropriated by the monasteries. These, too, were either leased or sold piecemeal, which led to the creation of many 'lay rectors' and lay tithe owners or impropriators, a situation which later became unacceptable. The advowson, or right to present a cleric to a living, was often sold separately from other church property – a well-endowed church living was a useful item of patronage, enabling the owner to present a member of his family, or even himself, to the living, and was an attractive purchase which raised money for the Crown.

Swindon illustrates the classic situation where the lord of the manor was patron of the local parish church. It was unaffected by the dissolution, and the patronage continued in the hands of the lord. In 1551 the patron was Henry Clifford, and the rectory income was £13 6s. 8d. In contrast, Leckhampton, Prestbury, Cheltenham and Charlton Kings all illustrate the more complicated arrangements which could follow the dissolution, as the Crown sold the property piecemeal. The advowson of the rectory of Leckhampton was held by Fécamp and then Syon abbey as lords of the manor of Cheltenham, together with glebe land in the township.[9] A small portion of the tithes belonged to Llanthony Priory, and another to Cirencester Abbey in respect of Cheltenham rectory lands. In 1535 the income of the rectory was £18 13s. 4d. and the glebeland was leased by Ralph Norwood, lord of the principal manor; he purchased the advowson in time to present Sir Rhys Jones to the living in 1549, and the Norwood family and their successors in the manor remained the patron. The rector was the major tithe-owner in 1778, but the former Cirencester Abbey tithes had been sold with the rest of Cheltenham rectory estate to Baptist Hicks and thence to the Capel family, Earls of Essex; it is not clear who purchased the Llanthony tithes, but as they were from the manor's own farmland or demesne, it was probably Ralph Norwood. Prestbury rectory and the patronage of the vicarage had belonged to Llanthony; the vicar's income in 1535 was £11, and he had half the tithes of

On the 1806 enclosure map of Cheltenham township, the site of the former Parsonage, Rectory or Farm can be identified, in number 606. It was owned by Joseph Pitt, who had purchased the Cheltenham tithes in 1799. The Parsonage buildings were extensive, and at that time part was used as a lodging house. Numbers 604 and 605 were the Cambray meadow. A lane separated the Parsonage from T. B. Hughes' Assembly Rooms and Powers Court, and adjacent to this property was Abraham Byrch at the *Plough*. Along the High Street frontage of Cambray meadow there was what could well have been a speculative development by Cirencester Abbey of a row of houses on narrow plots, reminiscent of Tewkesbury Abbey's fifteenth-century development of merchants' houses and shops called the Abbey Cottages.

GLOUCESTERSHIRE ARCHIVES D2025

the parish. The Crown retained the rectory estate for some years, selling it in 1608; Thomas Baghott, a local landowner, purchased it in 1622 with the advowson, which had been leased for some time previously by members of the family.[10] The Dean and Precentor of Hereford retained their portion of the Prestbury tithes, and continued to collect them until commuted to a corn rent in 1838.

Cheltenham rectory remained in the Crown's hands for a hundred years,[11] bringing income to the crown by being successively leased to Sir Henry Jerningham, followed by Sir W. Greenwell, and then in 1598 to Francis Bacon, later James I's Lord Chancellor. His lease for 40 years was specifically of the *church* of Cheltenham and the *chapel* of Charlton Kings at a rent of £75 13s. 4d. The Crown's lawyers continued to refer to Charlton Kings in legal documents as a chapel, although in the 1550s Bishop Hooper had considered it a parish church. Bacon was obliged to support two priests and two deacons to celebrate divine service, allowing them a yearly stipend of £40 each once he gained possession of the rectory. He also had to provide the communion bread and wine; to repair the chancel, which was the responsibility of the rector, whether lay or clerical; to supply straw to the church, which would have been used regularly to put a clean layer on the floor and help to make it less cold and damp; and to provide ropes for the bells. The crown retained the advowson. Long before the expiry of Bacon's lease, James I sold the 'reversion' – a lease for the next term of years – to Sir Baptist Hicks, later Viscount Campden, who would come into possession when Bacon's lease expired; but because of his pressing need to raise money, James I then sold Cheltenham rectory outright to Baptist Hicks in 1612, together with Campden rectory. The sale did not cancel Bacon's lease and the advowson remained with the crown until the lease expired. Baptist Hicks would eventually have become the impropriator but he died before Bacon's lease expired.

The men taking leases directly from the crown did not farm the land themselves, but sub-let to a local person who actually farmed the land and collected the tithes. At each stage of sub-letting, a payment to the lessor was required; the last in the chain made the most profit. Edmund Benbowe was the farmer in 1552 and 1554, when he was in dispute with the parishioners of Charlton Kings about tithes. In 1563 Thomas Higgs was the local farmer, and the churchwardens of Cheltenham complained that the chancel was in ruins and he ought to repair it.[12] Members of the Higgs family rented the rectory estate for many years thereafter. In the early seventeenth century, a major dispute broke out between the Higgs and the churchwardens and parishioners of Charlton Kings over the stipends paid to the curates. John Stubbes, a resident of Charlton Kings, copied relevant documents and letters into the manor court book.[13] The dispute lasted for sixteen years, between 1609 and 1624, and involved several petitions and court cases.

It was certainly true that the curates of both Charlton Kings and Cheltenham were being very poorly paid. Mrs Baghott or Badger (her name after her second marriage) and her two Higgs sons were paying the two curates, of Cheltenham and of Charlton Kings, £10 each, the minimum stipend for a parish clergyman, which only attracted 'reading ministers' – who were allowed to read services and homilies, but not to administer the sacraments or preach because they were not qualified by having an MA degree.[14] The two lay deacons were being paid 4 marks (£2 13s. 4d.). The rectory estate, by contrast, was said to be worth £400 and later £600. The parishioners wanted the stipends to be increased to £40, in order to attract 'learned' ministers. When the bishop of Gloucester, Miles Smith, complained that he had been forced to appoint 'some very mean ministers to supply cures as mean', the curates of Cheltenham and Charlton Kings may have been among those he was thinking of.

After Protestantism was established following the accession of Elizabeth I in 1558, there was a general reforming movement to improve the status and pay of the clergy. At the same time opinion was divided on how far the conduct of church services should be reformed; the Puritans favoured more freedom and less adherence to the old Prayer Book forms, but many parishioners were conservative, and wished to retain the older traditions of formal worship. Puritanism tended to be stronger in the towns than in the countryside. These two strands became inextricably entangled in the Charlton Kings case. The parishioners appear to have been the conservatives, while wanting well-qualified and resident preaching ministers. Stubbes was their spokesman, or perhaps he took it upon himself to complain of the Higgs' parsimony. The Higgs apparently favoured the Puritan cause. In 1609 Stubbes drew the bishop's attention to the obligation to pay 'two fit and discreet chaplains and two deacons' and requested his help in securing preaching ministers. In a subsequent petition there were said to be near 2,000 communicants, which looks like an exaggeration to increase the force of the case, as it is a much larger figure than was returned to the bishop in 1603.[15]

The case made no progress. In 1620 the parishioners petitioned Lord Chancellor Bacon, still the lessee, pointing out that the rectory estate was worth £600 a year to the Higgs – an increase in value in the last decade; Bacon was paid a mere £75 a year. They repeated the request for £40 for the two ministers as well as £10 to the two deacons (or 'reading' ministers), but Mrs

Fécamp Abbey and then Syon Abbey had left Cheltenham and Charlton Kings without an endowed vicarage, and this meant also that there was no vicarage house. Perpetual curates lived in rented accommodation or in their own house. When Revd Francis Close was appointed to Cheltenham, he quickly became very popular, and his parishioners subscribed to build him a house, 'The Grange' next to Christ Church in Lansdown. It was not a benefice house, but its size and style reveal the status of the perpetual curate by the early nineteenth century.

Badger was intransigent. In 1621 the curate of Charlton Kings left, and another man lacking an MA, Robert Walker, was appointed on the understanding that he would leave when better stipends were agreed. The dispute was settled in 1624 by deed of covenant, confirmed by a decree in chancery, that both ministers were to be paid £40, and this remained the accepted obligation on the owner of the rectory until the nineteenth century. Walker, however, refused to leave. He was unpopular because he tended towards Puritan ideas. He complained of persecution by people setting up maypoles and holding church ales on Sundays, which the Puritans particularly disliked for their roistering nature, and dancing and beating a drum during church services. He was being tormented in a manner which was part of popular culture before widespread use of printed material. He was finally induced to go when an alternative curate was presented, and Walker was physically prevented from entering Charlton Kings church by Stubbes and a body of parishioners.

Just before his death in 1629, Baptist Hicks made an elaborate arrangement for these parish clergymen with Jesus College, Oxford. Whenever there was a vacancy, the college was to recommend three candidates, who had to be masters of arts of at least two years' standing, fellows of the college, and unmarried. Lord Campden's heirs would then choose one of the three to present to the bishop. Hicks also required that £40 should be paid from the rectory estate to each incumbent. The ministers were to preach once every Sunday, not to be absent simultaneously, not to hold any other living, and not to stay at Cheltenham for more than six years.

Stubbes did not trust farmers of the rectory to carry out the agreement, and in 1633 wrote to Dr Mansell, principal of Jesus College, asking him to send a copy of Lord Campden's deed, 'that I may enter it in my book wherein I have registered all the passages of this business, to the intent that posterity may hereafter know how to inform you of any thinge that shall be here done contrary to the intent of our ho[nourable] and pious Benefactor'. Stubbes had succeeded in improving the pay of the local clergy, but he did not ensure that the next curate of Charlton Kings lived there; on being given another church position, he did not surrender his Charlton Kings curacy, probably paying a substitute no more than the old rate the curates had been paid.

The Puritans were in the ascendant for a decade after the end of the Civil War, and the well-qualified curate of Cheltenham, Dr English, whose wife was the aristocratic daughter of Lady Sandys, was ejected from the living. He had been appointed by the bishop before Bacon's lease expired and Baptist Hicks' peculiar arrangements came into force. As the war ended, the parliament's Committee for Compounding considered how much the royalist Sir Edward Alford should pay to regain his confiscated estates; he was the lessee of Cheltenham rectory, and was responsible for paying £80 a year to Jesus College for the stipends.[16] A proclamation concerning 'delinquents' was read in Cheltenham in August 1647, and the parishioners begged the Committee to settle £80 on the minister, 'the parish being very great and there being 2,000 communicants'; as in Stubbes' petition to the bishop in 1609, the figure was certainly an exaggeration. The committee responded that the stipend could not be altered because Sir Edward only had a lifetime lease. Sir Edward eventually 'compounded' (that is, paid that sum as a fine to parliament) for £1,284 15s. to regain his estates. John Dutton of Sherborne, the lord of the manor, was also a royalist, and he had to pay no less than £5,216 4s. to regain his estates.

A survey of church livings, compiled for the Commonwealth government in 1650, described John Cooper at Cheltenham as a 'preaching minister', and Richard Harrison at Charlton Kings as a 'constant preaching minister'. At Leckhampton and Prestbury the ministers also preached, but not so Anthony Guise at Swindon.[17] In 1653 the parishioners of Cheltenham

Dr John English, perpetual curate of Cheltenham, was a traditionalist loyal to Charles I at the time of the Civil War. He was appointed by the bishop of Gloucester before the arrangements made by Baptist Hicks requiring incumbents to be celibate came into force. As a royalist, he was taken in 1643 for eighteen weeks' 'close imprisonment', which he claimed caused his wife's death in August 1643; his love for her, he said, would last until he breathed his last. Some two months later his daughter died. In 1646 he was removed from his living, and died the following year, but the date is not entered on the memorial he composed to his wife and daughter. The memorial was originally immediately behind the Communion table, then was moved elsewhere in the chancel when a new altar piece was erected, and is now on the south wall of the nave.

PHOTOGRAPH: CARNEGIE, 2009

returned to the battle, asking for £100, as 'our town [is] a great market town', and claiming that the inhabitants themselves paid for a lecturer as a substitute for a preacher. Sir Edward Alford conceded £50. The restoration of Charles II brought the traditionalists back into the church. Because of Baptist Hick's arrangements, there was a steady turnover of Welsh clerics from Jesus College for the rest of the century and the next; these arrangements lasted until 1816 for Cheltenham and 1832 for Charlton Kings.

MID-SIXTEENTH-CENTURY ENCLOSURE

The potential disadvantages of the common fields are evident in the few court rolls that survive for the period 1527 to 1529, which have been deciphered and translated by the Cheltenham 'Latin Research Group'.[18] 'Roads' were tracks through the fields, and were convenient unploughed areas for a dungheap, or a ditch to serve an adjacent tenant's land. Without hedges or ditches around fields, it was easy to let sheep wander freely, as John Higges did on Sandford field, or to take six cows, four bullocks and a heifer from Nashmead in Alstone as Henry Stile was accused of doing. Ralph Norwood paid a jury to inspect a hedge dividing his land in Kingsham in Sandford from one of the rectory meadows belonging to the abbot of Cirencester, presumably because it was not where he thought it should be. William Keke's misdemeanour was ploughing up three acres in Milkwell furlong in Charlton which, it was asserted, did not belong to him. The major disadvantage of the open fields, however, was the uniformity required as to which crops were grown: each tenant had to sow the same in each field, and reap at the same time, and it was difficult for any one individual to put his strips down to grass instead of arable cultivation or to alter his cropping.

Ecclesiastical owners tended to be conservative forces in the open fields, reluctant to alter the particular donations made to them. Was it just coincidence that in 1557, less than twenty years after the dissolution of Cirencester and Syon abbeys, the tenants in Charlton Kings agreed to enclose some land? Some years later the Lygons secured enclosure of land in Arle, followed by the tenants of Westal and Sandford, and then of Cheltenham. These enclosures were limited, but were a step towards the creation of individual farms.[19] Enclosed land was by definition strongly demarcated with hedges and ditches, and only the owner and his animals had access to it.

As noted in chapter 2, each tithing had separate open field systems. In 1557 Charlton Kings had a three-field system. Two-thirds of the fields which had been ploughed and used for arable cultivation were opened to the manorial tenants for pasturing their animals from the end of harvest until Candlemas (2 February), when ploughing recommenced. The other third lay fallow and available for grazing the whole year. Pastureland was open as commons from Lammas (1 August) by which time the hay harvest would have been gathered, until Candlemas. But by this time the old balance of interests, governed by careful regulation, was under pressure:

For reformacion of which unreasonable kinde of Common many suites and contencions grewe betweene the tennantes and inhabitantes of Charlton Kings aforesaid touching the taking up of certaine groundes into severall.

Land in several or severalty was not subject to other men's rights of common, but belonged absolutely to its owner and so could be enclosed.

John Stubbes, himself a landowner, copied into the manor court books a great deal of information from earlier rolls about enclosures.[20] Under a three-year agreement made in 1557, for every ten acres held in the common fields, a tenant was allowed to enclose one acre. The lords of the manors of Ashley and Cheltenham had to agree because their strips were intermingled, as did all freeholders, copyholders, and 'base tenants', the successors to the villagers once obliged to do work on the lord's land in return for a holding. Seven men were appointed to measure and allot each man's proportionate amount. Out of a total of 3,500 acres in the parish, 1,482 acres of common field were surveyed. Eventually, 47 men were given allotments, and thereby 162 acres were taken out of the common fields. A process of 'engrossing' had already started, some men having increased their holding and others giving up land, but it had not yet gone very far.

The list of holdings in 1557 is particularly interesting because it was organised by manor. Ashley manor contained more than half of these common fields, 724½ acres; Charlton manor 395 acres; and 363 acres were held of both Cheltenham and Ashley manors, including land in Naunton in Cheltenham. But not everyone was happy with the arrangement and at the end of the three years some people pulled up the hedges and put their animals into the newly enclosed fields. The disputes were brought before the council of the Marches: by an amended agreement of 1564 some three acres were to be enclosed for every twenty held in the common fields, and the enclosures were to last for the lifetimes of the tenants and twelve years after. This gave a larger amount of private enclosed land, suggesting that some earlier allocations had been considered unfair, rather than the principle itself being objectionable. However, Ham and Battledown were brought within the agreement, including 55 acres on Battledown which was glebe, so adding some 450 acres to the total in common field. Most of Ham and Northfield were already enclosed, but this decision meant its owners had to reduce the amounts they held in enclosures. Over 2,000 acres were surveyed this time, 292½ acres were taken out of the common fields, and in the following year an order was made for the enclosures to be hedged.

The decisions were not welcomed by everyone. The owners of land in Ham and Northfield attempted to retain the enclosures they had made previously and refused to abide by the new agreement to open other lands. Probably wanting more commons for their numerous sheep, they tried to put their animals 'throughout all partes or ends of the towne', and it was said that neighbouring townships brought their cattle and sheep into Charlton Kings, buying ricks of hay in order to over-winter 'great flocks of sheep'. At one case in the manor court in 1566

About 1845 a 'cottage' in Charlton Kings caught Mrs George Rowe's eye. Her drawing (*above*) shows the 'King's House', formerly known as 'Hawthorne's', a yeoman's house of the early sixteenth century, when close studding was a fashionable method of timber construction. The ostentation of the close studding, the decorative woodwork and the jetties at each end all demonstrate the owner's status. The separate tall chimney is an intriguing feature, which was still in existence in 1902. Hawthorne was not a common name in the area, but in 1522 Robert Hawthorne was assessed on £5 of goods, and Thomas Hawthorne on £2, both in Charlton Kings. Thirty years later John Hawthorne held a copyhold in Ashley manor called 'Partridge's meese'; his holding of 26 acres in the open fields enabled him to enclose 4 acres, and the house may be built on this enclosure above the Hearne brook. John Hawthorne, yeoman, was mustered in 1608 and Robert Hawthorne tenanted one third of Northfield Down in 1617. The modern photograph (*left*) shows the west end of the house; the original entrance appears to have been where it is today, but is here hidden by the modern extension. The decorative panels on the north and east corner are still exactly as shown in Mrs Rowe's drawing.

GLOUCESTERSHIRE ARCHIVES A76-14 AND PHOTOGRAPH AUTHOR, 2009

these claims were rejected, on the grounds that while some might have messuages and lands 'lying in every ende of the towne' and so had rights of common everywhere, only those who had lands in any particular field had a right of common there, 'for that our commons are recyprocall, we have common in other mens Landes, bycause they have the lyke Common in ours'. Here is a very clear statement of the co-operative nature of the common fields, over-riding individual ownership.

In 1607 John Stubbes, who had been the under-steward, became steward of Cheltenham manor. He was trained in the law, as well as being a landholder in Charlton Kings, and appears to have been of a very litigious turn of mind. His unpopularity with the Higgs family because of the meanness of the stipends paid to the curate has already been described. He was also the leader of a campaign to protect the arrangements made in the previous century for the common fields, and he was a champion of better husbandry and opposed to the sheep farmers. The same year as the case about stipends was raised with the bishop, Stubbes secured an order of the court to 'stint' the common fields, limiting the animals who could use the commons to 30 sheep, 6 beasts and 2 horses (or equivalent substitutes) for every twenty acres of a holding in the common fields. A few months later the court agreed that Charlton Kings tenants were to be permitted to enclose all their pastures but not their arable. This decision was challenged immediately. Not surprisingly the Higgs family, together with Mrs Elizabeth Grevill, were Stubbes' main opponents.

Two years later a survey was made of common field holdings, to enforce a reduced stint of 20 sheep, 4 beasts and 2 horses for every twenty acres. This survey identified 865½ acres of common fields, divided among 56 people, of whom those with the largest holdings were Mr Grevill, Roger Houlder and Richard Pates. When compared with the 1564 survey, a reduction in the area of common fields is apparent.

Comparison of open-field holdings in 1564 and 1611
in Charlton Kings (and some of Naunton)

Acres	1564 Number	1611 Number
under 5	5	14
5 to 9	10	9
10 to 24	13	22
25 to 49	21	8
50 to 99	11	3
over 100	2	0
Total	62	56

Bitter disputes continued. Enclosures made by John Stubbes were attacked, his hedges 'daily thrown open', and Mrs Grevill put her oxen into his fields. There were prolonged legal battles and court cases. Finally, in 1620, some 41 people signed a petition to William Norwood, farmer of the manor of Cheltenham, and to Giles Grevill, lord of the manor of Ashley, asking to keep the enclosed grounds private at all times of the year for plough cattle and milk cows, 'for the necessary maintenance of their tillage'. 'The greatest part' of the tenants of Charlton Kings were said to agree, and an order was accordingly made. Anyone not having sufficient pasture for these animals was to be allowed to exchange grounds, and the number of animals pastured in the remaining open fields was to be stinted. A significant part of Charlton Kings was now enclosed, and although small common fields survived into the nineteenth century, there was no Enclosure Act for the parish.

Some years after Charlton Kings started on the fraught process of enclosure, an agreement was made in 1580 by the landholders of Arle, signed by Mrs Eleanor Lygon and eight others, to allow 4¾ acres to be enclosed for every 20 acres held in common.[21] Those concerned also agreed to exchange lands within the same field, 'goodness for goodness', as judged by four impartial persons in the tithing. This suggests some apprehension that, in exchanging strips, land might be allotted which was poorer than that held before the enclosures. The equitable principle of sharing both good and bad land had been the basis on which open fields were established centuries before. The Arle tenants agreed that no man's 'proper way' was to be obstructed, and that each man was to make 'sufficient mounds' and enclosures adjacent to his land to prevent animals straying. Two years later the agreement was recorded in the manor court book, after Eleanor Lygon's son, Arnold, had asked for it to be ratified.[22]

The 'whole tithing of Westal and Sandford' followed Arle's example, and agreed in 1581 that part of the tithing should be enclosed. 'Certain orders hereafter to be kept,' within the tithing of Cheltenham in 1582, show a similar trend towards ending the communal system: 'No persons hereafter shall keep any beese or sheepe within the Corn fields of Cheltenham or in the lands near unto the said fields but only upon their owne grounde.' The manor court confirmed that burgesses 'shall have and keep their Marsh to themselves until harvest be done'.[23] When in 1617 John Norden asked what enclosure of common fields had taken place in the manor, the jurors said that former common pasture fields were the only ones enclosed, and that this had been done with the consent of the lord and the freeholders. The scattered but substantial rectory lands, and the unwillingness of the owner of the rectory to alter the payment of tithes, held up any general reorganisation of the arable strips for another two centuries.

THE 1617 SURVEY OF CHELTENHAM MANOR

After the dissolution of the monasteries, Cheltenham manor had reverted to the Crown. James I transferred the estate to his son Charles in 1616, and in the following year the celebrated surveyor and cartographer John Norden undertook a full survey, assisted by his son. During the previous 15 years he had undertaken extensive survey work for the Crown and the Duchy of Cornwall, and in 1607 published *The Surveyor's Dialogue*. He produced early guidebooks and ambitious county maps, and in 1623 listed no fewer than 176 manors which he had surveyed. His work for the Duchy of Cornwall improved the management of the estate greatly, and the purpose of the Cheltenham survey was clearly to see whether revenues could be increased and to estimate what the manor would be worth if sold. He concluded that the powers of the lord of Cheltenham manor were much diminished, as was the income which should come from the tenants.[24]

A jury of 32 men was presented with a list of thirty questions. More questions followed the survey, as the Nordens had gone through manorial documents and found field and messuage names missing, and the jurors did their best to find answers to these. A manor court book contains a copy of the survey.[25] Freeholders were listed first, followed by burgesses, tenants of the demesne (in the table below, all these are categorised as 'leaseholder'), and then the large number of base tenants, 'othewise called customary tenants'. There was a maximum of 230 recorded properties, but many owners had more than one holding, sometimes under different forms of tenure. Each separate block of land was described by name and, in the case of the arable, by acreage in each common field. The old system of yardlands had disappeared; all measurements were given in acres and roods (quarters of an acre). Altogether over 5,100 acres, including 237½ acres of demesne, were covered. In 1831 the combined area of Charlton Kings and Cheltenham was 7,800 acres, so the 1617 survey covered an impressive two-thirds of the two parishes. The estates or manors which were not surveyed – Ashley, Redgrove, Arle Court and the rectory manor – account for the rest; the rectory lands were 225 acres when they were surveyed for Lady Cooper, daughter and heir of Baptist Hicks, Lord Campden, closely matching the area of demesne.[26]

There had been a dramatic change in the number and distribution of manorial tenancies since the manorial survey of 1453.

Types of holdings in Cheltenham manor in 1453 and 1617

	Freehold	Burgages	Leasehold	Customary	Total
1453	28	119	33	163	343
1617	66	63	14	88	231

The number of freehold tenancies had more than doubled, but all other types (including leaseholds) had fallen, a pattern indicative of the engrossing of holdings. About half the holdings can be attributed to a township, because many people held land in more than one, but from this sample it seems that the disappearance of customary holdings was most marked in Bafford and Charlton. They were still common in the other townships.

Tenancies in townships in Cheltenham manor in 1617
(where known), excluding burgages

Township	Freehold	Leasehold	Copyhold	Totals
Bafford			3	3
Charlton	15		8	23
Totals in Charlton Kings	15		11	26
Cheltenham	12	5	20	37
Alstone	3	1	14	18
Arle	3	2	10	15
Westal, Naunton and Sandford	2		15	17
Totals in Cheltenham	20	8	59	87
Totals in manor	35	8	70	113

The acreages of 122 landholders can be plotted, excluding burgages. The concentration in the middle of the distribution probably reflects the enduring influence of the old yardland holdings of the early medieval period.

Size of holdings in 1617 in Cheltenham and Charlton Kings (excluding burgages)

Acres	No.
Under 5	25
5–9	8
10–24	27
25–49	28
50–99	19
100–199	12
200–299	2
300 and over	1
Total	122

THE FREEHOLDS

Sir William Norwood's manor of Leckhampton and Broadwell was listed first in the survey, followed by a holding of five messuages in Leckhampton belonging to Anthony Partridge, gentleman. Three more manors were noted: Comptons' and Powers' in Charlton Kings and Cheltenham, owned by Robert Packer; Ashley in Charlton Kings, owned by Giles Grevill, gentleman; and Ham, also in Charlton Kings, owned by Alexander Packer. Both Grevill and

Little is known of the history of Leckhampton Farm, although it was one of the largest in the parish. It does seem possible that it was associated with one of the manors, significantly being called 'Berry' Farm, as this could be a form of 'bury', a name often appropriate to a manor. Later it was a substantial freeholding reaching to the western boundary of the parish, and it remained a working farm until 1954. The largest of its barns is late sixteenth- or early seventeenth-century. On the end gable there is an inscription 'J. Clark builder 1810', indicating when the barn was partly rebuilt. As farms were consolidated and land used for building, the barn fell into disrepair, but is now well restored and has been converted into two dwellings. The later farmhouse, too, has become apartments.

© MARTIN WILLIAMS

Alexander Packer were expanding their estates, absorbing once independent holdings. Thus, in addition to his manor of Ashley, Grevill owned 65 acres of freehold land formerly attached to two other holdings. Alexander Packer of Ham owned 294 acres, consisting of four messuages with their arable and closes amounting to 78 acres, together with 116 acres in closes, 50 acres of the 'Languetts' with the water mill and millpond, and 50 acres of arable on Ham hill. He also leased some manorial demesne in Oakley Wood. A 'capital messuage called Arle Court' was recorded, owned by John Lygon, but no details were given.

There were 23 freeholders in the manor, most holdings no more than a few acres and some merely a cottage and garden. Thomas Nicholas was by far the most substantial, with 200 acres of pasture on Northfield Down, and 65¾ acres of arable land. Northfield Down, which totalled 300 acres, was not enclosed and had once been in common – Robert Hawthorne, a customary tenant of the manor, held the other third, and his customary messuage was described as 'the sheep house'. Thomas Nicholas also leased 50 acres of demesne in Oakley Wood.

Fourteen people, generally of similar social standing to freeholders, leased demesne land. The most important, Thomas Gough, had two ancient houses in Cheltenham, one known as the Court House, and lands (mainly in Cheltenham township but also in Arle and Alstone) totalling 107 acres. This was just under half the total demesne. Another survey of the demesne was made in 1637, which specified the townships more clearly.[27] The largest amount was in Arle (111 acres), with 59½ acres in Charlton Kings, 49½ acres in Cheltenham, and 18½ acres

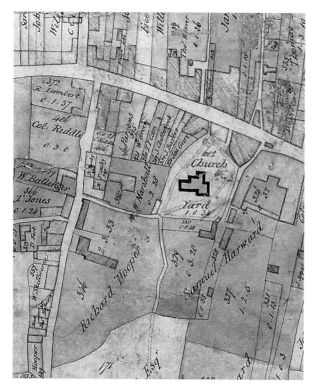

The site of Cheltenham's Court or manor house was where the Great House was built by Lady Stapleton in the early eighteenth century. On the 1806 map the Great House is number 346, and was owned by Richard Hooper. Its location close to the church is a typical position for a manor house. Across the lane now called Chester Walk, W. Marshall was also a freeholder with a substantial house. Church Meadow, number 171, is to the south, supporting the area's association with church and manor.

GLOUCESTERSHIRE ARCHIVES D2025

in Alston mead. It totalled 238½ acres, just one acre difference from the Nordens' survey. Two-thirds were enclosed, mostly in Charlton Kings, and one-third was common field. Richard Gough, gentleman, then had the largest share of the demesne, and there were ten other tenants.

John Dutton of Sherborne had bought the lordship of Cheltenham from Charles I in 1628,[28] but the 1635 survey shows that three-quarters of the land had been sold to other buyers. Some 51 acres were described as 'Not sold and so do come into the hands of John Dutton Esq on 24 June 1645'; this land, too, was sold at a later date, leaving the Dutton family with just the title to the lordship.[29]

THE BURGAGES

In John Norden's 1617 survey 52 whole burgages were accounted for, exactly the same number as in 1294, showing how carefully the record of each plot was kept, even though the majority had been divided.[30] It is clear that originally a burgage plot was an acre – as indicated by the corresponding acreage recorded for more than half of the holdings in 1617 – and the total in 1617 adds up to just over 50 acres.[31] Twenty-five were still undivided. Rents had originally been twelvepence a year for a whole burgage. The burgage owners also held the twelve acres of 'English moor' called the Lady Marsh, for which they paid 11s. 8d., and the Lower Marsh of 20 acres for which there was no particular payment. Every holder of a whole burgage was allowed to pasture two beasts on the Lower Marsh, and holders of a half-burgage one beast.

Because of subdivision there were 61 burgage-holders. John Benfield was exceptional in owning 3¼ burgages, and seven others owned more than one burgage or part burgage. Not all were listed continuously, so they were probably not contiguous. Many – perhaps even most – burgage-holders would not have been resident. Seventeen names may be identified with men in the muster list of 1608: a butcher, two glovers, five husbandmen, two maltsters, either a

Burgage plots became much sub-divided as the population of the town grew and the advantages of a freehold house in the High Street were appreciated. One such example is this site at the eastern end of the High Street, mapped in 1806 in connection with the enclosure of the township's open and common fields. Plots numbered 341, 409, 383, 310, 242, 382 and 259 were all described as 'old inclosures'. On the street side five tenements had been created; the largest, Mrs Millar's, also included half the garden plot to the rear. However, behind that again was another half of the original plot, with a messuage, garden and bowling green belonging to William Capstick Esq. To the side of the plot there is an alley giving access, linking with the Back Lane.

GLOUCESTERSHIRE ARCHIVES D2025

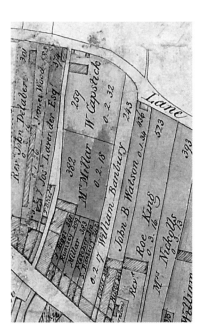

maltster or a cooper, two shoemakers, a smith, two tailors, and a weaver, giving a useful indication of traditional trades to be found in Cheltenham. Twelve burgage-holders held land in the surrounding townships, mostly of modest amounts, though William Gregory and Richard Pates had 85 and 207 acres respectively.

The jurors in 1617 asserted that the borough was independent of the manor, despite rents and reliefs being paid to the lord, and they emphasised that no 'exactions' were taken because it was 'allways alowed and taken to bee a Burrowe'. The profits and tolls of the market, and of the standings and stallages, valued at £6 13s. 4d. 'or thereabouts', did not go to the lord but to the town bailiff. Burgages passed either by inheritance at common law, or by purchase with a legal conveyance, and (unlike manorial tenancies) were not surrendered to the lord of the manor and reassigned. However, the bailiff of the manor witnessed a transfer to a new owner, reported it to the next manor court, and the steward entered it in the manor court roll, thus signifying a continuing manorial interest. On the death of an owner or on a sale, a 'relief' or small sum of money was payable to the lord, but no 'heriot' (the payment of the best beast or other item, a much-disliked symbol of a 'base' tenancy). After 1717 the transmission of a burgage did not have to be recorded by the manor court, when the civil law courts protected burgage-owners from being ejected by the lord for failing to follow the manorial procedure.[32]

CUSTOMARY TENANTS

In 1617 a large area was held by customary tenure – 3,418 acres, approaching half of the total acreage of the two parishes. There were 88 customary holdings recorded, and 72 customary tenants. It was not uncommon for an owner to hold three, four or five 'messuages', and to build up substantial properties – the existence of 25 customary holdings over fifty acres was indicative of the developing situation.

Only four freeholders also had customary holdings, outstanding among them being Richard Pates, gentleman, a juror at the enquiry and a nephew of the founder of Cheltenham grammar school. He was building up an estate, and had ten separate lots of land.[33] His five customary

Customary holdings in 1617

Acres	No.
Under 5	6
5–9	1
10–24	21
25–49	19
50–99	15
100–199	10
Total	72

holdings, totalling 172¾ acres, were scattered through the whole of Cheltenham manor, and he had a substantial burgage of two acres, four small freeholds, and a lease of two tenements in Cheltenham with some arable and a close of pasture. His largest holding was three copyholds in Alstone and Westal, totalling 53 acres, forty of which were scattered through four arable fields. He also had two watermills in Sandford, with their lands which lay mainly in Charlton. Some of his land was tenanted by others, but he was himself a working farmer. Unfortunately the original of his will, made in 1628, is lost, and the first page of a copy made in 1703 is also missing, while the rest is torn. But what is left confirms the spread of his estate. He bequeathed to his son Lynnett the house where he lived in Charlton Kings, subject to his wife's right of dower, and household goods and implements of husbandry which his wife was to have the use of for her lifetime provided she did not marry.

Lynnett Pates, gentleman, died in 1685. His house was full of furniture, and was probably the one bequeathed him. As well as the hall, parlour, cellar and closet, three bedrooms over these, a separate maids' chamber and men servants' chamber, a cheese chamber and a pott house chamber, there was a day-house or dairy and an old day-house, a kitchen, an 'old house', and a corn chamber. Forty acres of arable crops were on the ground in April, and he had 154 sheep, 12 cows without calves, fourteen other beasts and six calves, two yoke of oxen for ploughing, three mares and a colt for riding, and six pigs. He was a relatively wealthy man.

THE COPYHOLD ACT, 1625

Among the questions put to the jurors of Cheltenham manor by the Nordens, two concerned the customs operating with respect to copyhold tenure, and the jurors' replies are the only complete statement of the legal position. The most important feature was that they were 'copyholds of inheritance' and that heirs paid a fixed fine. The custom known as 'Borough English' was followed, whereby the youngest son or daughter or youngest of the nearest living relatives inherited the copyhold, but the copyholder could defer the inheritance by willing the property to another person for twelve years. Widows inherited for their lifetimes and also for twelve more years, provided a fine had been paid. There were customs dealing with what happened if a widow married again: provided the next husband paid the fine, which was double the normal rent, the copy became his and his child's, but if he had no children, the first husband's children inherited, and failing that, the kin of the second husband. Also important was the copyholder's freedom to lease his land for a term of years, and to make a grant of his land to another for a lifetime and twenty years more. When a copyhold was surrendered or a tenant died, a heriot was paid in money. There was no restriction on the marriage of a copyholder's son or daughter, as there had been in early medieval times, and there were no payments of cocks, hens or eggs. No customary tenant was required to carry the lord's letters, and no works were required, but money payments *in lieu* were still owed.

By the mid-sixteenth century, copyhold had become a form of tenure recognised by the courts, and protected by the royal justices. It had subtly changed from the medieval system of base tenure, but was still by definition governed by the customs of each particular manor, where they could be established, though there was a growing perception that instead the common law should govern the way copyhold tenure worked.[34] Attempts by Henry VII and Henry VIII to revive traditional feudal payments,[35] and the increasing complexity of the law, led the gentry, or those aspiring to gentry status, to send their sons to study law at the Inns of Court. They developed a greater awareness of the possibilities of legal protection for their estates, and of increasing their income if the legal status of copyholders could be made to revert to an older position.

Cheltenham copyholders may have feared that this was the likely outcome of the 1617 survey. The large amount of land held by customary tenure explains why they were anxious to secure recognition of their rights, and their particular concern with the 'certainty', or otherwise, of fines which were paid when taking over a copyhold. There was clearly local cooperation to bargain with the lord, Prince Charles, in order to secure safeguards for the future. This process cost the copyholders a good sum of money, but the agreement which was incorporated in an Act of Parliament in 1625 was generally favourable to them. There was another motive behind their desire to codify the customs of the manor. As more copyholds came into the hands of landowners who were also accumulating freehold estates, men like Richard Pates and the Grevills, they wished to pass their lands to one heir; as far as freehold was concerned, this was the *oldest* surviving son, or if no son then daughter. 'Borough English' made it more difficult for them to manage the transmission of their estates.

The Cheltenham copyholders appointed John Stubbes as their attorney, and once again his manor court book contains a full account of proceedings. A meeting was held at Denmark House in the Strand on 25 February 1625, with the copyholders of Cheltenham and Ashley manors 'attending the table' to discuss 'inconvenient customs' and the certainty (or otherwise) of fines. They offered his majesty £1,200, to be paid in three instalments during the ensuing year. All concerned contributed in proportion to their customary payments, and ten per cent more to defray expenses. Richard Pates was first on the list of Cheltenham tenants, paying £86 15s. and £8 7s. 1d. towards expenses, but his was not the largest contribution; John Packer paid £111 5s. and £9 15s. 5d. Nobody holding land in Ashley manor paid anything like as much, but Richard Pates paid another £15 16s. 8d. for his Ashley copyholds. There were 74 names recorded in Cheltenham and 31 in Ashley.[36]

By the time the Act was passed, Charles I had become king. The Act made several major changes to the nature of Cheltenham and Ashley copyhold tenure. 'Borough English' was given up. Copyholds were now to be held 'in fee simple, according to the rules of common law'; the eldest son would inherit, or failing a son, the eldest daughter. In place of the heriot, a fixed fine of 30s. was to be paid. The act protected the copyholder's right to surrender land to another's use, either in the manor court or before two witnesses, provided the transfer was reported to the court, and to grant land for another's lifetime and twelve years. This put the copyholder in the same position as a freeholder under common law, at the same time preserving the lord's right to a fine when land changed hands. Land could be assigned to a wife as a 'jointure', but again a fine was to be paid. If there were no jointure, a wife was entitled to 'dower' of one third of the estate, giving her possession for her lifetime, but this was not to apply to anyone married to a copyholder before the date of the Act. A wife's dower could not be claimed on lands granted away with her consent. Neither a husband nor a wife's individual copyholds could be granted away by the surviving partner, so heirs were protected.

In other manors, copyhold was steadily whittled away by owners who put pressure on tenants to enfranchise their property by buying the freehold, or who converted them into straightforward leaseholds when opportunity arose. But after 1625 Cheltenham copyholders had no incentive to change their form of tenure. Some wills from Charlton Kings show the copyhold rules in use. Richard Pates' will in 1628 referred to a lifetime lease plus twelve years. A complex arrangement was detailed in Giles Grevill's will in 1632 for a property which had come into his possession. William Baughan had granted the copyhold to Roger Holder for twelve years after his decease, but allowing Ruth Stubbes the use (or profits) of the property for the seventh year, the children of the late John Baughan deceased that for the eighth year, and his grandchildren Thomas Baughan and Samuel Stubbes that for the ninth year. Giles Grevill and his wife Sarah were living in Forden House, and his status was evident from the six servants, all of whom were given a bequest; typically his estate contained both copyholds and freeholds.

Increasingly a will was used to override the normal rules. Thomas Keare of Cheltenham, mercer, for example, in 1723 surrendered his customary tenancy and willed both customary and free lands to his three sisters for their lifetimes and then to a grandchild. Samuel Church of Alstone in 1715 wrote, 'I surrender two customary tenancies of the manor of Cheltenham and nominate them for my wife Jane for her life and then for my son Samuel', so avoiding the provision for dower. A more explicit example is the will of Francis Hurst of Cheltenham, butcher, in 1716. He left his wife a burgage at The Knapp for her life and surrendered several customary properties, including the house he lived in and some land, nominating his wife as his successor also for her life: 'I declare that the premises are devised to my wife in lieu of her dower or thirds at law.' [37]

The provisions of the Act governed a great deal of Cheltenham land for the next two hundred and more years, and were only gradually eroded as the town's development gathered pace. Not until the nineteenth century were serious questions raised about its operation. In one notorious case, Colonel Riddell, who was apparently a bachelor, came to live in Cheltenham about 1800 and made a number of grants of copyhold land. In 1830, five years after his death, his wife appeared and claimed her dower, and her attorney attempted to gain entry to numerous properties built on the land he had granted. After a struggle, she won her case.

Changes of lordship of the manor in the mid-nineteenth century led to two attempts to raise the level of fines paid on acquiring copyhold land. In 1843 Lord Sherborne sold the manor to James Agg-Gardner, whose steward thought that the lord was being deprived of copyholders' fees because several messuages were transferred at a time in one transaction and only one fine was paid. The copyholders resisted the demand for multiple fees, and took the case to the Queen's Bench. They proved conclusively that property had passed in this way many times in the past, and won. Soon after the death of Agg-Gardner, the manor was again sold, and in 1862 was bought by a solicitor, Robert Sole Lingwood. He sent notices to the copyholders pressing them to enfranchise their property to make it freehold, and threatened that if they failed to do this, he would revive old customary payments. He claimed that, for example, they should have sought the lord's permission to lease copyhold property, to fell timber or to dig earth for bricks, all which would have incurred a fee. The Cheltenham Copyholders Protection Association was formed, led by prominent townsmen including Sir William Russell of Charlton Park and William Nash Skillicorne. A test case was brought respecting William Gyde's property. At an enquiry held in the Old Well Music Hall, it was conceded that the cost of collecting pennies due when property was leased was uneconomic; however, this was the only part of the lord's claims that could be upheld. The copyholders were assured that the problem of leases could be obviated by using different legal forms and the lordship, now of small financial benefit, was sold back to the Agg-Gardner family. [38] Copyhold continued to be a feature of Cheltenham landholding until converted into freehold in 1926 by national legislation.

THE MANOR HOUSES

The location of the main house of a manor – the 'capital messuage' – was not fixed, but could be moved if the owner wished. This makes it difficult in some cases to establish the history of a particular site, while family settlements, life interests and reversions also create confusion. Furthermore, those with capital to invest might buy and sell estates, putting some together, splitting others, and separating houses from the manors of which they had once been the centre. Of the several manors and sub-manors in Cheltenham, four houses survive dating at least in part from the period of the 1617 survey, and have been given the title of 'Court House'. The history of other major houses is known, but they were rebuilt in the eighteenth or nineteenth centuries.

What was probably the most important of Cheltenham's manor houses, the Court House where the medieval manorial court presumably met, was next to the churchyard, with a meadow, the Lord's Close, adjacent. This was a typical position for a manor house, but it was not the centre of a compact manorial demesne. The medieval house was often repaired but there was no major rebuilding. In 1617 it was still part of the manorial demesne, and was described as an 'ancient house called the Court House'. It was sold some time after 1635, and replaced by Lady Stapleton's Great House about 1739.

Johannes Kip not only engraved, but also himself drew the sixty-five plates for Robert Atkyns' *The Ancient and Present State of Glostershire*, published in 1712, among which was one of Leckhampton Court. It is the only plate relating to the Cheltenham area. Atkyns was following the current fashion for topographical prints, and Kip, a Dutchman who had moved from Amsterdam, possibly through his work for William of Orange, had already proved himself with *Britannia Illustrata*. He was able to achieve an amazing bird's-eye view of each scene, and the detail of both house and grounds appears to be very accurate. The corridor with battlements had not yet been built in front of the oldest building (*see* page 56), and part of the north wing had not been destroyed by the fire in 1732; today only the west end of the wing survives with, on the north, its oriel window and two brick chimneys.

GLOUCESTERSHIRE ARCHIVES SR PRINTS 172-13 LOC 16-17

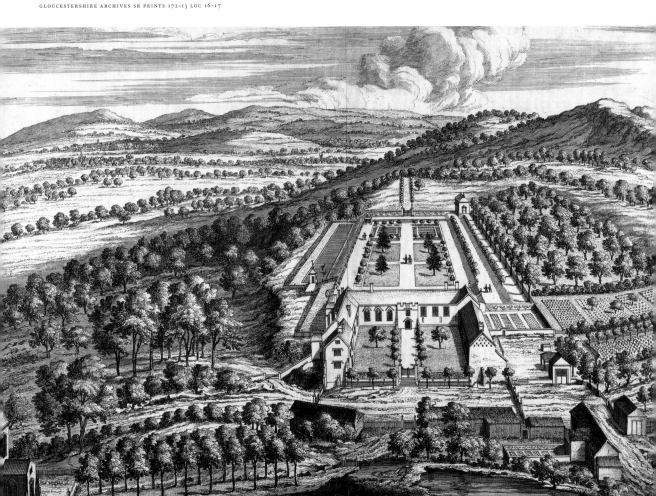

The long south wing of Leckhampton Court, with timber framing above a stone ground floor, was built about 1500, probably by John Norwood, and Kip indicates its timber-framing at first floor level. Other alterations were made to the Court later in the sixteenth century, as indicated by a doorway with the date 1582 carved on it which leads into the garden.

PHOTOGRAPH: AUTHOR, 2009

The most significant of the surviving manor houses is Leckhampton Court, which Verey thought 'a remarkable survival of medieval domestic architecture', and Kingsley 'one of the grandest medieval houses in Gloucestershire'.[39] It was the only house in the old Cheltenham hundred illustrated by Kip in Atkyns' *Ancient and Present State of Glostershire* (1712), which shows the pretensions of the Norwoods – they paid for the picture – as well as the status of the house. Now a Grade II* listed building, Leckhampton Court is built on three sides of a courtyard. On the east side there is a fourteenth-century hall, and most of the south wing has medieval timber-framing above the stone ground floor. A seventeenth-century coach house survives, though almost completely rebuilt, and most of the basic layout of the garden remains as drawn by Kip.

The manor and house were owned by the Gifford family or their descendants for more than 550 years, passing to John Norwood in 1486 and to Charles Brandon Trye in 1797; Henry Norwood Trye sold the property in 1894. Sir John Gifford may have built the great hall about 1320–30. John Norwood built the long south wing about 1500. William Norwood married Elizabeth Lygon of Madresfield, who was 'possest of a very large Estate', about 1570,[40] and he extended the house; a small wing at the rear was added – the date 1582 is carved over a doorway at the south end – and another block added to the north wing. Part of the north wing was destroyed by fire in the early eighteenth century, and was rebuilt then, and again in the nineteenth. After standing empty for a number of years, Leckhampton Court was restored between 1979 and 1981, from a near-derelict condition, to accommodate a Sue Ryder home.

An interesting sixteenth-century court house or manor house in Charlton Kings, called from at least the early seventeenth century 'New Court', and now 'The Court House', survives though much altered. It was in Bafford tithing. The timber-framed house was a significant early or mid-sixteenth-century building with a central hall and two cross wings, though not on the scale of Leckhampton Court. It, too, is listed grade II*. The existence of a pigeon house over the barn, recorded in 1691, suggests manorial status.[41] Who built it and why was it a 'new' court? It was probably connected with 'Compton's manor' noted in 1617.

Sir William Compton, the first of his name associated with Cheltenham, became very wealthy through service to Henry VIII, and built Compton Wynyates in Warwickshire. Amongst his portfolio of manors, lands and tenements he had substantial property in Cheltenham, Alstone and Charlton Kings which had belonged to Syon abbey and was therefore part of Cheltenham manor demesne. The abbey had apparently been persuaded to surrender this land some years before it was dissolved; Sir William acquired other lands in the same way.[42] He was quite young when he died in 1528, and his only son, Peter, was four years old. The 1557 list of owners of common fields in Charlton Kings, which referred to 'Compton's heirs', suggests that Peter Compton himself had died. Henry Compton was the heir, named in 1564 as a freeholder, knighted in 1567 and granted a peerage in 1572.[43] New Court is likely to have been the manorial centre for the Charlton Kings property of the Comptons, and the central hall, later much altered, and one or two of the wings were perhaps built by Sir Henry Compton's lessee, Thomas Wye; he was probably related to the son-in-law of Judge William Grevill of Arle Court, and was named as a small freeholder in the common fields of Charlton Kings in 1557 and 1564.

About 1600 the house and a small amount of land was sold to Humfrey Harris, yeoman, and separated from the rest of the manor, and in 1617 the heirs of Harris had a freehold dwelling house, but Robert Packer owned the manors of 'Compton's' and 'Powers'. New Court was later occupied by Charles Holte, who had moved nearer to Cheltenham from Withington in 1613, and subsequently bought the house from Harris.[44] Holte had an improvement lease,

Despite rebuilding and alteration, the overall plan of the Court House in Charlton Kings, formerly New Court, reflects its original form of a central open hall and two cross wings. Chimneys were inserted about 1614 by Charles Holte. The cross wing on the left, which contained the parlour and main chamber above it, was a cruck-framed building, showing how common locally this vernacular method was in the medieval period; crucks can be seen inside. The Court House probably dates from the mid-sixteenth century. It was a high-status house, associated with 'Compton's manor' referred to in 1617. William Prinn constructed a fashionable brick front about 1700 in front of the original timber frame. On the right was the service wing, with a cellar later constructed underneath it. It is listed grade II*.

PHOTOGRAPH: AUTHOR, 2009

and probably ceiled the open hall, creating a room above, an improvement made possible by the insertion of a brick chimney which was a common development from the mid-sixteenth century. The house was called 'Newe Court' when sold by Holte in 1625 to Giles Atkins. Thomas Atkins paid tax for three hearths in 1671. Margaret Rich owned the house from 1686 until her death in 1692; prior to 1686 it is likely that she had lived with her brother, Thomas Rich, at Powers Court in Cheltenham. She had his portrait in New Court, as well as portraits of her father and mother and of Lady Bathurst.

Margaret Rich's will and inventory reveal much about the house, and show it as a residence for a gentleman or gentlewoman, but without practical farming interests. Like Fleetwood Dormer, referred to in chapter 5, Margaret Rich had a coach. On the ground floor of her house there was a hall, parlour, drawing room, kitchen and brewhouse, and two cellars. The best staircase gave access to the best bedroom over the hall and another staircase to two other bedrooms. Outdoors, there were what sound to be extensive grounds: a great and little garden, the latter where apricots, peaches and grapes were growing, a cherry orchard, a barn with a pigeon house above it, and a court 'hay' or enclosure. The hall was furnished with blue and yellow flowered hangings, and here were a number of pictures, oval tables, turkey-work chairs, and a clock. Her clothes were in the best chamber, 'lynnen, woollen silk and silver whoods and scarfs'. Five rings included one with an amethyst, and she had a comb box with two combs and brushes, a powder box, a silver-framed looking glass and 88 books. One picture in the parlour chamber was described as a 'landskip' or landscape, a modern fashion in painting.

This house was left to a very young woman, Margaret Rogers, who was living with her, but Margaret Rich was in debt when she died, and a few years later the mortgage on the property was assigned to John Prinn, who was able to buy it outright. Surprisingly, the transaction was not completed until 1735. Prinn probably built the brick façades to the central hall in contemporary style and raised its height, while retaining the old cross wings. The Cheltenham manor court book for 1692–98 shows that the manor court met there on at least four occasions while Prinn was steward of the manor.[45] When he purchased the Forden House in 1701, New Court became the dower house.

Powers Court in Cheltenham must have been associated with 'Power's manor'. It stood in the High Street, near the later Rodney Road. The origin of the name has not been identified, but William Pouwer was the second largest taxpayer in Cheltenham town in 1327, and that could push the date of a freeholding back to his time or even before. The site of Power's Court was certainly part of Sir William Compton's Cheltenham estate in 1535, when his heirs were paid a rent by Cirencester Abbey for water rights, confirming that he owned land near Cambray mill, part of Cheltenham rectory estate. A transfer of Powers Court from Henry to George Packer was recorded in the manor court book in 1573.[46] This almost exactly coincides with the purchase by Thomas Packer of the manor of Ham in Charlton Kings.

Like New Court, Power's Court may have been separated from the rest of the manor soon after this. The house was in John Dutton's hands in 1635, when he sold the capital messuage with gardens, orchards and premises to Edward Rich of Dowdeswell.[47] Thomas Rich, his son, inherited the house and was living there in 1672, paying tax on six hearths. Thomas made his will in 1678, and his witnesses were Edward Mitchell and William Prinn. He died in 1686, when his sister, Margaret Rich, who had probably been living with her brother, bought New Court in Charlton Kings, a tantalising link between the two. In 1695 Thomas Rich's heir, another Thomas, and his son Lionel conveyed Power's Court to Edward Mitchell of Cheltenham who was already the tenant.[48]

Edward Mitchell was well thought of in Cheltenham, witnessing several wills between 1678 and 1727 and appraising inventories. Always called 'gentleman', he was connected with John Mitchell of Northleach; the two men with one other guaranteed a bond for £2,000 when Samuel Arrowsmith, haberdasher, died in 1685.[49] Edward Mitchell purchased Ashley manor from Giles Grevill in 1697, and sold it in 1716 to John Prinn, then living at Forden House.[50] Atkyns in 1712 noted that Mr Mitchell had a 'good house' in Cheltenham, the only house he mentioned in the town. Edward died in 1727. A bond for £1,000 taken out by the administrators (his son John and John Prinn of Charlton Kings) indicates the size of his estate. John Mitchell died childless

There is no other picture of Powers Court before significant alterations were done to accommodate the Assembly Rooms in the later eighteenth century. Thomas Robins placed this picture on the reverse of the very fine fan which he painted in 1740 (*see also* pages 164, 169), probably for Lady Stapleton, and labelled it the 'Assembley Room'; there was a ballroom in the house. Powers Court was a high-class and substantial house, which appears to have been rebuilt in the late seventeenth century in the fashionable brick style associated with the reign of William and Mary. Its land extended southwards to the Chelt. It would have been a striking feature at the eastern end of the High Street.
COURTESY OF MONICA MAIMAN

Ham Court. In the late sixteenth or early seventeenth century a timber-framed house was built in Ham with elaborate decorative panels, similar to those on the King's House (*see* page 104). It was perhaps the work of Alexander Packer, who had bought the manor in 1574, and was wealthy enough to purchase Northfield together with Puckham Farm in Whittington for £2,000. The barn to the south-east of the house is about the same date. Both are listed grade II. Alexander Packer died in 1638, and his heirs were not good stewards, eventually losing the house to Andrew Percival to whom it had been heavily mortgaged.

The fashionable brick front on the house may have been the work of Percival, or perhaps it was the reason that the last Packer owner became heavily indebted. The house was owned by Mary Dodwell from 1734 until 1799, and she married into the prominent Tracy family. During these years more land was purchased, but after her death there was a long case in Chancery, as a result of which the estate was broken up and divided between claimants. Most of the land was separated from the former manor house.

PHOTOGRAPHS: AUTHOR, 2009

the following year and his estate passed to his sisters Mary and Martha. Mary, the widow of the Reverend George Stokes, owned other lands in Cheltenham, including Gallipot Farm. About 1734 the dining room of Powers Court was converted to a ballroom, and the house was featured as the 'Assembley House' on a fan painted by Thomas Robins about 1739. A fine red brick building in a 'William and Mary' style, it had possibly been built by Thomas Rich in the 1690s, replacing the large old house with six hearths occupied by his father. Mary Stokes was the owner until 1776, and the house was finally demolished about 1819.[51]

Ham Court in Charlton Kings survives, although the name 'Court' was not attached to this sizeable farmhouse until the early twentieth century.[52] The first record of the manor is in 1574, when Robert Goodrych of Ham, Edith his wife, Richard his son, a gentleman of Coberley, and Richard's wife Elizabeth, sold the manor to Thomas Packer of Cheltenham, gentleman. An indenture two years later confirmed the sale, after the final payment was made in the porch on the north side of the parish church. It referred to 'all that manor, capital messuage or farme of Hame with all its rights, members and appurtenances whatsoever sett, lying and being in Charlton Kings within the parish of Cheltenham'.[53] The smallholdings of several manorial tenants were included, and the estate contained 100 acres of meadow, 300 of pasture, 100 of arable land, eight messuages and three cottages, gardens and orchards, a water mill and two dovehouses.

The Packers were a long-established family in Cheltenham and Charlton Kings, and have already been mentioned in connection with Powers Court. One Thomas Packer first came to Cheltenham in 1516, almost certainly with his brother John and his father, another Thomas Packer.[54] In the Military Survey of 1522 there were two Thomas Packers in Cheltenham, one with a small amount of land but goods valued at £60, and the other with £8 of goods. The elder Thomas was doubtless attracted to Cheltenham by having a lease of Cheltenham Rectory from Cirencester Abbey, as noted in the *Valor Ecclesiasticus* in 1535 for the large sum of £73 13s. 4d.[55] The date of his death is not known. Thomas, his son, founded a family of importance in Cheltenham and Charlton Kings. John's family moved into royal service as clerks in the office of the Privy Seal, and his grandson, another John, became a trusted and important royal servant, being granted a coat of arms about 1600; John was helpful to John Stubbes's attempts to secure better stipends for the local curates.

All branches of the family seem to have had numerous progeny, and a tendency to call their sons by the same Christian names. The family also illustrates the increasing affluence of smaller landowners who moved into the ranks of the gentry in this period, were mobile in respect of where they lived, and intermarried with similar families across the country. Their

The Packer family came to Cheltenham in the late fifteenth or early sixteenth century, before the parish registers began to be kept, which record some of the later events in the family. The family was successful and bought several large properties in the area. One member of the family emigrated to America, where again the family multiplied, and this simplified family tree is based on the researches of a descendant.

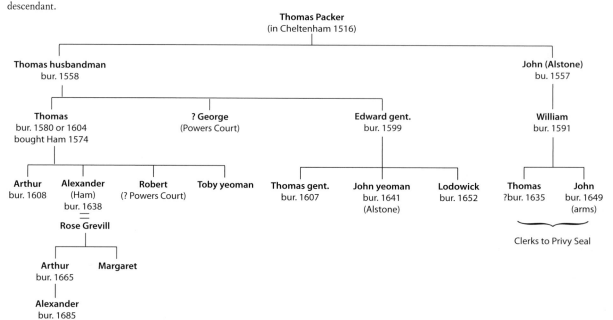

property often passed to brothers or cousins. Thomas died in 1558, and John died the following year. In his will Thomas called himself a husbandman; he left a burgage in Cheltenham, a house in Gloucester and other free lands and tenements.[56] His oldest son, Thomas, called himself a gentleman, and so did other members of the next generation.

Thomas's son and heir, another Thomas, bought Ham and the family owned it for more than a hundred years. His son Arthur was stated in the 1608 muster list to be joint lord of Charlton Kings with Giles Grevill – implying an equal status for the manor of Ham with the manor of Ashley. Arthur died later that year, and his younger brother Alexander inherited. Among many Packers in the muster list were John Packer, a woollen draper in Tewkesbury; John Packer, yeoman, in Alstone, a cousin of Alexander; and Toby Packer, yeoman, in Cheltenham, the brother of Alexander. The dividing line between a yeoman and a gentleman was a fine one. The existing Ham Court, with its decorative timber-framing dated to the later sixteenth century, was probably the work of Arthur Packer.

In 1611 Alexander Packer married Rose Grevill, another link between the local gentry families, and expanded the estate with the purchase of Thomas Nicholas's Northfield land. He died in 1638, and an *Inquisition post mortem* was held into his property as a landowner holding directly of the king.[57] It referred to 'the manor of Ham situate in Ham, Charlton Kings and Cheltenham'. Alexander had arranged that Ham should pass to his daughter Margaret as a dowry for 21 years, and thereafter to his grandson, another Alexander. His son Arthur had to become a member of the Society of the Gentlemen of the Middle Temple if he was to have an annuity of £50 from his father's estate.

In 1671 the younger Alexander paid tax on eight hearths. Only five hearths were indicated

Two drawings of the old manor house of Arle, one from the south-east and one from the north-west, were published in the *Transactions of the Bristol and Gloucestershire Archaeological Society* in 1913, to accompany an article by A. M. Welch. They were made about 1860 by A. B. Welch, close to the time the house was demolished. The main entrance was on the north-west, facing away from Cheltenham, and was approached by a long avenue from the Tewkesbury Road. There is a suggestion of two central timber-framed bays of three or four storeys of the Tudor period and two wings. The simple round-headed arch to the entrance suggests an older date, and there were steps up. On the south-east, however, the major feature was two gigantic chimney stacks. The drawings correspond well with the enclosure map of 1835. Arle mill was nearby, and the mill stream ran quite close to the house.

GLOUCESTERSHIRE ARCHIVES

in the inventory of his possessions made after his death in 1685, so three were probably in the 'cottage' or another part of the house let to tenants.[58] The inventory does not suggest a wealthy man, or indicate much farming activity. His clothes and money were valued at £25, and the books in the study at £20, but the pictures and maps in the parlour were not highly valued. He had some cheese, three horses and a colt, ten pigs, some poultry, and three stocks of bees. Most unusually, a summerhouse was listed. But the estate was being run down by this time, and would soon be forfeit to the holder of the mortgage. Ham Court was subsequently extended with a stone kitchen wing in the late seventeenth or early eighteenth century. The

In this painting Thomas Robins seems to have been attempting a bird's-eye view of Charlton Park. It was not as accomplished as the Kip engravings (*see* page 116), and the grounds seem to have interested him more than the house. Like Leckhampton Court, the vegetable garden in particular is a strong feature. The older timber-framed house built by Giles Grevill around three sides of a courtyard has been encased in brick by John Prinn after 1701 when he bought the house. The western block is dated 1732 on the gable, but was remodelled later in the century. Nevertheless, it is still a farmhouse, with barns and dovecote, although they were rebuilt by Prinn a little further away from the house. The spire of Cheltenham church is visible on the horizon.

BRIDGEMAN ART LIBRARY

The south front of Charlton Park, though not now completely visible, is recognisably the façade highlighted by Thomas Robins in his painting, which suggests that he was responding to Mr Prinn's own request to show clearly the newest block; this Mr John Prinn was the son of the purchaser of the estate.

PHOTOGRAPH: AUTHOR, 2009

front was rebuilt in brick later in the eighteenth century, probably after it was sold to the trustees of Sir William Dodwell of Brockhampton Manor and Sandywell Park in 1732.[59] It is now grade II listed.

Arle Court, like Ham, was a medieval freehold. It was close to the river Chelt (the older name of which was the Arle) and to the main road through Cheltenham to Tewkesbury. It passed to the Lygon family through Sir Richard Lygon's marriage to Margaret Grevill, daughter of William Grevill, and the Lygon family retained a strong interest in the estate. Either William Grevill or Sir Richard Lygon may have been the builder of the substantial house shown in two nineteenth-century drawings; William Gevill was certainly wealthy enough to have built or significantly extended the house. The sketch of the rear of the house (*see* page 123) shows two very large chimneys which could have dated from the sixteenth century, but the front, with its steps up to the entrance and stone base to some part of the walls, was perhaps more ancient.[60]

John Lygon owned Arle Court in 1617, and had to pay a large fine on admission to the property. When he died in 1644 he left monetary bequests to be paid from the rent charges issuing out of Arle Court.[61] He was buried in Cheltenham, as was Hugh Lygon who died in 1654 and John Lygon's daughter and heir, Catherine in 1678. She married Fleetwood Dormer, who became a prominent citizen of Cheltenham; his brother was Judge Robert Dormer. The Lygons tried to repossess Arle Court after Catherine and Fleetwood Dormer had died, and Arle Court had been inherited by Judge Dormer's daughter, another Catherine, but were not successful. Her friend and protector John Yorke, who had married a Lygon, helped her to secure her inheritance, and in gratitude she left Arle Court to him. In 1795 he sold Arle Court to Thomas Butt whose son, Thomas Packer Walter Butt, decided in 1855 to build a new Arle Court on a quite different site at Redgrove. Only a few traces of the old house now remain amid a large, post-1945 housing estate.

The most impressive surviving house in Charlton Kings or Cheltenham dating from the sixteenth century, listed grade II*, was not usually regarded as a manor house. Now called Charlton Park, it is the successor to a freehold house and messuage known as the 'Forden'. Forden Bank was part of a road which crossed Forden Brook, initially by a ford and later by a bridge and the name 'Forden mese' is recorded in 1504. The house was held by several successive owners named as 'de la Forde', before it was purchased by John Grevill in the early fifteenth century. The only occasion when the Forden was called a manor was in 1541, when John Hicks told commissioners from the council of the Marches that Robert Grevill had two manors in Charlton Kings, one called Ashley Court and one Forden Court.[62] In 1617 Giles Grevill lived in 'a mansion house' called Forden House, 'being freeland parcell of his Mannor of Ashley'.

The Grevill family had owned Ashley manor for a hundred years before acquiring the Forden, and from this time rebuilt and frequently occupied it, but it was not and could not become Ashley manor house because it was in Bafford tithing and Cheltenham manor. Walter of Ashley had no manor house in 1246, but there was one by 1599, when William Grevill leased 'the scyte of the manour or mannour howse of Ashley and the close where it stands'.[63] Mary Paget has shown that this house was in East End, west of East Court, and was part of the 'Old Manor House estate' sold in 1868. It was demolished soon after, to be replaced with a large and fashionable house called 'Newlands'.

Giles Grevill built the timber-framed house which is the core of the existing Charlton Park between 1562 and 1568. In the Hearth Tax returns of the 1660s 'Mr Grivill' paid for one house with five hearths and another with four. After 1701 Forden House was considerably altered and extended by John Prinn, who bought Ashley manor some years later. William Prinn inherited in 1743, and Thomas Robins painted the house and grounds soon after. Forden House became Charlton Park after it was inherited by William Prinn's daughter, who was married to Dodington Hunt. He created a deer park, where there were to be not fewer than fifty deer kept, and built an ice house in the grounds, which also still exists.[64]

CHAPTER FIVE

COMMERCE

CHELTENHAM was far from being a rural village at the beginning of the seventeenth century, as the increasingly plentiful historical records that have survived from this time show. The documentary evidence also makes possible more detailed comparisons with other Gloucestershire towns than in earlier centuries. Cheltenham was small, but it was prosperous. It had some distinct urban characteristics, and by the end of the century these became more developed.

POPULATION IN THE EARLY SEVENTEENTH CENTURY

At the beginning of the seventeenth century, Cheltenham's population was comparable with that of Winchcombe and perhaps half that of Cirencester or Tewkesbury. Over the next hundred years, all these places grew a little. Population estimates can be based on three ecclesiastical surveys; on the list of men mustered in 1608 in each township; and on the returns of those who paid the Hearth Tax in 1671, also compiled by township. None of these figures was in any way a modern-style census and each was made for a different administrative purpose, but they give a reasonable basis for calculating population.

The church surveys of 1603, 1650 and 1676 were made to examine the state of the Church of England, its ministers and their qualifications, and the loyalty of parishioners to the Established Church. In 1603 parish clergymen had to say how many communicants there were in the parish; in 1650, the question asked the number of families, although the Swindon return was specifically of persons; and in 1676 the questions were so confusingly phrased that it is not certain what was expected in reply. Some clergy gave numbers of communicants, some probably gave families, and some a count of the whole population.

The background to the 1603 returns was the upsurge of Puritan agitation following the accession of James I to the throne. The 'Millenary Petition', articulating their demands for more sweeping reform of the Church of England, was presented to James as he travelled south to his new kingdom's capital. Archbishop Whitgift wanted information to allow him to judge the weakness or strength of the church in the parishes.[1] In 1650, the Civil War between Charles I and the rebellious part of his parliament was over, the king had been executed, and there was a fresh opportunity for church reform. Since the episcopacy was suspended, this survey was conducted according to counties rather than dioceses. Recommendations for the adjustment of parish boundaries and the amalgamation of small parishes were made – though some of the suggestions were not implemented until the nineteenth century.[2]

Church surveys of 1603 and 1650

	1603 communicants	Estimated population	1650 families	ratio 1603/1650
Cheltenham	805	1,150	350	2.3
Charlton Kings	310	443	40 [140]	[2.2] 7.8
Leckhampton	93	133	40	2.3
Prestbury	300	429	60	5.0
Swindon	40	57	140 persons	
Cirencester	1,838	2,626	700	2.6
Tewkesbury	1,600	2,286	1,000	1.6
Winchcombe	862	1,231	340	2.5

Estimates of population in 1603 are based on the assumption that communicants were aged 16 years and above and that they formed 70 per cent of the total population. Two

There are not many early gravestones remaining in Cheltenham parish church, but two seventeenth-century stones were built into the outside of the north wall of the vestry when it was enlarged in the nineteenth century. One records Anthonie Machin Gentleman, who died in 1607/8. It has been re-cut. The second, becoming very worn, records Anthonie Machin's daughter Anne who died in 1615. Richard Machin, who died in 1509, had requested that he be buried in Cheltenham parish church, and another Richard was accused in 1559 of blocking three lanes round the High Cross and Market House with a door. Thomas Machin, gentleman, was recorded in 1608 in Cheltenham borough as having armour. There is, however, no record of Anthonie; perhaps he was one of the seven sons of Thomas Machin, mercer and alderman of Gloucester, who died in 1614. Margaret Machin, who owned half a burgage in 1617, may have been Anthonie's widow.

PHOTOGRAPH: CARNEGIE, 2009

Another early seventeenth-century gravestone is under a yew tree near the south porch. 'Here lieth the body of Robert Eckley deceased the XXV [25] day of February Anno Domini 1624 [1625].' He was listed in the 1608 Muster list for the borough of Cheltenham, and his occupation was 'maltster'. He was also a lessee in 1617 of a small amount of pasture land belonging to Cheltenham manor demesne, which no doubt was accommodation land for the horses used to pull the drays or collect the barley for malting.

PHOTOGRAPH: CARNEGIE, 2009

or three communicants might be expected in each family. If numbers of communicants are divided by the number of families in 1650, the ratio immediately reveals something wrong in the Charlton Kings figures – most likely a '1' was missed in copying; 140 families gives a more acceptable ratio of 2.2 communicants per family. The Prestbury ratio is also very high. Nevertheless, the 1608 muster list, made just five years after the first ecclesiastical survey, supports the relative accuracy of both.

These figures indicate that during the first half of the seventeenth century Cheltenham was still somewhat smaller than Winchcombe, and very much smaller than either Cirencester or Tewkesbury. Nonetheless, comparison with the approximate figures calculated for the beginning of the 1550s, and discussed in chapter 3 (pages 91–3), suggests that the population of Cheltenham itself had grown rapidly during the later sixteenth century, as had that of Prestbury. In contrast, Tewkesbury and Winchcombe, though still significantly larger, had seen relatively little growth over the intervening period. The implication is that Cheltenham was an increasingly dynamic community with important economic and demographic growth under way.

MEN AND OCCUPATIONS IN 1608

The 1608 muster list is a unique source for Gloucestershire history. It was compiled and preserved by John Smith of North Nibley, and has been published and analysed for particular places and various purposes.[3] A letter to the constable of Charlton Kings, explaining how he should prepare for the muster, was written by the bailiff and constables of Cheltenham and is preserved in the archives of Berkeley Castle.[4] 'Able' people aged 18 and above were to appear at Cheltenham on Saturday 24 September by 8 o'clock in the morning, to be viewed and enrolled, 'being ffytt to sarve his majestie in his warres'. The constable was to bring with him a roll of the names and surnames of these persons, noting of 'what quallytie trade or occupation everie of them are'. Servants were to be listed after their masters and able sons after their fathers. Available armour was also to be noted. 'And hereof ffaile ye not at your uttermost perill'.

The final roll, which has survived, indicated the ages of those mustered as 'about twenty', about forty' and 'between fifty and three score', which may suggest a quick visual assessment of each. An occupation was entered against most names but none at all was recorded by the constable of Arle, or for a variable proportion of individuals elsewhere (for example, 13 per cent of men in Cheltenham, 12 per cent in Gloucester, and 3 per cent in Tewkesbury, have no occupation stated). Cheltenham tithing was headed 'Cheltenham borough'; Sandford and Westal in Cheltenham were separately enumerated, but as always there was no separate return for Naunton. Lords of the manor were named – the king at Cheltenham and Winchcombe; Giles Grevill and Arthur Packer, gentlemen, at Charlton Kings; William Norwood esquire. and John Partridge, gentleman, lords of Leckhampton; Reinold Nycholas of Prestbury, and James Clifford esquire of Swindon.

Men mustered in 1608

Parish and tithing	No. mustered	parish and tithing	No. mustered
Cheltenham parish	220		
Cheltenham borough	172		
Alstone	19		
Arle	23		
Sandford	8	Cirencester	349
Westal	8	Gloucester	489
Charlton Kings	75	Tewkesbury parish*	502
Leckhampton	27	Tewkesbury borough	456
Prestbury	59	Winchcombe parish†	214
Swindon	21	Winchcombe borough	154

Notes:

* Tewkesbury parish included the tithings of Southwick, Myth and Myth Hook and Walton Cardiff.

† Winchcombe parish included the tithings of Greet, Gretton and Postlip.

Cheltenham could muster about half as many able-bodied men as Gloucester or Tewkesbury, but a similar number to Winchcombe, which is in keeping with the evidence of the returns of communicants. No allowance can be made for those too old to serve, but it seems that about half the males in Cheltenham and Charlton Kings were mustered, rather fewer than half in Prestbury, more in Leckhampton, while in Swindon every male appears to have been eligible for military service.[5]

	1603: half the communicants	1608: able-bodied men
Cheltenham parish	403	220
Charlton Kings	155	75
Leckhampton	47	27
Prestbury	150	59
Swindon	20	21
Tewkesbury parish	800	502
Winchcombe parish	431	214

From the occupations noted, it is clear that agriculture remained an important employment not only in the countryside, which of course would be expected, but also among town dwellers in the three boroughs of Cheltenham, Tewkesbury and Winchcombe – there it accounted for up to a third of adult males. At least 38 yeomen and husbandmen lived in the *borough* of Cheltenham, and among the towns only Gloucester was almost completely urban. An average of two-thirds of all males in the rural tithings were employed in agriculture. This was probably also true of Arle, where no occupations are given but at least eight of the 23 men named in 1608 were described as yeomen or husbandmen when they died. If Arle is counted as wholly agricultural, Cheltenham parish had half its able-boded employed in agriculture, and is thus typical of Gloucestershire outside the three bigger market towns.[6]

Men in agriculture in 1608

Tithing or parish	Farmers, servants and labourers	%
Cheltenham parish (less Arle tithing)	80	39
Cheltenham borough	56	33
Charlton Kings	40	53
Leckhampton	19	63
Prestbury	43	71
Swindon	15	71
Cirencester	100	29
Gloucester	38	8
Tewkesbury parish	197	39
Tewkesbury borough	162	36
Winchcombe parish (less Naunton tithing)	118	57
Winchcombe borough	55	36

Cheltenham borough nonetheless had a variety of trades and crafts. The later reputation of the town for malting, as reported by Atkyns in *Ancient and Present State of Gloucestershire* (1712), is certainly evident in 1608, with twelve maltsters and two maltsters' sons recorded (and no doubt there were others in that trade who were not of suitable age or ability). Other principal crafts were shoemaking (13) and tailoring (15). One silkweaver, six weavers and one tucker (that is, someone who fulled woollen cloth) indicate that textiles were made locally. There were four tanners and a miller in the borough, and two more millers outside, one in Alstone and one in Sandford. Among a scatter of craftsmen, a joiner made better quality furniture, with joints rather than rougher carpentry; a cooper met the local need for barrels. There were four tailors and four weavers in Charlton Kings, but otherwise almost no secondary crafts and trades in the rural tithings.

Thomas Milton was the only innkeeper mustered. A few years later he was in trouble with the bailiffs of Cheltenham for allowing a play to be acted in his premises, the *Crown*. The play

RIGHT

This painting shows Sandford Mill as it might have appeared in the Tudor period, when in the hands of the Pate family, and before it was rebuilt in the late eighteenth century; a date 1780 is recorded on the existing building, and the miller's house on the left-hand side was rebuilt after this. The scene is a thoroughly rural one, with the river flowing unregulated between low banks. The miller in 1608 was William Wayte, and his servant Walter Lane was also mustered; Henry Lane in Sandford tithing was a yeoman, and milling and farming were often closely integrated.

COURTESY OF MR AND MRS L. BAILEY

LEFT

The water drove one wheel, though a smaller arch at the back of Sandford mill may indicate a second wheel introduced later to run subsidiary machinery. By the end of the nineteenth century the mill was no longer in use, and the machinery was taken out in 1929. The building was restored by Leonard and Angela Bailey in 1986–87, work commended by the Cheltenham Civic Trust.

PHOTOGRAPH: AUTHOR, 2009

Fourways, the last house on the west side of The Burgage in Prestbury, displays timber-framing typical of the seventeenth century, the last period when this building technique was employed. It is said that there was a fire during the reign of Henry VII which destroyed Prestbury town, and there are at least eight houses on the west side of the street dating from the seventeenth century, but none that appears older; a sundial dated 1579 seems likely to have been reset from an earlier house. The east side of The Burgage is dominated by Prestbury House, built about 1700 by the Capel family, landowners in the parish for two hundred years. Fourways would go with a good-sized holding and the able-bodied men in the town in 1608 were mainly husbandmen.

PHOTOGRAPH: AUTHOR, 2009

was announced by a drummer going 'up and downe the towne' with seven companions causing proclamation to be made 'in divers places', a nice example of drumming up support! The excuse for suppressing the play was the presence of plague in nearby Tredington and Prestbury, but perhaps the bailiff's attitude was puritan-inspired. Undeterred, the little company moved with more drumming to a victualler's; probably they were mainly young apprentices or servants. They were fined five shillings each, a heavy punishment.[7] No victuallers were mustered in the borough, but this could have been a secondary occupation and so not recorded. Their business was supplying food and drink but not accommodation, and was on a smaller scale than an innkeeper's, as the example of Robert Mason, glover and victualler later in this chapter (*see* page 157) illustrates.

Cheltenham had a small service or tertiary sector, men who were not directly producers but were retailers, dealers, innkeepers or professionals. A scrivener and his son, four mercers, six butchers, two drapers, and the innkeeper were occupations in this sector. If gentlemen are included, it accounted for 10.5 per cent of the able-bodied. Although the exact nature of a gentleman's financial support is not known, he was much more likely to have been a lawyer or landowner than a shopkeeper.

From this point of view Cheltenham was still in the pre-industrial world, if services are seen as a sign of rising industrial prosperity.[8] Rather more of the men in the county town, about a quarter, were in service occupations, and nearly a quarter in Cirencester and Tewkesbury (22 per cent and 23 percent respectively). In Winchcombe borough a drummer and a musician

(perhaps at Sudeley Castle), four mercers, eleven butchers, a physician, victualler, hostler, and barber, comprised 14 per cent. Prestbury had a disproportionate number of gentlemen and their servants, and one barber, 30 per cent of the able-bodied. It is usually suggested that Prestbury became more socially exclusive in the nineteenth century, with the rapid growth of Cheltenham, but it seems that the superior style of the place was already evident two hundred years earlier. Certainly, Prestbury has a high proportion of larger than average village houses dating from the seventeenth century.[9]

Some of the men in the Cheltenham muster list can be matched with the probate records from the years 1608 to 1640. An inventory of goods and chattels had to be drawn up and exhibited to the ecclesiastical court before a will could be proved, but few of these documents have survived in Gloucestershire from this period. Both will and inventory often give the occupation of the testator. At best, 33 wills out of a total of 63 relate to men named in 1608; for one man no occupation was recorded in either source, and the identification of two is uncertain. Farmers were predominant among the will-makers; two-thirds were yeomen or husbandmen. Three men called 'yeoman' in their wills were described as 'maltster' in the muster list; certainly the two activities were often combined. Tradesmen and craftsmen are not well represented among the probate records: one was a mercer and one a maltster, and six were craftsmen. Nine yeomen or husbandmen, three maltsters, two innholders and one weaver were among those making wills who are not in the muster lists. Had it not been for the chance survival of the unusual 1608 muster list, Cheltenham would have appeared from probate records to have been an almost wholly agricultural community. That appearance would have been deceptive.

POPULATION IN THE LATER SEVENTEENTH CENTURY

Cheltenham's population had grown significantly by 1676, the date of another ecclesiastical survey known as the Compton Census. The census is named from the bishop of London who was responsible for obtaining returns of the numbers of those in each parish who 'conformed' with the Church of England, and of non-conformists and of papists. During the years of the Commonwealth government and the Protectorate under Cromwell, the Church of England had been dismantled; in some areas a puritan or presbyterian form of church government had been introduced, but there had also been a flowering of numerous individual Protestant sects. With the re-establishment of the Church of England under Charles II, from 1660, there was deep suspicion of, and hostility towards, the nonconformist groups, and the 1676 census was an attempt to assess their strength and influence.

The results were reasonably reassuring for the authorities. Most citizens had returned, at least nominally, to the Church of England.[10] However, urban areas presented greater worries than rural areas, for towns were easier places for nonconformists to meet without attracting the hostile attention of the rural élite who provided employment in the countryside. Typically, therefore, Cheltenham had a sizeable nonconformist community, as did Tewkesbury and Cirencester. The Quaker community in Cirencester was well known, while the minister of Tewkesbury was himself effectively a nonconformist who must have felt a surge of defiance when he recorded that only a quarter of the town's inhabitants were 'conforming' to the Church of England.[11]

Compton Census, 1676

Parish	Conformists	Papists	Non-conformists	Totals	Estimated population
Cheltenham	1,068	4	97	1,169	1,670
Charlton Kings	188	0	12	200	286
Leckhampton	90	1	0	91	130
Prestbury	177	0	10	187	267
Swindon	53	0	0	53	76
Cirencester	1,745	0	155	1,800	2,571
Tewkesbury	500	0	1,500	2,000	2,857
Winchcombe	1,226	0	35	1,261	2,102

If the Cheltenham return was of communicants, a reasonable assumption, and as in 1603 they were 70 per cent of the population, the total was close to 1670.[12] Goding in his *History of Cheltenham* published a count of the baptisms, marriages and burials in Cheltenham between March 1630 and March 1631: 44 baptisms, 7 marriages and 44 burials.[13] Accepting the usual assumption of a baptism rate of 30 per thousand would imply that the population had grown to about 1,500 before the Civil War, a figure which is quite plausible. In Charlton Kings, however, it appears that the return was of families, as comparison with the Hearth Tax in the next section suggests.

While Cheltenham's older houses have mainly gone, in the surrounding areas a larger proportion has survived. Moat Cottage in Leckhampton is an example of cruck construction, dating possibly from about 1600. There are two full pairs of crucks. The house seems to have consisted of just one bay, with a single fireplace and chimney, but would probably have paid the Hearth Tax because it represents a house occupied by a small farmer. Situated in the field called Moat Ground, the Cottage is near a medieval moated house site which was probably the manor house of one of the other Leckhampton manors. Moat Cottage and two other timber-framed houses nearby could be survivals of a second set of crofts and tofts similar to Collum End. Set well back from Kidnappers Lane, and facing away from it, Moat Cottage was approached from a lane, long disused, on the side where the front door is placed.

PHOTOGRAPH: AUTHOR, 2009

Brizen Farm in Leckhampton is a sixteenth-century farmhouse, which like Moat Cottage has retained its thatched roof. Warm in winter and cool in summer, the advantages of thatch have to be set against the need to repair or renew it more often than is the case with a tiled roof. Like other surviving houses of the period, it was probably once a hall house, and would have been a husbandman's or yeoman's, but no early records survive. On the western edge of the parish, part of the name Brizen probably derives from 'end'; it was known as Bray's End Farm in 1815, and belonged to the Leckhampton Court estate. The farmer at that time cultivated 208 acres.
PHOTOGRAPH: AUTHOR, 2009

POLITICAL ARITHMETIC

The restoration of Charles II in 1660 did not mean a return to the forms of financing the government that Charles I had used, which had, after all, contributed to the outbreak of civil war. Instead, there was a search for alternative ways of raising money. For three decades, a tax on hearths or chimneys was one stratagem that was tried. The idea of the tax reflects the extent to which many houses had been modernised by the insertion of brick chimneys into open halls, so that smoke from the fire no longer found its way out through the roof; the hall was then ceiled, and a room or rooms made above.

The tax was first collected in 1662, but its administration proved difficult. At first there were local receivers with staffs of sub-collectors known as 'chimney men', and petty constables prepared the lists which were presented at the county's quarter sessions. The tax was collected by tithings, with Charlton Kings treated as one. To try and improve the yield of the tax, for three years the administration was 'farmed' to some London merchants, a method subsequently tried again several times, but in Michaelmas 1669 the collection reverted to the original system and this was the framework for the one almost complete assessment that survives for Gloucestershire, covering the six months from Michaelmas 1671 to Lady Day 1672. Unfortunately much of the Winchcombe list is missing and Prestbury's is damaged.[14]

The Hearth Tax returns are a major source for the analysis of social structure in the seventeenth century, though without the interest of occupational descriptions which the 1608 muster list contained. The tax was one shilling for each chimney each half year (stoves were also charged, and ovens used to bake for public consumption) and was paid by the occupiers, not the owners or lessees of property. Two classes of occupier were exempted from paying the tax by the 1662 act: those not liable for local church and poor rates were automatically exempt; secondly, those occupying property with a rental value of 20s. or less, provided that the occupier did not have the use of lands or tenements of that amount, nor possessed £10 of assets themselves or in the hands of their trustees. In this second case a certificate of exemption had to be obtained, signed by the minister, a churchwarden and a parish overseer of the poor, and approved by two justices of the peace. The Gloucestershire lists of the exempt were headed 'These persons following weare discharged by legall Cert.'.

There was confusion about the overlapping nature of the two categories of exemption, and therefore it is not certain whether the 'exempt' listed in the returns included only those in the second category or also those in the first. Neither category implied that the person named was 'poor', in the sense of receiving poor relief or alms from the parish, but that they were unlikely to be able to pay taxes. A substantial number of people did not pay local rates. It is now known that in most areas of the country the really poor were simply ignored completely. As experience was gained, more instructions were issued in an attempt to clarify procedures but in fact they seem to have made the confusion worse. It was, however, realised that the lists should follow a topographical order.[15] No parish rating lists survive for Cheltenham to test the order, but it is obviously common sense.

A list of the exempt in Charlton Kings, dated 17 June 1672, has been discovered and published.[16] As lists were made at the end of the six-month taxation period, it must relate to the surviving return. It was signed by William Williams, minister, Giles Grevill and Anthony Webb, churchwardens, and John Holder and William King, overseers of the poor; the two justices of the peace, Edward Rich and Fleetwood Dormer, allowed the certificate 'containing sixty-nine names'. It matches almost completely the list of exemptions in the final return, the order being identical except for the last twelve names, though a copying error has exchanged two people's Christian names: was it Zachary Ireland or Zachary Harris, Charles Ireland or Charles Harris?

Charlton Kings had the largest number of exempt in the area, and comparison with the Compton Census suggests that there may have been another fifty households living close to or below the contemporary poverty line. Cheltenham's exempt appear to have been close to the national average of one in five: it was suggested by a contemporary that in the market towns of Gloucestershire more than a third of houses were 'poor', compared with a quarter in Oxfordshire, two-fifths in Worcestershire, but less than a tenth in Somerset with Bristol.[17] Gregory King, the famous contemporary statistician, who was described on his monument in St Benet's church, Paul's Wharf, as 'well versed in political arithmetick', allowed for one in twelve households to be omitted from the Hearth Tax, but he also noted the multiple occupancy of some houses, and that numbers of hearths do not exactly equate with either houses or households.

Hearth Tax, 1671–72

	Total listed	Discharged		% of hearths in groups		
		No	%	1 & 2	3 & 4	5+
Cheltenham parish	289	59	20.4	73.0	20.4	6.6
Cheltenham town	212	46	21.7	70.8	22.6	6.6
Rural tithings	77	13	16.9	79.2	14.3	6.5
Charlton Kings	149	69	46.3	81.2	14.8	4.0
Leckhampton	33	6	18.2	78.8	18.2	3.0
Prestbury	64	6	9.4	76.6	18.8	4.7
Swindon	15			66.7	26.7	6.7
Tewkesbury parish	483	186	39.0	70.8	19.1	10.1
Tewkesbury town	454	186	40.9	71.1	19.2	9.7
Rural tithings	29			65.5	17.2	17.2

Using the last Hearth Tax returns for 1689–90 as one of his sources, Gregory King estimated that there were 300 towns of 200 houses in the country about 1688, and between 120 and 140 towns which had 300 to 500 houses, the group in which Cheltenham may have come; five cities he calculated had 4,000 houses. He made a comprehensive analysis of the social structure and national income of England for the year 1688.[18] His first wife was from a Gloucestershire family, and after her death his second marriage took place in Sudeley church.[19] Among his calculations are figures for Gloucester city drawn from a return under the Marriage Duties Act of 1695: 1,126 houses and 4,756 people, that is 4.2 people per house; women were rather more numerous than men (2,627 to 2,129) which points to the many domestic servants which would be expected in the prosperous households of a county town. In his general estimates for the whole country he allowed for households to be larger or smaller in towns of different sizes and in the countryside. The average of 4.2 persons per household has been used below to calculate possible population size from the Hearth Tax returns, and comparison with the Compton census gives some indication of where the exempt were not all listed.

Goding published a table of population which he said was for Cheltenham *hundred* in 1666, giving 1,500 people and 321 houses, which is a ratio of 4.7 people per house.[20] He was normally scrupulous in stating the source of his information but not on this occasion. He may have had access to a Hearth Tax return which is now lost, or to calculations based on the return, or his figures could have been drawn from parish rating lists also now lost. His number of 321 houses does not match the 1671 Hearth Tax return for the four parishes in the hundred, though it may be the total of all households (including those which were exempt from the tax) in the parish of Cheltenham.

Population based on the Hearth Tax returns

	Total listed	Number multiplied by 4.2	Estimated population from Compton census
Cheltenham parish	289	1,214	1,670
Cheltenham town	212	890	
Rural tithings	77	323	
Charlton Kings	149	626	286
Leckhampton	33	139	130
Prestbury	64	269	267
Swindon	15	63	76
Tewkesbury parish	483	2,029	2,571
Tewkesbury town	454	1,907	2,857
Rural tithings	29	122	2,102

HEARTHS AND STATUS

The overall impression from the Hearth Tax returns is that modest one-hearth homes predominated in the Cheltenham area; about half those taxed in Cheltenham had one hearth, and nearly three-quarters in Charlton Kings.[21] As a rule of thumb, the more rooms which an occupier could heat with a fire, the more prosperous the household was likely to be, though this is much less true of the north of England. Cheltenham's larger number of households with several hearths suggests it was more prosperous than many places in the region. However, other factors are relevant: older houses mostly consisted of one main living room or hall with a fire; newly built houses tended to have more than one living room, for example a hall and a parlour. Arkell has suggested that the most effective comparison of one area with another is the percentage of occupiers charged on *three* or more hearths.

In the rural areas of Gloucestershire as a whole he calculated that about a fifth of occupiers were in this category; Gloucestershire was intermediate between the south-east, with nearly a third occupying houses with three or more hearths, and the north with only a sixth. In a detailed study of Kineton hundred in Warwickshire, Arkell showed that relatively few were taxed on three or more hearths in the rural areas but many more in the county town. In the Cheltenham area a quarter of occupiers paid for three or more hearths, and more in the towns than the rural areas. The match between Cheltenham, Prestbury and Tewkesbury supports a regional interpretation of the Hearth Tax numbers and highlights the important distinction between urban and rural house styles; modernisation reached the towns before the countryside.

Present-day Tewkesbury probably offers some insights into the appearance of Cheltenham at the end of the seventeenth century. Tewkesbury had more exempt persons than Cheltenham, nearly 40 per cent, but there were also more large houses. Today the three main streets still contain many timber-framed houses. Cheltenham, too, was a lowland timber-framed town, though possibly with fewer grand houses built by prosperous merchants in the fifteenth and sixteenth centuries than in Tewkesbury. It was said that at the lower end of the High Street a few thatched houses survived until about 1800, and Fosbrooke in 1798 commented on a single 'low thatched house with a gable end, and antique bay windows, of horn-coloured glass, and leaden reticulations'.[22] Moreover, Tewkesbury has retained many alleys and courts, which developed along the length of individual burgage plots behind the front houses. Cheltenham had similar alleys and courts, but while in Tewkesbury modest prosperity led to the replacement or refronting of only a proportion of the houses, in Cheltenham the old buildings were largely swept away, either in the great building boom of the earlier nineteenth century or during the twentieth century before conservation had become a concern. Gell and Bradshaw's *Directory* of 1820 noted a few old buildings in the High Street, commenting that 'in a short while the few humble cottages that still disfigure the western extremity of the row must give place to more spacious and elegant structures'. The change was far-reaching: most early nineteenth-century commentators on Cheltenham emphasise the number of new houses and the use of brick.

The large houses were notable but exceptional. Francis Norwood in Leckhampton paid for twelve hearths, and his was the largest house in the area. Mr Sturmy paid for nine hearths in Swindon, John Hobbs for seven in Prestbury. Mr Bates in Charlton Kings paid for ten hearths, Fleetwood Dormer of Arle Court nine. The largest house in Cheltenham town, with nine hearths, was the *George Inn* kept by Daniel Chester or Chestroe. Thomas Cox, a yeoman, had eight hearths, indicating a farmhouse rather than a town house, for a yeoman owned some or all of the land which he worked. Two men in the town paid for seven hearths: Thomas Cartwright and John Collett. Collett was also a yeoman; a Sarah Collett, who was probably his daughter and heiress as mentioned in his will, occupied a three-hearth house next to him, possibly even part of the same house (which would make it ten hearths). Thomas Rich (a local justice of the peace, with Fleetwood Dormer) lived in Power's Court and paid for six hearths, as did John Chester, yeoman.

Robert Blick, the Cheltenham constable in 1671, who himself occupied a three-hearth house, gave the title 'Mr', 'Mrs', or 'Esq.', to sixteen people in his Hearth Tax list. An 'esquire' was of higher status than a 'mister'. The titles are indicative of a gentleman or gentlewoman, one who did not work with his or her hands, but was able to live on rents from land, or follow an occupation (such as a lawyer) which did not involve manual labour. More simply, as William Harrison had noted a century earlier, a gentleman was someone who acted and lived like a gentleman. Most gentry in the constable's list lived in houses with three or more hearths.

'Mr' and 'Esq' in the Hearth Tax

| | Hearths | | | | | | | | | | | |
	1	2	3	4	5	6	7	8	9	10	12	Total
Cheltenham	1	1	4	4	3	2			1			16
Charlton Kings	1		4	3	2			1		1		12
Leckhampton				1							1	2
Prestbury			2	2	1							5
Swindon				1						1		2

Not many inhabitants of Cheltenham and area would be regarded as 'gentry' in the way that the College of Heralds would define the status, that is, a man inheriting his leisured position. At the heralds' visitation of Gloucestershire in 1623,[23] undertaken to establish who was entitled to gentry status, 'no gentleman' was recorded against many who put themselves forward, including Thomas Higgs of Cheltenham and Richard Pates of Charlton Kings. Two years later, when Charles I revived the custom of knighting men of gentry status at his coronation, and fined any who refused the status (and tax obligations), only three of the 82 Gloucestershire gentry fined were in the Cheltenham area: Giles Grevill of Charlton, John Lygon of Arle, and William Norwood of Leckhampton.[24] 'Pseudo-gentry' or town gentry were more numerous.

Gregory King was one of the two heralds who made a visitation of Gloucestershire and seven other counties in 1682–83, in order that 'every Person and Persons ... may be the better known in his and their Estate, Degree or mistery without Confusion or Disorders'. Aspiring gentlemen presented their family pedigrees and coats of arms, and paid £1 7s. 6d. for their title to be registered. JPs, baronets and knights paid more. The visitation had the useful effect of helping to finance the building of a new College of Arms in London.[25] In preparation for the visit, King extracted from the Gloucestershire Hearth Tax the names of all those with five or more hearths; he also listed all given the titles of Mr and Esq. and this brought into his net many with three hearths, some with two and a handful with one. He reckoned that many 'inconsiderable persons' would have to be struck out of his lists. Investigating Huntingdonshire in 1684, the heralds found the five-hearth criterion brought too many tradesmen or small estates into the net.[26] Cheltenham would appear to have been similar.

Quite a few women paid the Hearth Tax – 45 in Cheltenham parish, though only six were occupying houses with three or more hearths, five of them in Cheltenham town. Nineteen women were 'discharged' from payment. In Charlton Kings 23 women paid Hearth Tax, eight in Leckhampton and two in Swindon.

There are some large groups of householders in Cheltenham sharing the same surname, and some, if not all, were probably related.

Some large groups of surnames in the Hearth Tax

	Cheltenham tithing	Alstone	Arle
Ashmead	9	1	
Chester/Chestroe	6		
Gregory	7	1	1
Hyett	6		1
Milton	6		
White	6		
Charlton Kings			
Ballinger	6		
Clevely	5		

The wealthiest surname group was Chester or Chestroe: the innholder had nine hearths, one Chester had six, one four and two had three hearths. Mr Hyett was in Arle; about this time, Richard Hyett gentleman built Lower Alstone House, a 'good house and estate' remarked on by Atkyns in 1712 and still standing and recently restored.[27] There was a range of house sizes among most groups, but in Charlton Kings all the Ballengers and Cleveleys occupied one-hearth houses and five Ballengers out of six were exempt. One Ballenger lived in Leckhampton, but this was the only case of any of these names crossing parish boundaries. The concentrations of similar surnames is possibly related to copyhold tenure, where an heir lived locally rather than moving elsewhere when setting up a household.

INSIDE AND OUT OF DOORS

No late seventeenth-century source giving occupations is comparable with the 1608 muster list, but something of the lifestyle of Cheltenham's inhabitants can be learned from wills or administrations, and inventories where they are available. Most of those from the period 1660–1740 have been published.[28] In 28 documents the tithing is named, rather than the parish, suggesting a tangible sense of a more local identity, and where names can be cross-referenced with those in the Hearth Tax, they confirm the location. Individuals said to be 'of Cheltenham' were living in Cheltenham tithing. Nearly all the inhabitants of the rural tithings were engaged in agriculture.

Of the 231 documents which state occupation in those years, rather more than a third were for yeomen. Predictably, few were for husbandmen or labourers because among those less well-off groups not many people made wills or had probate taken out on their estates. An apothecary and two barbers were the only professional occupations. Members of the gentry accounted for one-seventh of the total – one knight, two esquires and 29 gentlemen. The rest of the testators, just under half, were in occupations typically associated with a country market town: maltsters (20) were the largest group; there were nine mercers, seven innholders, six carpenters, five bakers, five cordwainers, five glovers and four tailors.

For the thirty years at the end of the seventeenth century it is feasible to correlate names in the Hearth Tax with the probate documents. There were 139 such probate records, of which 119 stated an occupation. But matches can be found for only 58 of the 139, with 49 of these giving occupation details. Unfortunately, of the 65 probate inventories that have survived for the period, only 23 can be matched with names in the Hearth Tax. This implies considerable mobility, since 81 of the 139 Cheltenham will-makers between 1671 and 1700 were not living there in 1671. It is particularly difficult to identify widows, who might anyway have moved away from the house they had occupied while their husbands were alive. Some 31 wills and inventories relate to women, but only one can be clearly linked with a Hearth Tax entry.[29] Their personal possessions were important to them, but in some cases their copyhold property was already disposed of, and unless wealthy, as spinsters and widows they probably lived in another's house.

Ivy Cottage, Charlton Kings, dates from the seventeenth century, with the characteristic box-framing. It is situated on Ham Square, a name that probably relates to the square enclosure of pasture ground to the west. There may once have been several farmhouses around an area for pasturing animals, which was typical of some planned settlements.

PHOTOGRAPH: AUTHOR, 2009

Occupations listed in Cheltenham wills and inventories, 1671–1700

Occupation or status	Number	%
Professional	1	0.8
Tradesmen	6	5.0
Husbandmen and labourers	6	5.0
Gentlemen	14	11.8
Craftsmen	27	22.7
Women	31	26.1
Yeomen	34	28.6
total stated	119	100.0
not stated	20	

Occupations show a predictable relationship with hearths, and distribution probably represents the social structure and standards of living with some accuracy. Almost all tradesmen and craftsmen had just one or two hearths and, if five hearths did indeed mark a social divide, yeomen were most likely to be in the upper echelons.

Occupations in Cheltenham wills and inventories linked with the Hearth Tax

Occupations	Hearths									Totals
	1	2	3	4	5	6	7	8	9	
Husbandmen	1	2								3
Professional			1	2	1			1		5
Gentry	1			2	1	1		1		6
Craftsmen, tradesmen and maltsters	6	7	1	1	1					16
Yeomen	4	3	4	2	2	2	1	1		19
Totals	11	13	7	8	5	3	1	1	2	49

Many Cheltenham wills in this period no longer have an inventory, although the value of a testator's possessions is sometimes noted on the will. Conversely, there are a few inventories with no accompanying will. In general, the inventories are disappointing in the evidence they provide for living standards and number of rooms in the house, and in many there are few details of moveable goods. Furthermore, in the wills themselves property was rarely mentioned, perhaps because of the continuing strength of the manor in Cheltenham, where regular manor courts dealt with the transmission of copyholds, at this time still including burgages.

In checking the correlation between Hearth Tax and probate material, it is reassuring to find that a man charged in the tax for an oven was indeed a baker, and another, charged for a forge, was a blacksmith. The baker was Thomas Humphris, who died in 1695. His five hearths included an oven, but his inventory did not give any details of his house and listed only £20 of goods. He was an unusual example of a man of his class who owned books. The blacksmith, Thomas Adams, died in 1689. He had two hearths. His inventory suggests that he lived in a small two-room house, with a lower chamber and a bedchamber. If so, one hearth was his forge and the domestic hearth was in the lower chamber. He, too, had very few worldly possessions, valued at a modest £12, and there is no indication of tools. But 'in a tenant's house' he had a bed and some other furniture, and outdoors he had a pig, the traditional item in a cottage economy.[30]

CRAFTSMEN

Blacksmith, baker, candlestick-maker ... there were two documents for tallow-chandlers in the late seventeenth century, though neither was in the Hearth Tax and there is a minimum of information about them. Inventories for craftsmen generally are few, probably for reasons of mobility and poverty. There are very few for tailors or shoemakers, who were so numerous in 1608, and even fewer of these can be linked with the Hearth Tax. One tailor who occupied a one-hearth house was far from typical, for he had an estate at Gretton to leave to his wife, and a house and lands to pass on to his son. Thomas Farmer, tailor, was a poor man with only £9 of goods (several described as 'old') and he anticipated that there might not be any money left after his debts were paid. He was not named in the Hearth Tax, and neither was the only shoemaker, Anthony Smyth, though he was exceptional in having goods valued at £80, of which shop goods, leather and money owed to him came to £30. He had a shop and kitchen on the ground floor, two rooms above, and two cocklofts (rooms inserted in the roof and lighted with a gabled window – examples can still be seen in Tewkesbury). Thomas Ricketts, collar-maker, who made the harness for carthorses, had similar premises. The only mention of his trade was £3 of leather 'in the pitts [tanpits] with all working tools' and the total value in the inventory was £38. William Crowder, a cordwainer who made better-quality shoes, had £29 of goods, including a parcel of shoes and leather worth £8.[31]

Two carpenters can be linked with the Hearth Tax: Robert Milton, who paid for one hearth, and Richard Wills the elder, with two hearths. Milton had just £13 of goods, though his inventory specifically mentions a chimney in the hall, and he too owned books. In the shop were carpenter's tools, but of little value. Richard Wills the elder was better off, with £80 of goods, and it seems appropriate therefore that he had a two-hearth house. He bequeathed his wife land called the Court House in Cheltenham – though this is a clear sign of the declining status of what had been a prestigious property – and had £20 in clothes and ready money. He also had a weigh of malt and some wheat and french beans, ten sheep, two cows and three pigs, diversifying his sources of income. His carpenter's tools were worth £2.[32]

The one saddler who made a will was Charles Ireland, who paid tax for two hearths, and left £80 of goods. The house which he leased was well furnished, and his is an interesting inventory, listing various items of saddlery, though they were of surprisingly small value: six new saddles were worth £2. Among his possessions were two pigs and some hops.[33]

MALTSTERS

Malting was not confined to those calling themselves maltsters, but was a widespread, and often small-scale, activity; this is the explanation for the large number of malthouses which Goding said were revealed by the parish poor law accounts in the mid-eighteenth century.[34] Nevertheless, some of the maltsters were among the most prosperous inhabitants of Cheltenham town, and four of their inventories can be linked with the Hearth Tax. Malting was normally combined with farming, and there is some evidence of the accumulation of capital.

The inventory of Robert Hyett, maltster, who occupied a one-hearth house, mentioned the best chamber over the hall, but not the hall below. In the malthouse and malt chamber he had 6 weighs of malt and 4 weighs of barley worth £56, and there was wheat and barley in the barn. His total possessions were valued at £139.[35] Three maltsters were called White – William, Thomas and Walter the younger – and each paid tax on a two-hearth house. Walter's father, another Walter, had occupied a one-hearth house, but his son's possessions were valued at £280, of which £64 was in debts owing to him; he gave his father £10 and forgave him a debt. His 'free' lands were left to his brother. No copyhold was mentioned. He had a house belonging to Corpus Christi College, the lease of which was valued at £15. It appears to have been old and simple, with a hall and a second ground-floor room and one room above. Malt and barley, valued at £90, were stored in the malt chamber, as well as a bed, and outside there were 14 tons of wood for use in the malting process. A limited farming interest is evident in four and a half acres of pulse and barley in cultivation.[36]

William and Thomas White were Walter's uncles. William's inventory, although adding up to £225, is uninformative, but he had a malt chamber and lower malt house containing a

ALBION BREWERY

A handsome drawing of the Albion Brewery in Gloucester Road, close to the Gas Works, was included in Rowe's *Illustrated Cheltenham Guide*. He suggested that it was an old-established firm, 'which, for the supply of a good family beverage equal to home-brewed, has attained a celebrity as ancient as Cheltenham itself'. Its premises were probably moved to a site next to the tramway about 1820, and the smoke curling out of the chimney shows it made use of the facility nearby for the transport of coal. The brewery was demolished about 1876, and the site used for a market.

small quantity of green malt (sprouted but not yet dried). Thomas's moveable goods, valued at £311, were mainly in bonds, mortgages and £200 in ready money, but he owned part of a burgage in the borough, occupied by Richard Belcher (in 1671 Ralph Belcher, the only man with this surname, was discharged from payment of tax on one hearth). Thomas White owned a dwelling house and real property in Apperley, near Deerhurst in Gloucestershire; at Bedlam in Swindon; and in Cheltenham field. French beans and pease were stored in a chamber, barley, wheat and french beans in the barn, and he had three cows, a pig which was being fattened and two small store pigs in the cote, and 1½ acres of winter corn in the field.

Henry Mason, maltster, paid tax on four hearths in the town. He was worth £838 and left to his son Walter demesne land called Oakley Woods or Wood Grove in Cheltenham and a close called Inn close. His son was probably the wealthy Walter Mason, maltster, who died in 1697 – his moveables were valued at no less than £710, mainly bonds (£335) and mortgages (£250). The inventory of Mary Ashmead who died in 1690, widow of William Ashmead, maltster, shows comparably extensive money dealings; her possessions were valued at over £1,000, almost entirely book debts, bills, bonds and money. She had plenty of ordinary household goods, and a shop with chests, mortar and pestle, a silk press and 'wares' worth £28.[37] A widow Ashmead had five hearths in 1671 but she was a different woman, whose husband, William Ashmead the younger, died in 1688.

Yeomen and husbandmen

As already discussed, agriculture long remained important in Cheltenham, in the town tithing as well as the rural townships. Yeomen were, in general, likely to be more prosperous than most townsmen and so more likely to make a will. However, they might also have been less mobile than craftsmen and tradesmen, staying on their farms for long periods or for generations. This had implications for their accumulation of wealth. The seven available inventories cover quite

The 'large establishment' of Gardner's Original Brewery with a front entrance in High Street was also in the *Guide*. Rowe said that it was founded by the late J. Gardner Esq. 'when the prosperity of Cheltenham was in its infancy'; John Gardner was one of two brewers in Cheltenham listed in the *Universal British Directory* (1792–93). A deep well provided am ample supply of water. The brewery employed steam power, and used both 'scientific principles' and 'mechanical auxiliaries'. The front building of Gardner's brewery was demolished in 1967, together with the *Fleece*, to the left in Rowe's drawing. It stood on the corner of Henrietta Street.

AUTHOR COLLECTION

a range of wealth and situation, but suggest a pattern of mixed husbandry which appears to have been typical of Cheltenham – that is, not only sheep and corn, but also dairying. Crops and animals, as is invariably the case, accounted for a significant proportion of the moveable assets of any yeoman farmer. There is no evidence in these inventories that oxen were being used in the late seventeenth century in the Cheltenham area, whereas they were employed on some Cotswold farms even into the twentieth century.

Thomas Cox of Cheltenham and John Gregory of Arle were the wealthiest, with possessions valued at £414 and £434 respectively. Two men called Thomas Cox are listed in the Hearth Tax for the town tithing, one paying for three hearths and one for eight. Thomas Cox the younger, who died in 1684, had a well-furnished house: his inventory mentions the hall and chamber over the hall, little chamber and lower chamber, buttery, kitchen, brewhouse and corn chamber. There were utensils for brewing, making cheese and grinding malt. In July 1684 he was growing barley, wheat and pulses valued at £50 on 27 acres of land, and also had vetches and clover; five cows and a heifer; and 77 sheep and 27 lambs worth £39. His will mentioned an acre of freehold land which he had bought from Ludovick Packer and 2½ acres from Daniel Church, enough to justify using the title of 'yeoman'. Most of his land was not freehold, but he was clearly of high status.[38]

John Gregory paid tax on three hearths. His father left him land lately purchased called 'the demesnes', after the expiry of the lease which had about sixty years to go, and he in turn was able to leave to one son the 'title, interest and term of years to my demesne lands within the manor of Cheltenham … together with my lease and assignments of lease'; he also bequeathed his son the 'fee simple' (that is, outright possession) confirmation of the break-up of the manorial land earlier in the century. All his moveables, except a silver tankard, were willed to his wife, and as a result his clothes and the tankard were the only items appraised in the house, but outside, a considerable farming stock was valued: 138 sheep at various stages of their lives, four bullocks, and twenty cows. Two hundred of cheese was valued at £2. There were 36 acres of wheat, pulses and barley growing, valued at £41, and corn threshed and unthreshed, £47. He had six plough horses.[39]

The inventories of John Collett of Cheltenham, Thomas Higgs of Sandford and John Stephens of Alstone indicate less wealth. John Collett, who died in 1684, had a seven-hearth house. His inventory itemised a 'chattell lease' of demesne land worth £70, the main item in the total of £123, but the possessions listed in his inventory were limited. Thomas Higgs paid tax on four hearths and his possessions also totalled £123. He had a parlour, hall and kitchen and, upstairs, a chamber at the stair head, a chamber over the porch and another over the kitchen. The hall may have been open to the roof. Typically his most valuable item was the crop on the ground, worth £30, and he had wheat, rye, barley and pulses to thresh. His animals were horses, cows and calves, and sheep. John Stephens of Alstone, with two hearths, had £72 of moveables. Among his farm stock were 16 bushels of malt, four milch cows – he had cheese-making equipment in the house – and other cows, a horse, sheep and a pig.[40]

Two yeomen appeared to be rather poor but were perhaps old and retired. Anthony Ireland senior had four hearths in Cheltenham in 1671 but when he died had reserved only one room for himself and his wife in his farmhouse, where there was a meagre £8 of possessions; he willed to his wife 'the residue and profit of my leases during her life'. Thomas Hyett's possessions were worth only £14. He had a one-hearth house in the town, and left his brother his title in a Corpus Christi tenement on the north side of the street. The inventory listed 'an old College house', valued at £5, and two ridges of arable land in the Lower field of Cheltenham of about 1½ acres.[41]

An appreciable gulf of wealth and status would usually exist between yeomen and husbandmen. However, Henry Major, who had a two hearth-house, was called a husbandman despite having 'free' lands in the parishes of Cheltenham, Prestbury and Swindon. He had £38 worth of corn thrashed and unthrashed, one mare and three swine. His house contained a lower chamber adjoining the entry, an upper lodging chamber, a chamber next to it, and a hall and kitchen with hearths for which he had been taxed. The total value was £97. A second husbandman's will was endorsed with an inventory value of £63 but the document has not survived. At the upper end of the scale, therefore, a husbandman could in reality be more prosperous than a less successful or aged yeoman, while at the opposite end the level of income – if not the formal status – might shade into that of a labourer. It is indicative of this that in the only will for a labourer, that of Robert Avris, the testator used that label for himself, but the two men who appraised his goods called him a husbandman.[42] Unfortunately the inventory itself no longer survives.

THE GENTLEMEN AND THE GENTRY

In compiling the Hearth Tax the constable of Cheltenham gave more people the title of 'Mr' than claimed – or wished to claim – the status for themselves. One yeoman summoned to meet Gregory King at a herald's visitation disclaimed any aspiration in that direction, writing proudly that he and his father gave themselves no other description than 'yeoman'.[43] The distinction between a gentleman and a yeoman was that a yeoman was actively involved in the farming as well as the ownership of land.

'Mr Lane' of Arle paid tax on six hearths, but two men, Walter and Francis Lane, who made wills in 1682 and 1689 respectively, both called themselves 'yeoman'. The Lanes lived in a way fitting for a gentleman and may have occupied the same house. Walter Lane's gentlemanly status is implied by his bequest of a leather doublet and his second-best suit of clothes to his manservant. There is no mention of property, but he left the residue of his estate to his brother Francis, possibly the head of the household. His possessions were valued at £135. When Francis died, his estate was more impressive. Moveables amounted to £252. His real estate in Hayden, and meadows and pasture grounds leased from Lord Craven, were to go to his son Walter, together with the 'standards', that is, items to be left standing in his dwelling house in Arle. To Walter also went the furniture in the best chamber over the new hall, including the red chairs and stools, value £7. The old hall was furnished traditionally with settle and table; there was a parlour, kitchen, chamber over the parlour, and two cocklofts containing cheese, a dayhouse containing more cheese, a chamber over, and a servants' chamber. This number of rooms would match well with a six-hearth house. Arable and pastoral farming interests are very clear – there were four carthorses and corn worth £48; six cows, seventy sheep, forty lambs, and six pigs.[44]

Some inventories for those calling themselves gentlemen in fact give an impression of genteel poverty. Richard Banaster, gentleman, was charged for four hearths, and was perhaps elderly when he died in 1686. Although there was a little agricultural activity – 5 acres of wheat in the fields, hens and cocks, french beans and garden goods – he had only two 'very old decayed mares' and two 'very old decayed geldings', and all his ploughing tackle was likewise 'very old'. It is no surprise that his assets were no more than £31. He was also in debt. His son John, also charged for four hearths, was more clearly a gentleman because he employed a manservant to whom he left his clothes, and he also had an old sword. His stock of agricultural produce was larger: barley, pease, french beans, wheat and pulses, all told £91 worth, but nothing was listed in the house. Lodowick Packer, gentleman, an occupier of a five-hearth house and a relation of Alexander Packer at Ham Court, had land to leave to his children in the Ampneys near Cirencester and in Swindon, but there is no inventory.[45]

Gentlemen of higher social standing, such as Fleetwood Dormer and Edward Rich, had property in more than one diocese and their wills were therefore proved in the Prerogative Court of Canterbury, but few inventories have survived. It would be interesting to know about the furnishing of Fleetwood Dormer's large old house at Arle Court, with its nine hearths. Dr Parsons, chancellor of the diocese of Gloucester, thought it was sufficiently important to include a reference in his notes written sometime before the end of the seventeenth century: 'an ancient court house now belonging to Sir Fleetwood Dormer … with a pretty chapel in it'.[46]

In his will Fleetwood Dormer described himself as 'aged' – he was 81 when he died in 1696. He belonged to a different social stratum from most Cheltenham inhabitants, with his bequest of his coach and horses to his second wife, but notably *not* his property. At the time of the Hearth Tax, his first wife, Catherine Lygon, the heiress to Arle Court and Redgrove manor, was still alive. She died in 1679, a few months after Dormer became a knight, and as they had no children, he arranged, probably on the occasion of his second marriage, that the 'manor of Redgrove, capital messuage called Arle Court, and all my other real estate' should pass to his nephew Robert Dormer, the noted lawyer and, later, a prominent judge. In his later years Fleetwood Dormer looked after his nephew, the head of the family but a lunatic, at Arle Court. Fleetwood Dormer's family came from Quainton in Buckinghamshire, and this is where he was buried. His monument records his academic achievements in Hebrew as well as classical languages, his faithful service in the civil war and in Virginia … and that his wife brought him Arle Court.[47]

No woman was given the courtesy title 'Mrs' by the Cheltenham constable, and it was used of only one woman in her inventory, by her appraisers though not by herself. The status of Mrs Ann Carnall, widow, who died in 1698 was based on her possession of a 99-year lease from the Earl of Craven of lands and buildings in Washbourne. Her house in Cheltenham was well furnished with linen and she had twelve gold rings, value £7, and money, plate and bonds worth £50; together her possessions totalled £124, but there is no indication of the size of her house and she was not recorded in the Hearth Tax. The only woman who can be linked with the Hearth Tax, Edith Finch, occupied a one-hearth house and died that same year, leaving a parcel of land called the 'Moors', but there is no inventory. The meagre details in many of the sixteen inventories in the period relating to women suggest that they were living in one or two rooms in another's house, possibly with relatives or with the heir of a customary holding. Some appear pathetically ill equipped.[48] Margaret Rich of New Court, Charlton Kings, as described in chapter 4, was an exception.

RETAILERS AND INNKEEPERS

If gentlemanly status was not always supported by evident wealth, men engaged in retailing frequently handled much more money. This points to an already rising level of national prosperity, in which Cheltenham fits into the pattern of other Gloucestershire market towns – a trend even more marked in Gloucester itself.[49] Edward Johnson, mercer, died in 1670, too soon to be named in the Hearth Tax – though one Edmund Johnson had a four-hearth house. Edward's inventory was valued at £1,674, a huge sum and more than any other in the area during this period. He had a varied range of goods in his shop on the north side of Cheltenham street, although it appears that £150 of goods may have been entered twice, and

£449 was owed to him. His house was well furnished, and had such items as a looking glass and a brass clock and case. There was £60 of malt in the malt house, and crops growing in the field. But the main value was in shop goods: woollen cloth £214, linen drapery £234, silk £149, haberdashery £72 – all these might be expected of a mercer, but more surprising there was £57 of ironmongery goods and £60 of grocery wares.

He thought his wife and daughters might continue in his trade, and if so, his daughter was not to be charged house rent.[50] Edward Johnson was of sufficient wealth and standing to issue his own money after the restoration of Charles II, when there was a shortage of coin in circulation and wealthy tradesmen produced private alternatives. Several trade tokens with his name are known, one with the king's head; they could be used for small change not only in his shop but also in the town generally. John Mason, mercer, also issued a token in 1667 for 'his halfpeny'.[51]

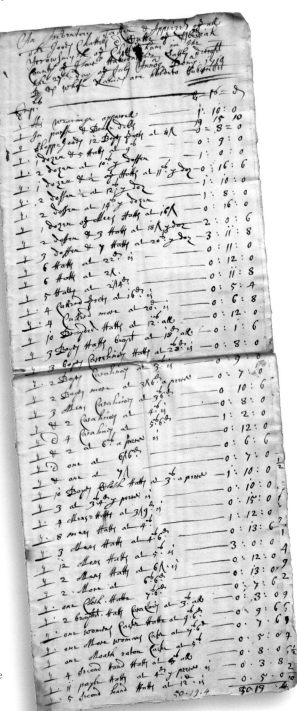

Another valuable set of worldly goods belonged to Samuel Arrowsmith, haberdasher, who issued a trade token dated 1663, with a coat of arms on it, confirmation of the status indicated in the inventory. Obadiah Arrowsmith of 'Tedbury' [Tetbury or Ledbury?], who also issued a token, was possibly his son. Samuel paid tax on four hearths. When he died in 1686 he bequeathed his wife for her lifetime land in Alstone, and Great and Little Barley Mead in Charlton Kings, but after her death the two meadows were to pass not to his son but to his grandson, another Obadiah Arrowsmith. His house had six chambers above the ground floor, and a hall, kitchen and pantry, millhouse, malthouse with 50 bushels of green malt and dried malt worth £56, and a cellar. His was a typical timber-framed town house of three stories, the top one described as a cockloft. He had diverse trading interests,

Probate inventories were compiled in connection with the process of proving a will; these recorded the moveable possessions at the time of death and constitute a vitally important source of economic and social information in the early modern period. Among several inventories that survive for Cheltenham residents is this one, made on 27 July 1710 for Obadiah Arrowsmith, haberdasher of hats. The two appraisers – the men who valued the items listed in the inventory – were John Hopley and Samuel Cooke.

GLOUCESTERSHIRE ARCHIVES GDR 1710 (98)

but his principal moveable wealth was money owed to him, £217 in 'hopeful' debts which could probably be collected, but rather more, £411, in the vividly named 'desperate' debts, contributing largely to the total inventory value of £744. A bond for £2,000, taken out by his son Obadiah as administrator of his will, shows that he had substantial real estate. But Samuel also had modest charitable intentions: he left sixpence each to fifty poor people of Cheltenham.[52]

Obadiah Arrowsmith the younger was a 'haberdasher of hats' when executor of his father's will but a 'gentleman' on the bond already mentioned – a nice example of upward mobility. He died in 1710 and the list of his 'shop goods' is a fascinating description of then current fashions in hats. There were felts, braided hats, carolinas, braided carolinas, cloth hats, women's 'caster' hats which were made of the finest beaver fur, a moth-eaten caster, second-hand hats, straw hats, hives, which were hats of plaited straw, child's brims and braid hats, none of them individually of great value. There were many varieties of ribbons and buttons and there were half-finished women's 'cases', which were coverings or perhaps boxes. He also had a shop in Winchcombe and his inventory detailed goods 'in the school', whether in Cheltenham or Winchcombe is not clear. Here there were furniture, linen, pots and pans and beds. His moveable estate was valued at £101 but his debts amounted to £135 – which was unfortunate for his wife.[53]

An extraordinary list of the creditors of James Smallpeece, gentleman, who died in 1714, enlarges the picture of the trades to be found along Cheltenham Street.[54] The man responsible for compiling the list, Thomas Keare, was a mercer. He declared in no uncertain terms that he was not personally liable to settle the bills which far outweighed the money owing to Smallpeece, whose household goods were of minimal value. Smallpeece was owed £434 by three men, one of whom was dead, one in gaol, and one the principal pauper in a case in Chancery. Thomas Keare himself was owed £156 15s. 3d., a figure stated first in the list, and was the largest individual creditor.

Smallpeece was in debt to numerous Cheltenham tradesmen and craftsmen: two saddlers, two maltsters, a grocer, a barber, a baker, two glovers, three butchers, four shoemakers, a brickmaker, three apothecaries, a collar maker, five innkeepers, a milliner, two mercers, a bodice-maker, a soap boiler, two tailors, a huckster, two haberdashers, a stone-cutter, two plumbers, two chandlers, two smiths, a bricklayer, joiner, labourer, mason, glazier, brazier, plasterer, two gardeners, a carpenter, woodseller, woolcomber, miller, postman, upholsterer and carver. In addition the list included his servant; a London innkeeper and tailor; his legal advisers and lawyers; Obadiah Arrowsmith of Ledbury; and others named but not their trade. Moreover there were bills yet to come in. He was obviously engaged in building work, and had some real estate which he had surrendered to trustees to sell in order to meet his debts, but the sale may have been disputed. He was a widower, and had no children. His sister was the wife of Thomas Rawlinson, of the city of London, and there is a hint here of development in Cheltenham which supported the opening of the first spa.

Innkeepers were among the aristocracy of a town. A census made for military purposes in 1686 revealed that Cheltenham inns could provide beds for 42 people and stabling for 73 horses, more than might have been expected in a small place off the beaten track – though larger towns might have several hundred beds.[55] The more important the inn, the more it had need of stables for travellers' horses, and an entrance from a back lane into the premises for the convenience of waggoners (and later of coachmen who could not easily reverse their vehicles and horses). No Cheltenham inns were on the scale of some along the Great North Road, or along a main road like that between London and Canterbury;[56] it was not on a major through route, and the roads to east and south were hampered by the steep climb up the Cotswold scarp. Nonetheless, there were weekly markets, and inns provided recognised meeting places for particular groups of merchants. The innkeepers also provided banking services, holding money from one trader's visit until his next, or possibly providing credit for purchases in advance of produce becoming available for sale. This may be the explanation for the long lists of debts owed to innkeepers.

There were two principal inns in Cheltenham, the *George* and the *Plough*. Gregory King stayed at the *George* in 1682 and again in 1683, when making the College of Arms visitation. The *George* is mentioned specifically in Daniel Chestroe's will in 1674, and his tax on nine hearths three years before gives an indication of the size of this building. He said that he lived in the house. Although there is no inventory, his will included interesting details about the arrangements. He left the remaining years of his 99-year lease of the *George Inn* with 'stables, outhouses, gardens, backsides, courts and ways to the same', and the furniture, to his brother, Anthony, and his kinsman, Henry Sturmy, mercer, probably one of the men given the title 'Mr' by the constable. The *George* was to be physically divided between his two sons, Daniel and Anthony. The line of division was carefully spelled out, through the house and through the garden. Anthony was to have the new part of the dwelling or inn. When a later Daniel Chester made his will in 1733, he left 'my new built brick house in the *George* backside in Cheltenham, wherein I now dwell' to his three daughters, or after their marriages or deaths to his son, John. Occupation of the premises by two men and their families had led to an expansion of the buildings on the site.[57]

In the fragmentary inventory of Anthony Chestroe, 1677, in the Canterbury Prerogative Court records, his goods were appraised at £1,031, making him one of the wealthiest men in Cheltenham in the period, and he was probably one of the joint owners of the *George*. His goods included pease, wheat, barley and beans, bullocks, horses and £85 worth of malt, and a lease of an acre of demesne land. The sum of his goods was £349. However, the striking feature of the inventory is the very extensive list of debts owed to him, mainly of small amounts up to £20, but amounting to £683, £72 of which were reckoned 'desperate'. Some of the men to whom he had lent money appear to have been local – one was from Prestbury, another from Charlton – which suggests that he was offering some sort of banking service.[58]

The 1700 inventory of Richard Cowles, innkeeper, similarly points to money-lending, though on a smaller scale, as one of a diverse range of interests; £115 was owed to him, out of the £356 which was the total value of his goods. Among those was 'the signe of the Bell', valued at 10s. The *Bell* contained a hall with two iron grates, parlour, pantry, measuring room, brew house, little room over the cellar, best chamber over the hall, a room over the parlour, one over the entry and one over the pantry, and the 'Chequer chamber'. A symbol such as a chequer was placed on inn doors so that illiterate visitors could identify their rooms. There was

The *Plough*, on the corner of Regent Street where the shopping mall of the Regent Arcade now is, was the pre-eminent hotel in the town, and centrally situated. The drawing in Rowe's *Guide* shows it 'about fifty years ago', that is about 1795, with its long High Street frontage and central carriage entrance; he said the High Street was then 'encumbered with an old Market House, over-shadowing the "Plough"'. There is some suggestion in the drawing of close-studding at the far or east end, and perhaps most of the building dated from the seventeenth century. As it was advertised for sale in 1795, it was probably refronted, or largely rebuilt, by the new owner.

AUTHOR COLLECTION

The façade of the *Plough* did not materially change after 1795, as the drawing in sales particulars of 1888 illustrates. Interestingly, it was still at that time part freehold and part copyhold. The very large yard behind was a complete workshop to keep horses and carriages on the road, and no fewer than 62 carriages could be accommodated at one time. There were 52 bedrooms, but just one bathroom, a graphic reminder of how the servants carried chamber pots and water jugs up and down.

PHOTOGRAPH: AUTHOR, 2009, COURTESY GLOUCESTERSHIRE ARCHIVES

brass, pewter and ironware and a great deal of beer, 11 hogsheads of ale and six dozen bottles of cider. Cowles was also a maltster, with several malt rooms and a malt house containing 96 bushels of wet barley (dampened to make it shoot) and green malt (with shoots but still to be dried), and 435 bushels of the final product, valued at £73.[59]

There was a gap between an 'innholder' who could accommodate travellers and a victualler who supplied beer and ale. Robert Mason was variously described as a victualler and a glover, and perhaps was indeed both, though there is no sign of gloving in his inventory. His goods were worth £182, and he appears to have occupied a one-hearth house (though this is not certain, as his name was not uncommon in Cheltenham). He had a cellar and brewhouse, a 'homestead' in the Street, and three pigs, one cow, and some barley and rye growing in his field.[60]

Two more inns or hostelries were referred to in wills and inventories of the period: the *Bull* in 1660 in Widow Elizabeth White's will, and the *Pelican* in 1690 in the will of John Banaster, gentleman, who had a parcel of dung there. Inns were a useful investment, as for William Freame of Cheltenham, gentleman, who in 1683 owned the *Crown* in Cirencester. Later it appears that the *Fish* in Ripple was owned by Charles Bagnell of Cheltenham, innholder (a reminder that the occupation given in a will may not have been pursued in the place where the testator lived at the time of his death) and the *King's Arms* in Prestbury was owned by James Wood of Cheltenham, maltster, in 1729.[61]

The *Plough* is not mentioned by name in probate documents, although it was the principal inn in Cheltenham in the following century, but it is very likely that Robert Smyth was the innholder when he died in 1686. His premises had many rooms, two with names, 'the Bear' and 'the Flower de Luce'. His brother also lived in the inn, and one chamber was 'Mr John's'; one John Smith was in the Hearth Tax with three hearths but no Robert Smyth. The gatehouse chamber contained most items of value; there was a great chamber, maids' chamber, earthen-floor chamber, room over wine cellar, chamber over the kitchen, little chamber, upper parlour and lower parlour, buttery, kitchen, hall, old brewhouse, day house, middle chamber and chamber over the beer cellar. A sign of superior status was the french and canary wine, beer and ale and silver plate in store. There was a set of ninepins and bowls, and the *Plough* had a bowling green, confirming the identification. Smyth's 'pseudo-gentry' status is indicated by his sword and gun and his employment of a personal manservant. Pictures of the *Plough* in the eighteenth century suggest that it consisted of at least five bays on the High Street frontage, though a modest size when compared, for example, with the 21 bays of the *George* in Sittingbourne, Kent.[62] This key sector of the late seventeenth-century economy of Cheltenham would help to support the great expansion of the town which took place in the earlier eighteenth century, long before the famous visit by George III.

MYTH

I N 1 7 0 0 Cheltenham was a typical small market town, not astride an important road, but pleasantly situated and serving a good farming district. In 1675 the Scottish cartographer John Ogilby published an important atlas of road maps; in it he had shown just one highway passing through Cheltenham, that from Gloucester via Winchcombe to Coventry. Neither of the two greatest travellers of the age, Celia Fiennes and Daniel Defoe, recorded any journey to or through the town. There was no famous abbey or great country house to attract the tourist. Dr Richard Parsons and Sir Robert Atkyns, when they were collecting materials on every parish in Gloucestershire, found little in the society or economy of Cheltenham worthy of comment. Yet long before the visit of George III in 1788 the town was acquiring some of the style and functions of a leisure resort and was attracting visitors and residents of gentry or aristocratic status. The King's visit generated a prevalent myth that Cheltenham's development started from this event.

The extraordinary growth of Cheltenham in the early nineteenth century has also deflected attention from the eighteenth century. In the terms of the time Cheltenham was not a village but certainly a 'town'[1] and, like many other English market towns in the Georgian period, it experienced an urban renaissance of the sort described by Peter Borsay, though on a smaller scale and later than many.[2] Some rebuilding or refronting of houses had already taken place by the time George III came to the throne in 1760. In the next decades, a Paving Act was obtained (in 1786, the year that Tewkesbury obtained a similar act)[3] instituting improvement commissioners who paved the High Street, removed the old market hall and installed oil lamps. Turnpike roads were sponsored and the coaching trade grew (in 1793 it was noted that 'The London coaches and post come in every morning, and go out every afternoon'),[4] and visitors were provided with cultural and leisure activities as well as the opportunity to drink the waters.

POPULATION IN THE EIGHTEENTH CENTURY

In 1712 Sir Robert Atkyns' study of Gloucestershire was published posthumously. In it he gave figures of population and houses, and noted the numbers of freeholders – that is, those qualified to vote. His figure of 321 houses in Cheltenham, of which 250 were in the town itself rather than the parish, can be compared with the Hearth Tax, and might suggest there had been some increase since 1671, but the same criteria could imply that the population of Charlton Kings had declined. However, if the two communities are taken together, the apparent changes disappear, which raises awkward questions about their common boundary and also about the definition of a 'house'. The ratio of people per house in Charlton Kings is surprisingly high: it was typical of urban conditions where many households were lodgers, but Charlton Kings was still a rural township. There are problems, too, in making a comparison because of the silent omission from the Hearth Tax of houses not required to pay local rates.

Population and houses in Atkyns' Ancient and Present State of Glostershire *(1712)*

Parish	Hearth Tax payers	Atkyns, Ancient and Present State of Glostershire (1712)			Ratio of people per house	Freeholders voting in 1741
		Houses	Population	Freeholders		
Cheltenham	289	321	1,500	200	4.7	182
Charlton Kings	149	102	550	60	5.4	64
Leckhampton	33	30	120	5	4.0	5
Prestbury	52	100	445	40	4.5	
Swindon	15	24	90	6	3.8	10

There was an unusually large number of freeholders in both Charlton Kings and Cheltenham. In the latter this reflects the pattern created by a medieval borough foundation, as was also the case in Prestbury, but in Charlton Kings it must reflect the break-up of freehold estates, giving opportunities to purchase copyhold land and make it freehold. A poll book for the 1741 parliamentary election, which records the names of voters in Charlton Kings, Cheltenham, Leckhampton, and Swindon, confirms the figures recorded by Atkyns.[5]

Goding referred to Atkyns's visit to Cheltenham in 1712 and plausibly suggested he had counted all rated premises including 'malt houses and out-buildings', which were certainly numerous.[6] Goding's comment was based on rating lists to which he had access but which are now lost; he mentions those for 1727, 1741 and 1763. He printed the list for 1727, which showed 158 heads of households paying the poor rate in Cheltenham tithing, and summarised that for 1763 when 490 premises were rated: 300 dwelling houses and 190 malt houses, stables, outbuildings and farm lands. Bishop Benson may have been supplied with more accurate figures of population for his survey of the diocese of Gloucester in 1735. Although the figures are clearly rounded, there is no reason to doubt that Cheltenham had grown significantly since 1712.

Parish populations in 1735, from Bishop Benson's Survey of the Diocese of Gloucester

Parish	Inhabitants
Cheltenham	2,000
Charlton Kings	700
Leckhampton	120
Prestbury	400
Swindon	8 families

Source: J. Fendley (ed.), *Bishop Benson's Survey of the Diocese of Gloucestershire, 1735–1750* (BGAS, 2000).

On the other hand, the statement by Samuel Rudder, in *A New History of Gloucestershire* published in 1779, that the population of Cheltenham was 'about 1,433', is difficult to reconcile with other information. He referred to the annual average of baptisms (45) and burials (37) from 1760 to 1769; his figure of 1,433 supposes a rate of 26 burials per thousand. Comparing his figure with Atkyns' 'it appears that population decreases and that one in about 39 dies every year'. For Charlton Kings it is clear that he worked back from the parish registers 'so that the annual average of burials is 10.7, and the number of inhabitants is about 458', which is close to 23 burials per thousand. He deduced that Atkyns' estimate of population was too high, but that the population was increasing.[7]

However, Cheltenham's inhabitants were strongly affected by nonconformity, so the parish registers were not a particularly good guide. Many may have chosen not to use the parish church to register baptisms and burials. George Whitfield preached to large numbers in 1739 and 1757, and John Wesley also in 1739 and on many occasions thereafter, and a Methodist

At The Crippetts in Leckhampton there is a pair of wrought-iron gates and gateposts; on top of each there is a pigeon, symbol of the discovery of the spa water in Cheltenham. Two stories about the discovery were told later. One attributed it to flocks of pigeons coming to feed on the salt left on the ground, and this seems to have become established as the accepted version because the pigeon is incorporated in Cheltenham Borough's coat of arms. However, another story has it that a horse was cured of illness by drinking the water, alerting William Mason to the spring's potential value. At one time there was a second pair. These gates and gateposts once stood at entrances to the Old Well Walk. Amina Chatwin, who has studied Cheltenham's ornamental ironwork, considers that they date from about 1829, at the time that the Well Walk was much improved.

PHOTOGRAPH: CARNEGIE, 2009

chapel was established in 1764.[8] The parish registers can also give a false impression because of inward migration, which tends to result in proportionately more burials than baptisms. The more plausible figure of 2,000 was given in the Cheltenham *Guide* of 1781, and the number of houses 400.[9] Goding reported a 'census' in 1797 which returned 530 houses and 2,700 people, a reasonable increase since 1735 considering the growing popularity of the town. The national census in 1801 confirmed continuing growth: 710 houses and 3,076 people in the parish, of which 618 houses and 2,639 people were in Cheltenham township.[10]

THE EARLY SPA

In 1718 or 1719, some six years after Atkyns' book on Gloucestershire was published, the first Cheltenham spa entrepreneur located the spring which was to make the town famous, railed it in, and erected a shelter over it. It is said that William Mason, a hosier in Cheltenham, had noted salt deposits on the ground in the Bayshill field which he purchased in 1704 from Thomas Higgs of Charlton Kings. However, Weedon Butler relates in the Cheltenham *Guide* that Mason was unable to find the source of the water in the first field, and in 1718 purchased the thin strip of land to the east of the Bayshill field, which is now contained between Bayshill Road and Montpellier Street, and here his quest for the spring was successful.[11]

The geological formation underlying the land between the Severn and the Cotswold hills is Lower Lias clay or limestone, and on this impermeable layer water collects, including the medicinal waters which were tapped in Cheltenham and also, though less successfully, in Gloucester. The Cheltenham spa water contains unusually large amounts of salts, in the form of chloride of sodium (Glauber Salts), sulphate of magnesia (Epsom Salts), sodium sulphate and bicarbonates of sodium and magnesium in slightly varying proportions. 'Chalybeate' water also occurs and contains iron.[12] Above the lower lias, there are varying superficial deposits of Cheltenham sands which are up to 50 ft in Charlton Kings. Only a few of the wells which have been sunk in Cheltenham, however, tap into the salty water, as the spa entrepreneurs soon discovered.

Advertisements for the newly discovered mineral water, with the added attractions of a bowling green and billiard tables, appeared in the *Gloucester Journal* in 1720 and in London newspapers.[13] The notice referred to a popular report that charges for accommodation in the town were exorbitant, but the 'gentlemen, tradesmen and innholders of the said town' united to counter the assertion. Nonetheless, exorbitant charges *were* possible because of the shortage of accommodation.

The water quickly attracted medical attention. It is easy to imagine how desperate was the search for medical treatments, which had long brought people to make pilgrimages to holy wells. But *drinking* the water was a relatively new practice which only became fashionable in the early seventeenth century.[14] In earlier centuries, as Defoe noted in Bath, the waters were applied externally for conditions such as skin or eye complaints, but by the 1720s 'many more come to drink the waters than to bathe in them'.[15] Drinking the waters led naturally to bottling and selling them further afield, a business which started in Cheltenham before 1721.[16] In that year, the well was leased to a Mr Spencer for £61 a year, a substantial rent suggesting it was providing a good income. A few years later, in 1727, the rateable value of the 'Old Wells', occupied by J. Mason, was £86, whereas the *Plough* was rated at only £8 6s. 6d., and the *Crown* and the *Lamb* each at £5 6s. 6d. The name 'Old Wells' implies that by that date, too, there was more than one well.[17]

Thomas Robins, the Charlton Kings painter, did not think William Mason made the original discovery. He painted a number of Cheltenham scenes and in a long caption to a picture of the 'Spaw', dated 1748, recorded that in 1719 Gabriel Davis, a mason, having himself been cured by the water, sunk a well and 'laid in stones which was afterwards palisaded round and wall'd in. But not in any great repute till 1740. Capt. Henry Skillicorne the present proprietor has since made a handsome walk and additional buildings'. It is possible that Davis was the tenant of the small field purchased by William Mason in 1718, and did indeed sink a well, but Mason then took possession and developed it further.

Henry Skillicorne came into possession of the Well through his wife. She was the daughter and heir of William Mason, who had retired to Bristol (where he died), and it was there that she met Captain Skillicorne.[18] Skillicorne is an unusual name, originating in the Isle of Man and still strongly concentrated there. Henry Skillicorne was a seafarer,[19] and had travelled

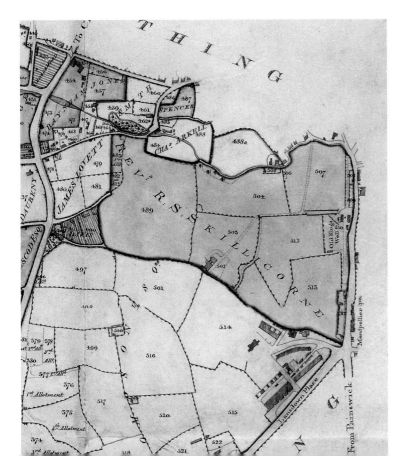

The enclosure map of Alstone and Arle of 1830 shows the fields before the general development of housing in Bayshill had begun in 1837, but after the Old Well and Bayshill House had been built. The first part of Lansdown is also shown. The 'Old King's Well' is marked, and the Well Walk running north-east to south-west is defined with dotted lines. Bayshill is numbers 502 and 503, and the drive from the house can be seen, joining a track leading to a crossing point of the Chelt, and to the Well.

GLOUCESTERSHIRE ARCHIVES QRI-41

The bright red
brickwork of the
enclosure around
the Old Well shows
how new it was
when Thomas
Robins painted
it on this finely
mounted fan. The
first planting of
trees that created
the Well Walk is
obvious, but as yet
the avenue does not
continue past the
Well towards the
church. Skillicorne
planted the second
avenue in the winter
of 1740, so it would
seem that this
painting was done
in the summer of
1740.
COURTESY OF MONICA
MAIMAN

ABOVE

The whole fan
COURTESY OF MONICA MAIMAN

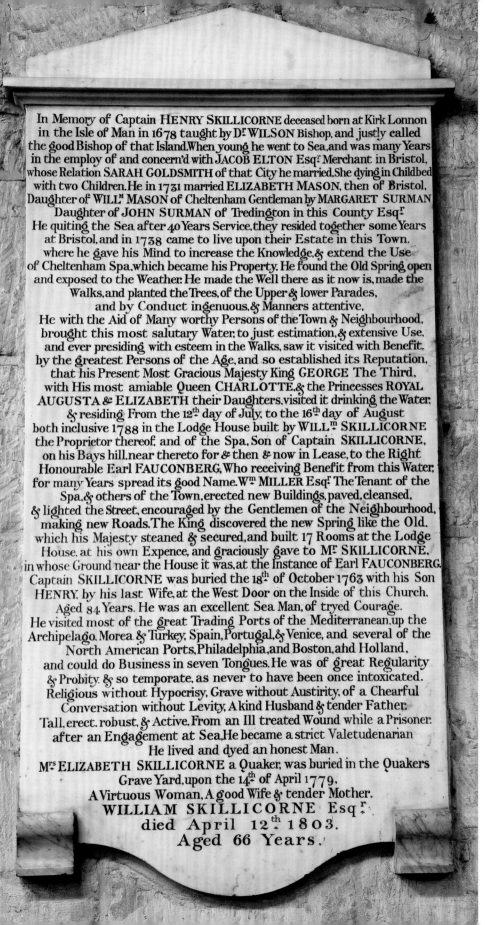

The story of Captain Henry Skillicorne's life and work was recorded on a stone in Cheltenham parish church by the wish of his son, William, and might constitute the longest ever church epitaph.

In Memory of Captain HENRY SKILLICORNE deceased born at Kirk Lonnon in the Isle of Man in 1678 taught by D.r WILSON Bishop, and justly called the good Bishop of that Island. When young he went to Sea, and was many Years in the employ of and concern'd with JACOB ELTON Esq.r Merchant in Bristol, whose Relation SARAH GOLDSMITH of that City he married. She dying in Childbed with two Children. He in 1731 married ELIZABETH MASON, then of Bristol, Daughter of WILL.m MASON of Cheltenham Gentleman by MARGARET SURMAN Daughter of JOHN SURMAN of Tredington in this County Esq.r He quiting the Sea after 40 Years Service, they resided together some Years at Bristol, and in 1738 came to live upon their Estate in this Town. where he gave his Mind to increase the Knowledge, & extend the Use of Cheltenham Spa, which became his Property. He found the Old Spring open and exposed to the Weather. He made the Well there as it now is, made the Walks, and planted the Trees, of the Upper & lower Parades, and by Conduct ingenuous, & Manners attentive, He with the Aid of Many worthy Persons of the Town & Neighbourhood, brought this most salutary Water, to just estimation, & extensive Use, and ever presiding with esteem in the Walks, saw it visited with Benefit. by the greatest Persons of the Age, and so established its Reputation, that his Present Most Gracious Majesty King GEORGE The Third, with His most amiable Queen CHARLOTTE, & the Princesses ROYAL AUGUSTA & ELIZABETH their Daughters, visited it drinking the Water. & residing From the 12.th day of July, to the 16.th day of August both inclusive 1788 in the Lodge House built by WILL.m SKILLICORNE the Proprietor thereof, and of the Spa, Son of Captain SKILLICORNE, on his Bays hill, near thereto for & then & now in Lease, to the Right Honourable Earl FAUCONBERG, Who receiving Benefit from this Water, for many Years spread its good Name. W.m MILLER Esq.r The Tenant of the Spa, & others of the Town, erected new Buildings, paved, cleansed, & lighted the Street, encouraged by the Gentlemen of the Neighbourhood, making new Roads. The King discovered the new Spring like the Old, which his Majesty steaned & secured, and built 17 Rooms at the Lodge House, at his own Expence, and graciously gave to M.r SKILLICORNE, in whose Ground near the House it was, at the Instance of Earl FAUCONBERG. Captain SKILLICORNE was buried the 18.th of October 1763 with his Son HENRY, by his last Wife, at the West Door on the Inside of this Church, Aged 84 Years. He was an excellent Sea Man, of tryed Courage. He visited most of the great Trading Ports of the Mediterranean, up the Archipelago, Morea & Turkey, Spain, Portugal, & Venice, and several of the North American Ports, Philadelphia, and Boston, and Holland, and could do Business in seven Tongues. He was of great Regularity & Probity, & so temperate, as never to have been once intoxicated. Religious without Hypocrisy, Grave without Austirity, of a Chearful Conversation without Levity, A kind Husband & tender Father. Tall, erect, robust, & Active, From an Ill treated Wound while a Prisoner. after an Engagement at Sea, He became a strict Valetudenarian He lived and dyed an honest Man. M.rs ELIZABETH SKILLICORNE a Quaker, was buried in the Quakers Grave Yard, upon the 14.th of April 1779, A Virtuous Woman, A good Wife & tender Mother. WILLIAM SKILLICORNE Esq.r died April 12.th 1803. Aged 66 Years.

extensively, probably meeting many proprietors of overseas estates. Having lived in Bristol for a few years, he appreciated how to develop the Cheltenham spa from his personal knowledge of the Hotwell in Clifton, mentioned as early as 1577 by William Harrison in his *Description of England*. As a merchant he also no doubt knew that the Society of Merchant Venturers owned half the manor of Clifton, including the well, which had become a useful investment.[20] Furthermore, he was helped in the Cheltenham project by Norborne Berkeley, whose house was near the Hotwell.[21]

A growing number of visitors came to Cheltenham after Skillicorne created more pleasant surroundings. In 1738 he erected a building to cover the well, and a 'room for the drinkers'. The planting of the Well Walks followed in 1739 and 1740, and in 1742 the erection of 'another room two storeys high', later called the 'Old Room', which seems to have adjoined the first building.[22] The Well Walk was aligned on the church spire; from the churchyard there was a path 'between quickset hedges' running between the Great House and a meadow, and then a gravel walk through Church Meadow to the bridge over the Chelt.[23] Skillicorne wished to extend the Well Walk through the meadow, but could not buy a small corner of land adjoining the bridge on the Church Meadow side. Landscaping had been introduced at other spas, as early as 1636 at Tunbridge Wells,[24] and is one of the pointers to their gradual transformation from simple centres of treatment for ill-health to holiday resorts.

Skillicorne was by no means the only person involved in financing these developments. In 1739 he received 41 private contributions towards the cost of improvements he was

making, amounting to £32 10*s.* 6*d.*: the lord of the manor, Sir John Dutton, gave five guineas and was the largest contributor; Jesus College, Oxford, and Madam Dormer of Arle Court, gave two guineas each; William Norwood of Leckhampton Court and six different clergymen, one guinea each. These details were

The portrait of Captain Henry Skillicorne suggests a man of more refinement than might have been expected for a strong and long-lived sea captain. However, Thomas Robins seems to have painted a man looking very like this promenading in the Well Walk, and it is more than likely that the well-dressed lady he is accompanying is Lady Frances Stapleton, the builder of the Great House. As the first developer of the Cheltenham Spa, Captain Skillicorne was of crucial importance. The Cheltenham Reference Library has annotated the photograph with a comment that the whereabouts of the portrait are no longer known.

© CHELTENHAM ART GALLERY AND MUSEUM

recorded in Skillicorne's journal, to which Goding had access though it is now apparently lost.[25] Fortunately, quotations from it were incorporated in his *History*. The local gentry were prominent in putting up money to finance improvements in the spa, both for speculative advantage through development of land, and because they were themselves able to take the waters and enjoy the social facilities. It was the usual practice for a visitor to the town who wished to enjoy social functions in the Pump Room and its surroundings, as well as to drink the waters, to pay a subscription, and so as it were join the club. Skillicorne's most successful year was 1741 when, he recorded in his journal, there were 667 subscribers at the Well, including (Goding reports) many peers. This encouraged him to build a second assembly room. The average annual number of subscribers between 1740 and 1749 was 566. Subscriptions to the Well or to the Assembly Rooms might make a profit for its owner or lessee, hopes which had encouraged the initial investment.

Numbers of subscribers to the Well

Year	No.	Year	No.
1740	414	1745	500
1741	674	1746	510
1742	667	1747	451
1743	644	1748	655
1744	502	1749	643

Source: Goding, *History of Cheltenham*, p. 250.

The principal sources of information about Captain Skillicorne are the journal extracts published by Goding, and the exceptionally long memorial tablet in St Mary's' church written by his son William. More, though, can be added from his will and from that of his son.[26] Both men were important entrepreneurs of the spa. Henry's will was modest, giving little indication of wealth, although he called himself 'gentleman' not 'Captain'. It was made in May 1762, eighteen months before he died, and referred to unspecified property which his wife was to enjoy during her widowhood, but not if she remarried, and which was then to pass to his son, as were his goods, chattels and personal estate. Some land was copyhold and some freehold. His daughter Elizabeth was endowed with £1,200, a useful dowry.

William's will was no more informative about the extent of the Skillicorne property, but in a version drafted in 1793 he included an account of his father's life which he required his executor, who in the event was his nephew Richard, to have inscribed on a marble monument in 'some conspicuous part of Cheltenham church at the west door on the inside whereof he is buried'. He said that his father was born in Kirk Lonan in the Isle of Man, and was taught the principles of Christianity and of 'Navigation and useful knowledge' by Dr Wilson, Lord Bishop of Sodor and Man. His parentage seems to have been unknown even to his son, or was not considered worthy of inclusion. 'He took himself to a seafaring life,' and was many years in the employ of a Bristol merchant, marrying a 'near relation' of his employer who died giving birth to twins. 'He became acquainted with Elizabeth Mason, then of Bristol, daughter of William Mason of this town hosier,' and in 1731 married her. He quitted the sea, became a merchant, and he and his wife settled in Bristol.

In 1738 they came to Cheltenham, 'where he turned his mind to increase the knowledge and extend the use of the Cheltenham spa water'. William said that he found the well exposed to the weather, 'sunk it as it now is', and made the two walks of elms and limes. He attributed the royal visit in 1788 to his father's conduct and manners in introducing Cheltenham spa water to 'just estimation' so that he saw it visited by 'the greatest persons of the age, and so established its reputation that his present gracious majesty King George III, the Queen, and two daughters spent five weeks in Cheltenham'.

After a short account of more recent events, William recorded his father's 'disposition very temperate so as never to have been inebriated', his honesty, his 'great health and strength', and that he died 'with the most beautiful set of teeth all sound even and white as ivory'. A good set of teeth was indeed a notable attribute, but one which Richard thought inappropriate to the church monument and omitted. William listed the ports to which his father traded, but not that he could speak seven languages, which Richard thought good to add. In the event William's draft was reduced a little and modified, for example his description of his grandfather as a 'hosier' was changed to 'gentleman'; Richard also added some information, for example that Henry was 'a tender father'.

Henry's second wife, Elizabeth Mason, was a Quaker. William Mason was one of three trustees to whom some garden ground in Cheltenham was conveyed in 1701 for the foundation of a Quaker meeting house,[27] which according to William 'first was created by one of my late mother's ancestors as that most respectable and much to be esteem'd Society of people called Quakers settled at Cheltenham and Worcester'. William himself bequeathed the Quakers his ground called 'William King's garden' with the dwelling-houses which he wished preserved, so that the meeting house could be kept in repair. Elizabeth did not live to see the ultimate accolade of her husband's work in George III's visit to Cheltenham; she was buried on 14 April 1779 in the Quaker burial yard, recorded simply by her name on a brass plate, and commemorated modestly by Richard on Captain Skillicorne's memorial as 'a virtuous woman, a good wife and a tender mother'.

Captain Skillicorne and Elizabeth had three children: Henry died young, William and Elizabeth outlived their father. They were conventional Anglicans. Henry was a churchwarden of Cheltenham and William, who died in 1803, similarly became a pillar of the church. Elizabeth married Reverend Thomas Nash DD, a graduate of Worcester College, Oxford, who was able to purchase the advowson of Salford rectory in Oxfordshire and present himself to the vacancy in 1800, immediately building a new and quite impressive house. Their son Richard inherited the Cheltenham estate and assumed the surname Skillicorne. He became chairman of the bench of magistrates and the first mayor of Cheltenham. The Skillicorne family had certainly entered the ranks of the gentry.

An upper-class clientele came to Cheltenham for the waters. While Captain Skillicorne was developing the Spa, Lady Frances Stapleton started to build a large property known as the 'Great House', looking across a meadow towards the Well Walk. She was the first, and Lord Fauconberg the second and better-known, aristocratic patron and builder in Cheltenham. The house was described in Butler's *Guide* as adjacent to 'The Grove', 'a pretty enclosure', but Moreau in his guidebook two years later said it was 'in' the Grove and it was sometimes known by this name. The Great House was on the site of the ancient Court House which had belonged to the Crown; the main entrance was to the west, from the land which was to

Thomas Robins painted two pictures of the Great House, an important building in Cheltenham on the site of the former manor court house. One, on the fan, shows the side facing south towards the Old Well. There is no certainty that the house existed exactly as shown; the painting may have been partly based on Lady Stapleton's plans. However, it gives every sign of being designed as a lodging house, with its two doors on each side of the central block. A second picture of the Great House by Thomas Robins shows the building from the other, north, side. Although the main entrance to the house was up a flight of steps, with a sweeping carriage way in front, the approach was from the west side. There is a grove of trees on the east, supporting the suggestion that the house was in a 'pretty grove'.

become St George's Place, but the house faced north. Although Ruff in 1803 said that the house was built as a family home, it seems just as likely that Lady Stapleton was investing capital in Cheltenham. She, or her son as her trustee, was purchasing copyhold property in the same area from 1741.[28] The coincidence of dates with Captain Skillicorne's development of the spa is striking.[29] Moreover, the Cold Bath, which was an added amenity, was part of the Great House property. It is difficult to see how Captain Skillicorne's investment could have been successful without Lady Stapleton's input of an upper-class lodging-house. It was certainly a place of entertainment by 1757, when Mr Pope was the lessee and a concert was followed by a ball. It became known as the Old Clarence boarding house when a second boarding house, in the garden of the Great House, was renamed Clarence Hotel.[30]

Lady Frances Stapleton also seems to have been an early example of that steady influx of visitors and residents who had lived in hot countries. She was an heiress to West Indian estates and her husband, Sir William Stapleton, the third baronet, was similarly the son and grandson of notably successful and wealthy sugar planters. They lived on one of their plantations in Nevis. Sir William died in 1699, leaving Frances with two very young children, and with them she returned to England. Some years later she married General Walter Hamilton, another West Indian planter, though she never used her second husband's name. She went out with him to the Leeward Islands after he became governor-general, but came back to England two years later. Hamilton died in 1722. She lived on until 1746, stating in her will that she was 'of Cheltenham'. She therefore enjoyed her Cheltenham house for only a few years, but she also had a lease of a house in Grosvenor Street, London, and property in Buckinghamshire. The list of visitors to Cheltenham Well in 1743 included Lady Stapleton, Sir William and Lady Codrington, Lady Archibald Hamilton and her daughter, and Lord A. Hamilton, surely a group brought here by kinship ties, and all with West Indian estates.[31]

Lady Stapleton's sons had predeceased her, but she had nine grandchildren, one of whom, Catherine Stapleton, inherited the Cheltenham house and her grandmother's jewels, though she was only twelve years old at the time. A long law suit was fought in Chancery over Frances's will.[32] Catherine Stapleton in time became the chief manager of the Stapleton estates, and leased the Great House to Mrs Field. In 1763 it was assessed for the relief of Cheltenham's poor at £60,[33] compared with the *George* inn assessed at £45 and the *Plough* at £46, and these were by far the largest rateable values among those recorded by Goding, apart from the Cheltenham tithes (£151 10s). The Cold Bath, also Miss Stapleton's, did not have a tenant and by 1781 it was 'much decayed'.[34] In 1780 Miss Stapleton was still the owner and Mrs Field the occupier of the Great House;[35] cards, tea-drinking, concerts and balls took place there and it was certainly a lodging house.[36] When she finally gained full possession of Lady Frances Stapleton's estate, Catherine sold the Great House in 1785 to Richard Hooper, gentleman and surgeon, who also purchased the Stapleton copyhold property with a mortgage, and at the end of the century was occupying the Great House.

Thomas Robins' pictures of Cheltenham

One guest at the Great House was Lady Somerset, a niece of Norborne Berkeley, Henry Skillicorne's collaborator in the development of the Well Walks. A pleasant picture of the view from the house looking towards the well, painted in about 1748 and with the cold bath as a prominent feature, was long thought to have been her work.[37] However, it is now considered more likely that it was painted by Thomas Robins. Two copies of the 'West Prospect of the Spaw and Town of Cheltenham' signed by Thomas Robins are known, showing the spa buildings, the two Well Walks, the Great House and the church set against the backdrop of the hills. One was used in the nineteenth century to make a lithograph, it is said by Thomas Phillipps of Thirlestaine House. Thomas Robins also painted two fans featuring the Spa and other buildings including the Great House, the first quite possibly for Lady Stapleton, and also painted the north façade of the Great House.

He was born in Charlton Kings in 1716 and lived there until 1760. His father moved from London, and was a maltster and small property owner. Also living in Charlton Kings was a man of French origin named Jacob Portret, a fan painter. In his will made in 1743 Portret described Thomas Robins as 'late his servant', presumably meaning apprentice, and he left Robins £200 and the furniture of his hall and parlour, items which do not appear in the inventory of his possessions made after his death. John Prinn of Charlton Park was one of the witnesses to his will.[38] Portret was a man of some sophistication, with French books and two coffee pots, but he also had apples and corn in the barn, and two pairs of garden shears. There is no indication there of his painting, but Robins had possibly acquired his materials. Robins will have learned from Portret his delicacy of brush stroke, and he continued to paint fans throughout his life. It is notable that a painter could make a living in Charlton Kings at this time, for this suggests affluent inhabitants and that the spa attracted visitors who could afford to sit for portraits or buy pictures. Robins travelled quite widely to fulfil commissions in neighbouring counties and he worked in Bath, making many drawings of the town. There he was patronised by Ralph Allen of Prior Park, a major figure in the town's development. He moved to Bath in 1760, and died there ten years later.[39]

Until relatively recently this Thomas Robins (the elder) was unknown, though his son of the same name was recognised as a flower painter. In the 1960s a number of works by the elder Robins were identified and, in response to an article in *Country Life* in 1972, a reader made known his possession of Thomas Robins's notebook, containing 133 drawings. John Harris incorporated this material in his rare and fine two-volume book, *Gardens of Delight*. Robins's pictures are mainly gouache and watercolour; only one oil is known, a panoramic view of Charlton Park, full of interesting details, including a small vignette of Cheltenham church and the Great House. The topographical accuracy of this picture has been noted by Mary Paget.[40] One patron led to another, and a common meeting place was Bath. Robins also painted watercolour views of the houses and estates of gentlemen. His paintings of

Painswick House, recently used to restore the Rococo garden there, and of Marybone House in Gloucester, were for Benjamin Hyett, an important early patron. He did a watercolour of Sandywell Park, Dowdeswell, in 1758, and shortly before he died sketched Haymes Place and a windmill seen from Cleeve.[41]

Robins was a young man when Captain Skillicorne and Lady Stapleton arrived in Cheltenham, and, though we should not assume complete accuracy, these early paintings and sketches are valuable evidence of the Spa. His first Cheltenham fan, titled 'South-east view of Cheltenham Well', was not known when Harris wrote his book. It must date from the summer of 1740 as it shows the two rows of very young trees of the Upper Walk, which had been

The first sets of lithographs of Cheltenham, published in March 1821, included this print of the Assembly Rooms. Shortly after he bought Powers Court, Thomas Hughes built new Assembly Rooms, a single-storey building probably where the earlier Fire Engine house had stood. Further alteration and rebuilding of the Assembly Rooms took place in the early nineteenth century, and this drawing by D. T. Egerton shows that by 1821 it had become a two-storey building. The lithograph was published by Williams' Library, which by 1817 occupied the east end of the building on Rodney Road, and was printed by a London firm. By 1800 three libraries had been established in the town.

© CHELTENHAM ART GALLERY AND MUSEUM

planted in the winter of 1739, but not the Lower Walk which Skillicorne records he planted in the winter of 1740.[42] As well as several fashionably dressed figures, Robins humorously includes himself sitting with a board on his knees drawing the scene, with a curious onlooker beside him. This fan is particularly fine and well preserved. The brickwork of the enclosure round the well is very bright and new, as it is on the small gabled building forming its west side, adjoining which is a three-storey tower-like block. From the appearance of the tower, with its unglazed windows, and its position outside the well enclosure, this could be new 'conveniences'. Another fan by Robins, now in Cheltenham Museum and Art Gallery, is later; it has the two Walks and what seems to be an extension to the gabled building which may be Skillicorne's second room built in 1742. Butler later described in his *Guide* the 'Old Room', as it had then become, with the billiard room above it, and noted that adjoining it was 'a dwelling house and offices for the proprietor's servants'.[43]

A unique feature of the earlier fan is that the principal buildings are identified: on the front, the Well and its conveniences, Lady Stapleton's House, Lady Stapleton's Dog Kennel, the church and part of the town, and on the reverse the 'Assembley House' and the 'Fire Ingine House'. Close to the Spa is an unlabelled and more modest brick house with three gables, so placed that it could be Well Cottage.[44] Robins did not include Captain Skillicorne's house, the 'Old Farm' which was near the Great House in what was to become St George's Place, where St Mary's Hall, later called Shaftesbury Hall, was opened in 1869.[45] Lady Stapleton's house appears to be largely brick, except for the prominent central bay which was stone. It is symmetrical, and the two wings, each with two front doors and three floors, suggest that they were designed as lodging houses. But this is an idealised portrayal, possibly even drawn from the projected plan of the house. In practice, the house was still being built in 1743 when Lady Stapleton made her final will, and one of the wings was not completed in Robins' picture of the other, north side of the house. The two outside doors on the south side also do not appear on his other drawings of the Great House.[46] Lady Stapleton's Dog Kennel is also brick, and is close to the River Chelt. The mention twice of Lady Stapleton's name strongly suggests that she had commissioned the fan.

The Assembly House on the reverse side of the fan is an impressive brick residence of four storeys, William and Mary in style, though with older buildings at the rear, and thoroughly symmetrical, with ranges of ten windows on each storey, the top ones gabled, and on the ground floor two windows on either side of two doors. This was Powers Court. From 1734 if not before, Powers Court contained a ballroom, and this function was obviously important in Robins' eyes. The house fronted the High Street; Lloyds Bank now occupies its site. The Fire Engine House which adjoins it and shares a boundary brick wall was on the corner of High Street and a lane which became Rodney Road, after Rodney Lodge was built on part of the Powers Court site. Sir John Dutton had given the town a fire engine in 1721 and in 1731 Lord Gage did the same, gifts which encouraged votes and also protected their property. Thomas Robins perhaps painted the Fire Engine house as a compliment to the lord of the

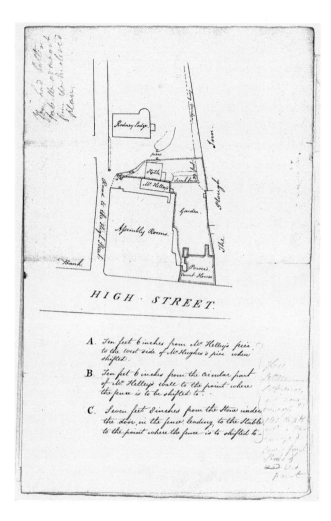

A plan of the Assembly Rooms and Powers Court made in 1820, when the house was sold to Robert Hughes and T. Smith, shows a very intricate arrangement of property boundaries as the site had been developed. The long garden running down the boundary of Rodney Lodge and the *Plough* is still clearly visible at the present day. The plan suggests that there might have been a ha-ha separating Powers Court from a meadow to the south.

GLOUCESTERSHIRE ARCHIVES

manor. Powers Court was purchased in 1776 by Thomas Hughes, perviously the lessee of William Skillicorne's well.[47]

Thomas Hughes was an ambitious man. He had been articled in 1749 to John de la Bere, a solicitor in Cheltenham, and about the time he finished his articles began to develop his business acumen by leasing the spa and selling bottled water. Two copies of a printed handbill were tucked into Skillicorne's journal when Goding saw it, apparently between pages relating to 1738, but relevant to a later date. In the handbill, Hughes made clear where 'genuine' water was being delivered: to several addresses in London, and one in each of Nantwich, Chester, Shrewsbury, Whitchurch, Oxford, Worcester, Gloucester, Bristol, and most surprising of all, Bath. In 1762 Hughes went into partnership with de la Bere and the following year married a wealthy bride, kin to the Duke of Chandos who was involved in building houses in Bath. By 1772 he had become recognised as an important county figure, becoming under-sheriff of Gloucester. But he may not have been in tune with William Skillicorne, and so transferred his interest to Powers Court where he built a new Assembly Room.[48]

William Skillicorne had inherited the Old Well in 1763. He was not as colourful a figure as his father, but he was responsible for two important developments. In collaboration with his lessee, William Miller, who came to Cheltenham from London, he built a new 'Long Room' on the opposite side of the Well courtyard in 1775–76. Of more importance in the long run, in 1781 he built Bays Hill Lodge, or Fauconberg House, Villa or Lodge as it was later called. This was the year that the first *Guide* to Cheltenham was published, marking a clear advance in the fame of the spa. William also took an active interest in the improvement of the town by acting as one of the commissioners for paving and lighting the streets.

EARLY GUIDE BOOKS

The publication of guidebooks started some thirty years before the first Cheltenham *Guide*. From the mid-seventeenth century there had been road books containing comments about individual places. In the eighteenth century a small but wealthy group of Englishmen travelled abroad, but an increasing number of the modestly affluent started to seek holidays and health in this country, travelling to seaside towns and 'inland watering places'. The *Tradesman's and Traveller's Pocket Companion; or the Bath and Bristol Guide* of 1750 was the first modern-style guidebook to cater for this market. Guides to Harrogate, Margate and Tunbridge Wells soon followed.[49] These guides promoted the places concerned, as well as helping visitors find their way about, and modern tourist guides are in a direct line of succession.

The first Bath guide was written for visitors but not, it seems, for aristocratic travellers. It was a slim book, suited to the coat pocket, and served as a general *vade mecum*, with road distances and the times of coaches, wagons, carriers and boats for both Bath and Bristol, and 'other useful observations'. A particular concern was information which enabled visitors to check on chairmen's charges for carrying them from place to place. Nevertheless the book's first chapter described Bath's waters, public buildings, churches, hospitals, squares, streets, and rooms for public assemblies, and the rules relating to the town. *The Prose Bath Guide* of 1778 lists artists, theatres, music, books and newspapers among the many attractions in that well-established pleasure town. Cheltenham would catch up with these facilities in time.

The *Cheltenham Guide or useful companion in a journey of health and pleasure to the Cheltenham spa* had a dedication to Lord Fauconberg dated July 1780. No author's name was given on the title page, but in fact it was written by Reverend Weedon Butler the Elder (1742–1823). He was a man of many parts, the keeper of Cheyne Walk school in Chelsea, amanuensis to Dr William Dodd before he was executed for fraud, morning preacher at the fashionable Charlotte Street chapel in succession to Dodd, and writer on miscellaneous subjects.[50] The *Guide* was a joint venture between four publishers, two in London (J. Ridley of St James's Street and Joseph Johnson of St Paul's churchyard, the friend and publisher of many writers and on one occasion of Samuel Johnson), with S. Harward of Gloucester – who became an important developer in Cheltenham – and W. Forty 'at the well in Cheltenham'. The *Guide* certainly demonstrates that Cheltenham was not unknown before George III's visit.

The descriptions of Cheltenham's environs in Butler's *Guide* were significant and continued to be a feature of its successors. Butler may be credited with advertising Cheltenham effectively as the 'centre for the Cotswolds', describing the 'stupendous ridge of hills, often visited by company on horseback, or sometimes in carriages, to enjoy the sublime and beautiful rural excursion', 'the majestic range of hills, which separates the vale from the Coteswould country', and the 'extensive views of the vale'. This might suggest that the amusements in the town itself were not enough to keep visitors occupied during their stay, and the same was true of guides to other newly established holiday places, such as Margate and Tunbridge Wells. But

in his dedicatory preface, Butler wrote of the restoration of his own health and spirits after a visit to Cheltenham and 'the parts adjacent', and of his wish to hang up 'a votive tablet' by communicating to others the pleasure and profit he had experienced. He suggested the *Guide* was not written for pecuniary gain (a claim which might be viewed with scepticism) but he hoped it would open a new sphere of enjoyment to the 'alert and healthy' as well as the 'sick and sorrowful'. The Earl of Fauconberg would be sympathetic to his objectives – the town of Cheltenham had been long rendered happy 'in your lordship's repeated visits to its salutary springs'.

Butler started with a short history of Cheltenham reminiscent of Atkyns's account in *Ancient and present state of Glostershire*. He went on to extol the mild air (contrasting it with the 'sharp and chill' air of the Oxfordshire wolds), the productive surroundings of the Vale, and the nature of the soil. The church was described in some detail, with a number of monumental inscriptions. The main street of the town was said to be 'regular, spacious and handsome', with most houses of brick, but some of stone. Butler had little time for some 'old coarse buildings supported on stone pillars', and hoped that the Corn Market, Butter Cross and an old uninhabited house belonging to a Mr Hayward would be removed. He noted the prison or cage further down the Street inscribed 'Do well and fear not'. Four inns were noted, a market and five fairs; the St James's Day fair was for lambs and the Michaelmas fair was also a hiring fair. Butler suggested that the malt trade was declining, and the only manufacture in the town was of white cotton stockings which were sold in great quantities; 'The women and children of the poorer sort comb and spin woollen yarn for the clothiers about Stroud'. Charities, Pate's almshouses, schools, and a boarding school for boys and another for girls, were all mentioned, the latter many years before Cheltenham College and Cheltenham Ladies' College were founded. Many residents did not let lodgings, he wrote, and moreover the ancient houses were too small for that purpose, but more lodging houses were being erected. The comment is rather contradicted five years later in the Paving Act, which made special provision for the

John Flower (1793–1861) was a Leicester painter. Apprenticed as a framework knitter, his artistic talent was recognised and he was sent to London, probably in 1815, to have lessons with Peter de Wint. Returning to Leicester, he drew many of the picturesque and old buildings in the town. He also travelled, searching for subjects for drawings and watercolours, and many topographical pictures are known. At least one visit was made to Cheltenham. His view of old buildings near the church appears to be a sketch rather than exact architectural drawings, which on occasions he did in Leicester. It shows the timber-framing that was general in the town before the building boom of the early nineteenth century. The tall chimney might imply that one building was a malthouse. A large water pump supplies the houses.

© CHELTENHAM ART GALLERY AND MUSEUM

rating of houses 'which are kept in hand by the Owners or Lessees therof, ready furnished, for the Purpose of letting out in Lodgings to the Company resorting to the said Town during the Water-drinking Season, and may not be occupied during the Remainder of the Year'.

Detailed measurements were given of the well area and of the walks. The Old Room had a billiard room over it and the New Room had three rich glass chandeliers. Balls were held on Monday nights, and they were 'free from disagreeable restraints' and less encumbered with form than elsewhere, which sounds like an implied criticism of the excessive formalities of Bath and its authoritarian master of ceremonies. The Avenues were illuminated on Ball evenings. The qualities of the spa water were described at length, drawing on Dr Short's treatise. The Playhouse was said to be beautified and neat but not large enough. The traveller to Cheltenham was encouraged by commendation of the inns in Dowdeswell, important because those without their own carriage had to take a post-chaise from the Frogmill to Cheltenham; at this date only a stage-waggon plied once a week between London and Cheltenham. In summer, he noted that there was a good bridle road from Dowdeswell to Cheltenham which saved two to three miles. The existence of 'summer roads' is a graphic sign of the state of winter roads, with their rutted, muddy surfaces. Butler was honest enough to print in an appendix a letter published in a London paper criticising the High Street as dirty and the inhabitants of Cheltenham as indifferent to visitors and preferring obscurity, but he offset this with a second letter drawing attention to improvements in the road to Cheltenham and in the paving of the Street. Cheltenham, this writer said, could be compared with Brighton 'which improves daily'.

The 'environs' of Cheltenham described in this first *Guide*, suitable for walks, rides, sightseeing and tea-drinking expeditions, included Charlton Kings, Leckhampton and Swindon, and stretched as far as Bishops Cleeve, Winchcombe, Sudeley and Hailes to the north, Coberley to the south, and Whittington to the east. Unfortunately the road to Prestbury was 'almost impassible'. Expeditions to Gloucester, Tewkesbury, the Malvern Hills and Worcester, as he said, did not 'properly come in under the head of airings'. Cheltenham could thus cater to the new trend for holidays 'for the alert and healthy'. The few had enjoyed the continental 'tour'; more could take shorter trips in Britain.

Weedon Butler was the first to publish a guide for the growing spa town, but his book was soon overtaken by the greater experience, and skills in self-aggrandisement, of Simeon Moreau, who had arrived in 1780 and offered himself as master of ceremonies. He presided over all the social facilities in Cheltenham from 1781. Thomas Hughes may have encouraged him to come in order to boost the popularity of the Powers Court assembly room and shortly after this, in 1784, Hughes opened the new Assembly room, possibly designed by a famous London architect, Henry Holland.[51] Moreau's *A Tour to Cheltenham Spa; or, Gloucestershire displayed* was published in 1783, without Moreau's name, but printed for the author in Bath. Many of the early visitors probably gained their first knowledge of the place from information acquired in Bath.

Moreau's account was much more extended than Butler's, including the natural history of the county, and description of a wide area around Cheltenham: the City of Gloucester, Cirencester, Tetbury, Tewkesbury and Fairford. It had a guide to calculating when the Severn crossing at Aust could be used, and 'the new passages', which were other places where a boat crossed the estuary, subject to wind and tide, to link up with the road system on either side, 'the whole interspersed with explanatory historical, chronological and genealogical notes carefully selected from the best authors'. Over the next fourteen years this guide was reprinted many times. The fourth edition in 1789 carried S. Moreau's name. The seventh edition was printed in 1793 with an interesting amendment to its title, *A Tour to the Royal Spa at Cheltenham*; to the eighth edition in 1797 '*is prefixed, An account of the Royal visit to Cheltenham in 1788*'. The second edition gave the printer's name, Richard Crutwell of Bath, who was responsible for a number of similar productions. He had a substantial printing business and was the proprietor and editor of the *Bath Chronicle*. He died in Cheltenham in 1793, though the firm carrying his name continued, and in partnership with another Bath printer, William Mayler, in 1803 published *The history of Cheltenham and its environs including an inquiry into the nature and properties of the mineral waters, and a concise view of the county of Glocester*, 'intended as a useful and amusing guide to the visitor and traveller', and printed by H. Ruff. This book acknowledged drawing on Moreau's account of George III's visit to Cheltenham.[52]

LORD FAUCONBERG AND GEORGE III

By 1781, when Butler published his *Guide* and Lord Fauconberg commissioned a house to be built on Bays Hill, Cheltenham was becoming established as a resort for 'the nobility and gentry'. In 1774 Wesley had noted in his journal that Cheltenham was 'full of gentry'.[53] It is indicative of the increasing number of well-to-do living in Cheltenham *before* George III's visit that in 1775 a petition was presented to the bishop by sixteen men, 'some of the principal inhabitants of Cheltenham being possessed of some of the best houses in the said town', who wished to sit in an exclusive area in the church. Thomas Baghot, William Skillicorne and Richard Hooper were among the petitioners. The vestry resolved that a gallery should be built over the north aisle. Plans were made for fourteen pews but fifteen names were recorded. Some years later, in 1787, the vestry resolved to close up the door in the chancel 'in order to the erecting a certain number of pews for the accommodation of the Nobility and Gentry that frequent the Cheltenham spa'.[54] The Paving Act of 1786, passed two years before George III's visit, also referred to 'great numbers of Nobility and Persons of Distinction' who resorted to Cheltenham, with large sums of money spent each year by the company. It may be that Cheltenham was a rather exclusive resort because only carriage folk could travel conveniently to the town; the roads, and especially those to the north-east and south-east which climbed the Cotswold scarp, were notoriously bad, and there was no direct communication by coach with London until after 1785 when a turnpike trust developed a route from Cheltenham up Dowdeswell Hill to Kilkenny to join the Gloucester to London road.[55]

A large boarding house was built in the grounds of the Great House about 1820, known at first as Liddell's. Cheltenham was proud of the royal visitors who, after an interval of a few years, followed George III; the Duke of Gloucester stayed in Royal Crescent and brought his niece Victoria to stay with him; the queen passed through Cheltenham station on a train but otherwise did not revisit the town. Adelaide, Duchess of Clarence, the consort to the future William IV, came in 1827 and stayed at Liddell's. As a mark of royal favour, the newly laid-out Great House Road was renamed Clarence Road, and the boarding house was renamed Clarence Hotel, but is now known as John Dower House. The Great House itself subsequently became known as the old Clarence Boarding House.

PHOTOGRAPH: AUTHOR, 2009

The royal coat of arms was placed above the entrance to the former Liddell's Boarding House after it was renamed Clarence Hotel in recognition of the visit there of the Duchess of Clarence.

PHOTOGRAPH: CARNEGIE, 2009

Henry Belasyse, 2nd Earl Fauconberg (1743–1802) was an
important figure in the development of Cheltenham spa. His
portrait by John Singleton Copley was copied and published
in 1794 by Anthony Fogg, an artist who was working between
1793 and 1806. Earl Fauconberg was a regular attender at the
Cheltenham well, so much so that he decided in 1781 to finance
the building of a house near it, and secured a site from William
Skillicorne on Bayshill a short walk away. A few years later he
suggested to George III that he try the waters, and the king and
his family squeezed themselves into the house, which was rather
smaller than their usual palaces.

© NATIONAL PORTRAIT GALLERY, LONDON

Henry Belasyse, Lord Fauconberg, is a shadowy
figure in histories of Cheltenham, but of the many
nobility and gentry who came to the town he was
particularly important for two reasons. The most
obvious is that in the summer of 1788 he offered George
III the use of his house, which was new and close to
the well. Less attention has been paid to the fact that,
even before this, Fauconberg had commissioned the
building of a house on a greenfield site at Bayshill and
had been staying in Cheltenham for some years. According to the *Gentleman's Magazine* for
1788, the earl used it as a summer residence.[56] It saved him travelling for his summer holiday
from London to Yorkshire, where his main residence was Newburgh Priory near Coxwold.
Fauconberg was lord lieutenant of the North Riding and had been MP for Peterborough from
1768 until he succeeded his father in the earldom in 1774. The following year he was made a
lord of the bedchamber, which for £700 a year involved attending at Court, and it was said
that he was a great favourite with George III.[57] He earned popularity by defending the King's
Civil List in 1783, and by speaking in favour of coercing America's 'deluded inhabitants'.

In his portrait he looks to have been a kindly man. What attracted him to Cheltenham? The
proximity of Fauconberg Lodge to the first spa suggests that it was health reasons, perhaps on
behalf of his wife as well as himself. As *The Gentleman's Magazine* noted, Lord Fauconberg's
house was 'a delightful seat about a quarter of a mile from the town, and 200 yards from
the Spa'.[58] In 1781 he was quite a young man, 38 years old, and his wife was just six months
younger; she died in 1790 and he followed her in 1802 at the age of 58 – the *Gentleman's
Magazine*, in its notice of his death, reversed the digits in his age and made him an old man.
Lord Fauconberg's Bayshill house shows that the *Gentleman's Magazine* was mistaken in saying
that Cheltenham waters were 'long-neglected' before the king's visit, though this is perhaps
the source of that view of Cheltenham's history.

In her diary Fanny Burney, later Madame d'Arblay, wrote a graphic and detailed account of the royal visit to Cheltenham. It was published in 1843, three years after her death. The King's illness had started in June 1788 with 'a pretty smart bilious attack'. When it continued for several weeks, Sir George Baker recommended Cheltenham water, which was supposed to be good for bilious complaints. The illness, as it continued, made the king appear insane – Fauconberg was one courtier who at this time assured the king that he had suffered an attack of insanity, but was completely cured.[59] This became the accepted diagnosis, though in 1966 two medical historians put forward the now widely accepted theory that it was a rare hereditary disease, porphyria, which was endemic in the Stuarts and reached George III through Sophia, Electress of Hanover, the granddaughter of James I.[60] The king's earlier illness in 1765 was probably not this, but the apparent insanity did recur in 1801, 1804, and at the end of 1810, and from this time George III had very few periods of clarity.

Fanny Burney's account of the royal visit is well known, recording the small size of Fauconberg Lodge (so that the pages slept in the outhouses and most servants elsewhere in the town); the sudden influx of visitors who had to be accommodated in neighbouring towns and villages; the informality of the king; the routine followed with respect to drinking the waters; the visits to neighbouring gentry and to the Worcester Music Festival; sightseeing expeditions; and attendance at the theatre. But the letters of Mary Yorke, wife of the bishop of Ely, who with her family was staying at the time in her country house, Forthampton Court, on the opposite bank of the Severn from Tewkesbury, are less familiar, and include 'some little trifling rural anecdotes that are perfectly local'.[61] On 18 July she wrote to her sister-in-law, the Marchioness Grey

> their life at Cheltenham is perfectly quiet, the King rises and drinks the Water at six every morning, and at nine appears upon the Publick walks with the Princesses, but they none of them appear again at any Publick meeting except Church, where they all attend; the Bishop of Gloucester preached last Sunday. A wag was much entertained with the Psalm that the singers chose to entertain his Majesty with, namely the first verse of the seventy second Psalm.

The psalm begins 'Give the king thy judgements, O God, and thy righteousness unto the king's son'. Mary Yorke's niece, Amabel, Lady Polwarth, was given a more extended account a month later, on 14 August:

> Our very great Neighbour leaves us on Saturday; his condescension and affability have endeared him to all Ranks in this Neighbourhood. The Papers so faithfully detail all and indeed more than all relating to him of any consequence, that nothing is left for me to tell you unless you will accept of some little trifling rural anecdotes that are perfectly local. One of our tenants mentioned a visit he made to an acquaintance of his, where he went to see sheep and purchase a horse, the one he told her was too dear for him, it might do for

some Lords and Dukes – the sheep were too large, he wanted little sheep – he had indeed lately bought some <u>little</u> sheep at a <u>great</u> price but that was not quite what he wanted. On riding off after this conversation he seemed rather at a loss about the road; the farmer <u>kindly</u> said, 'shall one of my fellows show your majesty the way?'

There is support for this story in Fanny Burney's *Diary* though these particular details were not included. Mary Yorke's letter continued

He rewarded the activity of our butcher's boy who kept off the Mob with an oaken stick with commendations and a Guinea. This boy is not the only one of our dependants that have benefited, for the man that keeps the gate to the drive down to our house from the turnpike road, carried some of his fine flowers the first day to offer to the Princess Royal, but just as she was taking them the coach drove away; the next visit to Tewkesbury he repaired there again and presented himself at the coach side, the Princess recollected him, said she was afraid she should not have seen him again, took the remainder of his flowers (which he had this time stuck in moss, more to catch the eye) and gave him a <u>Guinea</u> which in the joy of his heart he brought immediately to our house to shew, being a nice new Guinea.

As to his Majesty's health I cannot really say what benefit it has really found from the Waters, he still looks thin and of a dark red complexion. His Spirits however are very good, and being addressed by a lady the other day on the walks with kind enquiries, he assured her he was much better, for now he could eat four pieces of mutton, when he came he could only <u>two</u>.

She was right to be doubtful about the king's health, as his relapse shortly confirmed. Her conclusions on the visit were contained in a letter to Marchioness Grey on 11 September:

But let me quit the subject of influenzas, and begin upon the more brilliant one of <u>Kings</u>, <u>Princesses</u>, and <u>Titles</u> ... all this Neighbourhood are now composed into their usual state of quietness, and were it not for the reinstating of the <u>wooden</u> house, we should hardly recollect, the very great honour this part of the world has received. But this operation now begun, will put us from time to time in mind of the power and authority which first moved the building from its natural foundation. I must say the satisfaction given is general; everybody speaks with pleasure (I may add with feeling and affection) of the great attention and desire shown to please: and I hope on the other side the little returns were not unacceptable. I am told, none of the entertainments were more approved than one given by Sir George Paul; who very ingeniously contrived to make the Mob (who in most places are so troublesome) form a part of the show of the place, by making them take their stations regularly on the side of a hill where they could both <u>see</u> and be <u>seen</u>.

The Gentleman's Magazine reported that the king had noticed a neat-built timber house at the end of the town, and as he was short of rooms at the Lodge, he ordered the building to be moved.[62] His illness recurred soon after his return to Windsor and continued for the next five months. On 14 February 1789 the sensible and well-informed Mary Yorke noted the improvement, writing to Marchioness Grey from the Bishop's Palace in Ely:

> I cannot conclude my letter without expressing the Bishop's and my own great comfort and satisfaction in the gradual improvement in our poor King's health within the last ten days which not only the Papers, but private accounts assure us of. God grant they may continue!

However, a little later she saw cause for concern; in a letter to her niece on 4 April she made reference to the service of thanksgiving to be held for the king's recovery:

> Why [the Queen] and the King undertake and promote so much hurry and bustle of all sorts I cannot conceive, surely it must be wrong for him! Even before his illness last summer at Cheltenham I regretted the eternal fuss they lived in, and now it seems to me perfectly improper, and of all the schemes that of moving through the City to St Pauls strikes me as the most so.

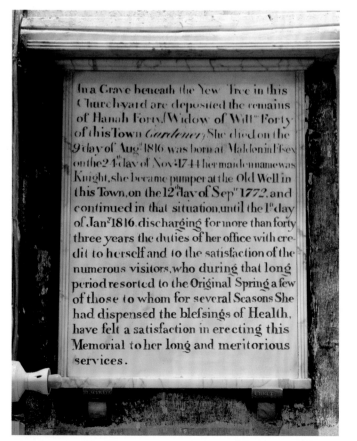

Then, probably on 11 June 1789, she wrote to the Marchioness from Forthampton:

> I learn by the Papers we are not to be honoured by Royal visitors in our Neighbourhood; this I am glad of, as it always seemed a useless scheme though I believe it was dictated by

Perhaps the long memorial plaque in the parish church about Hanah Forty, widow, was inspired by the even longer one about Captain Skillicorne. Hanah Forty was born in Maldon, and married Will Forty, gardener. She was appointed 'pumper' to the Old Well on 12 September 1772 – the precision is interesting. As such, she would have served the royal family when they took the waters. She continued to 'pump' for forty-three years, until the end of 1815, and died eight months later. She was buried under a yew tree in the churchyard. 'Satisfied' customers to whom she dispensed the blessings of health erected the memorial.

PHOTOGRAPH: CARNEGIE, 2009

Earl Fauconberg's house on Bayshill was a tall, thin building, with behind it some smaller buildings which may have existed before the earl's development of the site. Fanny Burney gives a graphic description of the difficulty of accommodating the king's household, and the whole town was brought into service, but informality was the keynote of the visit. Earl Fauconberg and his wife both suffered ill-health, and, like the king, it has to be admitted that the waters did not cure them, although perhaps may have prolonged their lives a little. While a number of houses in Bayshill carry Fauconberg's name, Bayshill House was replaced with what for Cheltenham is a relatively unusual red brick building called Sidney Lodge, erected by Baron Ferrières in 1860.

good nature; the Cheltenham People much wished it, though only for a week or ten days (thinking, why I do not know) it might remove the odium they lie under. This is certain, the place has been thinner than for some seasons; and a Lady of my acquaintance in London, who is coming down there says she can hardly get over her apprehensions; though the faculty assure her, she has nothing to apprehend. In short there is no accounting for whims and fancies, which though they appear like affectation, do really produce serious anxiety in some minds.

Is there here a suggestion that the king's visit and his continuing illness had not helped the cause of the spa, or was there an infection such as smallpox in the town? The effect of the royal visit can easily be exaggerated, though there is no doubting the immediate publicity which the king's visit brought. Information was published in the *Morning Post*, and the *Gentleman's Magazine* included many details of the visit in the volume covering the second half of the year 1788.

But the king was not restored to health, and once recovered, he did not return to Cheltenham, as local people hoped (which contradicts the view that they were entirely uninterested in the spa and its visitors, as Butler's correspondent had indicated) but instead took sea air at Weymouth, where he returned a number of times. Even in 1788 the number of visitors to Cheltenham was tiny when compared with Bath, which it is estimated had about 10,000 visitors as early as 1766.[63] Subscriptions to the Cheltenham Pump Room were between 500 and 600 in the 1740s,[64] and were building up from 1786 but, as Mary Yorke suggested, actually fell immediately after the king's visit. Ruff's record of the number of visitors was presumably based on subscribers at the Wells or to the Assembly Rooms. There were quite large variations from year to year.

Numbers of visitors to Cheltenham

Year	No.	Year	No.
1780	374	1786	1,140
1781	500	1787	1,320
1782	460	1788	1,500
1783	560	1789	860
1784	650	1790	1,100
1785	910	1791	1,350
		1792	1,560

Source: Ruff, *The History of Cheltenham* (1803) p. 124.

He suggested an average of 1,700 visitors a year between 1793 and 1800; 1,860 visitors in 1801; and in 1802 for the first time visitors exceeded 2,000. The size of Cheltenham's population helps to explain the relatively small numbers: there simply were not enough houses in which visitors could stay. Bath had about 23,000 inhabitants in 1801, Cheltenham and its outlying hamlets a mere 3,000. Weymouth was bigger than Cheltenham, with a population in 1801 of 6,454 including Portland, or 4,835 in Weymouth itself.

In fact, this was just what appealed to George III, who liked a country retreat rather than a big city. Bath Corporation could not tolerate their much longer established and more extensive facilities and amenities being neglected by the royal visitor to spas and resorts – the mayor led a deputation which went to Cheltenham to invite the king to visit Bath, but they did not persuade him. Not for a hundred years would Cheltenham's population rival that of Bath – in 1901 both were close to 53,000.[65] The town's attraction in the eighteenth century was precisely its exclusive, sober and quiet style, which contrasted with the busy and rakish character of Bath.

An unusual small town

The year after George III came to Cheltenham, John Wilkes was granted a royal patent to publish a national directory, and the first parts of the *Universal British Directory* appeared a year later.[66] Cheltenham was in volume 2, probably compiled in 1792 and issued in 1793. The prospectus claimed that the *Directory* covered every 'city, town and principal village in England and Wales, in each of which the gentlemen, clergy, tradesmen and persons occupying official departments are correctly entered and methodically arranged'. In practice, Wilkes relied on local contributors as well as paid researchers, and the published material was not completely uniform. The *Directory* also had lists of mails, post coaches, stages, wagons and common carriers. Few towns had a directory by 1791 – indeed, 1,500 of the 1,600 places included in the *Universal British Directory* had never appeared in one before. A small national directory had been published by Bailey in 1784, but it did not include Cheltenham among Gloucestershire towns.[67]

Most entries in the *Universal British Directory* were of named individuals, with only a few businesses. It was organised under the headings of gentry, clergy, physic, law and traders; there is an occasional overlap in names in the various categories. Gloucester had 576 entries, Cirencester 207, Tewkesbury 188, Cheltenham 127 and Winchcombe 86. Its coverage of Cheltenham may have represented between a quarter and a fifth of all the households in the town.[68] Each place was introduced with a description. Cheltenham, 'deservedly celebrated for its mineral waters', was 'a handsome, well-built town' mainly consisting of one mile-long street. Attention was drawn to the long gardens behind the houses, giving it a 'great beauty'. There was a description of the walk to the well itself and of the two buildings there, the library on the right and breakfast room on the left which occasionally became a ballroom. Nearby, Cleeve Hill 'raises its awful head, clothed almost to the summit with hedge rows of elm-trees, which enclose corn-fields, arable lands, and orchards', a very different prospect from that of the twenty-first century. One aspect of the town is notable: even before the nineteenth-century expansion, nearly a third (32 per cent) of those named were gentry, more than other Gloucestershire towns, and significantly more than Cirencester, Tewkesbury or Winchcombe. Even in the county town only a fifth were gentry, although the cathedral meant that there was a good number of eminent clergy and lawyers. Not all Cheltenham gentry were constantly resident; John Yorke at Arle Court and the Earl of Fauconberg, for instance, mainly lived in London and their Cheltenham houses were holiday homes.

Cheltenham also had a larger proportion of inhabitants engaged in the occupations which catered to affluent residents. As well as two bankers, four attorneys, three surgeons and physicians and five clergymen, the *Directory* lists a lady keeping a boarding school, a jeweller and goldsmith, a manager of the theatre and a master of ceremonies, seventeen retailers of food, including a wine merchant, and thirteen selling or making clothes, including a peruke-maker. The compiler of the Cheltenham entry did not notice those engaged in the traditional occupations of a market town, such as shoemakers, nor did he mention any farmers. A substantial number of freeholders was noted, 39 in all, who had the potential to develop their gardens and fields as the numbers of visitors increased. There were 42 inhabitants letting lodgings, twenty of whom were classed as gentry, showing, as Hembry noted, an elastic concept of gentry status.[69] In Bath, 91 people offered lodgings out of a list of names eight times larger than Cheltenham's.

Percentages in particular categories in the Universal British Directory *(1792/93)*

	gentry	clergy	physic	law	miscellaneous professional	trades	total named
Cheltenham	32	4	2	3	5	54	127
Cirencester	14	2	2	3	1	78	207
Gloucester	21	7	3	3	2	66	576
Tewkesbury	13	2	2	3	2	79	188
Winchcombe	6	4	2		1	87	86

As towns became more prosperous, so the tertiary sector of employment, the service sector, expanded and the food and textile processing trades in relative terms declined.[70] While the *Universal British Directory* does not give a strong basis for generalising, it suggests that Cheltenham had a profile indicative of rising prosperity. Winchcombe was described as 'a populous town, but carries on very little trade, owing in a great measure to the badness of the roads in its vicinity, which are by far the worst in the country'. Improvement of the roads was a function of the amount of traffic and so of the opportunities to make a turnpike pay; it was something of a vicious circle.

Percentages in sectors in the Universal British Directory

	Secondary	Tertiary
Cheltenham	54	14
Cirencester	78	9
Gloucester	79	8
Tewkesbury	66	14
Winchcombe	87	7

A few years later, in 1800, Cheltenham's first local directory was published by J. Shenton, whose printing shop was on the north side of High Street in Counsellor's Alley, nearly opposite the parish church. The *Cheltenham Directory* was sold at Mr Buckle's stationer's shop in the Street. It ranged more widely through the trades of the town, but was confined strictly to the town itself, so gentlemen's houses outside the area of the main street were not included. The *Directory* gave specific addresses for those listed, and indicated where lodgings were available. It is not easy to analyse. As the list was made geographically, people were named more than once if they occupied more than one property, and only where properties were adjacent was this sometimes clarified, but the similarity of surname alone is not enough to assume duplication. Some men were given several trades; they included a tailor, salesman and wine dealer; a grocer and postmaster; a hairdresser and dealer in hats, gloves, perfumery etc.; and a cooper and carrier. Fifteen women had a business, and nine businesses are listed in their own

Griffiths prepared a fine plate of the Well Walk for his *History of Cheltenham*, first published in 1826. The elm trees were about 100 years old, and made an impressive and shady walk. He captured it just before the Bayshill Company was about to build villas in the area, and the trees were sacrificed.

BY COURTESY OF ERIC MILLER

THE ROYAL OR ORIGINAL WELL WALK, CHELTENHAM.

Printed & Published by S.Y.Griffith & C.ᵒ Chronicle Office, Cheltenham.

The *Plough*, *George*, *Fleece*, *Crown*, and *Lamb* were the five hotels in Cheltenham listed by Ruff in 1803: 'at the first four good chaises and horses are kept ... The Plough drives to the King's Head, and the George to the Bell in Gloucester.' Rowe waxed lyrical about the food and the wine at The Lamb. He said it stood in the High Street on the north side, close to *The George*, and about where the 'old rickety Shambles' had been.

GLOUCESTERSHIRE LIBRARIES

right, rather than under the names of individuals. Public buildings such as the market house, the two ballrooms, nonconformist meeting houses and theatres were noted.

An 'L' (for 'lets lodgings') was placed against 156 names and addresses in the 1800 *Directory*; the 42 lodging houses in the *Universal British Directory* may therefore have been an understatement. Could the number of suitable houses have increased in nine years as rapidly as the figures appear to indicate? A handful of people had more than one lodging house, most notably Mr Harward, an important entrepreneur in the early development of the town. He had started to build the Colonnade in 1791, the same year that the colonnade in Bath was begun. It was probably inspired either by the Bristol Hotwells or by the Pantiles at Tunbridge Wells, and Earl Fauconberg laid the foundation stone. Here, Harward had three lodging houses, with another three at the corner of the churchyard, and one in the Street. Mr Lambert had four lodging houses in St George's Place, where he also had his coach houses and stables, but he lived in the High Street. Some 22 people owned two lodging houses each. Many women let lodgings, seven of whom were 'Miss' and thirty-four 'Mrs'. Three premises were described as' board and lodging' or 'boarding', but were not marked with an 'L'; presumably they were guesthouses rather than holiday houses or apartments. There were also fourteen other addresses where visitors could have been accommodated: six inns, the *George* which was both inn and hotel, the *Plough* hotel, and six public houses.

Looked at from the point of view of premises rather than individuals, and excluding the seven public buildings, a picture emerges of a large tertiary sector in Cheltenham at this date

– more than the *Universal British Directory* suggests. This is partly because of the inclusion of no fewer than forty laundresses and clear starchers, suggestive of the status and style of Cheltenham visitors and inhabitants. The only people listed in primary occupations were eight men and one woman who were gardeners. The secondary sector was not of major importance, either. Cheltenham no longer appears as a typical market town serving a rural hinterland. Few occupations were connected with agriculture, such as blacksmith, saddler or harness maker, and those few could have served the coach and carriage trade rather than farmers in the area. There were twelve shoemakers and one who was also the constable.

Sectors in the Cheltenham Directory, 1800

	Primary	Secondary	Tertiary	'Gentry'
Number	9	87	140	110
Percentage	3	25	41	32

Shenton's description of Cheltenham included the significant comment that 'there is no particular manufactory in the place, and but little trade in the winter; the chief dependance of the inhabitants is on their lodgings, and the business that is done by the nobility and gentry that resort here'. In this it was like other holiday resorts. The picture of Cheltenham and its society is one of some sophistication.

The 'gentry' included twelve 'esquires' and two 'Hon. ladies'. Samuel Harward was catering for this clientele. He was a man of education and some capital. Between 1760 and 1775 he printed a large number of chapbooks in Tewkesbury and in 1790 generously subscribed for 100 copies of W. Dyde's *History and antiquities of Tewkesbury*.[71] As a printer in Gloucester he contributed to Butler's *Guide* to Cheltenham. At that time he was proprietor of a circulating library in Cheltenham, opened three years earlier. He hired out harpsichords, pianofortes, and other musical instruments, could arrange for them to be tuned, and also sold patent medicines. He was one of the first Paving Commissioners in 1786.

Before 1800 he was investing in Cheltenham property, owning seven lodging houses, including those in his newly built Colonnade (where he also had a circulating library), and a house in the High Street where he ran his business as a bookseller, stationer, and printer and had a second circulating library where daily newspapers could be read. In 1803 his library in the Colonnade was commended by Ruff for the variety and standard of the books but criticised for its lack of organisation, 'the majesty of Lord Bacon, in a quarto dress, insulted by the last duodecimo edition of a modern novel'. Harward died in 1809, but his land would be further developed by relatives in the 1820s.

THE ATTRACTIONS OF CHELTENHAM

The building that
now houses the
Playhouse Theatre
in Cheltenham
was erected early
in the nineteenth
century by Henry
Thompson as a suite
of fourteen warm
medicinal baths
and one large cold
bath, together with
a manufactory for
the production of
Cheltenham salts. It
was then known as
Montpellier Baths.
In 1899, in what
was the heyday
of Cheltenham
Borough Council's
demonstration of
its newly acquired
status, it purchased
the baths and
placed its also
newly acquired
coat of arms on the
decorative central
stone feature above
the entrance.

PHOTOGRAPH: CARNEGIE,
2010

The spa waters acted as the point of attraction, drawing society to Cheltenham rather than to another country retreat, but there were at least two other aspects to Cheltenham's attractiveness. In the provision of social facilities – ballrooms, assembly rooms for concerts and plays, cards, billiards, public breakfasts, theatre, and tea rooms – the town could hardly rival Bath, which had developed much earlier as a centre for fashionable society; Bath's only rival was Tunbridge Wells.[72] Nonetheless, these are a clue to a notable increase in the number of people taking holidays in England during the eighteenth century. Celia Fiennes had shown the way as an early exponent of travel. She had started her journeys in 1685 'to regain my health by variety and change of air and exercise' as she said in a preface to her manuscript description of her travels.[73] There was a growing interest in the 'picturesque' and the 'past', even before the French and Napoleonic wars cut off access to the continent – George III was a keen and patriotic sightseer. In any case, holidays in England appealed to the new 'middling' classes who were not as wealthy as the aristocracy but enjoyed incomes which allowed them leisure. Londoners of means, who did not or could not afford a country estate, sought to leave the smoke and heat of the summer months and take lodgings in a town such as Cheltenham. The smallness of the town was part of its attraction, as visitors were not surrounded with large numbers of poorer people.[74] The scenery around, increasingly regarded as being of special charm and quality, and viewed with a Romantick eye, added to the attraction.

Cheltenham offered both town and country pursuits. Holidaymakers looked for ways of occupying their time, and a spa offered an extension of the activities of the London 'Season'. In Cheltenham, according to Shenton, the season was from 1 June to 1 October. During these months, tradesmen from London and Bath opened shops in Cheltenham and the spa town provided activities for the idle – for example, two billiard rooms where the '*ennui* of a dull

Aesculapius (*left*), the god of healing and medicine, is one of three figures on the front pediment of Pittville Pump Room; he holds what looks to be a baseball bat, but is presumably his traditional staff. The god symbolises the hoped-for medicinal power of the spa water in Cheltenham. The inspiration, as for a number of new buildings in Cheltenham at the time, was Stuart and Revett's *Antiquities of Athens*, published between 1762 and 1830. The prominent Bath sculptor, Lucius Gahagan, carved the statue; the other two figures on the pediment represent Hygeia (*centre*) and Hippocrates (*right*). By 1937 the statues were badly eroded and were taken down. R. L. Boulton & Sons Ltd made copies in 1965, financed by private donations.

PHOTOGRAPH: CARNEGIE, 2009

morning may not be felt' and backgammon could also be played. For younger folk, the country town or spa town offered an opportunity for finding a marriage partner, which was why a master of ceremonies was so valuable; he organised the social contacts. As Ruff noted in 1800, Cheltenham provided 'a happy mixture of London elegance and rural delight'.[75] Moreover, Cheltenham was cheaper than other resorts, particularly Bath.[76] Edward Pigot, who kept a diary of his travels which is now in an American library, noted that in Cheltenham 'a person that is fond of public places will be very much pleased here and at a very cheap rate'.[77]

The French wars, with the consequent loss of opportunity for travel on the Continent, gave impetus to the development of many English holiday resorts. In the longer term, the king's visit may have given some notable Cheltenham entrepreneurs the notion that there was a development opportunity. But it was limited until land suitable for building became available. The earl of Essex, who owned the Rectory lands and tithes in Cheltenham was, like Lord Fauconberg, a lord of the bedchamber. He would probably have supported the idea of George III's visit, noticing that it could lead to rising land prices and development opportunities, but he died on 5 March 1799 before any real expansion of the town had taken place. It was the decision of his son to sell the Cheltenham property that opened the way to the really significant growth of the town.[78]

As an artistic device the sculpted female figures that act as architectural columns – known as caryatids – date back to ancient Greece and Phoenicia. At the beginning of the nineteenth century Lord Elgin removed one ancient, armless example from the Acropolis, which was housed in the British Museum. This might well have served as one inspiration for Cheltenham's fine set of 32 caryatids which decorate the shops in Montpellier Walk, adjoining the first major spa development, of Montpellier, on land purchased by Henry Thompson at the turn of the nineteenth century. It was many years before the full array of fashionable buildings here was completed. All 32 caryatids are slightly different.

PHOTOGRAPH: CARNEGIE, 2010

CHAPTER SEVEN

POWER

A T THE BEGINNING OF THE EIGHTEENTH CENTURY, power within the ancient parish of Cheltenham, which included Charlton Kings, was both dispersed and distant. From the agricultural point of view, the parish consisted of a town, a village, and five hamlets; the pattern of landownership and of occupation varied according to the type of settlement but in most the land was much divided, and few people had a dominating share. For political influence, particularly in parliament, it was ownership that mattered. An owner or freeholder with property worth forty shillings (£2) or more could vote in county elections, while a member of parliament had to own land worth £600 if aspiring to represent a county, and £300 if a borough. Crucially in the eighteenth and early nineteenth centuries, if enough landowners were in agreement, sweeping powers could be obtained from parliament to alter or remake roads and collect tolls, cut canals, create railways, and enclose the land. Enclosure was the single most important factor in the nineteenth-century development of Cheltenham, and it was governed entirely by the power and influence which ownership brought.

When George III visited Cheltenham at the end of the 1780s there were at least 160 proprietors in the township alone, most of them with small plots of land. There may have been economic oppression of the labourers by the farmers, and in the town itself of the labourers by nascent 'capitalists', but neither group had overall authority, either to control or to change the structure. Only the owner of the tithes of the parish could exert a large influence through enclosure by Act of Parliament, and it was the decision of the earl of Essex to sell the Cheltenham tithes and rectory land which opened the way for a new and more thrusting entrepreneurship.

In all the townships in the parish, the medieval system of landholding had been whittled away over several centuries in a piecemeal fashion. Agreements had been made to allow small amounts of land to be enclosed with a fence or hedge, or land to be exchanged in order to give each owner a larger plot. Enclosure by Act of Parliament was an altogether more drastic and wholesale reorganisation of the remaining open and common fields in a parish. Nationally, the number of Enclosure Acts increased markedly in the late eighteenth century. An act gave authority to commissioners to make new roads, to create or redraw field boundaries, and to decide which pieces of land should be allotted to each owner. The ordinary tenants who cultivated the land were largely irrelevant to the process, and might be greatly disadvantaged by it. Enclosure by Act of Parliament affected Cheltenham, Alstone and Arle townships, together with Leckhampton and Prestbury, but not Westal, Naunton and Sandford, nor Charlton Kings and Swindon.

The occupiers of land – that is, those who actually worked the farms, though not necessarily owning them – had power and influence in the administration of parish affairs. Those farming more substantial amounts of land, or with larger trading interests, naturally had the most influence. Not least, they were the more substantial ratepayers who financed local services. Smallholders, however numerous, could not have the same influence because they paid less. The ratepayers met in the vestry of the parish church to exercise their responsibilities, and hence their meetings, and the institution itself, became known as 'the vestry'. Their earliest task, dating back to the Middle Ages, was the maintenance of the main part of the church building, though not the chancel which was the responsibility of the rector, whether lay or clerical. A rate of so many pence or shillings could be levied by the churchwardens on occupiers

Imperial Square is one of the most important early developments in Cheltenham, with its large garden beside the Promenade. The east and north sides of the square were built in the mid-1830s, on land south of the Chelt that had been purchased by Samuel Harward as the town began to attract more and more visitors. From the gardens, the terrace on the north side is now obscured by the Town Hall and by constant traffic. These were lodging houses, now mainly converted into offices. The balconies display the frequently used 'heart and honeysuckle' motif (*see also* the photograph on page 229) cast by the Carron Company, and possibly designed by Robert Adam.

PHOTOGRAPH: CARNEGIE, 2010

according to the value of their land, houses or goods. Repairs to the fabric were necessary from time to time, as was reorganisation of the interior of the church to fit changing procedures for public worship. But from the mid-sixteenth century the parish was also required by parliament to organise the maintenance of the roads and to give relief to the poor. The vestry was empowered to raise rates for these purposes, too. The county justices of the peace exercised a limited supervision of the vestry, which continued to carry out these duties while *ad hoc* and specific authorities were being created by Act of Parliament to look after other parts of local affairs. Thus, the powers granted to a body of commissioners to improve Cheltenham's roads applied only to the small area of the town itself – the vestry supervised the remainder.

There was another source of authority in Cheltenham though with limited power – the lord of the manor and the manor court; it was a remarkable survival of the medieval manorial system even after enclosure had removed the manor's remaining agricultural functions, and despite rapid urbanisation in the early nineteenth century. The lord of the manor had some influence on the provision of market facilities in the town but, more importantly, purchasers and sellers of copyhold property had to go to the manor court to register every change of 'tenant'. Many properties in Cheltenham parish consisted of both copyhold and freehold land. When, in 1832, parliament made some modest changes to the methods by which members of parliament were elected, copyholders were given the right to vote in the same way as freeholders. There were significant numbers in Cheltenham and more copyhold voters than freehold in Charlton Kings.

LAND OWNERSHIP

Like the Hearth Tax in the previous century, records of the Land Tax survive for the whole country in the later eighteenth century. A tax based on the annual value of land was imposed in 1692 on 'proprietors'; also taxed was the value of stock-in-trade, and income from tithes and from various types of government employment: three officers of excise in Cheltenham were taxed on the profits (or income) of their office. By 1697 this new tax was specifically called the 'Land Tax', reflecting the predominant source of wealth. Valuations were made by two local assessors, who wrote down the appropriate amount for each person judged 'able' to pay.[1] Property valued at less than 20 shillings (£1) was exempt. Though assessments were subjective, contemporaries had a fair notion of values, and amounts could be adjusted for a variety of reasons (including, less objectively, family connections or political expediency). Initially the tax was set at 4*s.* in the pound, but after a few years the amount to be raised by each county was fixed centrally, and that amount subdivided locally between parishes. From 1780 a list of those assessed had to be deposited with the clerk of the peace for each county, and hence most records begin at that date, including those for Gloucestershire. From 1772 'occupiers' of property were also recorded, helping to identify particular holdings. Locally, all the 1780 returns included the names of occupiers except that for Charlton Kings (where the information is included in that for 1783). The Land Tax is not a perfect survey of land-ownership: it does not include by any means all owners, and furthermore 'proprietors' listed were not always owners – some were leaseholders or tenants for lives. Nonetheless, the lists are a valuable way of gauging the general situation within each particular parish and tithing.[2]

Important differences between communities in the Cheltenham area are clear. There were two main groups. Cheltenham and Charlton Kings had many small proprietors. This, as noted earlier, made large-scale development more difficult but, on the other hand, cottage-building on a small scale could readily be undertaken. In Cheltenham, development was always possible by crowding inhabitants in small cottages along the length of the burgage plots. In the second group of tithings, proprietors were not so numerous but on average owned more land, most notably in Leckhampton, which might be described as a 'closed' parish, because more than half the land was controlled by Henry Norwood esquire, the lord of the manor. There, opportunities for work and for speculative building were correspondingly limited.

The large number of proprietors in Cheltenham township reflected the quantity of urban property, much of which was small in size and relatively low-rated. The tax lists also show that, in a number of cases, more than one house was owned by a proprietor – perhaps several small terraced tenements in a row, but sometimes a group of highly rated houses. Even before George III came to the town, there was a surprising number of the latter, which it would be reasonable to assume were 'villas' or large houses rather than land. William Skillicorne and William Meekings were among the higher rated, as were the officers of excise. There was no dominating proprietor of land. The rectory tithes of the earl of Essex were given a rating assessment of over £18, rather more than the next twelve taxpayers whose assessments ranged between £5 and £11, but Essex was not a major landowner, although his tithes were to lead to a big land allotment when Cheltenham tithing was enclosed. The practice in Gloucestershire of compensating the tithe owner at enclosure by allotting him land created new holdings, sometimes of considerable size.

Proprietors in the Land Tax in 1780 (1783 for Charlton Kings)

Tithing	Total tax paid	Proprietors paying tax	Proprietors responsible for about 50% of total	Proprietors rated at under £1
Alstone	£47	40	5	26
Arle	£77	35	5	13
Cheltenham	£228	162	15	105
Westal	£59	19	2	10
Charlton Kings	£210	83	4	48
Leckhampton	£94	12	1	1
Prestbury	£119	53	2	35
Swindon	£53	18	3	7

Arle House, shown on this plate prepared for S. Y. Griffiths and Co. in 1826, was built about 1806 by the young John Gregory Welch. On the left, however, there is an older and more modest house, known a few years later as 'Gregory's' or Home Farm. The Gregory's had farmed in Arle for several centuries; four men of this name were in the 1608 Arle Muster list. The last Gregory was buried in 1782. His daughter Mary had married Walter Welch of Brimpsfield, and John Gregory Welch, born in 1775, was their eldest son. He built the new Arle House following his marriage in 1797 to a wealthy wife, but the building and an extravagant life style bankrupted him. It was his son who benefited from consolidation of the family's holdings at the enclosure in 1835, among which was a farmstead and 24¾ acres called Aysters Way Orchard, the basis of Hester's Way.

The tithings of Alstone, Arle and Westal in Cheltenham parish were clearly distinguishable to the local administrators at the time, though less so to historians subsequently. The fields of Alstone and Arle were partly intermingled and there were numerous owners. Corpus Christi College and Mr Critchet were the two more significant proprietors in Alstone, but neither had a dominating share; William Skillicorne, who was so important in the early development of the spa, had quite a modest estate. John Yorke of Arle Court, who had inherited his estate from a Lygon heiress, was the most important proprietor in Arle. He paid one-fifth of the tithing's total Land Tax; John Gregory was next, contributing half as much. In this tithing there was a large number of smallholders. Westal, Naunton and Sandford were not clearly defined but were dominated by one large owner; John Delabere was responsible for 40 per cent of the tithing's tax; William Prinn of Charlton Kings was a second important proprietor, though paying less than half as much. John Delabere had earlier purchased land and tithes from the earl of Essex, and his consolidated land was to be important in opening the possibility of building development. Charlton Kings had a larger number of small proprietors, and here William Prinn was an important though not dominating proprietor, who paid a little over a quarter of the parish's tax.

Information about occupiers in the Land Tax is more problematic. Tenants were less important to the tax collectors than proprietors, 'occupiers' might further sub-let the property, and not all the tenants of any one proprietor were named; for example 'John Greenwood and others' was recorded for some property of John Yorke in Arle. Such entries are treated as referring to the named person, who was perhaps the most important. Furthermore, if a tenant occupied land or houses belonging to more than one proprietor, his name is scattered through the returns and entries have to be gathered together, and similar names may be mistakenly conflated. In Arle 'Mr John Gregory' and 'Mr Gregory of Alstone' were distinguished but less prominent people with the same name may not have been. Holdings sometimes crossed township boundaries: the Richard Hooper who appears in the lists for Alstone, Cheltenham, Leckhampton, and Westal was very probably the same man.

Occupiers in the Land Tax in 1780/1783

Tithing	Number listed	Occupiers of larger properties (rates equal to about 50% of total)	Occupiers of property rated under £1
Alstone	48	5	36
Arle	30	3	12
Cheltenham	134	14	77
Westal	19	2	6
Charlton Kings	73	9	36
Leckhampton	16	2	2
Prestbury	45	4	21
Swindon	26	3	13

Some larger landowners had more than one major tenant: John Yorke in Alstone leased his land to John Greenwood and William Davies, and in Leckhampton the Norwood estate was divided between Henry Norwood himself and Edmund Ballinger. More commonly, larger farmers occupied the land of more than one proprietor, assembling strips scattered through the common fields into more compact blocks. Josiah Cook and William Laver in Alstone, for instance, both held land from three proprietors; in Charlton Kings, John Lawrence was the tenant of six proprietors, Edward Greenwood of four and William Buckle of three. Such tenants were a small minority numerically, but were significant figures.

In Cheltenham, the three men occupying the highest-rated properties were Samuel Aston, who leased the tithes from the earl of Essex in Cheltenham, Alstone, Arle, and Charlton Kings, William Meekings and Thomas Buckle. Only William Meekings, 'gentleman', was listed in the *Universal British Directory*. In the *Cheltenham Directory* for 1800 there were two Mrs Meekings living in Meekings Passage and one in High Street; Thomas Buckle was a stationer, perfumer and tea dealer, and ran the circulating library; and Samuel Aston was again not listed. Several other people paying over £5 Land Tax can be identified from these directories: Mr Pope, a surgeon; Thomas Snelus, fishmonger and distributor of the *Gloucester Journal*; and John Hayward, Charles Hathaway and William Benfield, 'gentlemen' with no stated occupation. This lends support to the idea that larger assessments represent big houses. William Benfield was one of the occupiers of William Skillicorne's property, as was Mr Harward, but Skillicorne himself did not occupy property in Cheltenham. Thomas Hughes, who at one time leased the Old Well, appears as both proprietor and occupier of his property, the Assembly Room which he had built in High Street. The vicar, the Reverend John Chester, was one of a middling group of taxpayers.

A nineteenth-century print of Cheltenham parish church shows it before restoration and the removal of the railings on the left which appear to enclose some table-top tombs, and also before the cross was moved to a different location near the rose window. The old base for the cross appears to exist still where it was shown in this picture. A chimney provides for a fire in the vestry where the ratepayers held their meetings.

ST MARY'S CHURCH, CHELTENHAM.

The Vestry

From the time of Henry VIII's reforms, the church had little power in Cheltenham. The curate did not have the authority of a rector or vicar, he was not a landowner, and neither did he collect tithes from his parishioners. The rectory was simply a source of income for a layman. The much greater influence of the Reverend Francis Close in the earlier nineteenth century was the result of his personal style and popularity as a preacher, while the contemporary surge in church-building and educational provision which he stimulated was a voluntary movement, described in Chapter 9. But the vestry was the local government of each parish, and it continued to carry out its traditional tasks into the nineteenth century.

The churchyard had not been the vestry's concern because it had belonged to the impropriator, and in 1799 was part of the rectory property purchased by Joseph Pitt. As the population of Cheltenham grew, there was an urgent need for a larger burial ground, and in 1812 the vestry asked Pitt to sell some adjacent land to enlarge the churchyard. Subsequently the vestry was able to purchase the old churchyard as well, but the extension was soon found to be inadequate. At the same time there was a national campaign to prevent burial within the built-up area of a town, on grounds of public health. In 1829 His Majesty's Commissioners for the building of new churchyards required Cheltenham to address the problem, an early pointer to increasing control over local government by central government. Some land for a new burial ground was accordingly purchased at the lower end of the High Street and a small chapel erected. Thirty years later the Paving Commissioners, who had some of the functions of a town government, purchased land for a much larger cemetery at Oakley.[3]

The vestry's duty of caring for the poor, placed on the parish by several Acts of Parliament in the sixteenth century, culminating in the great Poor Law Act of 1601, was not only most onerous (because the needs of the poor were constant) but, in the eighteenth century, was increasingly expensive. The vestry annually elected – from among the ratepayers – overseers of the poor, whose responsibility it was to implement and manage the system. From relatively simple beginnings, involving the payment to paupers of small sums of money in relief, or finding them some paid work, the financial burden steadily increased, especially at times of general difficulty when harvests were poor or corn prices rose, and bread became correspondingly dear. Poor rates were a heavy tax on parishioners and as they increased, rates were levied several times a year. Occasionally the justices of the peace ordered the overseers to relieve some poor person to whom they had refused relief, but generally the system operated here, as elsewhere, largely on local decision-making.

In 1757 Cheltenham vestry purchased a house to serve as a workhouse, where the possibly workshy (the 'able-bodied paupers') could be placed and made to earn something; for example, pin-making was tried in 1796. The vestry resolved that only 'extraordinary cases' should be relieved 'out of the workhouse', a test which was clearly intended to deter the poor from applying for relief.[4] In 1809 a purpose-built workhouse was erected.[5] The number and needs of the poor nonetheless increased, particularly because of the widespread economic and social hardship caused by the prolonged wars with France from 1793 onwards. In 1812, therefore, the vestry decided to experiment with a salaried Guardian of the Poor, and a salaried Governor of the Workhouse, to be appointed by the justices of the peace. This solution had been encouraged across the country by Gilbert's Act of 1782. According to Griffith, writing in 1818, this did improve the finances of the parish, and in 1819 Cheltenham adopted the Sturges Bourne Act, which allowed parishes also to employ a salaried overseer and to elect a committee to manage the poor. The rates did not fall.

The problem was a national one, and after an enquiry into the various ways in which parishes were managing poor relief, the Poor Law Amendment Act was passed in 1834. This removed the duty from individual parishes, and created Poor Law Unions, groups of parishes with a collective responsibility. The unions were managed by elected Boards of Guardians, a certain number being elected by each parish involved. A central Poor Law Board would supervise and coordinate the implementation of the new law. The legislation of 1834, and the policy enforced by the Poor Law Board, was based on the principle of strict deterrence: relief was not to be available to the poor in their own homes, and assistance meant entry into the workhouse, a policy Cheltenham had tried almost a century before. Local workhouses were closed, and each union was to build a new central workhouse ('the union house'). Cheltenham became the centre of a rural union which included Charlton Kings, Leckhampton, Swindon, Prestbury, Uckington, Badgeworth, Shurdington and Great Witcomb. At first the Board met in Cheltenham workhouse, and its new workhouse was opened in 1841.[6]

Another duty laid on the parish in the mid-sixteenth century was maintenance of the highways. Under legislation of 1554, each year highways surveyors were elected, and they organised the amateur efforts of the parish labourers in filling up potholes and digging ditches. In a large parish like Cheltenham, individual townships were required to maintain their own roads. As the built-up area of Cheltenham spread outwards from the central High Street, there were disputes about who should maintain certain roads. The landholders in Westal, Sandford and Naunton were sometimes in trouble for this reason. Pearson Thompson took them to court about Hatherley Lane in 1831. When the common and open fields of a township were enclosed, an important concern was setting out new roads and determining which owners of adjoining lands were to make, and maintain, them. The same responsibility attached to landowners even where enclosure occurred through agreement. In 1819, for example, the inhabitants of Westal tithing objected to being required by the surveyor to mend Well Lane and the road through Sandford field from Old Bath Road to the new Bath Road. They won the argument, because the owners of newly enclosed land adjoining the road had not put it in good repair.[7]

The vestry also had responsibility for the drainage and cleansing of roads not under the jurisdiction of the Paving Commission. In 1821 it appointed its own commission to report on the condition of these highways, and this provided evidence of some very dirty streets. Rutland Street, which was to be a problem for the next hundred years, was particularly singled

The constable and the vestry had very limited means of disciplining parishioners, but putting a man in the stocks where his jeering neighbours could throw things at him was probably quite effective. Part of Cheltenham's stocks have been preserved in the parish church.
PHOTOGRAPH: CARNEGIE, 2009

out. The task was larger than the vestry could tackle, but an appeal to owners to cooperate in better maintenance was issued.

TURNPIKE TRUSTS

The weakness of the system by which parishes were responsible for their roads was early acknowledged, and from the late seventeenth century more professional road-making was undertaken by turnpike trusts – though only for a limited network of major inter-urban and through roads. In each case a group of local businessmen and gentry combined to secure a private Act of Parliament, giving them powers to form a trust and erect barriers across roads to be improved, collect tolls, and repair or reroute the roads concerned. Each act only lasted for a set number of years, and then had to be renewed. Turnpiking added confusion about who was responsible for highways, though it was a relatively successful way of dealing with the needs of travellers on the main road system.

Nationally, the first road to be turnpiked was the section of the Great North Road (now the A1) south of Peterborough, in 1663. Over the next thirty years other key sections of national trunk routes, linking major provincial centres, were tackled. It is no surprise, therefore, that the first Gloucestershire turnpike was for a road from the county town. An act was passed in 1698 to turnpike the Gloucester to Birdlip road, part of the main London road which went through Lechlade and Abingdon. A road of more significance to Cheltenham was turnpiked in

Before the engineering improvements made by the turnpike trusts in the eighteenth century, roads were often deeply rutted and very muddy. Especially where a road went uphill, heavy rain running down would carry any gravel away. The higher reaches of Sandy Lane, deep-set between banks, illustrate this process today. Prior to the turnpike road being made from Cirencester through Seven Springs to Charlton Kings in 1827, on the line of an older track and also the modern road, Sandy Lane was one of the ways south towards Coberley; as early as 1755–56 it was included in a Turnpike Act. It had earlier been known as Highbreach Lane or the road to the Windarse, which sounds like a description of the hill at this point.

PHOTOGRAPH: AUTHOR, 2009

1723. This was the route from Gloucester up Crickley Hill to Burford and Oxford and thence to London, and it soon became the preferred London route from Gloucester.[8] It allowed major improvements to the coach services from Gloucester to London: travellers to Cheltenham left the Gloucester coach at Puesdown and proceeded to Cheltenham by post-chaise. The first turnpike involving Cheltenham directly was set up by the Tewkesbury Trust and concerned the road through Swindon; an act was passed in 1725 but then lapsed.[9] In 1756, the Gloucester to Cheltenham road was turnpiked, branching off the London road just outside Gloucester at Wootton; a petition to parliament the year before said that the road was nearly impassable to carriages in summer and never passable in winter (though the English have always complained about the roads, and such terminology was almost invariably used in advance of a turnpike Act). In the same year a new Tewkesbury turnpike Act authorised improvement of a number of roads, including the route which started from the Cheltenham Market House in High Street, then went up Harp Lane and over Northfield Hill, through Whittington and Syreford to Puesdown, where it linked with the London road.

In 1764 the Cheltenham turnpikes were effectively separated from the main Tewkesbury trust and a new act was required to continue their turnpiking. It was not passed until 1774. By then, Cheltenham residents were becoming aware of the handicap posed by the difficulties of the link with the Gloucester–London road, and in 1785 an act was promoted for an alternative route past Dowdeswell Court, by Kilkenny and so to the London road; the Act also covered a road to Painswick leading towards Bath which became the New Bath Road. From this date onwards the two earlier turnpikes from Cheltenham, to Piff's Elm towards Tewkesbury and to Puesdown, were included in this trust's responsibilities.

The result of the alternative turnpike road towards Kilkenny, despite the steepness of Dowdeswell Hill, was immediately apparent. In 1781 the first *Cheltenham Guide* made no mention of coaches leaving Cheltenham for London, but noted the stage coach and the diligence leaving every weekday and Saturday from Gloucester; Cheltenham had to be content with one waggon a week going to London. When volume two of the *Universal British Directory* was published about 1793, 'The London coaches and post come in every morning, and go out every afternoon', and the London waggon set out from the *Plough* every Monday morning. By 1803 the daily mail coach called at the *George* and then went on to Gloucester, the 'Old Heavy Coach' arrived daily at the *Lamb*, the 'Original Post Coach' arrived at the *Crown* on Monday, Wednesday and Friday, and the London waggon still ran once a week. From this time road transport steadily increased. The route from Gloucester to London through Cheltenham gradually became the preferred route, and Pigot's *Directory* of 1822 shows more coaches going to London from Cheltenham than from the county town, while the construction of Haw Bridge in 1825 and Mythe Bridge in 1826 aided the growth of Cheltenham but tended to encourage the bypassing of Gloucester.[10]

Although there were improvements in the eighteenth century, their effect should not be exaggerated. William Marshall, who moved to a farmhouse 'near the center of the vale of

Glocester' in 1783 and travelled round the county preparing a report on *The rural economy of Glocestershire* which was dated 1789, was scathing:

> The roads of the vale are shamefully kept. The Parish roads mostly lie in their natural flat state, with the ditches on either side of them full of water to the brim. The toll roads are raised (generally much too high) but even on the sides of these I have seen full ditches ... The road between Glocester and Cheltenham (now become one of the most public roads in the island) is scarcely fit for the meanest of their Majesties' subjects to travel on, AND PAY FOR; and is much less suitable for their Majesties themselves, and their amiable family, to trust their own persons upon.[11]

Such polemical writing was typical of the agriculturalists of the period, but contains more than a grain of truth.

The life of the Cheltenham Trust had been extended in 1806 but in 1824 a new act was necessary to allow some alterations to the routes. Thomas Telford, the greatest road and bridge engineer of the age, had reported that a major road should not go up Dowdeswell Hill. Therefore a new route was engineered through Charlton Kings and from the foot of Dowdeswell Hill to Andoversford, close to the present-day route. Amendments to the turnpike trust's routes, as new residential roads were built, were agreed by parliament in 1831 – for example relating to St Paul's Road, St. Margaret's Road, Swindon Road, and the Old Bath Road. But here, as in many parts of rural England and Wales, competition from the railways drastically undermined the traffic on the turnpike roads from the 1840s onwards. Tolls had to be cut to compete with railway rates, yet the amount of traffic fell sharply. The result was insolvency, and although in 1863 the trust obtained another amending act, it could not survive. In November 1878 it was wound up, and the roads reverted to parochial control.

THE PAVING COMMISSION

PEOPLE AND POWERS

The first stage towards establishing a town government, separate from either manor or parish administration, was an Act of Parliament in 1786 which gave powers to a body of commissioners to pave, light and clean Cheltenham's streets and raise a rate to finance its work.[12] Only parliament could create a new authority with power to raise money from householders, and to override the power of owners with respect to their properties. The act named 58 commissioners, of whom forty can be found in the *Universal British Directory* of 1792–93, who almost certainly lived in Cheltenham, but as the *Directory* did not record Christian names one or two may be mis-identified. At least fifteen were described as gentlemen, and eleven might be regarded as 'pseudo-gentry': five attorneys, four surgeons and apothecaries, and two clergymen, one the master of the grammar school. Thirteen were tradesmen: a baker, two grocers (one also the postmaster), a brewer, builder or ironmonger, butcher, currier, hatter, linen-draper, plumber, printer and bookseller, and saddler.

Other commissioners not in the *Directory* can be identified: the Hon. John Dutton was the son of the lord of the manor, who had recently been created Lord Sherborne; John Delabere was the steward of the manor, and lived in Cheltenham; his son, the Reverend John Delabere, probably lived with him, although he had been appointed vicar of Teynton in 1784; the Reverend Hugh Hughes was the incumbent of Cheltenham; William Skillicorne was the son of the builder of the first Pump Room and Well Walk, and at this date was one of the largest landowners in the town; and Thomas Pope owned the *Plough*. All the commissioners had to be the owners of real estate of £400 or have an income of £40 from rents, so the great majority of Cheltenham inhabitants were not qualified to serve. Although tradesmen were represented in the list, the commission in practice was the organ of the town's gentry or pseudo-gentry. Vacancies were filled by nomination, so the commission was a self-perpetuating oligarchy.

The fourteen men who attended the first meeting on 26 June 1786 at the *Plough* were obviously the keenest advocates for 'improvement', and apart from the two grocers, no other tradesmen were present.[13] John Delabere was chairman, a natural continuation of his role as steward of the manor. Two of the 'gentlemen', Thomas Hughes and William Miller, were the proprietors of the Assembly Rooms, and it is clear that the major driving force behind the scheme for improvements was the desire to make the town more attractive to visitors who might stay in the lodging houses and enjoy the holiday facilities. Larger property owners, with an eye to speculative building, were also probably interested in improvement.

The Paving Act provided for the demolition of the old Market House or Corn Market and the Booth Hall or Butter Cross in High Street and the erection of a new Market House and Butter Cross which were to be vested in the lord of the manor. A total of 120 oil lamps were to be erected in the streets (replaced by gas lights in the High Street in 1818, with power supplied by a private company formed that year), a scavenger was appointed to remove household waste and refuse, and householders were required to remove 'excrescences' and to place their water spouts closer to their houses. Every householder was to pave his frontage as far as the roadway and a surveyor was appointed to see that the work was done properly. The High Street would not become a paved pedestrian precinct, for only the footways were paved and carts and wagons, coaches and carriages continued to pass along the road as before. The street, dusty in summer and muddy in winter, was the responsibility of turnpike trustees. It was already cleansed occasionally by diverting water from the river Chelt to flow along it, and the Commission tried to negotiate the continuation of this practice, but it was subject to interruption because of the unwillingness of the miller at Cambray to stop the flow of water to other mills lower down the stream.[14] A limited area, mainly around High Street, enjoyed these improvements; not all the new houses along the London Road were considered to be within the town, and the lack of defined boundaries to the borough caused considerable dispute which was not settled until 1806.

In 1806 the commissioners obtained a second Act which extended their powers.[15] It coincided with completion of the enclosure of Cheltenham township's open and common fields. The commission was still an unelected oligarchy. The act named a further 71 commissioners to add to those appointed under the first paving act who were still surviving. At the head of the list was Thomas Howard, Viscount Andover, the eldest son of the earl of Suffolk who had purchased land and built Suffolk House.[16] Joseph Pitt, who had purchased the tithes and rectory land in Cheltenham in 1799, and Charles Brandon Trye who had become the owner of Leckhampton Court in 1797, were similarly new landowners in the area. Dr Edward Jenner, who lived in Cheltenham during the season and carried out smallpox vaccination, was a commissioner. Notable are the ten clerics on the list, including the dean of Worcester, Thomas Nash, who was Henry Skillicorne's son-in-law and rector of Salford in Oxfordshire; and Reginald Wynniatt who was rector of Stanton. It was not uncommon for clerics to live in a pleasant town like Oxford or Ludlow and ride out to serve their country churches on Sunday;[17] this may have applied to the Reverend John Delabere, while other town-dwelling clerics, perhaps living in Cheltenham for their health, left their churches to a curate. Most of the enlarged body of commissioners appear to have been merely adding weight rather than being actively involved. Twenty-four men attended the first meeting after the Act; the Reverend Richard Skillicorne, who had inherited the Old Well, Henry Thompson and Charles Brandon Trye were among those present.

The purposes of the Act were to extend the control of the commissioners to new streets, to establish a watch to patrol the streets at night and keep order, and a 'proper and effective Police', and to set up a system of licensing for hackney coaches, chairs, porters and basketmen and basketwomen. It also provided for the sale of the Market Hall. One of the first tasks of the new commissioners was to order the measurement of distances between various points in the town so that an appropriate table of charges for transport could be instituted, which emphasises the importance of the tourist trade in stimulating town improvement. Another early resolution was to build a carriage road linking the intended new Crescent development in Church Meadow, started in 1805 and one of Joseph Pitt's first enterprises, with the 'new well' named after Lord Sherborne which was at the end of the Old Well Walk in the vicinity of Henry Pearson's later Montpellier spa.[18] The road would involve a bridge over the 'brook', as Henry Skillicorne had wanted. There was immediately a debate about whether to build a road from the Colonnade instead, which Thomas Jameson's map of 1809 shows as the projected route. The Commissioners were encouraged to go for this route by the failure of the new well and the opening of the Montpellier Spa in 1808–09; later this route offered the opportunity to link with Samuel Harward's development of The Promenade. The limits of the town were agreed by the new commissioners in November 1806; they resolved that the 'several public wells shall be considered within the limits of the town', although Pitt's new town when it was developed was not included, nor was the Bayshill estate, so depriving the commissioners of valuable rating income.[19] A watch was not set up until 1815.

An Act to allow
the installation
of gas lighting in
Cheltenham was
passed in 1819,
one of the first in
the country. Coal
wharves had sprung
up close to the
tramway to meet the
growing domestic
requirements of
the town, and here
was the natural site
for the Gas Works.
The tramway
carried a significant
amount of coal
until the middle
of the nineteenth
century, and then
railway sidings not
far away took away
its main function.
The photograph,
showing smoke
belching out of
the chimney, one
full gasometer and
one empty one,
was taken in the
twentieth century.
© CHELTENHAM ART
GALLERY AND MUSEUM

There was some further increase in the powers of the Paving Commissioners in 1821. A new act authorised the sale of the existing Market House and the negotiation of a new lease of the tolls. It confirmed the commission's authority to examine the plans of new buildings, which they had started to do in order to control fire risks, and permitted them to widen existing streets. It also clarified the duty of householders in new roads to put down pavements in front of their houses, after which the road became the responsibility of the commission. It also gave the commissioners power to supply gas, but no use was made of this power and a private company continued to supply gas until nationalised in 1948. Similarly the construction of sewers fell naturally into their remit, as they were essential to the cleansing of the streets, but here too the commission failed to act in any significant way. The commission's focus was still the town's roads. Not until 1852 were their powers materially altered, by which time the whole context of urban government had changed.

MARKET BUILDINGS

The project at the top of the commissioners' priorities after the first Paving Act of 1786 was passed was the demolition of the old market buildings, and this was agreed almost immediately. The act had effectively overridden the power of the lord of the manor, who owned the buildings and collected the tolls paid there; his manor court had met in the room over the

Corn Market. The removal of market buildings had taken place in Gloucester some twenty years earlier, and was an aspect of the 'urban renaissance' in many places. It exemplifies the 'rationalisation, commodification, and the construction of a "public sphere"'.[20] Eventually it was agreed to build a new Market House on the site of the old 'Blind House' or prison, to replace that with a new prison on the site of the Pound, and to provide a new Pound for stray animals at the edge of the Marsh. The lord of the manor continued to collect tolls. The new Market House quickly proved inadequate and seems to have been very poorly built, since only twenty years later, in 1808, another was built. This one was more substantial, faced in stone, of three storeys with a room on the top storey for the commissioners' meetings. The lord of the manor agreed to lease the market tolls to the Paving Commission for 21 years. The older Market House was left standing, if not for very long; three years later it fell down.

The population of Cheltenham was growing fast in the early nineteenth century, as was the number of visitors, and correspondingly more produce was brought for sale in the market. For a third time the Paving Commission sought powers to build a new Market Hall as Lord Sherborne was unwilling to agree. There followed long negotiations, at the end of which he consented to buy the existing market building and in turn erect, at his own expense, a new one on a different site further down the High Street. This had a rather unusual entrance design suggesting Indian influence, and was built between 1822 and 1823; it was demolished in 1867. Lord Sherborne collected the tolls, but leased them and the management to Baynham Jones. For

When in 1826 Pruen, Griffiths and Pruen, solicitors, took over the building vacated by Messrs Hartland & Son, bankers, they intended to use it both for their own offices and for a magistrates' office. A local clockmaker, John Denne, suggested that a large, double-sided town clock should be installed outside the Magistrates' Office, and the Town Commissioners took up the idea. Mr Denne was commissioned to build the clock, and it was erected in 1828. A further proposal to light it with gas did not materialise. After 130 years, the thick, zinc-covered beam supporting the clock was found to be completely rotten, and the borough council thought it was too expensive to replace it. In consequence a notable feature of the High Street was lost.

AUTHOR COLLECTION

LEFT

The Muffin Man was a well-known and colourful figure on the streets of Cheltenham about 1830, and a number of drawings were made of him in his beaver hat, white apron nearly down to the ground over his round jacket, basket for muffins (shown empty here) and stick. He was about 3 foot 6 inches tall, and it was said that the stick was used to chastise cheeky children as well as to help him walk. His name may have been John Milbank, and pictures of him may have been sold as souvenirs. Much later it was suggested that his round was Great Norwood Street, Suffolk Parade, Suffolk Road and Bath Road. This muffin man may have died in 1834.

RIGHT

Another drawing of a street hawker, a woman with a basket of wares, was made by J. Thomas in 1841, a little later than the Muffin Man pictures, but it also portrays a second rather stout figure who was a dwarf, possibly on crutches. One John Thomas was born in Gloucestershire, and became an architect and sculptor. A second muffin man called Henry Clarke is known, dying in Cheltenham Workhouse in 1851. Street hawkers such as these three lived close to destitution. Henry the muffin man's coat is threadbare, but they all have neat shoes.

a short while Sherborne allowed the commission to meet in the upper room of the older market building and then, when it was taken over by Hartland the bankers, he paid for accommodation at the *Fleece* until the commission's 21-year lease of the tolls had expired. Hartland's refronted and altered the building. In 1827, after Messrs Pruen, Griffiths & Pruen took over the premises, the town clock was installed on the front, provided that the commissioners maintained it, and the justices of the peace held petty sessions there. After 1852 the building became the Public Offices, where the Commissioners and then the borough council met.[21]

ENCLOSURE

Enclosure by Act of Parliament was a demonstration of the power of larger landowners. It gave an opportunity to extinguish tithe payments due from their land, and larger landowners could afford to surrender land in order to achieve this. Smaller owners settled for annual money payments. Medieval Cheltenham had been largely in open and common fields; Charlton Kings, Leckhampton and Prestbury had not been so completely organised in that way, and Swindon possibly not at all.

Prestbury was the first to be enclosed by Act of Parliament, passed as early as 1732. It affected a little under half the parish,[22] where landownership was dominated by Lord Craven. His ancestor, early in the seventeenth century, had acquired the bishop of Hereford's former manor; Prestbury Park was largely 'in several', not subject to common rights, and his allotment in lieu of common field was only 10 acres, though he also gained 100 acres for his manorial rights over the extensive 'waste' on Prestbury hill. Prestbury Park was to be useful in the nineteenth century in developing the racecourse. Lord Craven did not live in Prestbury, and though in 1780 his Land Tax payment was twice that of Thomas Baghot Delabere, the Baghot family (also important in Cheltenham) was probably the prime mover in the enclosure. An ancestor, Thomas Baghot, had bought Prestbury 'rectory' in the same year, 1622, that Lord Craven bought the manor, and two brothers, William and Thomas Baghot, were allotted nearly 500 acres at enclosure in 1732; William subsequently inherited the Delabere estate in Southam in 1734, and added that name to his own. Sixty-one smallholders in Prestbury were given allotments of less than 20 acres each, though some probably also owned land already

It is clear from Henry Lamb's print of Prestbury High Street and The Bank sweeping round to the right, that this was still very much a rural scene. Lamb's *Views of Cheltenham* and its vicinity were published about 1825; they were produced by a well-known lithographic printer in London, Charles Hullmandel. Lamb was born in Worcester, but was in Cheltenham by 1819. His business flourished, but then he moved to Malvern in 1834; the growth of the spa presumably attracted him to a new set of clients. Some of the houses he drew in Prestbury are still there, and trees hide the hillock.

GLOUCESTERSHIRE ARCHIVES A254

enclosed.[23] Enclosure must have stimulated the building of new houses, but the number of smallholders had fallen by about half when the 1780 Land Tax list was made, a reflection of the general tendency towards 'engrossing' during the mid- or late eighteenth century as small owners sold out to larger ones. This was especially true of those people given one small field at enclosure to replace their grazing rights, for grazing one field month after month was not a viable husbandry option. William Baghot certainly bought at least two hilltop holdings of an acre or so after 1732.[24]

The holdings of the Delabere family in 1780

Township	Proprietor	Occupier	£	s.	d.
Alstone	John Delabere Esq	Richard Hooper	3	0	0
Cheltenham	Mr John Delabere	Mr John Delabere	0	5	4
	Thomas Baghot Delabere Esq	Richard Hewet	3	12	½
	John Ballinger	Mr John Delabere	0	4	9
Westal	Mr Delabere	Josiah Cook	0	0	11
	Mr Delabere	Mr Delabere	0	7	6
	John Delabere Esq	Richard Hooper	20	10	7¼
	John Delabere Esq	Richard Hooper	2	17	8
	John Delabere Esq	Richard Hooper	0	2	8
Leckhampton	John Delabere Esq	Richard Hooper	1	4	0
Prestbury	Thomas Baghot Delabere Esq	Revd John Delabere + 3 others	18	1	5
	Revd John Delabere	Revd John Delabere	4	2	2½

The open fields in Leckhampton were enclosed in 1778. The whole parish was some 1,330 acres and the Enclosure Act dealt with 344 acres, indicating that most of the parish was already enclosed. After enclosure, Henry Norwood, the lord of the manor, could reorganise approximately 100 acres which he had held in the common fields, and, more important, free all his land from tithes, which was probably the main purpose of this enclosure. Tithe was paid on nearly all Leckhampton land. The act provided for compensation to the tithe owner at the rate of one-sixth of the arable, a generous allocation; land had to be surrendered by each tithe payer in proportion to the amount owned. The extinction of Leckhampton tithes revealed a curious anomaly.[25] Some parcels of land were in Leckhampton township but were in Cheltenham parish and had to be dealt with separately. These appear to have been two fields which abutted the Hatherley Brook, and had probably been held by Cheltenham church at the time when Leckhampton parish was defined.[26] Tithe from this area was owned by the earl of Essex, though it was leased to Leckhampton's rector, Reverend Edward Draper,

George Rowe probably drew Swindon Hall at the same time as he drew the church. The house was at the centre of an estate that was built up in the eighteenth and early nineteenth centuries. John Surman gentleman was living here when he died in 1730. His wife had been the daughter of Lodowick Packer of Cheltenham. John Surman came into money from the banker and well-known miser, Jemmy Wood, in what were regarded as suspicious circumstances, and he enlarged the house greatly between 1845 and 1850. There is a second large house in the parish also still standing, Swindon Manor, which had belonged to the Sturmy family, and like Swindon Hall is converted into apartments.

GLOUCESTERSHIRE ARCHIVES A 324/5

and he was allotted 8 acres in lieu. Great and Little Mearstones, part of Gallipot Farm in Westal, were the property of John Delabere, and he was required to pay the rector a 'corn rent', the equivalent of the tithe he owed, but valued year by year as a money sum. Three other proprietors similarly paid small corn rents. This was the origin of some of the tithe payments still due from properties as late as 1936 when this last vestige of an ancient system was abolished by Act of Parliament.

The main allotment of Leckhampton's rector was 150 acres in compensation for his tithes, which made him a significant landowner, and he had 10½ acres of glebeland in the common fields. Two minor landowners were concerned in the enclosure, allotted 28 and 20 acres respectively. In the Land Tax returns for 1780 Henry Norwood was the only major landowner. Cheltenham was several miles away, but when the town started to expand, his large block of land adjoining the Westal brook on Cheltenham's boundary offered scope for the ambitious development of The Park.

Swindon was a small parish. There may once have been some common fields, but if so they were enclosed by agreement and not under an Act of Parliament. The Land Tax showed one man, Mr Thomas Beale, paying three times as much tax as either of two other larger taxpayers. The rector, Mr Joseph Hayward, and Mr John Surman were the other more substantial contributors, and there was a relatively large number of small taxpayers. Because there had not been an Enclosure Act, Swindon tithes were commuted into money payments in 1839, following the 1836 Tithe Commutation Act. John Surman of Swindon Hall, who had been buying land in the parish, owned nearly 300 acres out of the 673 which were subject to tithes.

BARRIERS TO EXPANSION

CHURCH LAND AND TITHES

There were two major constraints to the physical expansion of Cheltenham. The first was the former church ownership of land immediately to the south of the High Street and in the Cheltenham tithings; and the second was the continued existence of substantial amounts of commonable land north of the High Street. Their removal opened the opportunity for large-

A map of Gallipot and Westal farms, dated 1765, was copied by George Strutt in 1817, and his copy was copied again in 1822 by Hall and Trinder, surveyors, to show the lands purchased by the late John Delabere Esq. The eastern section of the map shows the common fields in Sandford, and reveals the Delabere holding scattered among the various furlongs. The nearly square field called Whitecross, which was not divided into strips, may be the explanation of the narrow street rather strangely called Whitecross Square, where the first houses had been built by 1841.

GLOUCESTERSHIRE ARCHIVES D8244

scale development, realised in the early nineteenth century by Henry Pearson and Joseph Pitt.

No longer in clerical hands since the dissolution of the monasteries, the church lands or the 'rectory' had passed by 1700 from Baptist Hicks' heirs to the earls of Essex, and comprised not only rather more than 200 acres of glebe land, but also the right to collect tithes from all the townships in the ancient Cheltenham parish which included Charlton Kings.[27] Glebeland was tithe-free, since the profits of the land already went directly to the church or, as in Cheltenham, to the impropriator, but tithes were paid by all other proprietors. The 'impropriate rectory' remained with the earls of Essex until the later eighteenth century. The earl's decision in 1778 to sell some land and tithes to John Delabere was the first loosening of these fetters. It opened the way to 'the most spirited improvements the town has undergone', as Goding commented with respect to the early nineteenth-century development of the Lansdown and Montpellier estates, but the Delaberes themselves were not the entrepreneurs.[28]

In 1756, John Delabere had purchased 'Gallipot Lodge' from Mrs Stokes of Powers Court, and 160 acres of land, mainly in Westal tithing, but extending into Alstone and Leckhampton. In 1778 he purchased, from the earl of Essex, glebeland in Westal tithing formerly known as 'Naunton Meese',[29] together with the right to collect tithes due from his own lands and from other proprietors' lands in Naunton tithing.[30] Essex accepted a legal obligation on his remaining estate to pay the stipends of the ministers of Cheltenham and Charlton Kings. Tithes in Alstone, Arle, Charlton Kings and Cheltenham are clearly indicated in the Land Tax assessments; in Alstone, Delabere was assessed on part of the small and great tithes, and Lord Essex on the rest. No tithes remained in Westal, but John Delabere paid a substantial amount of tax on his land, which was tenanted by Richard Hooper. There were several of this name in Cheltenham: Mr Hooper, surgeon, was the occupant of the Great House and let lodgings, and William Hooper and Thomas Hooper also lived in the town.

Joseph Pitt's first building project in Cheltenham was Royal Crescent, started in 1805. He was able to develop this site near the church because he had bought it from the Earl of Essex at the time of the rectory sale. The terrace was designed by an architect from Bath, Charles Harcourt Masters, an interesting link with the more famous Royal Crescent there. This is the conventional concave crescent; the convex crescent in Lansdown had not yet been started. The houses were smart enough for the Duke of Gloucester and the future Queen Victoria to stay in the end one, number 18.

PHOTOGRAPH: AUTHOR, 2009

Tithes in the Land Tax assessments in 1780/83

Township	Proprietor	Occupier	£	s.	d.
Alstone	Earl of Essex	Samuel Aston tithes	0	8	2
	Earl of Essex	Widow Neale great tithes	6	14	8
Arle	Earl of Essex	Samuel Aston	0	12	0
	Earl of Essex	Richard Bendall great tithes	6	8	0
Charlton Kings	Earl of Essex great tithes	J. & R. Bastin	10	4	10
	Earl of Essex small tithes	J. & R. Bastin	2	0	6
	Farm Battledowns	Samuel Aston	2	0	6
Cheltenham	[Earl of Essex] tithes	John Bastin	0	15	2
	William Meekings for Ld Essex	William Meekings	5	7	7½
	Richard Newman for Ld Essex	John Wells	0	10	5½
	Earl of Essex	John Cock	8	7	9½
	Earl of Essex	Samuel Aston	18	9	9
	Earl of Essex	John Hayward	0	17	1

Lord Essex continued to own extensive glebeland and tithes. In 1799, when the entire property was advertised for sale, the glebe amounted to 'upwards of 214 acres of rich arable, meadow, pasture, orchard, garden ground, and common field land', and two-thirds of Cheltenham was still tithable: 700 acres in Alstone, 800 acres in Arle, 650 acres in Cheltenham township, and 2,700 acres comprising the whole of Charlton Kings.[31] This estate was sold at auction on 6 and 7 August 1799 at the *Plough Inn*. As the auction particulars noted, the land was divided into 54 small lots, 'for the convenience of purchasers who may be induced to cultivate a favourable soil, or to build in or near the much frequented and fashionable resort of Cheltenham'. The only large block of enclosed church land was the 56 acres of 'Battledons' in Charlton Kings.

From the point of view of the future development of Cheltenham, the most significant lot was number 54, the Cheltenham tithes, which were sold together with 'The Farm'. This term was usually applied to church or manor demesne land 'at farm', that is, leased out. The house, which was alternatively known as the Parsonage, was in the High Street, stone-built with stone slates on the roof: 'A considerable part' was 'usually let off as a Lodging House, to Persons of the first Distinction'. There were extensive outbuildings, an orchard and Cambray meadow, amounting to nearly 10 acres. The property was said to be capable of 'great improvement' by letting on building leases. These parts of Lot 54 were 'in severalty' (that is, not subject to any common rights), but lot 54 also included about 25 acres in Cheltenham's open and common fields. It was purchased in its entirety by Joseph Pitt.

He also purchased the four acres of lot 20, Church Meadow, a 'Lammas' meadow open to commoning by Cheltenham's burgage owners from 1 August each year, and occupied by Richard Hooper. It was available in two lots if purchasers preferred to bid for it that way, divided by the walk leading to the footbridge over the Chelt. The earl of Essex had allowed a gravel walk to be made, winding across the meadow to link the Old Well Walk with the path from the churchyard, but a tiny corner of meadow adjoining the bridge was not glebe. A previous owner had refused to sell it to Captain Skillicorne, so preventing him from extending the Well Walk towards the church. However, before the enclosure of Cheltenham, Pitt was able to buy that corner of meadow from Samuel Harward.[32] Together with the land bought in 1799, therefore, Pitt had acquired the whole of Church meadow, which was where his first development, Royal Crescent, was started in 1805, before the award under the Enclosure Act was finalised. In addition, he purchased another 44 acres of the church's common field holdings, making him the owner of some 83 acres of land in addition to the Cheltenham's tithes.

No sooner had he bought the tithes than Pitt proceeded to promote an Enclosure Act, passed in 1801, in which he was named as the surveyor of roads. An important motive for enclosure at the end of the eighteenth century was rising corn prices because of the war with France, but this was insignificant in a town environment. In places such as Cheltenham enclosure 'at the

Henry Thompson was probably the first entrepreneur to recognise the potential for development in Cheltenham. He purchased land from the Delabere family. It was his son, Pearson Thompson, and then the Jearrad Brothers, architects, who brought his concept of a smart residential suburb to fruition. The twenty-three houses of Lansdown Parade were built between 1838 and 1841, and were designed by R. W. Jearrad.

PHOTOGRAPH: CARNEGIE, 2010

urban fringe' led to clarification of property rights so that developers could extend the urban area into the countryside.[33] As a solicitor in Cirencester and a banker both in Cheltenham and London, Joseph Pitt appreciated the speculative advantages of owning tithes when the land was still unenclosed, and also the investment opportunities in Cheltenham. He emerged four years later as a major landowner in Cheltenham and with a cash sum as well.

CHELTENHAM ENCLOSURE, 1801–06

The continued existence of common and open fields was the second major constraint on development. Even if only one or two owners of burgages would not give up their right of common on the Marsh, or one or two owners of arable strips did not want to risk losing good land in the general exchange which enclosure involved, the common fields could not be abolished by mutual agreement. But parliament could, and would, override the objections of a minority provided that the owners of a significant proportion of the land, usually two-thirds, agreed.[34] Most important was the agreement of the tithe owner. In the preamble to the 1801 Enclosure Act for Cheltenham, Joseph Pitt was named first as having a share in the open and common fields, and two other men were named, Thomas Markham esquire and Sir William

Lansdown Terrace is also by the Jearrad Brothers. The whole Lansdown development was unusually bold, and this terrace is the boldest. The first ten houses were completed by 1834; numbers 11 to 22 were added in 1837–38, and the row was planned to be longer. It was partly financed by the East India Company for its retired employees.
PHOTOGRAPH: CARNEGIE, 2010

Hicks. Markham lived in North Street, Cheltenham, and Hicks on the north side of London Road; both appear to have had a rather small share of land, but both were gentlemen. William Skillicorne, who owned 39 acres, was the only other owner of significant quantities of land in the open fields. Four men had larger holdings than anyone else but their lands were already enclosed: Thomas Baghot Delabere, who owned 55 acres adjacent to Prestbury; Robert Cox, gentleman, who lived in High Street and owned 45 acres; James Agg owner of 34 acres at Hewletts; and Anthony Ellis, who owned 23 acres.

Most of the land was essentially 'accommodation' land, divided into smallholdings for the craftsmen and tradesmen who owned the burgages, and had probably become further subdivided as properties were inherited or sold. It was complicated work to enclose Cheltenham's common fields. Francis Gibbs of Salisbury, the commissioner appointed under the Act, not only had to adjudicate on the claims of owners and find suitable allotments within the common fields to satisfy those claims, but also had to fix the course of numerous roads, bridges and watercourses, arrange for them to be fenced, and determine in every one of the 230 separate allotments who was responsible for its boundaries. Each allotment had to be specified with its abutments to the land of other owners or to roads or watercourses. Eighty-nine owners of freeholds or copyholds were dealt with, most having no more than a few perches of land (a perch was 1/160th of an acre), and 65 claims to 'beast pastures' were accepted. Not all those concerned had a holding in the open fields; some were compensated with as little as 5 perches of land.

Moreover 220 properties were subject to payments of tithe, and in each of these the commissioner had to determine the amount of money which should be paid to exonerate them for the future. It was not practicable for most such owners to surrender land, as they either had very small holdings in the common fields or no land except their gardens. The amount was calculated taking into account quantity, quality and situation, and was equal to the value of one-fifth of the arable and one-ninth of other land. This brought Pitt the very useful sum of £2,325, though he may have had difficulty in actually collecting all the money. Seven owners, however, were required to give up old enclosed land, the commissioner considering that it would not be harmful to them; they included Thomas Baghot Delabere, who surrendered 5¼ acres adjoining Bouncers Lane, and Samuel Harward. Finally there were 155 houses, gardens, orchards and lands – and 150 owners – neither subject to common rights nor tithes, which were mapped although not included in the enclosure award. At least 300 acres was in old enclosure. As well as the larger holdings mentioned, Samuel Harward had 9 acres adjoining the Colonnade, where the most important road in Cheltenham, the Promenade, would be developed, and Abraham Byrch had 8 acres at the *Plough*. The process was complicated and time-consuming, and it is hardly surprising that more than four years passed between the passage of the Act through parliament in 1801 and the final award in January 1806. The commissioner redrew the map of Cheltenham's fields, creating a new set of property rights which would determine the future building patterns of the town.

Some owners gained compact blocks of land through the enclosure, but there were still many small plots scattered through the township. Even Joseph Pitt's allotments were not all in one place, but he did acquire several large blocks of land: 130 acres in lieu of tithes, 77 acres of which was in the former common called The Marsh on the north side of the town, and 47 acres in the former Lower Field at the west end of the Street, on which the obligation to pay Cheltenham's minister his £40 a year was placed. This land continued to carry that cost at least until the end of the nineteenth century.[35] Pitt was also allotted 73 acres in place of former church glebe, which had been scattered throughout the township; his enclosure allotments in Whaddon field, Great and Little Leechcroft, and Maud's Elm were also quite scattered. Another 30 acres represented copyholds which he had purchased at some time prior to the final award.[36] With the enclosed land bought from the earl of Essex in 1799 this brought his total landholding to 243 acres.

The open fields, meadows and pastures remaining in Alstone and Arle were enclosed under an Act of Parliament of 1830 (and in 1834 a further act was required to protect copyhold tenures), for which the final award was made in 1835. This was also a very complicated enclosure to implement, involving many proprietors and an intricate calculation of the lands which were still tithable. For this reason a full survey was made of all the lands in the tithings, and names of owners and acreages they held were recorded, whether or not they were involved in the enclosure. Forty-four proprietors had bought the tithes of their estates before the enclosure; they included the Reverend Richard Skillicorne Skillicorne and Pearson Thompson, and these nominal tithe obligations were extinguished by the Act. A great deal of Alstone and Arle was in fact already enclosed – for example, most of Thomas Packer Walter Butt's land (about 160 acres), 156 acres belonging to Pearson Thompson, and all that 71 acres owned by the Reverend Skillicorne at Bayshill. Eighteen proprietors agreed to put some of their old

Samuel Harward was a man of vision concerning the future development of Cheltenham, though of limited means to accomplish it, and he built up a significant land-holding which would eventually become The Promenade and Imperial Square. He died in 1809. In his will he encouraged his wife to complete the last house in the Colonnade, now occupied by Martins the jewellers, and furnish it like the others as a lodging-house, and to maintain all the houses in good condition, also to maintain his public library. Numbers 2, 3, 4 and 6 The Colonnade were copyholds purchased in 1787, and mortgaged to his cousin John Harward; other property was mortgaged to John Pitt. This is the only one of the six houses of the Colonnade to survive, the others were replaced by an undistinguished block in 1935–37.

PHOTOGRAPH: CARNEGIE, 2009

enclosures into the general re-allotment of holdings to facilitate reorganisation, among whom John Gregory Welch was the most significant. At this date Thomas Butt owned the original Arle Court; W. H. Prescod (and by 1835 James Pritchett) owned the enclosed Grove field, part of Redgrove wood and the house and pleasure ground which Butt's son, another T. P. W. Butt, would convert into the modern Arle Court. On the other hand John Gregory Welch esquire, of Arle House, owned an estate in Arle and another in Alstone, and held most of his land in the open fields, altogether over 300 acres. He was one of the prime movers in the enclosure, but subsequently became insolvent.[37] Two men, Devereux Bowly and Samuel Sadler, jointly owned most of what was left of the impropriate rectory and were allotted 158 acres in lieu of tithes; Reverend Skillicorne had a very small share of the rectory, for which a mere 1½ acres

After Thomas Packer Butt built his new house in Grove field on the western edge of Cheltenham parish about 1855, he demolished most of the old Arle Court. A. M. Welch said that old oak panelling, a beautiful staircase and some good tapestry work 'were removed to the new Arle Court'. There is much panelling, and a grand staircase that owes much to archaic inspiration (*right*), but it is uncertain that any of it is older than the house itself, with the exception of the overmantel in the dining room (*left*) with the date 1689; even this could be a reproduction, but would date from the period when Fleetwood Dormer owned the house.

PHOTOGRAPHS: CARNEGIE, 2009, BY COURTESY OF THE MANOR BY THE LAKE

John Prinn set out at the end of the seventeenth century to buy up land in Charlton Kings, and built up a significant estate. His son continued the process. By 1723 there was a consolidated block of land, and by 1746 it had been divided into three farms, of which Hill Farm covered land, bounded by Sandy Lane on the east, which had been in the open fields. In 1748 Hill Farm, later Southfield Farm and now Southfield Manor, was occupied by William Ballinger, yeoman, and there was a house, barn, stable and garden. Probably in the late eighteenth century a modern house was built around or onto an older core. The attractive mid-nineteenth-century farm buildings have been converted. The gateway in Sandy Lane (*right*), the old road to Cirencester, led to The Elms, the predecessor of Lilleybrook House, and was perhaps erected when the house was considerably extended in the 1890s.

PHOTOGRAPH: AUTHOR, 2009, BY KIND PERMISSION OF MR JOHN WRIGHT

were allotted him. Fifteen people gave up land in order to extinguish the tithes, and 25 small proprietors paid cash sums.

The Cheltenham enclosures did not bring an end to the ancient system of tithes and open fields. Naunton and Sandford tithes had been sold by John Delabere's son about 1804, when he succeeded to his father's estate, each proprietor buying a share in proportion to his landholding. However, because of the particular legal form in which this was done, tithes were recorded separately from title to the land itself, an anomaly only removed in 1849 and 1850 under the Tithe Commutation Act of 1836.[38] An area of 600 acres was dealt with. There were 24 tithe owners, among whom Dame Jane Eliza Prinn (127 acres) and Pearson Thompson, son of Henry Thompson (131 acres) were significant. The number was partly the result of subdivision of land among developers, and included the Cheltenham College (the proprietary college) and Cheltenham General Hospital and Dispensary. There was no need to include Westal, where tithes had been extinguished through John Delabere's 1778 purchase.

There was no enclosure by Act of Parliament in Charlton Kings, and the tithes of the parish were not commuted until 1848 under the terms of the 1836 Act.[39] The whole parish was subject to tithe payments with the exception of four fields, 'well-known by their accustomed metes and bounds', of 'Battledon or Battledowns', 50 acres in all, which were 'by prescription exempt from the render of tithes'. More than two-thirds of the parish was meadow and pasture, and only 810 acres were arable, but four small fields with strips still existed, and were only gradually eliminated. It was said in 1835 that no commoning had been practised on Ryeworth field from about 1800, and the Lilleyfield strips were still open in part and still arable in 1848. There were 84 owners who occupied their own land, house or cottage. They had bought the tithes of their land in the rectory sale, often quite small amounts, and these were accordingly legally extinguished by the commutation award. There were two substantial tithe owners, Jane Eliza Russell, who had inherited Charlton Park and owned the tithes of the estate, 1,335 acres, and Conway Whithorne Lovesey, of Coxhorne, who owned much less land – 400 acres – but collected tithes from 102 small owners.[40] He accepted a rent charge of £260 in total. Another eight people were awarded small rent charges. One-third of the land in the parish remained subject to rent charges. The tithe commutation survey emphasises how dominant the Prinn family had made the Charlton Park estate.

CHAPTER EIGHT

REALITY

LEFT

The photograph of the south end of The Promenade was taken at the end of the nineteenth century. Two carriages are driving up the road, one going towards the Queen's Hotel, visible in the background. The trees, which contribute so much to the important streets in Cheltenham, are still young. This southern part of the Promenade has always had a different character from the part nearer the High Street and north of the Chelt. On the left is Imperial Square. The division between the two halves is emphasised by the flow of traffic crossing the Promenade.

© CHELTENHAM ART GALLERY AND MUSEUM

I N   T H E   S E N S E   T H A T Bath thinks of itself as a Georgian town, Cheltenham is a Regency town, even though the decade of most rapid population growth was between 1821 to 1830, when the Prince Regent had finally become George IV. It is particularly surprising that Cheltenham became such a fashionable inland resort in the early nineteenth century, because it lacked three important features of Bath's appeal: an historic foundation of real importance; a splendid former abbey church; and a remarkable outpouring of hot water. There are no obvious signs of Cheltenham's foundation in the Roman period; its church may once have been an Anglo-Saxon 'minster', but if so had not attracted wealthy benefactors and was not architecturally outstanding; and its spa waters were neither prolific nor hot. Nor was there much to satisfy growing antiquarian interests.[1] When the Bristol and Gloucestershire Archaeological Society visited Cheltenham in 1879 its president, Mr Gambier Parry, began his inaugural address by saying that 'the town in which you have chosen to meet offers but little for your purpose beyond its pleasantness, convenience and hospitality', and members found nothing to see in the immediate vicinity but Cheltenham church and Leckhampton Court. Yet Cheltenham attracted not only notable visitors, particularly George III whose visit in 1788 has generated a potent myth, but also, and possibly more important, it attracted well-to-do residents. What was the secret of its attraction?

Bath was developed on a grand scale in the eighteenth century – large houses, long terraces, some splendid squares, streets and the Circus, inspired by Roman architecture. It could offer a mild climate, hot baths, assembly and pump rooms which were gracious, civilised, and grand, and a large and beautiful church. But the topography of Bath was hilly: the ailing found it impossible to walk up to terraces such as Lansdown. Bath was also expensive, and 'urban' in style. Cheltenham, in contrast, could offer an equally mild climate, as the town is sheltered by the hills from 'the bleak and piercing blasts of the north and east',[2] it had strongly medicinal spa waters, and in the town itself the conditions, as Gell and Bradshaw noted in 1820, were level. In addition, hilly and picturesque countryside was within reach for those who wanted to ride out. Indeed, Cheltenham later presented itself as 'the centre for the Cotswolds'. But perhaps more important than anything else, it was *cheaper* than Bath, appealing to the next rung of society down from the top, the class which was in search of holidays but unable to afford its own country house as the aristocracy could. For some years it was also less crowded.

For some, at least, the noise and bustle of Bath acted as a deterrent – Jane Austen, for example, seems to have disliked its crowds, and when her sister Cassandra visited Cheltenham in September 1816 she wrote 'but how very much Cheltenham is to be preferred in May', which was before the season began; she had herself tried the waters for her failing health in May the same year. However, she was pleased that Cassandra found so much there to be satisfied with, although noted that bad weather may have meant that her sister would perhaps 'not have been able to get to the Pump'. She commented less favourably on the premium added to the price of a lodging house because it was in the High Street. The Austen family and their circle of friends and relations quite often visited Cheltenham, but Jane's own views of the town did not feature in her letters to her sister, as she had been there with Cassandra.

One feature of Cheltenham in 1800 was that building had mainly taken place on the north side of the High Street. Fewer than a third of the population described in the first *Directory* lived on the south side, and twelve of those premises were new. There were obstacles to development on the south – the blocks of church land, and the marshy pasture through which the River Chelt flowed. A small amount of church land had been released in the later eighteenth century, and new streets such as St George's Place, Portland Place and the Colonnade were begun. Cobbett accurately noted in 1821 that, as well as the mile-long High Street, 'at some distance from this street, there are rows of white tenements, with green balconies, like those inhabited by the tax-eaters round London'.[3] But in the early nineteenth century development took place on green fields at an astonishing pace. Much building was designed as spacious lodging houses with public gardens nearby. A continuing trend was for a leisured class of residents, either retired or enjoying income from investments, to come to Cheltenham – they came to live, not merely to sojourn. It was for them that Joseph Pitt's more dramatic vision of an estate of 'urban villas' as well as terraces was designed. He contributed largely to the character of Cheltenham in the nineteenth century. Montpellier and the Park were also shaped in the image of parkland and gardens, walks and rides rather than bricks-and-mortar

The design of a small development of town houses in Trafalgar Street by Stanley Partnership (*right*) picks up interestingly the much earlier small row of three truly Regency houses of about 1820 (*left*), Nelson Cottage, Nelson Lodge and Nelson Villa, set back behind small gardens, with delicate wrought-iron balconies. The Civic Society in 2005 commended the modern row.

PHOTOGRAPHS: AUTHOR, 2009

Balconies in Suffolk Square display the heart and honeysuckle theme (*see* page 196). Iron balconies are very much a feature of Cheltenham's nineteenth-century houses. Early examples were of wrought iron, and some builders used both cast panels and wrought-iron canopies. Suffolk Square was built on land owned in the late eighteenth century by the Earl of Suffolk. His estate was based on Gallipot Farm, where he built a grand house, and, like Earl Fauconberg, it seems he bought the estate for his personal use, rather than for development. A number of roads in the area record his one-time ownership, or refer to his son, Viscount Andover.

PHOTOGRAPH: CARNEGIE, 2010

townscape. Henry Thompson's grand terrace, significantly named 'Lansdown', was not immediately successful. In Bath the 'promenades' were along streets, but Cheltenham offered more 'country-style', tree-lined walks and, as it was not on a supposed Roman pattern, it was free of the 'history' that determined the Woods' plans for Bath.

Early accounts of visitors to Cheltenham give the impression that the town consisted of just one street, the High Street, but this is misleading. There were lanes, alleys or passages off that thoroughfare, crowded with families not of sufficient status to be included in a trade directory. The ways through from the High Street to the common land to its rear were called 'lanes', like Fleece Lane,[4] and Bell Lane which became Winchcombe Street after the road to Winchcombe was turnpiked in 1792. Alleys and passages gave access to the buildings behind High Street frontages – examples included Counsellor's Alley, Dod's Row, Meekings Passage, Coffee House Yard, Crown Inn Yard, Post Office Yard and Rose and Crown Yard. Building along the length of a town plot (a former burgage) enabled the owner to gain income from rents, and may sometimes have been forced by the pressure of economic difficulties.

Alternatively, an alley or long back plot might have accommodated the owner's workshop, and possibly also his workforce. The poor and the unskilled labourers were those who physically built the large houses, and it was from among their families in the lanes and alleys that the prosperous occupants recruited servants. But their crowded conditions, minimal water supply and primitive sanitation were gradually perceived as threats to the health and prestige of the town's more affluent residents.

As the population expanded, terraces of modest artisan houses represented some improvement on the living conditions in older properties, although in due course some became public health hazards. Stylistically these terraces made a superficial bow towards the 'classical' façades of larger houses. The curved line of Naunton Crescent with its stucco houses is one among many examples. It was started about 1840. By 1851, when 31 houses were occupied, nine of the heads of households were labourers and one was an agricultural labourer. There was a shoeing smith, gardener and pig dealer. Seven men were connected with the building trade: one builder, two carpenters, a journeyman painter, a plasterer and a brickmaker. Four women headed households, only one of whom had an occupation, and she was a laundress. A cordwainer, tailor, baker, hawker, fly driver, bailiff and stable man also lived in the street.

THE AGE OF BUREAUCRACY, 1801–21

The first national census in 1801 introduced a new age of bureaucracy. From this time ever more statistics were collected by parliament, describing whole communities, not just the élite which was recorded in early directories. Thus, 710 houses in Cheltenham were recorded in the first official census, twice as many as the local *Directory* included the previous year. One was the workhouse with its 58 inmates, while 65 houses were unoccupied, suggesting that census day, Monday 10 March, was too early in the year for holiday homes to be in use. The 1786 Paving Act had specifically noted that many houses were only occupied during the 'Water-drinking Season', though it specified that owners or lessees should pay the rates nonetheless. Another complication was revealed later in the century, throwing a surprising light on census statistics: it was noted of the census taken in April 1861 that 'the houses returned as unoccupied were not so in reality'. A special note explained that they were occupied during the day and rated to the poor, but not slept in, the owners having residences in adjoining parishes. These people must have used their town houses as their base for daytime enjoyment of the facilities of Cheltenham out of season, and then let them in the season. The number of positively unoccupied houses in the town was remarkably small and belonged to the class 'to let'.

The inadequacy of the 1800 *Directory* as a guide to Cheltenham's occupational structure is shown when compared with the census, which attempted to find out, in a very basic way, how many persons in each parish were employed in 'agriculture' or in 'trade, manufacture or handicraft'. The census did not count those in professional and service employments such as bankers, lawyers or doctors, nor servants. The *Directory* listed only 86 people with occupations such as baker, builder, saddler or tailor, while the census returned 459 persons employed in trade, manufacture and handicrafts – although manufacturing was insignificant in Cheltenham until the mid-twentieth century, while the commercial sector was relatively small, a statistical consequence of a large leisured class. The *Directory* concentrated on the township of Cheltenham, so the eight gardeners listed naturally gave little impression of the mainly agricultural occupations of the other townships. It might, however, hint at the importance of market gardening; the 1801 crop returns reported nearly 400 acres in Cheltenham under potatoes, peas, beans and turnips, three times more than in Charlton Kings.[5] The census

'Houses' in 1801 and 1811

| | 1801 | | 1811 | |
Place	Inhabited houses	Empty	Inhabited houses	Empty
Cheltenham	645	65	1,568	109
Charlton Kings	122	3	149	11
Leckhampton	29	1	48	3
Prestbury	118	9	138	0
Swindon	27	4	33	0
Cirencester	837	48	902	24
Gloucester	1,325	43	1,509	20
Tewkesbury	859	28	959	33
Winchcombe	283	18	287	9

Percentages of 'families' in the 1811 census

Place	In agriculture	In trade, manufacture, handicrafts	Remainder of population
Cheltenham	22	41	37
Charlton Kings	64	22	14
Leckhampton	74	20	6
Prestbury	63	27	10
Swindon	85	15	0
Cirencester	22	56	23
Gloucester	1	77	23
Tewkesbury	7	87	6
Winchcombe	31	50	19

The first terrace in what is now Montpellier Spa Road was developed from 1820 as 'The North Parade', being on the north side of Montpellier Gardens, on the edge of Henry Thompson's land, with south-facing frontages. This gracious row was built as lodging-houses. There were ten numbered houses occupied in 1851, but thirteen households. Six were lodging houses, with just six lodgers in total, five in one house. A colonel in the Royal Artillery, a captain in the Royal Navy, and a doctor of divinity with their households occupied three other houses, and, typically, five households were headed by women.

PHOTOGRAPH: AUTHOR, 2009

returned 284 people in as being employed in agriculture. In 1811, and again in 1821 and 1831, 'families' were counted, which meant in practice heads of households, giving a better indication of the overall social structure.

Some interesting papers relating to the 1821 and 1831 censuses were preserved among the Cheltenham parish records,[6] including the tally sheets for the 1821 census. In 1821 counting started on 28 May and continued until 7 June. The enumerator was Edward Hatch, the overseer of the poor, assisted by Samuel Piff and John Hutton. Hatch was paid five guineas, while 'Bishop at the Old Swan Inn' was paid £3 2s. 6d., the final tallies being made up, it seems, accompanied by refreshment. The men seem to have walked from house to house, entering in their books the numbers in each category. They recorded 2,463 children under ten years of age, which was 18 per cent of the parish's population, a notably low proportion at this date (when nationally the figure approached 30 per cent). One person was over 95 and two over 90, but only 34 people in total were over 65 years. The numerous incomers into Cheltenham were predominantly of working age. These statistics were required for the analysis of ages in each hundred, but the age structure of Cheltenham alone was not in the printed reports.

The population of Cheltenham in 1801 had been smaller than in the three major market towns of the county, but ten years later it had overtaken all but Gloucester. The population more than doubled in just ten years, and almost doubled again by 1821. From that point onwards Cheltenham grew with extraordinary speed and far outstripped every other Gloucestershire town with the exception of the county town, a position which has become more pronounced ever since. In 1841 Cheltenham's population was more than ten times that of 1801, a rate of increase that was not only far greater than anywhere else in Gloucestershire, but more than matched that of most of the mushrooming industrial centres of the North and Midlands. From a much smaller base Leckhampton, too, experienced rapid growth, but before 1851 the surrounding parishes had not yet been drawn into Cheltenham's orbit. Eventually, a sequence of boundary changes would bring more of their areas into the borough.

Population, 1801 to 1851

	1801	1811	1821	1831	1841	1851
Cheltenham	3,076	8,325	13,396	22,942	31,411	35,051
Charlton Kings	730	1,005	1,707	2,478	3,232	3,174
Leckhampton	225	242	318	929	1,770	2,149
Prestbury	485	667	906	1,231	1,283	1,314
Swindon	116	162	201	225	204	221
Cirencester	4,130	4,540	4,987	5,420	6,014	6,096
Gloucester*	7,029	8,280	9,744	11,933	14,497	17,572
Tewkesbury	4,199	4,820	4,962	5,780	5,862	5,878
Winchcombe	1,256	1,936	2,240	2,514	2,613	2,824

Source: *VCH Glos.*, iv, p. 171.
* From 1831 the data relate to the municipal borough, which was enlarged under the Municipal Corporations Act, 1835, to match the parliamentary borough.

In 1831 the printed census report, based on the local enumerators' comments, noted that 'The town of Cheltenham has experienced an extraordinary increase in Population (9,546 Persons) attributable to the Mineral Springs, which cause a great influx of Visitors, particularly from the East Indies, the Colonies, and the Continent. Leckhampton has likewise increased in Population (611 Persons), owing to its proximity to the Town of Cheltenham'. The *Cheltenham Chronicle* enlarged on this, noting that

the inhabitants of the numerous houses on the London, Bath, Painswick, and Winchcomb roads, may be considered as forming part of the *Town* of Cheltenham; the populous suburbs of which extend even to a greater distance, although they are situated in the adjoining parishes of Leckhampton, Charlton and Prestbury. The *whole* population therefore, may, with these suburbs included, be fairly estimated at 25,000 souls.

From this time onwards, parish boundaries become less relevant to the history of the town. In 1831 Cheltenham's population, 22,942, was

This Victorian pillar box is at the north end of Montpellier Walk. Hexagonal boxes were designed by J. W. Penfold, a Surrey architect and surveyor, for the General Post Office, and first cast by Cochrane, Grove & Co. of Dudley in 1866. Of the twenty originals known to survive, Cheltenham has eight; the only collection of similar importance is in London. The design of the pillar box was subsequently modified, and continued in production until 1879. They were all painted bright red from 1874. Their siting in locations such as College Lawn, Lansdown Place and Pittville Circus Road evoke thoughts of well-to-do visitors in these houses who would write to friends and relations while enjoying the summer season in Cheltenham.

PHOTOGRAPH: CARNEGIE, 2009

twice that of Gloucester, although it should be noted that Cheltenham parish was larger in area and allowed for more expansion than was possible within the boundaries of the city of Gloucester.

THE 1831 CENSUS

Each census was more ambitious than the last in terms of the questions asked. More detailed information on occupations of men aged 20 years and over was required in 1831, and also

CENSUS

OF THE

Population of Cheltenham,

Taken May 30th, 1831, and following Days.

[From the Cheltenham Chronicle, June 9th.]

Shortly after the orders of Goverment had been received in this town, to take a census of the population, and the necessary official forms of return had been supplied, a Meeting of the Churchwardens, Visitors, and Overseers of the Poor, was convened for the purpose of making arrangements to number the Inhabitants. Mr. Hatch, as Chairman of the Meeting, detailed the mode in which the census had been taken under his superintendence in 1821, and furnished a tabular statement of the returns; but on examining the Government Papers, they were found to contain a great number of additional questions; and that the precise fulfilment of the order would require great exactness, not unattended with difficulty. It was therefore resolved that the Parish should be divided into four districts, according to the King's Books; and that Mr. Hatch and the Overseers should obtain the assistance of the Collectors of Assessed Taxes in their respective districts, and that two persons should undertake to number each division.

Pursuant to these resolutions, handbills were issued, requesting the inhabitants to facilitate the progress of the census, by furnishing all the information in their power; and it is but justice to add, that the officers have met with every civility and readiness to comply with the orders of Government on the part of their fellow-townsmen. They commenced their arduous undertaking on Monday, the 30th ult. and we have much pleasure in furnishing the following statement as the result of their labours.

The following table, taken from official documents, will shew the population at three different periods during the last thirty years:

Taken by Mr. Buckle in 1801:
Houses, 710.—Males, 1405; Females, 1671: Total, 3076.
Taken by Mr. Hall in 1811:
Houses, 1566.—Males, 3780; Females, 4545: Total, 8325.
Taken by Mr. Hatch in 1821:
Houses, 2297.—Males, 6083; Females, 7305: Total, 13,388.
Taken as above by the Parish Officers and Collectors in 1831:
Houses, 4013.—Males, 10,048; Females, 12,997: Total, 23,045.
Shewing an increase, since 1821, of 9657.
Ditto since 1811, of 14,720.
Ditto since 1801, of 19,969.

So great an increase of inhabitants within so short a period of time, is, we believe, unparalleled in any town in the kingdom, and we are happy to observe that it is principally to be attributed to the influx of wealthy and respectable families, who, during the last ten years have made Cheltenham their residence. It is truly gratifying to us to be the medium of publishing a statement to our fellow-townsmen, that must in every way convince them of the growing prosperity of Cheltenham; and when we contemplate the numerous and pre-eminent advantages she possesses over every rival Watering Place, we are fully justified in anticipating that the census of 1841, will again record a similar augmentation of numbers, rank, & opulence, in her residents—*Esto perpetua!*

DISTRICTS.	Houses Inhabited.	Males.	Females.	Total.
SOUTH SIDE. Enumerated by Mr. HATCH and Mr. BRIDGEWATER.	1056	2672	3565	6237
NORTH SIDE. Enumerated by Mr. A. GARDNER and Mr. W. HAINES.	2132	5474	6605	12,079
WESTAL, INCLUDING LANSDOWN PLACE. Enumerated by Mr. RIDLER and Mr. COX.	633	1397	2194	3591
ALSTONE and ARLE, EXCLUSIVE OF LANSDOWN PLACE. Enumerated by Mr. E. WALWYN and Mr. H. FORTY.	192	505	633	1138
GRAND TOTAL	4013	10,053	12,889	22,942

[☞ In addition to the above enumeration, the inhabitants of the numerous houses on the London, Bath, Painswick, and Winchcomb roads, may be considered as forming part of the *Town* of Cheltenham; the populous suburbs of which extend even to a greater distance, although they are situated in the adjoining parishes of Leckhampton, Charlton, and Prestbury. The *whole* population therefore, may, with these suburbs included, be fairly estimated at 25,000 souls.

[From the Cheltenham Chronicle, June 16th.]

In our last week's paper we published an account of the Population, males & females, with the number of Houses. We are now enabled to lay before our readers an *exact* copy of the Schedule to be returned to Government:

Inhabited Houses.	By how many Families occupied	Houses now building.	Other Houses uninhabited.	Families chiefly employed in Agriculture.	Families employed in Trade, Manufactures, &c.	Families not comprised in the two preceding Classes.	Males.	Females.	Total Persons.
4013	4766	90	246	135	1875	2756	10,053	12,889	22,942

Number of Males 20 years old.	Occupiers of Land employing Labourers.	Occupiers not employing Labourers.	Labourers employed in Agriculture.	Males employed in Manufacture, &c.	Males employed in Retail Trade, Handicraft, &c.	Wholesale Merchants, Bankers, Professional Persons, and other Educated Men	Labourers employed by the 3 preceding Classes, not in Agriculture.	All other Males 20 yrs old, retired Tradesmen, superannuated Labourers, &c.
5375	10	9	210	2	1935	667	1725	253

Male Servants upwards of twenty years old ... 564
.... under twenty years old 139
Female Servants 2334
The population of Leckhampton is 929.

With Messrs. Cunningham and Cox's Respects.

Cheltenham Vestry preserved in the parish chest a copy of the returns for the 1831 census from each division of the parish, taken from the *Cheltenham Chronicle* on 9 June, and printed by Messrs Cunningham and Cox.

counts of servants. A meeting of 'the churchwardens, visitors and overseers of the poor', convened to make the necessary arrangements in Cheltenham, was somewhat taken aback by the 'great number of additional questions', claiming that 'precise fulfilment of the order would require great exactness, not unattended with difficulty'. The parish was divided into four districts and two men numbered each; the collector of taxes was asked to assist. A manuscript preserved in the parish chest gives a summary for the four districts: the South side, the North side, Westal, and Alstone and Arle. The 'North side' was more densely developed than the 'South side': over 12,000 people lived north of the High Street and 6,000 to the south. Westal, Naunton and Sandford had 3,591 inhabitants, and Arle and Alstone 1,138. Distinguishing the townships in the parish was abandoned shortly after this, as their boundaries had no real relevance to what had now become a major town.

Occupations of 5,312 men of 20 years and over in the four divisions of Cheltenham in 1831*

	South side	North side	Westal, Naunton and Sandford	Alstone and Arle	Totals
Occupiers of land employing labourers	0	2	1	7	10
Occupiers of land not employing labourers	0	0	9	0	9
Labourers employed in agriculture	82	3	68	57	210
Totals in agriculture	82	5	78	62	229
Males in manufacture	0	2	0	0	2
Males in retail trade, handicrafts etc.	476	1,254	198	7	1,935
Wholesale merchants, bankers, professional persons, and other educated men	163	303	177	24	667
Labourers not in agriculture	320	1,161	167	14	1,662
Other males	183	67	3	0	253
Male servants	236	146	175	7	564
Totals	1,460	2,938	798	116	5,312
Male servants under 20 years	68	39	29	3	139
Female servants	758	970	568	38	2,334

* There were 5,375 men of this age, but the total in the summary was 63 fewer.

The north side was overwhelmingly the area of shopkeepers. There was a concentration of general labourers in this area, too, easily overlooked in studies of the more affluent houses and their occupants. There were a few small farmers in Westal, Sandford and Naunton; all but one of the larger farms were in Alstone and Arle.

Cheltenham was not typical of English towns at this time. Of Gloucestershire towns, Tewkesbury was perhaps closest to the national norm.[7] There were more 'capitalists, bankers and other educated men' in Cheltenham than was usual, though Prestbury shared this characteristic; 'educated' men included 51 military gentlemen, of whom six were generals, and Admiral Montague at Cambray New Lodge.[8] Cheltenham was also distinguished by more general labourers, many of whom it may be assumed worked on the building sites in the town: the *Gloucester Journal* remarked in November 1823 that 'upwards of 4,500 workmen are in daily employment on houses and buildings now erecting.'[9] There was an imbalance between the sexes, with 13 women to every 10 men, a disparity that continued to increase, partly because of the influx of female servants from other parishes, and to a lesser extent because of the tendency of well-off single women to live in the town.

Considered the finest of the early, purpose-built masonic halls to survive in England, this example in Cheltenham was built between 1820 and 1823, and was designed by George Allen Underwood, who was responsible for a number of Regency buildings in the town. Underwood had himself been admitted to Cheltenham masonic lodge in 1818, a year after it had been founded, perhaps through the patronage of his architect master Sir John Soane. The commission to design Holy Trinity church probably also owed something to masonic patronage. This Cheltenham Masonic Hall contains many masonic symbols, but also demonstrates architecturally the secrecy of the Freemasons.
PHOTOGRAPH: CARNEGIE, 2010

Percentages of men aged 20 years and upwards in specified occupational groups, 1831

	capitalists etc.	retail trade and handicraft	agricultural labourers	general labourers
Cheltenham	12	37	4	31
Charlton Kings	5	37	15	25
Leckhampton	6	35	33	14
Prestbury	12	12	21	10
Swindon	5	22	37	19
Cirencester	8	49	13	16
Gloucester	9	54	4	25
Tewkesbury	7	38	6	17
Winchcombe	6	29	39	9
Urban averages*	8	39	6	22

* D. A. Gatley, 'Urban and rural England and Wales in the 1831 Census', *Local Population Studies Society Newsletter* (2004), pp. 9–11; these figures relate to 707 towns defined as having a population greater than 2,000, and London.

Oriel Place or Terrace consists of eleven houses built in 1827. It is much less grandiose than some of Cheltenham's new terraces of this period, and is an attractive example of design for occupants of more modest status. Instead of balconies, the architect used iron for the porches. In 1851 a number of households were of independent means, and two were keepers of lodging houses.

PHOTOGRAPH: CARNEGIE, 2010

The numerous male servants underline the status of Cheltenham's inhabitants. Resident servants in a household are a reasonable index of affluence, though the ability to employ one servant girl could extend quite a long way down the social ladder. Not all servants worked in the houses in which they were resident; some worked by the day and lived elsewhere.

Numbers of servants, 1831

	Male servants over 20 years	Male servants under 20 years	Female servants
Cheltenham	564	139	2,334
Charlton Kings	27	17	153
Leckhampton	9	2	24
Prestbury	10	4	43
Swindon	1	1	12
Cirencester	43	9	298
Gloucester	109	72	746
Tewkesbury	41	26	195
Winchcombe	12	10	61

The published census report presented a list of the actual occupations of men aged 20 years and above in the retail trades or handicrafts in selected towns, of which Cheltenham was one of three analysed in Gloucestershire, the others being Bristol and its suburbs, and Gloucester. This is itself an indication of the increased importance of the town. Dividing these occupations between secondary and tertiary sectors, Cheltenham appears to have been very like Gloucester in its economic structure. More than two-thirds, 73 per cent in Cheltenham and 71 per cent in Gloucester, were in the older traditional trades, skilled craftsmen producing food and clothes or in the building trades; a quarter, 26 and 28 per cent respectively, were working in the service occupations. Neither Cheltenham nor Gloucester was yet dominated by those catering for the leisured and affluent. Numerically, the three largest groups in Cheltenham were shoe- and bootmakers, tailors, and carpenters, accounting for a quarter of the men in employment. In the tertiary sector publicans, hotel and innkeepers were the next most numerous group; there were five printsellers, eight booksellers, fourteen clock- and watchmakers, fourteen jewellers, sixteen tea-dealers, and seventeen druggists and chemists catering for the well-to-do. The presence of four nightmen or scavengers, six pawnbrokers and four old clothes dealers tells its own story.

Pigot's *Directory* of 1830, which gave addresses, allows 1,191 of the more important businesses and individuals to be traced.[10] Tradesmen and craftsmen were given simple Christian name and surname, while 269 people were dignified with a title (mainly Mr or Mrs), over a third of whom were women. Though categorised by Pigot as 'nobility, gentry and clergy', they were not gentry in the sense that the term was used in previous centuries for the 'gentle born', nor 'pseudo-gentry' which has been suggested as a term for urban professional men as well as those not earning their living.[11] Now, they might more accurately be termed 'leisured'. These people were scattered through the new streets of the town, with larger groups living in Berkeley

Place, Gloucester Place, Lansdown Place, Montpellier, North Place, Oriel Terrace, Oxford Parade, the Promenade, Priory Street, and Rodney Terrace. There were only four 'leisured' in the High Street and two in Pittville, where development was just beginning.

Thirty-seven physicians and surgeons, 24 attorneys and 23 people running schools formed the town's professional class recorded in the *Directory*. The majority of the schools were boarding schools; two were mixed, one run by Cheltenham Union and the other by the National School Society; thirteen catered for girls. Charlton Kings, Prestbury and Swindon together had six schools. There were eight booksellers and stationers. George Arthur Williams was advertised as a bookseller and stationer, but also ran a library on the corner next to the Assembly Rooms. In about 1823 he had published *A catalogue of Williams's library*, affording an unusual glimpse into the interests of Cheltenham's inhabitants or visitors. He had 'a valuable

The photograph of one side of Swindon Passage or Swindon Place was probably taken when its demolition as a slum was under discussion. The terrace was built about 1820, and a block of houses in this narrow plot of land behind one of the High Street houses was an example of back-to-back housing in the town, a type of construction more usually associated with the industrial North. It was one of the areas mentioned particularly by Cresy in his Report in 1849 on the public health of Cheltenham. The houses were cleared in the 1930s, and the Royal Mail sorting office now occupies the site.
© CHELTENHAM ART GALLERY AND MUSEUM

An early terrace of stone-fronted houses at the eastern end of High Street, divided into two blocks of five houses separated by Berkeley Street, was started about 1820 and completed six years later. Berkeley Place remains almost unaltered. Standing well back from the road, the gardens used to be railed all round. The houses have fine wrought-iron verandas. Typically, in 1851 four households were headed by women: one an officer's wife and three fund-holding or land-owning gentlewomen; an 'independent' major, a gentleman fund-holder, and a justice of the peace completed the occupants resident on census night.

PHOTOGRAPH: AUTHOR, 2009

collection of books, both ancient and modern', and took in 'London, Irish, Scotch, Welsh, and Provincial newspapers'. Cheltenham's own newspaper, the *Cheltenham Chronicle*, was started in 1809, sixty years after a similar venture in Bath. The *Cheltenham Journal* followed in 1824. Williams expressed interest in 'the spread of knowledge', suggesting that novels and romances were no longer sufficient as they had been to the circulating library. He had books in French, Italian, German, and Spanish, there was much history, some classics, books of interest to soldiers and sailors, adventures, and a vast number of basic and surprising works by a variety of authors. The Clarence Library was in the Colonnade; in 1803 it had also contained a wide range of books. These libraries are a reflection of Cheltenham's style, attracting the leisured and educated. Jane Austen was delighted to know that the second edition of *Sense and Sensibility* in 1813 'was very much admired in Cheltenham'.[12]

Fewer than expected businesses and craftsmen were in the High Street – only two-fifths of those listed by Pigot, though nearly all the grocers and butchers were there, the market place being occupied exclusively by the two fishmongers, six poulterers and nine butchers. However, bakers and confectioners, of whom there were no fewer than 136, were scattered throughout the residential streets, with just twenty in the High Street. Tailors were concentrated in the High Street. Clark & Debenham was in the Promenade, in premises soon to become known as Cavendish House, but the Promenade was mainly occupied by the leisured classes. The Colonnade had nineteen varied commercial businesses, and Albion Street, Henrietta Street and Winchcombe Street running north from the High Street were also busily commercial, with 73 enterprises and only two 'leisured' residents recorded by Pigot.

Directories do not usually include poorer people. One fairly typical example of this problem, described by Maggie Blake, was the houses of Swindon Place, in the lane known as Swindon

Passage.[13] In the late eighteenth century there was one front house here, on the High Street at the lower or west end; in 1800 it was occupied by a gardener.[14] Behind the house was a good-sized burgage plot of an acre, reaching to the back lane which gave access to the High Street plots. It probably represented the standard medieval burgage in the town. Early in the nineteenth century, two brothers inherited the property, and the front house was divided. One brother was a tailor and one a gardener, but neither was listed in Pigot's 1830 *Directory* (though one was enumerated in the 1841 census returns). Both brothers began to build cottages on their ground, with a narrow passage from the High Street passing between the two halves of the front house, and another at one side giving access to the rear part of the plot. John Snelus, the gardener, was the more enterprising of the two brothers – or the more desperate.

John Snelus bought out his brother, borrowing money on mortgage, and between 1821 and 1825 built at least twenty more cottages, so that by the early 1830s there were 38 dwellings

Although not a chartered borough until 1876, Cheltenham became a parliamentary borough in 1832, at the first large-scale reorganisation of parliamentary constituencies for several hundred years. A commission established the boundaries of each parliamentary borough, and in the case of Cheltenham they were coterminous with the parish. The map, based on a survey by the Ordnance Survey, gives a good indication of the extent of development outside the main historic town centre, and is probably an accurate indication of what had been built by this date. Privately produced plans of the town included projected developments as well as existing buildings.

© BODLEIAN LIBRARY, UNIVERSITY OF OXFORD

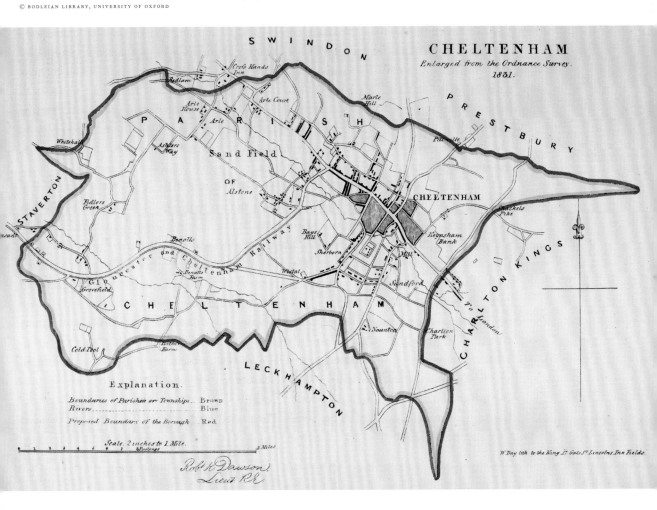

on the one-acre plot, in addition to the two front houses. Of these, 28 cottages were back-to-back, a layout economical of space and of building costs, with their common back walls. Nonetheless they were sufficiently well built to pass the Cheltenham surveyor's inspection, although categorised as 'of the lowest class'. But John Snelus was over-ambitious, and in 1840 became insolvent. The whole property was purchased by one of his creditors, whose family continued to own it until it was demolished in 1934. In 1844 nine of the occupiers of the cottages were general labourers, and five were porters, but the other sixteen men apparently had a trade – although the maltster was certainly not the master of a business but rather a worker in a maltings, possibly the local Albion brewery. Ten men were in the building trades. Six women were heads of households; two were laundresses. In his public health report of 1849 Edward Cresy particularly noted Swindon Place for its deplorable conditions, but it was not condemned until 1933, and demolished the following year.

POLITICS

The 1831 census confirmed how out of date the system of parliamentary representation had become. Parliaments were in principle a means of consulting major 'interest groups' in the country: the Church and aristocracy through the House of Lords, the landed interest through the election of two members for each county, and the trading and commercial community which elected members for each significant trading place or town, the parliamentary boroughs. But over many centuries the size and importance of towns changed: some shrank to mere villages, and other villages flourished and grew into important centres. In the mid-seventeenth century, during the Commonwealth period, there was a brief period of reform, but the older system was one of the structures restored with the monarchy in 1660. It was already anachronistic then – by the early nineteenth century it bore little relationship to the social, economic and demographic realities of the greatest commercial power in the world.

In the counties, those owning land worth a modest forty shillings a year in potential rental value were able to vote, and they were a relatively numerous group. Some seventy landholders in Cheltenham parish actually cast their votes in the county elections in 1776, thirty in Charlton Kings, three in Leckhampton, five in Swindon and 26 in Prestbury. Not all lived in the place where they were qualified to vote. In the parliamentary boroughs, however, there were many and various ways in which property-owners might be entitled to vote, ranging from an extreme in a borough like Westminster where everyone could vote who was a householder – a pot-walloper, originally a pot-boiler – or Preston where it was only necessary to sleep in the town the night before the election, to the 'rotten boroughs' where there was a handful of voters or even just one, like Old Sarum which had been deserted for Salisbury, or Old Dunwich which had fallen into the sea. Joseph Pitt, the developer of Pittville, was the owner of a rotten borough, Malmesbury, which had just thirteen voters, and of a pocket borough, Wootton Bassett, with 250 voters. He himself sat as MP for Cricklade from 1812 to

1831, as a result of 'influencing' (which means bribing) sufficient of the 1,200 electors, but he anticipated the end of his influence and in 1831 retired aged 72.[15]

Pressure for reform built up after the Napoleonic Wars and in 1832, after a dramatic struggle between the House of Commons and the House of Lords, a modest measure of reform was agreed. A mid-1832 petition from Cheltenham in favour of reform contained 3,787 signatures, and a second 5,000.[16] Rotten boroughs were abolished by the 1832 Reform Act, and unrepresented towns with large populations were made parliamentary boroughs in their place. Cheltenham was one of those towns whose population qualified it to become a parliamentary borough, and by the terms of the 1832 Act it was given one representative. The boundaries of the new constituency matched those of the parish but did not include Charlton Kings. The voting qualification in the boroughs was standardised, to comprise every male householder owning property worth at least £10 a year, provided that he paid poor rates and had possessed it for a year. It was still not necessary to live in the borough.[17] Cheltenham celebrated its enfranchisement by erecting a statue of William IV in Imperial Gardens, it has since been moved to Montpellier Gardens.[18]

For the first time it became necessary to register as an elector before being allowed to cast a vote. The first electoral register of 1832–33 for Gloucestershire named 415 men in Cheltenham, although the previous year, in a survey probably instituted to see how the £10 franchise might work, there were over 3,000 occupiers of property rated at £10 and over.[19] Of those on the register 33 were copyholders who between them owned 89 houses or cottages and six plots of land; twenty copyhold cottages, owned by six men, were in Gas Green, and copyhold land was scattered through Cheltenham, at Granley, Cakebridge, 'Fair view garden called the Lippiates', the Promenade, Maidenhom and Bath Road, and Maul's or Maud's Elm. Eighty-seven registered voters did not live in Cheltenham, among them Robert Jenner (the son of the pioneer of smallpox vaccination) whose 'place of abode' was Berkeley but who owned 7 Portland Street, and Richard Skillicorne Skillicorne, who lived in Salford Rectory but was a voter through ownership of Bayshill Lodge and lands.

The new borough could hardly be described as 'rotten' as the term had been understood before 1832, but it did not have a large electorate, and there were considerable scandals about bribery; voting was not secret until 1872. Nor was Cheltenham a 'pocket borough'.[20] Under the old electoral system, a pocket borough was one where voters were responsive to pressure; usually they worked for one of the candidates or lived in a house which he owned. Colonel William Berkeley (later Lord Segrave and from 1841 Earl Fitzhardinge), the brother of Cheltenham's first MP, was a patron of the town; he continued the family tradition of maintaining a pack of hounds there. But in terms of owning property, the Berkeleys were not significant.[21] Craven Fitzhardinge Berkeley relied on giving electors generous entertainment on election day in order to win and retain his Cheltenham parliamentary seat, which he did in 1832, 1835, 1837, 1841, and in the second election of 1852, thereafter holding the seat until his death in 1855. Some of the bribery may in practice have been unnecessary.

Borough constituencies had the reputation of being radical and nonconformist, and the most sympathetic parliamentary group was the Whigs who had introduced the Reform Act. Berkeley sat as a Whig, and his majority was large in 1835 and 1837, but in 1841 the result was close. That probably explains the considerable efforts made to secure enough votes in 1847 and 1848, efforts detailed in his rival's election petitions; one William Cull, for example, enjoyed continuous entertainment on election day, eating and drinking at Berkeley's expense in a variety of hostelries.[22] In 1847 Berkeley was defeated by the conservative Sir Willoughby Jones, a Norfolk man, but Sir Willoughby was unseated the following year, and after the subsequent election, Berkeley in turn was unseated. Berkeley was excluded from standing in 1848 (he gave his occupation as 'ex-MP' in the 1851 census for Cheltenham), and another family member sat for Cheltenham instead. After Berkeley's death, the Cheltenham seat was sometimes won by a Conservative and sometimes by a Liberal.

Among the voters on the first electoral register who can be traced in Pigot's 1830 *Directory*, about half were working men and half professional, a total of 148; twenty were 'leisured', but they were a tiny proportion of the town's male population of 10,000, and most voters did not feature in the *Directory*. Yet 24 voters were qualified by owning very poor properties in Rutland Street, an interesting indication of the modest ownership which could confer the franchise and half those owners lived in the street. Rutland Street was started in 1806 on a former section of the Marsh in the area which became St Paul's, and was the first major development of artisan housing. As early as 1821 it was singled out for condemnation for its filth, 'reflecting disgrace

St Paul's church is a complement to the Pittville Pump Room – both were designed by John Forbes in neo-classical style. While the Pump Room catered for the affluent, St Paul's was designed as a free church to cater for a much less wealthy district of the town north of Swindon Lane. Joseph Pitt provided a site for a nominal payment, and the Church Building Commissioners provided half the cost of the building, but financing the other half locally was not easy because of the financial crisis of 1825. As a result only the front façade was encased in ashlar. The church opened in 1831 with 1,230 free sittings, all in pews to prevent any distinctions of rank.

PHOTOGRAPH: CARNEGIE, 2010

In the nineteenth century local authorities did not have powers of planning to prevent or control the intermingling of residential and commercial uses within the urban environment. As elsewhere in the country, such as Bath or London's Mayfair, the back streets behind the grand façades were packed with coach-houses, service entrances and small-scale commercial premises. This photograph shows the corner of Lansdown Place Lane and Lansdown Walk.

PHOTOGRAPH: CARNEGIE, 2010

on the inhabitants'.[23] The classical temple of St Paul's church which overshadows the area was erected specifically at the instigation of Revd Francis Close to serve the poor of the district, and was newly completed in 1831. It was known as the Free Church, 'where the poor could be certain of a welcome'.[24] As well as individual freehold houses, two voters owned groups of three cottages, and three people were qualified by owning an undivided one-sixth share of a house. Two of these were James and Thomas Boodle, hence the development of Boodle's Passage. The voters in the copyhold cottages in Gas Green were even poorer than those in Rutland Street. The cottages, off the north end of Gloucester Road, adjoined the gasworks established a few years earlier, and had been built by 1826. Twenty were noted in the 1832 electoral register as conferring a vote on their owners, in groups of two, three, four or five cottages and four of the six owners lived in Gas Green.

Disappointed at the limited nature of the 1832 Act, the radically inclined were attracted by the simple message of Chartism with its six point agenda for parliamentary reform, the most important demand being for universal manhood suffrage. Founded in 1838, Chartism was relatively strong in Cheltenham. It was said that a thousand men attended a Chartist 'sermon' on a field on the London Road in 1839, and 151 subscribed in 1847–48 to the Chartist Land Company.[25] John Goding, the writer of the first substantial history of Cheltenham, was a Chartist, and became a Unitarian, a church strongly associated with reform. Chartism attracted considerable opposition in the town partly because it was linked with Socialism; Robert Owen lectured in Cheltenham in 1838. The Chartist George Holyoake was accused of blasphemy by the *Cheltenham Chronicle* after he had lectured at the Mechanics Institute in 1842; he was tried and imprisoned for six months in Gloucester goal. His biography made much of this event. The Mechanics Institute, founded in 1834 as a middle-class initiative to diffuse useful knowledge, had quickly been captured by a lively political lecturer, William Penn Gaskell, a member of Francis Place's Radical Club and a keen Chartist.[26]

In the 1840s, attempts were made to increase the number of eligible radical voters by creating small freeholdings, as the Anti-Corn Law League was doing. It was suggested that the League already had 'a preponderance in the boroughs'. Three societies were formed in Cheltenham in 1843–44 with the aim of enabling men of modest means to become freeholders by paying monthly subscriptions until a share was large enough to buy a house. One had a notable Whig, W.N.S. Skillicorne, as a trustee, and the other two had the Conservative James Agg-Gardner, who had purchased the manor of Cheltenham in 1843. A fourth society, the Cheltenham and Gloucester Freehold Land Society, was formed in 1849, with the stated aim of enabling members to 'become the proprietor of a piece of freehold land ... so that he possesses a stake in the country and a voice in the election of MPs'. In 1850 the Society bought land near Lansdown railway station, which was named the 'Libertus estate'.[27] But although these societies, together with the Chartist Land Society, were pioneers of a property-owning democracy, they made a rather small contribution to the number of voters over the next decades.

The number of registered voters did increase: in 1843 there were 2,100 on the register, and in 1856, with 2,485 registered voters, it was claimed that Cheltenham was 'the largest constituency in England returning but one member'.[28] By 1861 registered voters were still less than 5 per cent of the population, an indication of the prevalence of rented property. The franchise was reformed for a second time in 1867 to allow all male householders in borough constituencies to vote: 3,536 were registered in 1868, when a Liberal was elected, and 7,169 in 1895 when a Conservative won the seat. The introduction in 1918 of manhood suffrage, and limited suffrage for women aged 30 and over who were householders or married to householders, made a huge difference. Some 23,217 were registered in Cheltenham in 1918, and the introduction of the 'flapper' vote in 1928 for all adult women on the same terms as men brought the electorate to 35,712.[29] Interestingly, there was then a run of Conservative members of parliament elected on the wider franchise.

EXPANSION

In early eighteenth-century country towns the better-off lived side by side with the poor, as they did in Cheltenham High Street, and often the front house had the poor crowded in an alley behind. With a few exceptions, such as almshouses, properties were built individually, rather than being designed in larger schemes for urban streets, and there were open spaces between. Cheltenham, on a smaller scale, was probably much like the Cirencester shown in Kip's engraving of 1712, where vegetables were grown behind the houses on the typical burgage plots of the town centre. It has been said that the wide streets of some exceptional eighteenth-century towns represented 'ordered elegance amidst a sea of vernacular idiosyncrasy'.[30] Until the early nineteenth century Cheltenham, a lowland country town, had been built mainly of brick or timber.[31]

The concept of town planning in England owed much to the rebuilding of London after the Great Fire, the devastation giving an exceptional – though mainly unrealised – opportunity for large-scale design, and the mid-eighteenth-century terraces of Bath are notable examples of planning in a provincial context. Planning led to the separation of social groups. Terraces such as Lansdown and Montpellier in Cheltenham were designed solely for the leisured and, because they were large houses, a great many have survived and give the town a distinctive character. Cheltenham's prosperity and population grew so rapidly over a short period that a large number of houses were built in congruous styles, and idiosyncratic vernacular buildings were either swept away or refronted. George Rowe in 1845 wrote in his *Illustrated Cheltenham Guide* that 'a visitor would imagine, on reviewing the Town, that it had arisen in a single night from some fairy's magic influence' but he also noted that in 'the lower and older portions of the town … the march of improvement has not been so rapid'.[32]

At that period of rapid expansion, building was much influenced by London fashions. The revival of classical styles was important, and so was the recent introduction of stucco which, because it was used by prominent London developers, had rapidly achieved fashionable appeal. Liardet's cement, patented in 1773, was described by Clifton Taylor as 'a widely serviceable substance' for covering brickwork and acting as a substitute for stone, and was at once taken up by the Adam brothers in London. Roman cement, patented in 1796, was more successful, being strong, durable and able to withstand damp. Nash used it extensively in London and between 1810 and 1850 its use spread all over the country. It was colour-washed to look like stone, but after oil paint was introduced about 1840 the fake stone joints marked on the stucco were abandoned in favour of painted surfaces. It needed repainting every six to eight years.[33] Many of Cheltenham's houses in this period were covered with Roman cement – builders had to use it in Pittville, or alternatively 'well-washed freestone', which was much more expensive.[34] In mid-century, Roman cement gave way to Portland cement. Cobbett was accurate in noting in 1821 that 'at some distance from [the High Street] there are rows of white tenements, with green balconies, like those inhabited by the tax-eaters round London'. The houses were designed by men who had lived in London, for others who were moving out of London.

Early census returns suggest the remarkable pace of development, which is clear despite some uncertainty about how each enumerator interpreted the apparently simple word 'house'. Between 1801 and 1811, during the Napoleonic Wars, an average of nearly a hundred houses was built each year. There is confirmation of the building boom in the few surviving rating assessments for 1811.[35] When the Cheltenham overseers of the poor drew up their lists that October, they were obviously keeping track of houses which might be rateable in the future. They noted no fewer than 80 building plots in the 'first division' of the parish, and 279 in the 'third division', a total of 359. Unfortunately the lists for the other two divisions of the town are missing. Another pointer to accelerating economic activity in this first decade of the nineteenth

Rodney Lodge (*left*) and 'Formosa House' (*right*) are two examples of houses with a Regency 'bow', of which there are a number in Cheltenham, giving relatively modest houses more impressive façades. Rodney Lodge, listed grade II, was built in 1809 for Robert Hughes on ground behind the Assembly Rooms. It is described as a 'distinguished villa design'. A plan of 1820 to accompany the purchase of Powers Court (*see* page 174) shows that Rodney Lodge then consisted of the bow and the block on the right with the two gables; the entrance to the house was on the end to the left or west and the driveway swept round between it and the Assembly Rooms. The house is now occupied by Inlingua, a college for foreign language training. 'Formosa House' is dated to about 1820, the year George III died and the Prince Regent became George IV, though with later additions; it is listed grade II. It stands between Northfield Passage, to the left of the house, and Northfield Terrace on the right, reminders that one of Cheltenham's open fields was here. Northfield was recorded as early as 1372. Following enclosure in 1806, the land became available for development. The more modest row of Northfield Terrace behind Formosa House was built in the 1820s. The theme of the bow has been echoed in a number of modern buildings.
PHOTOGRAPHS: AUTHOR, 2009; CARNEGIE, 2009

century is the construction, in about 1800, of a plateway (an early form of railway with flanges on the rails rather than the wheels) to bring building-stone down from Leckhampton quarries to the foot of the hill. Excavation work for the Leckhampton plateway may have created the Devil's Chimney, which was described as early as 1803.[36] A few years later, in 1809, a horse-drawn tramway between Gloucester quay and a wharf at the lower end of Cheltenham High Street was authorised by Act of Parliament. The tramway opened between Leckhampton and Cheltenham in 1810, linking up with the plateway, and reached Gloucester the following year. It carried coal and stone. The Railway Company was given a very large rating valuation in October 1811 of £550. This, and the Spa in the occupation of Mr Edward Smith at £297, were far and away the highest valuations in the two surviving lists.

The rate of house-building slackened between 1811 and 1821, with an average of seventy-five houses a year, but accelerated again in the following decade, to 183 houses a year. This is perhaps surprising considering that in 1825–26 there was a banking crisis, with about 100

London and provincial banks collapsing, but the removal of the ban on joint-stock companies in 1825 and the formation of new joint stock banks the following year allowed more liquidity. It is notable that at least one major entrepreneur in Cheltenham, Joseph Pitt, was a banker. There was a slight slackening of activity between 1831 and 1841, the annual average dropping to 156 houses, while the 1840s was a period of general economic difficulty and the sharp fall in the number of new houses in that decade comes as no surprise.

The third Cheltenham Act (1821) required that plans of new buildings should be submitted to the surveyor of the Improvement Commissioners for approval, and that he should enforce regulations concerning the thickness of party walls and prevent the use of thatch.[37] It is perhaps unexpected that in a town such as this houses were still being built with thatched roofs. The intention of the legislation was to minimise fire risk, not to secure the welfare of the occupants. The introduction of building certificates was the initiative of a particularly energetic surveyor to the Commissioners. After inspection, a certificate was issued and a considerable number from the years 1824 to 1840 have survived.[38] They give the names of the developers and indicate the completion dates. This evidence shows how many builders and entrepreneurs exploited the popularity of Cheltenham. For example, Anthony Major built most of Oriel Place, William Gwinnell 40 houses in Lower Bath Road, the Jearrad brothers 34 Lansdown properties, John Boles Watson and then Colonel John Riddell developed Cambray, and Thomas Billings St James's Square.

With its striking tower, Cornerways in The Park (*left*) may have been designed by Samuel Daukes as the entrance to his pleasure grounds on the site of Thomas Billings' failed project of the Zoological and Botanical Gardens. The house plots had been laid out by 1835, and several large villas built. But if the present house is compared with a print of 'The Lodge' (*right*) it appears that the actual building was not quite as portrayed by a contemporary print maker. In mid-century the house was known as 'Park Spa'. It is now part of the University.

PHOTOGRAPH: AUTHOR 2009; PRINT COURTESY OF ERIC MILLER

Much house-building after 1806 was on freehold land to the north of the High Street, allotted in small amounts of two acres or so at enclosure in compensation for loss of common rights on the Marsh. These plots were ideally suited to small building developments. An example is the Portland Square area.[39] In the enclosure award, William Wills was allotted 2¾ acres in Sandfield alias Prestbury field alias Whaddon field. The land is near the modern Pittville Circus. Joseph Hughes, a butcher, bought the land in 1824, and drew up a modestly ambitious scheme for a square with a central garden. Unfortunately, the banking crisis, and Hughes's lack of capital, quickly led to bankruptcy after he had built some six houses. Other small entrepreneurs then took over his plots and plans, and the Square was completed, but it was significantly altered when the restriction on building on the central garden was lifted. In 1835–36 Charles Wilson, a stonemason, planned a layout and arranged details with each speculative builder who took on house plots there.[40] In 1832 six voters lived here, and in 1851 nearly a hundred houses were occupied; a wide variety of people lived in the area, some professional, some leisured, some craftsmen, and ten kept lodging houses.

EARLY NINETEENTH-CENTURY ENTREPRENEURS

Joseph Pitt has seized the headlines, with his colourful personal history and undeniably imaginative development of Pittville, the most grandiose scheme of the period. Furthermore he had become a major landowner and was unique in the number of years in which he was involved in Cheltenham developments. Henry and Pearson Thompson, who were responsible for the ambitious estates of Montpellier and Lansdown, were also for a time major landowners. They are typical projectors – by their access to capital and their willingness to assume greater risk they were distinguished from the body of speculative builders who bought a limited site and erected a few houses at a time to a uniform design.[41] However, as with other speculative builders, the financial strains might prove overwhelming. Important estates were also developed by Samuel Harward and by his nephews, who together with Thomas Henney were responsible for the Promenade, arguably the single most important street in Cheltenham, and for Imperial Gardens. Smaller-scale but still significant building was achieved by James Fisher, who developed Suffolk Square; and Thomas Billings and S.W. Daukes, who between them laid out and developed the Park. A group of gentlemen formed a company and developed the Bayshill estate. A proper sense of the shape of these estates has been much reduced by the inexorable tide of traffic which flows along some of the roads, cutting off one part from another, although the impression of open spaces and gardens remains.

THE HARWARDS AND THE JEARRADS

To the visitor, the Promenade and Imperial Gardens are more likely to form their impressions of Cheltenham than either Lansdown or Pittville. The Promenade was developed after the death in 1809 of Samuel Harward, who had built the Colonnade. His nephews, the Reverend

John Harward and his brother Thomas, were the sons of Michael Harward, gentleman, of Hartlebury, near Worcester.[42] Neither lived in Cheltenham – between 1796 and 1855 John was rector of Icomb near Stow on the Wold in Gloucestershire. Living at 'a great distance', the brothers relied on John Cossens, the postmaster, as their agent, and on Thomas Henney their partner, who lived in Cheltenham.[43] This group saw an investment opportunity for another Pump Room which did not require an enormous capital outlay, but generated income from visitors. The Sherborne Spa had been built in 1804 at the top of Old Well Lane on land belonging to the lord of the manor, but the well proved inadequate. A new site was found on land purchased from Lord Sherborne by Samuel Harward, and a more ambitious Sherborne Spa was completed by 1818, later renamed 'Imperial Spa'.[44] Gardens and an approach road from the High Street, with an avenue of trees like the Old Well Walk, were laid out across the marshy area to the south of the High Street. The road soon became known as 'The Promenade';[45] the conception, style and position justify a capital letter for the definite article – The Promenade has proved a defining feature of Cheltenham. Possibly not coincidentally, Henry Thompson started his development of a Montpellier spa in the same year. But times were changing. The Harwards or Henney saw that more residential roads and lodging houses for the leisured were needed. The fine terrace on the west side of the Promenade, Harwards Buildings, designed by George Underwood, architect and county surveyor, and, towards the Colonnade and High Street, the impressive Imperial Hotel and terrace, were built in 1823–25.

The Imperial spa was sold in 1825, and by 1834 had been taken over by the Jearrad brothers, London architects who, with their father, were based at 260 Oxford Street from 1806 to 1852; they also leased Montpellier Spa and much of the Lansdown estate.[46] It is a measure of the growing reputation of Cheltenham as a fashionable residential centre that these two architects invested heavily in the town's development. They had recently built fourteen houses in Bedford Gardens and their father had carried out extensive works for the 4th duke of Portland at his mansion of Welbeck Abbey in Nottinghamshire. In 1836 the Imperial Spa was dismantled and removed to a position lower down the Promenade, and replaced by the outstanding Queen's Hotel, which they designed. The Jearrads also laid out Imperial Square. A number of villas along the Promenade were built by Thomas Henney. He was a very active figure in Cheltenham, serving on committees and commissions, including the new Board of Guardians elected under the Poor Law Amendment Act of 1834. In 1830 he lived in Promenade Villa, and was given the title 'esquire'; in 1851 he was described as a magistrate, and his address was Clarence House, where he lived with his wife and son (a clergyman and tutor at Pembroke College, Oxford) and four servants, while another son, a solicitor, was at Imperial Lodge. In this way, a crucial Cheltenham feature was the result of successive developers seeing the potential, and having the capital and enterprise to implement their conceptions.

A map of Samuel Harward's property dated 1817 shows the complex pattern of boundaries around the churchyard, and his larger block of property south of the Chelt; he had bought two meadows in 1795, while three pastures which he had purchased were not transferred to the estate until after his death in 1809. The line of what became The Promenade as far as the Chelt was called The Colonnade, and there were gardens on either side. The map does not include Harward's dwelling house and printing office, which, along with premises in Eastgate Street, Gloucester, he left to his wife; the property that was mapped passed to his relations.

The map suggests that Samuel Harward was planning an extension over the Chelt before his death, but it was his cousins, Revd Thomas Harward and his brother, John, who held mortgages for part, who built The Promenade and part of Imperial Square, the largest of Cheltenham's squares. Harwards' Buildings, at present the municipal offices, eclipse all others in the area by their splendour: 'the great terrace, equal to any in Europe' as David Verey claims in *The Buildings of England*.

PHOTOGRAPH: AUTHOR, 2009

Building of the unusual row of shops in Montpellier Walk started from the Montpellier Spa end in 1829, but work was halted for seven years. Then a few buildings at that end were added, and in 1844 the ostentatious entrance to the parade at its northern end, the Rotunda, seen here; the entrance to the Walk was beneath a first-floor link to the shops on the right. R. W. and C. Jearrad were responsible for this design, incorporating the decorative caryatid figures which give a uniquely distinctive appearance to the Walk (*see* page 194).
BY COURTESY OF ERIC MILLER

THE THOMPSONS AND THE JEARRADS

In about 1801 Henry Thompson bought nearly 400 acres of Delabere land adjoining the Old Well and Bayshill, with the immediate intention of developing a new spa and rides, and set about a series of trial borings to find another source of the mineral water.[47] Goding said that he paid only a nominal purchase price. This is hardly credible, but may indicate that he was a substantial creditor to Delabere. As early as 1804 he had built Hygeia House as a spa house, subsequently converted to be his private residence, and now called Vittoria House, but he did not live in Cheltenham until 1809.[48] Finding a better water supply led him to build a small pump room at Montpellier in 1808 or 1809, and also a laboratory for concentrating the salts. However, there was not enough water from his existing wells to enable him to use machinery to concentrate the salt, so 'upwards of 70 wells' were sunk and several thousand feet of pipes installed. In 1817 a larger pump room was erected at Montpellier.[49] But Henry's speculative streak also led him into some disrepute. He claimed that the wells which he had sunk on his land each yielded water with distinctive chemical constituents. As it was observed that Epsom salts were added to some other wells, and that a certain black wagon departed from his salt manufactory for Epsom every week, his claim was doubted. 'Be this as it may,' Dr Granville

Of all the buildings associated with the early history of Cheltenham as a spa, Thompson's Montpellier spa with the slightly later Rotunda has most often been the subject of prints and later of photographs. The print (*above*) is of Henry Thompson's Montpellier Spa before the Rotunda was added in 1825–26. G. A. Underwood designed the building, but after Henry Thompson's death, J. B. Papworth made it far grander with the addition of the Rotunda. The photograph (*below*) probably dates from the last years of the nineteenth century, between 1892 and 1898; the flower show was advertised for Wednesday 11 May, and this date occurred five times in this period, while the horse and rider make it more likely to be an earlier rather than a later date. There is no sign of a motor car to suggest it might be 1904 or 1910.

The lion, which has been restored along with the rest of the Montpellier Spa building by Lloyds TSB plc, is visible on the earlier print opposite showing the building before 1825. The Rotunda has become one of the iconic images of 'Regency Cheltenham'.

PHOTOGRAPH: CARNEGIE, 2009

wrote in the *Spas of England* in 1841, Henry Thompson 'is looked upon as the regenerator of Cheltenham.'[50]

Henry Thompson is a rather mysterious figure. He appears to have been an adventurer, whose enterprising spirit according to Dr Granville led him early in his life to various parts of the world. He married Judith Techmaker, a granddaughter of a wealthy German émigré to England.[51] Thompson has a reputation as a London banker but does not appear in *A Handbook of London Bankers*, compiled in 1890–91; Hart suggests that he was a merchant and underwriter.[52] He certainly had the eye of a skilful speculator; he saw what might be done in Cheltenham 'by energy and some ready cash' and arrived in the town, Granville said, with £10,000. He died at Hygeia House in 1820, aged 72 years. His wife was allowed to have the furniture and one year's residence, and then the property passed to his two sons jointly.[53] One, resident in Cockermouth Castle, was called Henry Techmaker Thompson; his younger son was Pearson Thompson, who lived in Cheltenham and further developed that part of his father's estate.

Pearson Thompson and his brother were anxious to protect Montpellier Spa, and made a bargain with James Fisher, a boarding-house keeper, who in 1820 had purchased Suffolk House and proposed to develop the grounds. The Thompsons owned the land between Suffolk House and the new turnpike road from Cheltenham to Painswick, the Bath Road.[54] Fisher undertook not to dig for mineral springs in return for a right of access, but he had to put a gate across his driveway marked 'Private Road to and from Suffolk House and Grounds'. Part of the driveway was 'not to be used for servants to exercise horses nor haul wagons of bricks, stone, timber, coals or heavy [loads] nor throw offensive matter on it nor for wheel barrows on footpaths'. Fisher was responsible for mending Engine House Lane and Trafalgar Street and the Home Acre Road, while the Thompsons accepted responsibility for other roads and paths.[55] Engine House Lane became Rodney Road and in 1827 was adopted by the Cheltenham highways surveyors.[56]

Pearson Thompson, a solicitor until he took over his father's Cheltenham property,[57] seems to have taken on the development of the estate with enthusiasm. He secured the services of a notable architect, John Papworth, to add a rotunda to the Pump Room in 1825–26, and to draw out a design for new roads and houses for the Montpellier and Lansdown estates and Gardens. John Papworth (he adopted the additional name Buonarotti in 1815 in a vainglorious reference to Michelangelo) was a man with many skills: architect, artist, furniture designer, landscaper designer, writer and town planner. He designed other estates, at Dulwich, St Bride's Avenue off Fleet Street, and Dover, and a model town near Cincinnati. Among his achievements was the design of the first Gin Palace on Holborn Hill (1829–32) for a firm called Fearon and Thompson; his work on the Montpellier spa might have contributed to his understanding of the requirements for a higher class, ornate shop with a bar for selling gin and wine.[58] Papworth also assisted with building St James's church, Suffolk Square and St John's church, now demolished, proprietary churches where the seats belonged to the subscribers. A significant extension of Cheltenham to the south was begun in 1826 with Lansdown Place. The original plans appear to have been for detached 'villas' but the enterprise was not immediately successful, and progress was slow, both in building and also finding purchasers for the houses.

In 1830 Pearson Thompson leased the estate to the Jearrad brothers, who considerably modified the design, substituting terraces for villas, and eventually bought the estate.[59] The Jearrads wanted to create a good approach to Montpellier from the High Street and Promenade, and immediately began to build shops in Montpellier Avenue, close to the Imperial Spa. Montpellier Walk was started later, in 1843, and the shops were flamboyantly separated by caryatids, armless female figures based on the classical Greek sculptures supporting the porch

of the Erechtheion on the Acropolis; two in painted terracotta were certainly sculpted by Rossi, and the other thirty were carved in stone locally in Tivoli by W.G. Brown.[60] However, the link between the Promenade and Montpellier was considered 'crooked and narrow' by Dr Granville, and is still obviously not part of a single coherent layout.[61] The flamboyant Lansdown Terrace, which was building in 1832, was said to be for retired East India Company servants.[62]

Willoughby was the first house in Suffolk Square, a development started in 1823 by James Fisher. Suffolk House itself has been demolished. There is a fine terrace running eastwards from this house towards St James's church, and another on the east side of the square, while the south side is occupied by two very large houses, now linked together and divided into apartments. Sir Robert Smirke, a leading architect of the Greek revival, and particularly notable for designing the British Museum, lived in one from 1859 to 1867, and his residence here is marked with a blue plaque. He was buried in Leckhampton.

PHOTOGRAPH: CARNEGIE, 2009

Pearson Thompson's first development of his property to create the Lansdown estate was slow to achieve success. When the map of Alstone and Arle was made in 1835, only the smaller section of the convex Lansdown Crescent, to the left in the aerial photograph, had been completed, and this was all that Papworth had planned. The rest of the estate was conceived as semi-detached villas. However, the Jearrad brothers extended the arc of the terrace to three times its original length, to comprise forty-five houses on a gradual curve, completed about 1838, and these are now a strong feature in Cheltenham's early nineteenth-century architecture. Also clearly visible in this aerial view are the smaller-scale residential, commercial and service premises behind the grand façades (*see also* page 245).

Lansdown Crescent was intended to be a circular set of semi-detached villas,[63] but the Jearrads considerably modified the design to make it less expensive, building groups of houses in an austere, long sweep of curved terraces, although they retained the classical columns and pediments. Only half the circle was completed, resulting in a convex crescent, the opposite of Royal Crescent in Bath which must have influenced the original design. Pearson Thompson himself lived in Lansdowne Villa in 1832, but had moved to Hatherley Court by 1839, from where he published an election address opposing Craven Berkeley's more liberal views on who should be permitted to vote.

JOSEPH PITT

Although Pittville was sometimes called a 'new town', as its name implies, it was centred on gardens and the Pump Room, not the usual urban facilities which were placed on the periphery. It might better be characterised as a pioneering example of the garden suburb. A small number of leisured and 'town gentry' were building villas on the edge of a town, and the pleasure of this type of urban living could here be adopted by those less wealthy than the aristocracy. As in the twentieth century, in Cheltenham and all large towns, the suburbs would accommodate the more modestly affluent.[64]

It was said that Joseph Pitt had 'a sharp eye for advowsons'.[65] He had purchased several before he secured the Cheltenham tithes, but could not buy the advowson of Cheltenham itself as the arrangements for presentation, there and at Charlton Kings, which had been made by Sir Baptist Hicks as long ago as the 1620s still stood. An advowson was valuable where the glebeland and tithe income of the parish church were substantial; just one presentation could be sold, for example to a father wishing to present a son to a lifetime's secure position. Pitt had bought the advowson to the rectory of Rendcomb and presented his first son, Cornelius, and subsequently gave him the advowson. He had probably already paid for Cornelius's presentation to the rectory of Hazleton and chapel of Yanworth and thought him adequately provided for. Pitt also bought the advowsons of the vicarages of Malmesbury and Ashton Keynes, presenting another son, Charles, to Malmesbury and bequeathing him the advowson to Ashton Keynes. However, in the case of Cheltenham, it was the glebeland and tithes which Pitt valued and purchased in 1799, before promoting enclosure.

This was probably the most successful period of his career. In 1807 he bought a 'respectable old mansion', Eastcourt House in Wiltshire,[66] where he lived for the rest of his life. His building plans for Cheltenham were purely a speculative venture. In 1812, when he became a member

The wonderful interior of the Pittville Pump Room was drawn soon after it was completed in 1830. Building had started five years before, but the resignation of the architect, John Forbes, led to a delay in finishing it. The drawing shows the central square gallery high up, open to the assembly room below, and also the edge of the dome above it. At the 'high' end of the room there is a recessed ceiling. These unusual features help to create the exceptionally good acoustic. There are other rooms for entertaining, and the spa water may be taken here. Cheltenham values John Forbes' design, and, newly redecorated, it is a delight to eye as well as ear.

of parliament, he retired from his solicitor's practice. His family were of yeomen farming stock near Malmesbury and he remained rooted in this area. Though he no doubt exaggerated his rags-to-riches story by recounting how he held the heads of horses for gentlemen in Cirencester, the tale suggests an early desire to make money.

In 1812 Pitt purchased the advowson of Bagendon, which he was to use to alter the patronage of Cheltenham church.[67] An Act of Parliament was required to transfer the advowson of Cheltenham from Jesus College to Pitt, and to allow Jesus to accept that of Bagendon in exchange. The act was obtained in 1816, and Pitt immediately sold the advowson to the Simeon Trust, which in pursuit of Charles Simeon's evangelical aims, was buying advowsons in order to present evangelical clergy who were not acceptable to most patrons. The Trust bought the advowsons to Bath, Bridlington and several large industrial towns, including Birmingham and Bradford. They presented Francis Close to Cheltenham in 1826. One of Pitt's motives may have been to remove the onerous restrictions on the incumbents of Cheltenham and Charlton Kings imposed by Baptist Hicks. The sale may also have brought Pitt some money in excess of his costs. In 1812 he had sold to Cheltenham vestry the churchyard, which was his by virtue of buying the rectory, and some additional land for an extension to the churchyard. In 1843 he even sold the chancel of the parish church to a firm of Cheltenham solicitors.

Some years after the Cheltenham enclosure Pitt embarked on his new town project. He had made further purchases and land exchanges in order to acquire a favourable site, including 48 acres in Prestbury on which he built the Pump Room and planned to build houses. He also widened Portland Passage, now Pittville Street, to make a convenient access from the town centre.[68] Granville noted in 1841 that the distance of the Pump Room 'from the centre of buzzing life, the shops and the hotels' had operated to reduce 'the merited success of that establishment'.[69] Pitt grasped an opportunity to design a smaller-scale Regent's Park or Hyde Park estate, with gardens, walks and drives, centred on a classical Pump Room with spa water available, but where the houses would not be as expensive as in London. In 1824 the plans

The fountain from which the medicinal water is still dispensed (into plastic cups!) is the original one, possibly designed by J. C. Mead of London who completed the interior of the Pump Room after John Forbes resigned. It is made of marble and scagliola (coloured and polished plaster), and, as David Verey comments, is rather like a Grecian altar, a fitting design in the light of the miraculous benefits attributed to the water.

PHOTOGRAPH: CARNEGIE, 2009

for his new town, modestly named after himself, were drawn by John Forbes, an architect and projector who had been working in Cheltenham for some time. He was apparently a difficult man and resigned after a few years; he was also under-capitalised, and financial problems led him to forge a signature for which he went to gaol. The layout which Forbes created for Pittville was masterly, and he designed the generally admired Pump Room and a particularly fine terrace in Pittville Lawn.[70] Pittville was a private gated estate, and only house-owners had access to the pleasure grounds. Restrictive covenants protected the status of the properties, and shops were only to be built in Segrave Place and Prestbury Road.

The original scheme provided for between 500 and 600 houses, both individual villas and terraces. Many builders were involved, mainly constructing single houses on a speculative basis, but one man, Abraham Tyler, built the 23 houses which constitute most of Pittville Parade and Pittville Villas. Builders and architects had to follow Pitt's master plan, and if any wished to alter a façade, had to agree the design with his estate surveyor. By the time of Pitt's death in 1842, 177 houses had been completed. As the houses went up, the Paving Commissioners realised that the boundaries of their authority were annoyingly limited; they were unable to collect rates from any of the new houses built on former glebe or land granted at enclosure in lieu of tithes. The provisions of the Enclosure Act protected the land. In 1839 they proposed applying to parliament to extend their area of authority. Pearson Thompson and the Jearrad brothers were in favour – they were building outside the old Cheltenham township

The architecture of the Pittville Pump Room externally has been criticised as oddly unbalanced, but it combines Greek inspiration with idiosyncracy and individuality. It is therefore immediately recognised, and has formed an integral part of Cheltenham's appearance and attractions. Its restoration after the Second World War was costly, and its maintenance continues to be so, but it is a very important contributor to Cheltenham's ethos.

PHOTOGRAPH: CARNEGIE, 2009

82754. (JV.) PITTVILLE PARK GATES , CHELTENHAM .

boundary – but Pitt and Thomas Billings were vigorously opposed, as their new houses would then be rated. They won. In 1843 the vestry examined the same problem, since church rates, too, could not be collected from these houses. The vestry recorded 505 houses built on church land, mostly in Pittville, with an estimated rateable value of £20,042.[71] The commissioners and the vestry successfully altered the situation in 1852 with a new improvement act.

Pitt had borrowed extensively to finance both the layout and the builders. His eldest son, Cornelius, predeceased him, but Cornelius's son Joseph, who became rector of Rendcomb, was one of his grandfather's creditors. Pitt had already given all his children financial resources for their futures, and he left the rest of his estate to his own son Joseph. Unhappily for the uncle's prospects, he was sued by his nephew for satisfaction of moneys owed him and the other creditors from his grandfather's estate. As a result, between 1843 and 1845 the property at Pittville was sold in four auctions. Some occupiers or intended occupiers bought plots, but many others were bought by the County of Gloucester bank, which had absorbed one of Pitt's own banking businesses, and the bank effectively became the manager of the estate, and the Pump Room and gardens, and continued in this capacity for over forty years. Building proceeded more slowly after the auctions: 216 houses were completed by 1860. Thirty years later, in 1890, the County of Gloucester bank sold Pittville Pump room and the gardens to Cheltenham Corporation on condition that both were preserved. Joseph Pitt might be gratified that the exceptionally good acoustic of the Pump Room is much appreciated by players and audiences alike, and that it has been restored and beautifully decorated by the borough council. Pittville has continued to be an important element in Cheltenham's attractions.

DR GRANVILLE'S SPAS OF ENGLAND

The description of Cheltenham by Dr Granville captures the achievements of the developers before 1841. By that date the shape and style of Cheltenham had been established.[72] Granville (1783–1872) had an Italian father, and an English mother whose surname he adopted. He graduated in medicine at Pavia University, and for the next ten years led an adventurous life before settling in England in 1812 with his English wife and building a respected medical practice in London. Having published *The Spas of Germany* in 1837 and then being chided by a manageress in Buxton that he had not written about English spas, he set about travelling throughout England during 1839 and 1840 to remedy this. He said he had first visited Cheltenham fifteen years earlier. He stayed at *The Plough*, described as a large country inn which was nearly always full, and not as expensive as the new *Queen Hotel*. The Midlands

Cheltenham Ladies' College was founded in 1853, and at first occupied Cambray House. In 1870 The far-sighted Dorothea Beale suggested that the proprietors buy Faconberg House, the large house on the corner of St George's Road and Bayshill, built in 1847 and designed by Samuel Onley. Other parts of the original Well Walk had been developed a few years earlier, including four Fauconberg Villas about 1860, also by Onley, of which three remain within the school, and another terrace that has been demolished. Some of the Walk remained. Gradually the school acquired more of the site, as property became available, and finally purchased Onley's Theatre Royal which was on the site of an early pump room. What remains of the Well Walk is the open space within the school precinct, seen here; the range on the right is part of the first new buildings on the site, 1871–73, and the continuation to the left is a few years later.
PHOTOGRAPH: CARNEGIE, 2009

The postcard dates from about 1910, and shows the former Imperial Hotel, built in 1823, after it became the Post Office and received an extended porch in 1906. Dr Granville in 1841 commented on the occupants of the hotel, a number of single gentlemen. Waterstone's have restored the building and opened up the original central staircase. This end of The Promenade is busier than the south end, and is built up on both sides. The shops were already infiltrating this residential street by 1845, notably Cavendish House, which was so named already when it was the silk mercery establishment of Debenham, Pooley and Smith.

© CHELTENHAM ART GALLERY AND MUSEUM; PHOTOGRAPH: CARNEGIE 2009

volume was published in 1841, and an engraving of the 'Old Well Walk' appeared on the title page.

His observations, both general and particular, are astute. He recognised the transformation from health cure through aristocratic social centre, 'the urban equivalent of the great country house', to popular holiday resort, and then to a residential centre as seaside resorts took on the holiday function. As a spa, the reputation of Cheltenham was waning, he said; only 82 names were recorded at Montpellier Pump Room in the month that he was in Cheltenham. Leamington was becoming more popular. But Cheltenham 'has become a town of great resort and importance'.

The building of entire new districts, 'so many little new towns', he thought was paralleled only by Newcastle, and he noted that inmates for the houses were found as soon as built. He feared that the beautiful avenue of elm trees at the Old Well would be levelled to the ground by the joint stock company developing the Bayshill estate, a fear that was realised. He reported a trenchant view of Cheltenham society overheard in a hotel: 'we have the reputation of possessing more spinsters and old maids, more widows and half-pay yellows from the Indus and the Ganges, together with lots of methodists and tee-totallers, than are necessary to render the place as dull as ditch-water'. He felt that Cheltenham exhibited more of the 'worst symptoms of a fashionable spa' than any other English watering place, but that a permanent as well as a transitory population made it the only 'fashionable watering place to rival Bath'.

The *Imperial Hotel* in the Promenade was particularly noticed by Granville. The widow Susan Joseph kept the hotel which was a 'rendezvous of, and is supported by, Old Bachelors, many of whom dwell in it permanently, and rule the roast', so controlling the carving of the joint rather than the chicken coop. They did not like ladies at their dining table so Widow Susan had established quiet and civil boarding houses on each side of the *Imperial*. The veracity of this observation is largely confirmed by the 1841 census, which showed ten single men in the hotel. There were also three independent women, attended by two men and seven women servants, and Widow Susan herself. Seven more 'houses' under the same *Imperial Hotel* address contained small independent families and their servants, and these were conventional boarding houses.

Dr Granville's informant had some justification for his view of the marital status of Cheltenham's inhabitants. Assuming that once a woman reached 30 she was considered unlikely to get married, there were slightly over 2,000 'old maids' in Cheltenham in 1851, not including any spinster visitors. Out of a population of 35,000 this was not an extraordinary number, but to the observer these people were noticeable because many lived independently in their own houses. Bachelors were less numerous.

What of the comment about half pay officers retired from service in India? As early as 1820, Gell and Bradshaw commented that Cheltenham's name 'is become as familiar in the British East and West Indies as in London'. The Cheltenham tradition may have started eighty years earlier, when Lady Stapleton and Captain Skillicorne established the first spa. The houses at Daylesford and Sezincote in the Cotswolds may also have influenced the

Edward Cope designed a number of houses in the Pittville area, including the large sweep of Pittville Circus, about 1840, which has a number of villas in assorted styles round it, but was not completed. In spring time the circus green is a particularly attractive open area. Only two houses were occupied in 1851, one by a colonel in the Bengal army with his family and three servants, and one by Charlotte Pitt and her four sons and two servants.

PHOTOGRAPH: AUTHOR, 2009

casual observer. Warren Hastings, the celebrated former governor-general of Bengal, bought Daylesford in 1788 and employed Samuel Pepys Cockerill to design a house with echoes of Indian architecture. Cockerill's two brothers had served in Bengal, and in 1805 one purchased nearby Sezincote and remodelled it in more flamboyant Indian style. But it was the mild climate and nature of the waters which brought men who had worked in India and the West Indies to Cheltenham. Like the old maids their numbers hardly justified the apparent prominence which they assumed in accounts of the town, but they were clearly important for its image and reputation.

The 1851 census recorded 215 men in Cheltenham with either a military, naval or Indian service connection: some were visitors, relations or lodgers, but 151 were heads of households. They ranged from a 19-year-old in the Madras Civil Service to an 87-year-old 'Late Major'; 63 of them were aged under 50, and 72 had been or were in the East India Company's employment, or were serving in the Indian army. There were also four women who were East India Company or Indian army pensioners. They were scattered through the town, though the largest groups (27) were in Pittville, in Clarence Square (10) and Imperial Square (7). A few people had been born in the West Indies, and there were two West India merchants. But some occupations or birthplaces in the census did not reveal colonial service. A professor of Oriental Languages at Oxford University, Adam Durnford Gordon, who was an early member of staff at Cheltenham College, had served with a cavalry regiment in India, although the 1851 census does not reveal this, and the chairman of the first Cheltenham College committee, George Swiney, who had served in the Bengal army, was described in the census as 'retired medical officer'. David Hartley, surgeon at Cheltenham General Hospital, had earlier worked for the East India Company. So the census understates the Indian connection. It is notable that during the Indian mutiny in 1857, the *Cheltenham Examiner* had a special column headed 'the Bombay Mail'.[73]

It has been a matter of comment that Cheltenham architecture does not reflect Indian styles, though the entrance to the new Market Arcade in the High Street, built in 1823 and demolished in 1867,[74] had Indian echoes. Indian army and East India Company servants served on a number of commissions in the town,[75] and an area of the Old Gloucester Road, now St George's Road, was called Calcutta. The names Calcutta Terrace, Calcutta Place, Calcutta House and *Calcutta Inn* (demolished in 2003), and an occasional house-name recorded the connection, but these reflections are not many. The most important legacy of the Indian connection is Cheltenham College. Several retired officers were important in its founding in 1841, as a proprietary college, funded by subscribers, for day boys and boarders who were 'gentlemen's sons. One of its professed aims was to prepare boys for university, the army and entrance to the East India Company's colleges at Addiscombe and Haileybury; it was particularly successful in respect of Addiscombe.[76] Having founded a school for gentlemen's sons, a matching institution for their daughters, Cheltenham Ladies' College, followed twelve years later.

CHAPTER NINE

IMPROVEMENT

THE FIRST, and arguably the most important, phase in Cheltenham's development had been completed by 1851. The second half of the nineteenth century was a period of consolidation and sometimes reluctant improvement. The town had gained significance when it became a parliamentary borough in 1832, though it did not become chartered until 1876, by which time counsel could say, when arguing for Cheltenham to become an incorporated borough, that only 29 boroughs in the whole country had a population greater than Cheltenham's 43,000.[1] The parliamentary borough did not always match the area of the town's local government, but was revised on several occasions in the nineteenth century to take in parts of Charlton Kings and Leckhampton.

PUBLIC HEALTH

Cheltenham's Paving Commissioners had limited their work to cleaning, lighting and widening the streets in the central area around the High Street, and to the provision of larger market halls. They did not extend their efforts to the provision of other basic and essential services. From the first outbreak of cholera in 1832 public health gradually became a major national concern, and by the end of the 1840s it was increasingly appreciated that the whole population of a town was at risk from disease spreading from poorer areas, because of water which was contaminated through lack of sewers. This was a problem in all rapidly expanding towns, in Cheltenham as much as any industrial centre in Northern England or South Wales. There is a reference to a medical officer in the Paving Commission's papers for 1819,[2] long before such posts became standard nationally. In response to the threat of cholera in 1831 the government authorised the formation of Boards of Health, temporary bodies intended to implement the rudimentary medical and sanitation measures then available. At Cheltenham a Board was formed that autumn and, among its somewhat inadequate actions, 'stationed constables at the outskirts to turn away mangy-looking itinerants'.[3]

As a town devoted to the search for health, Cheltenham should have had a particular interest in adequate drainage, but the Paving Commissioners were found wanting in this respect. They had mainly provided for the removal of surface water from the roads. Twenty-two medical practitioners met together and signed a resolution, dated 14 December 1831, to be presented to commissioners from the Board of Health of Cheltenham; 'Resolved that common drains or sewers are very much wanted in the town of Cheltenham and that it is highly expedient and necessary the same should be made without delay', most of the streets

inhabited by the labouring classes in Cheltenham being without the advantage of any drains or sewers whatever and exposed to the great nuisances arising from dry wells or cesspools and the continued emptyings thereof which occasions a great want of cleanliness in the said town and are highly dangerous to the health of the inhabitants more particularly in case of fevers and other pestilential diseases.

That more effectual draining of Cheltenham is the more strongly recommended by this Board at the present time as a protection against the extension to this town of the disease which now exists at Sunderland.

There was some provision for the health of the poor of Cheltenham from 1813, after the vestry convened a meeting which resolved to open a dispensary. A casualty ward was later added. It moved to new premises five times at least before the new hospital was built on a two-acre site in Sandford fields. The immediate impetus to this move was compensation paid by the Cheltenham and Oxford Railway Company in 1848, because their proposed line would pass through the hospital premises in the High Street. Many charitable donations enabled the hospital to work. The classical design by D. J. Humphries was commended as 'one of the neatest, most commodious, and compact little hospitals'. The postcard shows it before extensions were added on all sides. The west wing with its staircase was for men and the east wing for women and a museum; offices were in the centre. The importance of a generous supply of hot and cold water in the bathrooms was appreciated.

This was cholera, the terrifying threat of which had prompted the formation of the Board of Health. Nothing was apparently done, and two years later a group of inhabitants were preparing a bill to be presented to parliament to authorise the formation of a private Sewers Company. The Paving Commissioners discussed the bill in February 1833. They were anxious to protect their rights, and intended to retain a power to inspect the company's work, but they agreed to vest their existing sewers in the company. The bill was passed later that year. Twenty-eight men subscribed £7,600 in £100 shares, mostly gentlemen or esquires. Eight men put up £500 each: Thomas Henney, the developer of some of the Promenade, William Pitt, banker, Samuel Sheddon, mercer, John Gardner and Robert Capper, Esquires. Robert Capper lived in Marle Hill house outside the town, and a smaller subscriber was James Agg of Hewletts, also out of the town; they were not going to benefit directly from the sewers, and their motive could have been philanthropic, unless they seriously thought they would make a profit. Another subscriber was Edward Hatch, the overseer of the poor, who perhaps knew better than most the situations concerned.

Having made the sewers and reinstated the roads and pavements, the company charged all those connected an annual rate. But fine words about the need for sewers where the labouring classes lived, particularly on the north side of the High Street, were not heeded. In 1848 the Paving Commissioners offered to buy the company out for £12,000, but the offer was rejected. The Improvement bill, three years later, included a clause authorising the purchase of the company, but was dropped because of a technical objection to stating in the bill the amount to be paid. The new Improvement Commissioners then proposed building their own sewer system in parallel with the company's. However, negotiations continued, and in 1857 Henry Dangerfield for the commissioners reported that the company had 5 miles of sewers and 1,007 houses were connected (out of 7,000 in the parliamentary borough in 1851). He valued the company at £6,820. The company held out for a better price, eventually selling for £9,000. The Improvement Commissioners agreed to levy a uniform rate on all property, but owners on private estates such as Pittville were granted a reduction.

The Cheltenham Waterworks Company was first formed in 1824 to supply households which could afford the cost of connecting to, and paying for, water drawn from the newly constructed Hewletts Reservoir. The Company applied to parliament in 1847 for power to raise more money and extend its waterworks;[4] at that date it claimed to supply 1,941 houses out of the total of 7,677, recorded in the poor-rate assessment books for Cheltenham, Charlton, Leckhampton, Prestbury and Swindon, which it could potentially supply. A committee heard evidence from Cheltenham residents both in support of and against the bill. Samuel Higgs Gael esquire said that he lived in the neighbourhood 'part of the year' and with the Board of Guardians had recently enquired into conditions in Cheltenham and Charlton Kings. They had found a great number of alleys and courts 'many of which had only one pump or well to perhaps, on an average, six or seven tenements, and some where ten tenements shared one pump'. He noted that the district around Bath Road was on the clay, a large district of small tenements with a very inadequate supply of water. One common standcock was supplied from Leckhampton Hill. The rest of the buildings on the clay were of a better sort and could afford water rates. John Goding also gave evidence. He lived in Burton Street and drew his water from a well. 'It is of good quality, and being a tee-totaller, I drink very freely of it'. He said he supplied water to perhaps ten families. Much discussion centred on a supply to the Paving Commissioners for fire-fighting and to water the roads. To modern eyes, accustomed to tarmac road surfaces, this seems a profligate use of water; but when the roads were gravel, mud and dust, watering them in summer was an important amenity. The company gained its act, but continued to make slow progress towards extending the number of houses it supplied.

Edwin Chadwick, one of the great figures in Victorian health reform, became aware of the national deficiencies in public health and sanitation through his work at the newly constituted Poor Law Board, set up following the Poor Law Amendment Act of 1834.[5] Illness and ill-health were frequently the reasons why people had to ask for poor relief. His seminal *Report on the Sanitary Condition of the Labouring Poor*, published in 1842, horrified many people. A further enquiry into the health of towns in 1844 and 1845 led to parliamentary action, against the background of a renewed threat of epidemic cholera. The first Public Health Act in 1848 created a General Board of Health and made provision for local boards of health to be established, disregarding local wishes where mortality exceeded 23 per thousand. Cheltenham's death rate, variously given as 23 and 24 per thousand for the three years 1841 to 1844, may in fact have exceeded this level. The all-purpose description 'fever' was commonly given as the cause of death of Cheltenham citizens – but it hid a multitude of sins. It was evident that the public health situation in the town was very unsatisfactory, and this triggered a formal investigation.

The General Board of Health sent an inspector, Edward Cresy, to survey the town and its sanitary condition. His report highlighted the many failings in the poorer areas of the town. Cresy reported that the Waterworks Company then supplied 2,021 houses out of 6,541, and that by no means all houses even of a 'superior kind' had adequate drainage. His opinion of the Sewers Company was low. 'The Chelt and every other stream has been given up to the Sewers Company and made the receptacle of all the filth they could pour into it'.[6] 'Having personally surveyed the streets, alleys, courts and dwellings in the town of Cheltenham, and particularly those situated in the quarters most subject to epidemic, endemic and other fatal disorders', Cresy recommended first and foremost 'the establishment of a local board of health, the laying down of a system of main sewers, and the draining of every house by means of tubular drains'. He also recommended the enlargement of the area covered by the Improvement Commissioners to include a circle of radius 1½ miles from Cheltenham parish church.

'I can only enumerate a few of those streets which were evidently in a bad condition, and to which the medical reports more particularly apply,' Edward Cresy reported. Rutland Street was the first to be described. 'There is a well for the supply of water to every five or six houses. This street as well as the several small courts leading out of it, have privies and ashpits common to several houses; and Boodle's, Harper's, Green's, and Hampton's Passages are ill ventilated, and apparently seldom visited by the scavenger.'[7] The narrowest alley was 4 feet wide, and the street was 30 feet wide. Cresy detailed seventeen more streets, ending with Swindon Place, which 'consists of forty houses placed back to back, with three sets of privies, wash-houses, and pumps; it is without sewage, carriage way, or pavement; the gutter-channels on the surface are always full of filthy fluid; and the place is never free from fever; wanting in ventilation, the houses are always in an unhealthy condition.' Such conditions were not confined to the industrial towns of the Midlands and the North, whatever the popular view might have been.

Cresy's report stimulated the Commissioners into promoting an improvement bill, which would also have the not coincidental advantage of bringing the whole town under their authority. The monster Improvement Act of 1852 had 136 sections and incorporated relevant clauses from numerous national acts, dealing among other things with town commissioners, town police and cemeteries. Septimus Pruen, a local solicitor, produced a summary which was published locally.[8] He believed that a simple provisional order made under the Public Health Act would have enabled the commissioners to take all necessary powers, instead of spending £4,000 on securing the Act. But many argued that anything was better than the continuation of a self-elected and self-electing body of commissioners, with jurisdiction over various and often detached parts of the town, while surveyors of different hamlets and private parties had jurisdiction over other parts. The 1852 act introduced a modest element of democracy into the government of Cheltenham.

The new Improvement Commissioners were given responsibility for public health and authority to buy out the Sewers Company. A sewerage and drainage committee was established and a medical officer of health appointed. The General Board of Health advised the committee that an accurate plan of the town should be made.[9] Of 3,600 acres surveyed, 1,700 were mapped in detail and the remainder, the suburbs, in outline on the very large scale of 44 feet to the inch. It took until 1857 to be completed, and 84 of the sheets of this ambitious mapping scheme still survive. From this time onwards, a steady stream of annual reports by the medical officer of health listed the houses and streets where the lack of water, sewers, and flush toilets was worst. Only when these conditions had to some extent been ameliorated could attention shift to the poor physical condition and standard of the actual houses, and ways of tackling the often acute over-crowding.

In 1865 the Cheltenham Waterworks Company was advised that extraction from the River Severn was the only long-term solution to an adequate water supply, and after securing the enabling Act of Parliament the company set about building a waterworks at the Mythe at Tewkesbury. It soon proved its worth in supplying Tewkesbury, where the problem of wells and drainage in the old town was even worse than in Cheltenham, and there the death rate fell markedly, but the Improvement Commissioners blocked its introduction to Cheltenham.[10]

The private company was more farsighted than Cheltenham's commissioners, but it claimed that lack of revenue hindered the provision of water to the poorer parts of the town. Moreover, the supply in existing pipes was intermittent: it was neither available at night nor for the whole of the day.[11]

The Waterworks Company maintained its independence for another quarter of a century. It was finally purchased, compulsorily, by the new borough council in 1878. In 1886 a reservoir was built at Dowdeswell, which also helped to reduce flooding in Cheltenham.[12] The Chelt is a small river but it carries a great deal of water as the extensive floods in the town in July 2007 demonstrated. But the council, too, moved very slowly to extend the pipes to the north side of the town. In 1893 there was an outbreak of typhoid, and Dr J. H. Garrett, who had been appointed Medical Officer of Health the year before, prepared a special report on those Cheltenham houses which still relied on well water, a large number notwithstanding the borough council's fifteen-year ownership of the Waterworks Company.[13] He carried out a house to house inspection in the North and Central Wards, where the greatest number of wells were known to be, and found that 2,233 houses were supplied by 1,730 wells. In the East and South Wards he estimated there were 860 wells. He did not review West and Middle Wards as there it was known that few houses relied on wells. Garrett observed, as had been noted many times before, that wells, sewers and house-drains were close together, and pollution frequent, and also that the drains had little fall and ran through the sands. Where water was drawn from wells, it was inevitable that flushing of toilets was inadequate. His conclusion was that a major and comprehensive scheme should be undertaken, rather than piecemeal improvement. He had in mind the scheme of the 1860s for piping water from the River Severn at Tewkesbury.

Garrett's report persuaded the Corporation to pump from the Severn to Hewlett's reservoir; by 1898, 500,000 gallons a day was being supplied and fever ceased to be a frequent occurrence in the town. By 1900 few shallow wells remained. Even so, in 1902 only one-third of the water supply of Cheltenham came from the Severn.[14] As Cheltenham has grown, so has reliance on the Mythe Waterworks. This was painfully apparent when the exceptional rise in the level of the Severn in July 2007 flooded the works and interrupted supply for two weeks.

The Cheltenham Waterworks Company had foreseen that Gloucester, too, might be supplied from Tewkesbury, but the joint Cheltenham and Gloucester Water Board was not formed until 1936, following Gloucester's failure to secure authority to bring water from the Wye. The Water Board continued to increase its capacity and to innovate in water treatment, but so great had become the demand nationally that larger river systems needed to be managed collectively. First the North West Gloucestershire Water Board was formed in 1965, and then Severn Trent in 1974, one of ten nationalised regional authorities. The insatiable demand required a scale

Cheltenham's better houses were connected to a sewer provided by a private sewer company. The company claimed that it could not connect houses in poorer districts because the occupants could not pay the sewer rate. Eventually in 1857 the Town Commissioners instructed their surveyor to estimate the value of the company's works with a view to buying them out. This map was prepared to accompany the bill presented to parliament giving them the necessary powers. The red lines show the Cheltenham Sewers Company's sewers and the dotted lines the proposed new main sewers.

TOWN of CHELTENHAM.

The Red Lines denote the Sewers of the Cheltenham Sewers Company.
The Dotted Red Lines denote the course of the three projected Main Sewers.
The division of the Wards is shown by the Blue Colour.
The Parish Boundaries are shown thus——

SCALE OF CHAINS

of investment which proved politically impossible for the nationalised companies, and the water authorities were reorganised as privatised companies in 1989. From small beginnings in Cheltenham a very large water authority has gradually developed.

In the railways' most successful period, around 1908, there were eight places in Cheltenham where people could board a train, and four companies that provided services locally. Lansdown is the only remaining main line station for the town, and the lines which were opened in the later nineteenth century are the ones now closed. Enthusiasts forming the enterprising Gloucestershire Warwickshire Railway in 1984 have relaid the track from Toddington to Cheltenham racecourse.

RAILWAYS

The 1830s and 1840s were not only marked by concerns about public health; these were also the decades when the railway caught the public imagination, following the success of the Rainhill trials in 1829 which had demonstrated the viability of locomotive steam engines. Railway development followed the same pattern as turnpikes in the previous century; local interests secured the construction of relatively short lengths of line until gradually the numerous companies coalesced into larger concerns. Isambard Kingdom Brunel, like Thomas Telford in the turnpike period, was unique in his larger vision of what might be achieved. The Great Western Railway from London to Bristol was projected in 1833, and Brunel, through his successful engineering work in Bristol, became the chief engineer; he immediately envisaged the line joining up with a steam ship to cross the Atlantic and terminate in New York. He designed his railway on a broader gauge, 7 feet, than the 4 ft 8½ inches adopted elsewhere in the country.

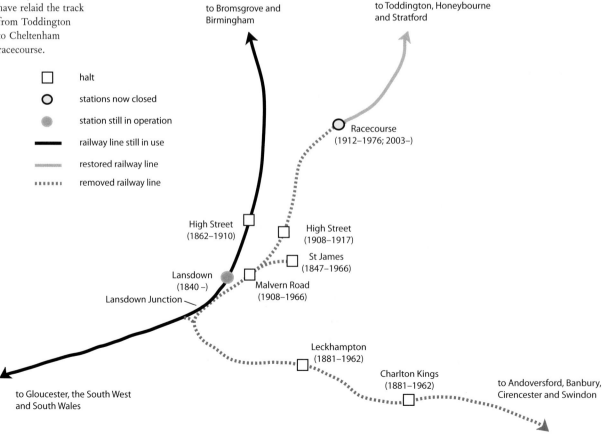

Some gentlemen from Cheltenham, Gloucester, Stroud and Cirencester were stimulated by the issue of the Great Western prospectus, in 1835, to propose a link with that railway at Swindon, in order to secure a direct line to London; clearly this was the major source of Cheltenham visitors, though the gentlemen suggested the agricultural, manufacturing and commercial classes of Gloucestershire would all benefit. Brunel suggested the linking line should go through Gloucester and Stroud. The Cheltenham and Great Western Union Railway was approved by parliament in 1836. The Cheltenham terminus was to be in the vicinity of St James's Square. Gloucester gentlemen subscribed £18,000 towards the initial expenses, and Cheltenham gentlemen £212,800, but this company was not really successful, though the necessarily circuitous route did eventually materialise.[15] The most important subscriber to this railway was Lord Sherborne, who contributed the notable sum of £10,000. Joseph Pitt subscribed £1,000, the Earl of Suffolk, Sir William Hicks and James Agg, £500 each. These were men with a strong interest in the development of Cheltenham. Altogether £26,000 was subscribed.[16]

Geography placed Cheltenham not far from the proposed route of a railway between Birmingham, Gloucester and Bristol. Projectors had first considered a Birmingham and Bristol railway in 1824, but the scheme petered out.[17] Birmingham traders then engaged Brunel to survey a more limited line between Birmingham and Gloucester, but found his estimate of its cost too high. In the event, it would have been much more practical than the eventual choice of Capt. W. S. Moorsom, which went straight up the steep gradient of the Lickey hills. In 1835 this railway project was also put forward, and two committees were formed, one for Gloucester and one for Birmingham. Initially there was no intention of bringing this railway to Cheltenham, nor to Tewkesbury, which also lobbied for access to the line; the early driving force for railway development was trade — in this case the bulk carriage of Birmingham's manufactures and of coal — not passengers. The company was persuaded to bring the railway nearer Cheltenham partly by learning that a rival company was also wishing to build along the obvious route from Cheltenham to Gloucester, so eventually a wide curve was substituted to bring the line closer to the town. While not as close as the Cheltenham and Great Western wanted, it had the great advantage of continuing on to Birmingham. The Gloucester to Cheltenham plateway was a further inducement to come to Cheltenham, because it offered an access to Gloucester docks, and both companies intended to buy it.

The Birmingham and Gloucester railway bill was also approved by parliament in 1836, on the basis that the two companies cooperated on the Cheltenham to Gloucester section of their lines, which had to be both narrow and wide gauge, narrow for the Birmingham line, wide for the Cheltenham and Great Western, and for some years both people and goods had to change from one gauge to the other at Gloucester. Pearson Thompson was on the Gloucester committee, and he offered land for a station. As a result, Lansdown station (now called Cheltenham Spa) was built in a convenient position for the occupants of his Lansdown development, but not as near the town as people at the time or since would have liked; an omnibus service was provided into town. Thompson also provided the land for what became Queen's Road, linking the station with the Leckhampton road. The Cheltenham and Great Western Union started building the Cheltenham-Gloucester section of the line but failed to complete it to time and the Birmingham and Gloucester took over. The first part of the line to Birmingham, between Cheltenham and Bromsgrove, was opened on 24 June with two first class carriages and two second class. By August 1841 the whole line was open. The Cheltenham and Great Western struggled on with its Swindon line, which was opened in July 1844, just as it was wholly absorbed by the Great Western. These two lines remain to serve Cheltenham. The Cheltenham and Great Western had announced early in 1843 that it was going to build a branch line to a station on Jessop's Nursery Garden in St James's Square, and this it proceeded to do, opening a grand and more practical terminus in 1847.[18]

H. Davies of Montpellier Library had started weekly publication of the *Cheltenham Looker-On* 'A note book of the sayings and doings of Cheltenham and containing a list of the arrivals and departures' in 1835. As soon as trains were running between Birmingham and Cheltenham, the *Looker-On* in 1841 printed a timetable. Most of the page was occupied by a timetable for the nine stagecoaches, but there were four trains a day to Gloucester or to Birmingham and two night mail trains. One year later, two goods trains, two mail trains, and six passenger trains were running; the 11.15am train had first and second class carriages but no third class! By 1847 five trains a day and two mail trains were also running from Cirencester to London via Swindon; coaches from Cheltenham started regularly for Cirencester two hours before the departure times. It was pointed out that '*The times set forth in the following tables* are in every instance, the London or Greenwich times, which, it must be borne in mind, are in advance of Cheltenham some seven or eight minutes'.

Passengers had now been recognised as an important reason for railway lines, and Cheltenham was recognised as an important destination for many travellers. Several years

Lansdown station may have been convenient for inhabitants of Pearson Thompson's new estate, and for the Earl of Suffolk who subscribed to the Gloucester and Cheltenham Railway, but it was not convenient for most townsfolk. Many rival routes into the town had been suggested, but eventually in 1847 a broad gauge spur was built from near Lansdown station to a station near St James's Square. St James's station was extensively enlarged in 1894. It was used a great deal and had longer platforms than Lansdown, which was built on a curve. But later railway development left St James's station to one side. The Lansdown platforms were lengthened in 1965, and St James was closed in 1966; the buildings were almost immediately demolished.

THE ROYAL TRAIN LEAVING THE CHELTENHAM STATION.

Queen Victoria's train passing through Cheltenham in 1849. The Birmingham to Gloucester Railway had been open nine years when Queen Victoria travelled through Cheltenham on her way to Osborne in the Isle of Wight after a visit to Balmoral. The royal carriage is distinguished by a crown on top, and the Royal Standard is flying above the station. The queen thoughtfully asked for the train to pass slowly through the station. The bridge over the line and the up platform are packed with spectators, and others are pressing up to the railings outside, but the down platform is clear of all but three people who form a select welcome party. The *Illustrated London News* published this woodcut, drawn by a local wood engraver, G. F. Bonner of Winchcombe Street. An astonishing amount of detail is included: all the small figures of spectators are animated.

of 'railway mania' followed the first successes. In September 1845 the *Looker-On* wrote 'Cheltenham appears at length in a fair way of becoming a victim to the malady'. Cheltenham's name was included in the titles of many projected companies, although in most cases existing lines would make the actual connection. A public meeting was held in the Town Hall to promote the idea of one central terminus in Cheltenham, a far-sighted idea which would have been of great benefit, and a committee was formed, but unfortunately all the different interest groups failed to compromise.

Coal freight remained a major concern for railway companies, and remained so for the rest

Forty years elapsed from the construction of the first railway line to serve Cheltenham and the construction of a more direct line from the town to Swindon; Brunel had no doubt recognised the difficulties of this route, and opted for a line from Swindon to Gloucester and thence to Cheltenham. In 1881 the Cheltenham to Andoversford line was opened, linking a number of small Cotswold places and providing stations in Leckhampton and Charlton Kings. The Dowdeswell viaduct took the railway across the valley. The line was not economic, and was closed to passengers in 1962 and to freight two years later; the viaduct was demolished in 1967.

of the century and indeed until after the Second World War. For some years the Gloucester–Cheltenham tramroad continued to carry most of the coal to light Cheltenham's fires; in the mid-1830s it had carried 25,000 tons a year, and demand was growing; in 1837, 56,000 tons were consumed. Despite the Birmingham and Gloucester Railway Company gaining full ownership of the tramway in 1840, it continued to operate for several more years as the convenient and economic route for coal, with its extensions to sidings very close to the centre of town. Its effectiveness was gone once the Birmingham and Gloucester railway company completed its branch to Gloucester docks in 1848. The fact that it ran along the road caused its final closure; the Improvement Commissioners came to an agreement with the owners, and in 1859 the Gloucester and Cheltenham Tramroads Abandonment Act was passed. Within two years the track was broken up. The Leckhampton quarry section continued in use as far as the *Malvern Inn* for rather longer; groceries were loaded there and carried up the hill for inhabitants of Coberley and Cowley to collect from the quarry. This section was taken up in the 1890s.[19]

Towards the end of the century Cheltenham had two more stations and a halt, and not far from town there were stations at Leckhampton, Charlton Kings and the Racecourse. In 1881 a railway was opened with broad gauge from St James's station through Andoversford to Bourton on the Water, and thence to Banbury, with stations at Leckhampton and Charlton Kings. It involved a dramatic viaduct at Dowdeswell. The Midland and South-Western Junction Railway also used Leckhampton station from 1891 when a line between Cirencester and Andoversford was completed. In 1906 the Honeybourne line was opened from St James's station to Honeybourne junction, through Bishops Cleeve, Winchcombe and Toddington to Stratford on Avon and ultimately to Birmingham, and two years later a station at Malvern Road, Cheltenham, avoided an awkward section into St James's station. The halt in High Street was on this line. The multiplicity of companies and duplication of routes obviously required rationalisation, which took place when four regional companies were organised following the Railway act in 1921 and then nationalised in 1948. Closures inevitably followed, most of which can be seen as justified, though some are regretted.

CHELTENHAM'S SOCIAL STRUCTURE IN 1851

Rutland Street in 1851 is representative of those districts whose inhabitants provided the services which were needed to support the town's affluent households. There were 104 households, and 523 people, an average household size of four. Nearly 40 per cent of the inhabitants were under the age of 14 years. There was also a sizeable number of lodgers – 60 scattered among the 104 households, bringing in a small income to hard-pressed families. In total, 75 households were headed by men and 29 by women. Of the men, twenty were labourers, twenty worked in the boot and shoe-making trades, six were tailors and five were carpenters. Of the women, four were charwomen, eight were laundresses and five were needlewomen, while two were 'boot binders'. Many of the wives were working – five as charwomen, thirteen as laundresses, and one as a 'washerwoman', an interesting distinction. Gas Green was not selected for particular criticism by Cresy, although this was a poor area in 1851. Among the 22 households and 78 people, six were on parish relief. One head of a household was described as an ash- gatherer and another a dung-gatherer, two were tripe butchers, one a brick-maker and one a match-maker. There were three charwomen and three dressmakers among the women.

Women significantly outnumbered men in Cheltenham: there were fourteen women to every ten men in 1851. This reflected two characteristics of the town – the presence of a number of independent women, and the amount of domestic service. Leaving aside all the resident domestic servants, nearly 4,000 women returned an occupation, a title or an independent income. Of these more than a quarter had a pension, were land or house proprietors or had money invested in the 'funds', but the majority did not head their own household.

One in every eight people in the town was a servant living in an employer's house, and the vast majority of this domestic army of over 4,000 people was female. Of the paupers in the workhouse, 106 had been servants, and nearly 1,000 servants were not living in their employer's house. Others in service occupations included footmen, butlers, and cooks. Servants came in small numbers from all over the world, but most were born in Gloucestershire or neighbouring counties. Some had perhaps been trained by the Cheltenham School of Industry, or Female Orphan Asylum, which since 1806 had taught a certain number of girls how to become 'upper servants' or 'ladies' maids'.[20] In Lansdown and Pittville (not including Pittville Street, which was very much a commercial street), nearly every house had resident servants: there were 214 houses and 474 servants living-in. Half of these households were headed by women. The two largest households were numbers 1 and 15 Lansdown Crescent: one was headed by a woman who gave her occupation as 'own affairs', the other by a magistrate and deputy lieutenant (a man, of course). By contrast, in Rutland Street, Swindon Passage and Gas Green, there were no resident servants at all.

If resident servants were an index of affluence, working wives were an indication of the opposite. Approximately one-fifth of wives had an occupation, and they were scattered through the town, with some larger concentrations in the new parish of St Paul's, and west of the Bath Road. By far the largest groups of working wives were either using their needle as

Queen Charlotte was influential in the founding of the female orphan asylum in 1806. It was maintained by voluntary donations, and upwards of forty girls between the ages of 8 and 15 were clothed, boarded and educated. 'Hundreds of good domestic servants and others ... have received their instruction at the Asylum.' Griffiths' plate shows the first Orphanage. A larger, two-storey building was erected in Winchcombe Street in 1833; at the top of the walls there was inscribed, on the left, 'Female Orphan Asylum', and, on the right, 'School of Industry'. Queen Victoria became a patron after being presented with examples of the skilful needlework.

The boys' Orphanage in St Margaret's Road was designed by W. H Knight, and built in 1865–66. It is unusual in Cheltenham, being in red-brick Victorian Gothic style. In 1881 it accommodated fifteen boys aged between eight and fourteen, apparently coming from all over the country. It closed in 1966, and the following year opened as Dowty House, a care home.

PHOTOGRAPH: AUTHOR, 2009

seamstresses, dressmakers, milliners, stay-makers, corset-makers or bonnet makers, or were laundresses. Some helped husbands in their crafts, and a few ran businesses. One woman was a tailor employing two men. There were some very unusual occupations, and it is clear that women were already taking on a wider range of employments than might have been predicted, although as yet in small numbers. For example, one was a supervisor in the Inland Revenue, one was a 'Clergyman Inspector'. There was a midwife, an umbrella-maker, and an assistant umbrella-maker, a stationer, a draper, a matron of the Training College, the principal of Back Street Normal School, a crêpe flower maker, and a flower artist. Thirty-six wives were shoe-binders, twelve were lodging house-keepers, 21 were teachers, and a few were grocers, greengrocers, and poulterers.

Dressmakers were a large group. The Children's Employment Commission in 1865 took evidence from three Cheltenham employers who were milliners and dressmakers.[21] The Commission uncovered the long hours and poor pay and conditions experienced by dressmakers who lived in their employers' houses, in what were effectively small 'sweat shops', and there is some evidence from the 1851 census which may substantiate this. Mrs Ann Gregory, who lived in Cambray Villa and gave evidence to the Commission, employed two milliner assistants and one dressmaker, aged 22, 24 and 25 years, for whom she did not enter any relationship to herself as head of the household. She also had four female apprentices living with her, aged between 15 and 23, three described as 'dressmaker' and one as 'milliner'. The household had one resident servant. This was not the largest such household. In one of the Promenade Villas, where the head was a Miss Allen, there were eight 'dressmaker assistants' with no stated relationship to her, their ages ranging from 18 to 28 years; here there were also a cook and housemaid. Two doors away was a similar establishment, with five assistants and one apprentice, and two more villas in the Promenade housed similar but smaller businesses. The conjunction with Clark & Debenham in the Promenade was obviously relevant. There were also two such businesses in the High Street, and one in Montpellier Street. Clothes were important to the leisured inhabitants or visitors to Cheltenham, and the number of clothes shops and supporting needlewomen suggest that the consumer society was already in the making. George Rowe's *Cheltenham Guide* of 1845 drew attention to 21 drapers, tailors and haberdashers; six years later in the census 168 people gave their occupation as draper or draper's assistant, and 310 as tailors.

PRIVATE ENTERPRISES

CHURCHES

Census Sunday in 1851 was the occasion not only for 'numbering the people', but also for taking a religious census. Clergymen were asked to state the numbers attending services that Sunday, how many could be accommodated on seats in the church, and how many seats were free. The results were a shock to the establishment. At a maximum, about a quarter of the population attended a Church of England service, but an unknown number may have been counted more than once because they attended more than one service. Another quarter of the population attended Nonconformist chapels.[22] It was a measure of Cheltenham's growth that it was one of 65 large towns for which detailed statistics were published in the census report, and the only one in Gloucestershire. Cheltenham was marginally more godly that the average of 29 towns of similar size, where 54 per cent attended a service but fewer than half were Anglicans. In Cheltenham 66 per cent attended a church and nearly two-thirds were Anglicans. The numbers attending Methodist, Baptist, Independent, and Roman Catholic services were relatively small. In Bath, with a larger population, religious observance was higher and the Anglicans more successful.

The results were also shocking with respect to free seats. Ministers relied quite heavily on the money paid by wealthier parishioners for their special pews, especially when, as in Cheltenham, the perpetual curate had no traditional sources of revenue from tithes, glebeland or the Easter dues paid by parishioners.[23] Pew rents were almost as common in Nonconformist chapels as in Anglican. A mere 31 per cent of 'sittings' were free in Cheltenham's Anglican churches, which included the parish church, and 40 per cent in the Nonconformist chapels. This was a matter of concern to all those wishing the Anglican Church to make more effort to reach the growing population. But church building was generally an expression of social differentiation. The affluent did not wish to attend a church where the poor were also present. A new – and exclusive – church was therefore an attraction in a new housing development.

A general programme of church building was everywhere under way, encouraged by parliamentary grants but owing much to private enterprise. There were seven Anglican churches in Cheltenham in 1851, all but the ancient parish church having been built in the previous 25 years. There were also seventeen Nonconformist chapels, one Roman Catholic church, one Latter Day Saints chapel, and one synagogue. The state of Cheltenham parish church in itself had stimulated church building, and Francis Close, the energetic and evangelical perpetual curate of Cheltenham was behind much of the effort. He first came to the town in 1824 as curate of Trinity in Portland Street, the first new church and one which had been built in part through Lord Sherborne's sponsorship, and became perpetual curate of the parish

This striking photograph is dominated by the tower and spire of St Matthew's church, which seem to have been inspired by a French château. Ewan Christian was the architect, and the church was built in 1876–79, with the tower added in 1883–84, and was effectively free-standing, with a porch on the northern side. It proved to be unstable. In 1952 the spire was removed, so this photograph must predate that event as well as any road works and major redevelopment of the town centre. The tower was further reduced in 1972, leaving only two stages. In the foreground is St Gregory's Roman Catholic church, and between these two churches is St Mary's Hall, later called Shaftesbury Hall. Behind St Matthew's is the parish church of St Mary. South of St Matthew's are the imposing premises of Barnby Bendall, behind which is the rear view of Clarence Hotel and to its right the beginning of Royal Crescent. The curved end of the Colonnade, Martin's, is clearly visible.

church two years later. Trinity was a proprietary chapel, belonging to trustees, as were three other Anglican churches built before 1851: St John's, St James's and Christ Church. They could generate profit for the owners, if large congregations paid to attend a notable preacher. Tickets were sold at the door of Trinity until 1857. St Paul's and St Peter's were built to serve less affluent congregations, and St Luke's was opened three years after the religious census. Francis Close was one of the trustees of Christ Church and lived next to the church in The Grange, a house given him by his grateful parishioners. The legal position of new Anglican

This interesting composite print was produced by Charles Knight of London in 1850, showing the parish church, Christ Church and St Peter's churches, Montpellier Spa, and Cheltenham College. Christ Church, designed by the Jearrad brothers to complement their work in Lansdown, was built in 1837–40, a proprietary chapel for the residents of Alstone, where there were 'many of the best houses in Cheltenham'. It was conveniently placed for the Bayshill estate as well as Lansdown. The tower has remained a dominating feature of the townscape. St Peter's, 1847–49, is in a rather different genre, an imitation Norman church designed by Samuel Whitfield Daukes, and intended to serve the relatively poor districts along the Tewkesbury Road. The first Cheltenham College buildings were designed by James Wilson of Bath, and built 1842–43. By 1861 the school had become notably successful, with 600 pupils, rivalled only by Eton.
BY COURTESY OF ERIC MILLER

CHRIST CHURCH ST MARY'S ST PETERS

MONTPELIER SPA CHELTENHAM COLLEGE

CHELTENHAM

churches was complicated, but gradually parishes were established to cover the areas served by these churches, and four more churches were built later in the century.

Francis Close's imaginative scheme for the restoration and enlargement of the parish church was never implemented. The vestry would have been required to raise a rate on all occupiers of property in the town, whether Anglican or not, and there was widespread opposition to church rates, which were finally abolished by Act of Parliament in 1868. The pew-owners also opposed change. Close wanted to open the view of the church to the High Street by demolishing two houses and when, in 1843, some houses adjoining the churchyard were offered for sale, it was suggested they should be purchased and the ground opened to the public. This, too, was turned down. What an opportunity was missed! There is still no appreciation of the possibilities for using the church and churchyard as an urban asset, and buildings are still planned to crowd round it.[24]

Close had left Cheltenham to become dean of Carlisle before any action was taken to improve and restore St Mary's. When that did happen, it was not for the benefit of the church itself but because of a public health problem. The floor of the church was collapsing in places where so many burials had been made: the odour pervading the building was offensive, and the pillars supporting the galleries were unsafe. The public health hazard had to be dealt with, so the next perpetual curate, Edward Walker, closed the church in 1859, and organised the rapid erection of a temporary church where the Great House had been. This served the congregation in what Walker considered a more satisfactory way than the parish church for the next two years. Indeed, it was so much liked that the congregation did not wish to return to the parish church when it reopened, and continued to use the temporary church. Walker was also responsible for purchasing the chancel of the parish church in 1863 from the solicitors Newman and Gwinnett, so legally converting Cheltenham's perpetual curacy into a rectory.[25] He died in 1872. His successor promoted the erection of St Matthew's church, built by public subscription on the site of the temporary church between 1877 and 1879. He intended it as a replacement for the parish church, an objective which was not accepted.

SCHOOLS

The Reverend Francis Close was 'one of the great figures of Gloucestershire educational history'.[26] By the time he left Cheltenham, he had 'built three churches and promoted the building of two others, he had revived and rehoused the charity school, he had played a leading part in the reformation of the Grammar School, the building of a Proprietary College, and the founding of the Ladies' College. He had conceived and built one of the first and most successful of the Training Colleges for teachers, that of St Paul and St Mary. He had also brought into being a dozen National Schools'. The school which commemorates his name, Dean Close, was founded in his memory in 1886. He had also introduced infant schools to the town.

The national census in 1851, in addition to counting the people and the churches, carried out a third survey, of educational provision in the country. A form was delivered to every school, and historians consider that the returns are more complete than any other survey in tracing those small private schools that had previously escaped notice.[27] Here again, Cheltenham qualified as the only 'principal town' in Gloucestershire, while the analysis generally was for registration districts or poor law unions. There were 5,195 children aged between 4 and 10 years in the borough. Eighty-one schools were recorded, 23 'public day schools' and 59 'private day schools'. Public schools were those supported 'in any degree' from sources other than payments by the scholars, and they were subdivided into various categories. The private schools were numerically in the majority, and included the two famous 'public schools', but they educated only 28 per cent of those children in Cheltenham who were receiving some weekday education. The contribution of the Church of England to public education was outstanding, reaching twice as many children as the other public schools: two National Schools and eleven other Church of England schools had 2,121 pupils, though no doubt this was an optimistic maximum. There was a workhouse school, with 120 children, both boys and girls, and a grammar school with 50 boys. Four schools were run by nonconformist churches and one by the Roman Catholic church. There was one non-denominational British school, an orphan school educating 58 girls, and a ragged school with 115 children. In addition, over 3,000 children received some minimal schooling in the Sunday schools attached to every church.

The variety and number of small schools was to be much reduced once a state-organised system of education began to provide larger and better-equipped schools and made elementary schooling compulsory. In Cheltenham, though, this happened much later than in many places. The 1870 Education Act required that where the existing provision was inadequate the local ratepayers should elect a School Board and raise rates to provide schooling. Perhaps inevitably, ratepayers tried to avoid the expense if they could. Charlton Kings was reluctantly forced to have a school board in 1883, because of lack of financial support for the church school,[28] and Winchcombe had one from 1875. But in Cheltenham and also at Tewkesbury the creation of a board was successfully avoided.

The 1902 Education Act led to the formation of an Education Committee for the county, although responsibility for elementary education was still with Cheltenham Borough Council. There were now 28 elementary schools in the town, educating about 6,400 children,[29] many still in early nineteenth-century buildings. The school attendance officers were somewhat slack in securing the presence of children in school, though in 1904 the three school attendance officers in Cheltenham visited the homes of over 1,000 absentee children. His Majesty's Inspector commented that 'educational efficiency and progress in the town are impeded by the large number of small schools in antiquated and unsuitable premises and in close proximity to each other, which are maintained at a cost out of all proportion to their educational value'. This was a sad reflection on a town with a reputation for pioneering educational advance. A few schools were immediately transferred to the control of the county council, and a county school built and opened in Gloucester Road in 1907. A county grammar school for girls was opened in a big house in St Margaret's Road in 1905 and the Pate foundation was enlarged to

Among the many small private schools in Cheltenham was one in a house in Westal called Casino; it was a boarding school kept by William Childes in 1830. When Griffiths published this plate, it was the residence of William Whitehead Esq. Casino Place preserves the name, but the house was demolished in the 1930s to allow construction of eleven houses on Painswick Road. The name, and the design of the house in Griffiths' plate, suggest it was possibly built originally as a grandstand for watching coursing.

Ham House school in Charlton Kings lasted rather longer than Casino. The house replaced an older one on the site about 1800, and by 1819 it was being used as a school, run by Revd John Tucker, a classicist, with the assistance of a mathematics tutor from Cambridge. By 1830 it was advertising courses in Persian and Hindustanee to prepare candidates for service in India, and offered year-round boarding for boys from India. The school continued under Tucker's successors until about 1888. In 1881 there were ten scholars aged between 9 and 14, and nine military students aged between 14 and 18 years.

include the girls' school, which was renamed accordingly two years later.[30] But the borough kept hold of its local autonomy. The first large new 'central' school was built on the Gloucester Road in 1920 and the council used its authority under the 1918 Education Act to raise the school-leaving age to 15 in the borough.

THE INCORPORATED BOROUGH

Incorporation in an important respect modernised the way in which Cheltenham's local government was constituted, yet in another respect it was a backward-looking measure.

Much of the artisan housing of the 1820s and 1830s in Milsom Street has been demolished. On the north side there remains a pretty mid-Victorian building of 1863–64, designed as a 'ragged school' by the fashionable Cheltenham architect John Middleton, better known for his churches and the Delancey hospital. The building was extended in 1886. Ragged schools, supported by charitable donations, catered for the very poorest children, sometimes providing board as well as schooling and practical craft skills. Mrs Guinness started the ragged school in Cheltenham High Street in 1849 'to teach the wildest rabble of the poorest quarter of the town'; in 1851 there were 65 boys and 51 girls. The school moved to Milsom Street, within a stone's throw of St Paul's College. It was purchased by Cheltenham Education Committee in 1903, and within living memory continued its craft functions for All Saints' school. With south-facing rooms and small courtyard, in 2009 it provides an attractive day centre for those with mental health issues, and is a locally listed building.
PHOTOGRAPH: AUTHOR, 2009

The steady expansion of housing in Naunton, and the constitution of a new education committee, led to the proposal in 1903 by the borough council to build Naunton Park Council Schools. A site was drawn out of Naunton Park, and the handsome red brick schools were opened in 1906. The first part of Churchill Road was developed about this time. During the First World War the school buildings were requisitioned for a Red Cross Hospital. In 1939 when railings were taken up as a contribution to the war effort, those round Naunton Park were removed, but not those round the school, as it was thought to endanger the children to have no barriers between them and the road.
PHOTOGRAPH: AUTHOR, 2009

The buildings of St Paul's College, now
Francis Close Campus of the University of
Gloucestershire, were designed as a new training
college for teachers by Samuel Daukes, and were
inspired by the old universities; they illustrate the
ambitious conception of the founders. Stimulated
by an educational entrepreneur, Samuel Codner,
Revd Francis Close took up with enthusiasm
the idea of a training college in Cheltenham.
Small enterprises for men and women were
started in 1847, and in 1848 an association was
formed; Miss Jane Cook's gift of six acres of
land between St Paul's Road and Swindon Road
together with government assistance enabled
buildings to be erected for 100 male students and
one master, with houses for principal and vice-
principal. When it reached its full complement,
it was the largest such college in the country.
Women students were housed separately.
PHOTOGRAPH: AUTHOR, 2009

For nearly seventy years after the 1786 Paving Act, the Board of Commissioners was a
self-perpetuating oligarchy. Had there been a borough council in 1835, it would have been
regulated by the Municipal Corporations Act, and the council would have been elected by the
modern democratic method of 'one man one vote' on quite a wide rate-paying franchise. But
the Improvement Commission was not subject to this act. The local Act of 1852 introduced a
method of election which was weighted heavily towards the property-owning classes – up to
twelve votes could be cast by one man according to the amount of property for which he paid
rates.[31] Commissioners were nominated in the Act for the first year only; half of them were
Liberal, half Conservative, but thereafter the majority swung towards the Liberals. By 1874,
when incorporation was being seriously discussed, twenty commissioners were in favour and
five abstained, an indication of the Liberal complexion of commissioners. It was suggested
that the Board was dominated by tradesmen and that the town's 'gentry' stood aside because
of the rowdy nature of elections. This is perhaps borne out by the evidence that 25 of the
commissioners were tradesmen and only five were professional men.

The royal charter of 1876, which created the municipal borough of Cheltenham, abolished
this system, and thenceforth the standardised method of election of councillors, as set out in
1835, was applied to the town. The charter gave the new corporation the same boundaries
as the preceding Improvement Commission, covering the whole parish. The borough was
divided into six wards, each electing three councillors, with one-third of councillors in rotation
being elected each year. The first election, on 14 November 1877, was a vigorous and even
bitter contest between Liberal and Conservative candidates, and resulted in an overwhelming
majority for the Liberals. The resulting political complexion of the first borough council

was thus not conspicuously different from that of the previous Improvement Commission. However, the social composition *did* change after 1876. Greater participation by the gentry was symbolised in the choice of William Nash Skillicorne, the great-grandson of Captain Skillicorne, as an alderman and first mayor. The ceremonial functions of a mayor, six aldermen and eighteen councillors now created a significant psychological focus for the town – a developing sense of civic identity had been reinforced.

However, the charter could be regarded as backward-looking because it established the borough with boundaries which were already out of date. From 1834, and the passing of the Poor Law Amendment Act, Cheltenham had been the centre of a Poor Law Union covering a group of rural parishes as well as the town. In 1837 this automatically became a registration district for births, marriages and deaths under the Civil Registration Act of the previous year. Moreover, in 1868, a few years before the charter was granted, Cheltenham parliamentary constituency was enlarged with the addition of a section of Leckhampton to reflect the growth of housing on the borders of the town, and it was enlarged again in 1885 to take in that part of Charlton Kings north of the Cheltenham and Banbury railway.

The new council's functions, as specified by the royal charter, were all those applicable since 1835 to municipal corporations, among which was the obligation to establish a Watch Committee and the power to form a police force. The Municipal Corporations Act had also obliged councils to publish budgets and accounts, and had enabled them to take over the duties of Improvement Commissioners. That the new Cheltenham Borough Council duly did. In addition the council had the important duty under the Public Health Act of 1872 of appointing a medical officer of health and it was also a responsible authority under the 1875 Housing Act. Other responsibilities accumulated as central government laid more burdens upon local authorities. An act passed in the year that Cheltenham received its charter required councils to set up school attendance committees, which implied that schooling had become compulsory. Special committees had long been organised by the Improvement Commissioners, and the practice was steadily expanded. Cheltenham continued to be governed under this charter until 1974 when it became a district council in the general reorganisation of local government.

Central government gradually reorganised local government in order that all areas were given the protection of national legislation. Urban and rural sanitary districts were defined in 1866 and made mandatory by the Public Health Act in 1875. In 1888 local government was completely changed by the creation of elected county councils, which took office from January 1889. With a population in 1881 of approximately 44,000, Cheltenham – in its then-existing boundaries – was not large enough to become an independent county borough, for which the determining size was 50,000, so for a range of important functions it remained under the control of the new Gloucestershire County Council. Charlton Kings had taken advantage of the local government Act of 1858 to set up a Board of Health, which could deal with roads, street lighting, nuisances and sewerage.[32] This latter function was particularly a subject of dispute with Cheltenham, which complained about Charlton King's effluent. As an existing

sanitary authority, Charlton Kings in 1875 became an urban sanitary district. Part of the
district was removed to Cheltenham borough in 1892.

At Leckhampton, also experiencing urbanisation where the parish adjoined Cheltenham,
there were similar local concerns over sanitation and the provision of basic amenities. In 1861
a Gas Fund Committee was established, with the aim of providing street-lighting for the
built-up part of the parish, and in 1870 a Leckhampton Sewer Authority was also constituted.
Such *ad hoc* bodies were unsatisfactory, and in 1873 they were replaced by the Leckhampton
Board of Health, under the provisions of the 1872 Public Health Act. The Board of Health
had much wider powers than those of its very limited predecessors, and over the next twenty
years made significant progress in improving the parish.

By the early 1890s the government was moving towards major reform of local government,
whereby (among other changes) local boards of health and urban sanitary districts would be
replaced by urban district councils (and their rural equivalents became rural district councils).
These changes were implemented under the 1894 Local Government Act, with effect from 1
January 1895. Charlton Kings then became an urban district, a status which it retained until
the sweeping changes of 1974; in 1971 the population of the district council area was 10,177.
At the same time Cheltenham became the centre of a rural district covering the surrounding
rural parishes, governed from, though administratively quite separate from, the borough.
But at Leckhampton, which would in other circumstances have become an urban district in

This view of the quarried edge of Leckhampton Hill was taken no later than 1915, as a postcard made from the same photograph was
postmarked. It shows a thoroughly rural scene, although Victorian development had taken place along Leckhampton Road. It was taken
from the lane which leads to Burrow's field. The buildings on the right of the lane, covered in ivy, are Collum End Farm. The garden in
the foreground to the left of the lane was known as 'the pansy patch'. Church Road, the modern road through Leckhampton, passes beside
Collum End Farm from left to right of the view shown here. It was once known as Collum Street.
© CHELTENHAM ART GALLERY AND MUSEUM

its own right, change had already taken place before the 1894 Act. By government order, on 9 November 1893 the parish was divided and its local board dissolved. Part was added to the borough of Cheltenham, the remainder to the Cheltenham Rural Sanitary Authority (which from 1 January 1895 was reconstituted as the rural district council). The part of Leckhampton transferred to Cheltenham borough was that included in the development of the Park estate and along the new Bath Road; this resulted in a substantial fall in Leckhampton's population.

The 1894 Local Government Act also instituted parish councils in rural areas. The historic ecclesiastical parishes had become less and less relevant during the nineteenth century as other administrative districts were introduced which overlapped but did not correspond with them, and as ecclesiastical parishes, too, were divided or altered. The term 'civil parish' was applied to all areas levying a separate poor rate and electing an overseer of the poor. The same term was given to historic parishes which matched these criteria. Hence Charlton Kings and Leckhampton civil parishes were not the same as the old parishes, but they could elect parish councils. Boundaries have since been altered many times to suit administrative convenience, so creating a confusing web of authorities. Ecclesiastical parishes continued to have a separate identity, but only in relation to church affairs, and their councils had to be called 'parochial'.[33]

From this time onwards it is difficult to find the most illuminating units for comparisons. Using the traditional parish before 1901, and then its civil successor, it is clear that the populations of parishes round Cheltenham fell slightly towards the end of the nineteenth century, after the steady growth of the previous seventy years, related to the agricultural depression and consequent exodus of labourers from the land. Cirencester, Tewkesbury and Winchcombe, though physically extensive, did not grow significantly. The county borough of Gloucester and the municipal borough of Cheltenham became the dominant urban centres in the county.[34] Another period of dramatic change was to occur after the Second World War.

Population, 1861–1921

	1861	1871	1881	1891	1901	1911	1921
Charlton Kings	3,443	3,680	3,950	4,187	3,806	4,495	4,379
Leckhampton	2,523	3,265	3,501	3,363	348	428	460
Prestbury	1,297	1,373	1,402	1,430	1,393	1,806	1,933
Swindon	227	239	201	243	233	297	256
Cirencester	6,336	7,079	7,737	7,521	7,536	7,631	7,422
Tewkesbury	5,876	5,409	5,100	5,269	5,419	5,287	4,704
Winchcombe	2,937	2,993	2,834	2,864	2,699	2,930	2,741
Cheltenham	39,693	41,923	43,972	42,914	44,805	48,942	48,430
Gloucester	16,512	18,341	36,521	39,444	47,955	50,035	51,330

SOCIAL STRUCTURE IN THE
LATER NINETEENTH CENTURY

The pattern of Cheltenham society changed little in the years before the First World War. It still appeared to be dominated by the professional and leisured people who employed the army of servants and the numerous artisans needed to build houses and supply goods to their inhabitants. The development of the Battledown estate in Charlton Kings in the 1860s is an example of their continuing importance. The estate was envisaged not as a group of spacious town villas but as a suburb of quasi-country houses. Battledown was in Charlton Kings parish, but the orientation of the estate was clearly towards Cheltenham, and the main approach was from Hales Road. The scheme was the vision of a Cheltenham solicitor, George Ridge.[35]

The nucleus of the estate was 'sundry Pieces and Parcels' of rectory land on the slopes of a hill to the north-east of Cheltenham. Several tenants of Cheltenham manor in 1564, including the lay rector, were allowed to enclose land here; in 1632, the rectory owned two pasture fields, called New Baddleton and Old Baddleton, measuring 51 acres;[36] in 1810 one enclosure was called 'The Castles' and three 'The Harps'. Described in the sale particulars in 1799 as 56 acres on 'a beautiful eminence' commanding 'an extensive Prospect of the River Severn, and the much-admired vale of Gloucester bounded by the Malvern Hills', the area had obvious

LEFT

Named because near the Great Western Railway's extension to St James's station, Great Western Road is on the edge of the central conservation area. The terrace on the north side was built in the 1860s in characteristic Cheltenham stucco style. Also typical, these relatively modest houses, which were for artisans and not for the poor, each had a decorative feature over the front door. Households living here in 1881 were headed by men with a wide variety of occupations: commission agent, musician, unemployed hotel keeper, plasterer, retired soldier working as a municipal sanitary inspector, cabinet maker employing one man and an apprentice, draper, upholsterer, retired railway guard, watch and clock maker, and two jewellers. In the background is the bridge for the cycle path which follows the former Honeybourne line.

RIGHT

Station Street is a terrace on one side of the street only, developed at the end of the nineteenth century where an extension of the Tramway to a stone-breaking yard had been; the yard had been taken over by the Great Western Honeybourne Line. The houses are fronted in brick, showing the change from the fashionable stucco general in the nineteenth century. A Roman ditch and Saxon pottery have been found here.

PHOTOGRAPHS: AUTHOR, 2009

charms and attractions but did not offer obvious potential for development until Cheltenham had begun to expand beyond its ancient boundaries.

A development scheme for 'first class residences' was announced by the *Cheltenham Looker-On* in October 1858, and in 1859 the Battledown fields were sold to three Cheltenham 'projectors': George Ridge, Somerset Tibbs and William Bain. The three men worked for the Cheltenham Equitable Building Society, Ridge as the solicitor, Bain the accountant and Tibbs, a dentist, a trustee. Tibbs had inherited some land between Battledown and Hales Road which was of significance in creating access to the estate. The three men also purchased a further 50 acres. One-fifth of the land was copyhold of either Cheltenham manor or Ashley manor, though the former rectory land was freehold and tithe-free. Plans were drawn up by Henry

An aerial view of Battledown taken in the late 1950s demonstrates the spacious layout of the estate and the slow pace of development. It is looking eastwards towards The Castles (Camp Hill), the area with a nearly circular boundary; two houses had been erected on its edge by this date. To the right is Battledown Manor, formerly The Knowle, which was not part of the mid-nineteenth-century estate. The straight road in the foreground is Ashley Road, a nod towards the Charlton Kings manor, and standing on the north side of the road is Battledown House, the one building already on the Battledowns before the estate was developed. There has been some infilling since this photograph was taken, but the estate retains its spacious and well-treed layout, with many large houses surviving.
CROWN COPYRIGHT, NMR

Dangerfield, surveyor and architect in Cheltenham, and as finally designed there were 83 lots, one as large as four acres but most of one acre, though the inclusion of the area known as 'The Camp', which looks like a hillfort, was evidently a mistake, as the plots there were not at that time attractive to buyers. Further purchases were made to secure more access roads, and the three originally laid out were tree-lined as were so many of the nineteenth-century roads with houses of 'the better sort', to create the desired visual and (by implication) social quality. Hewletts Reservoir was conveniently nearby to provide water to the estate, and happily Tibbs was on the management committee of Cheltenham Waterworks Company.

The first plots were sold in 1859 and within a year two-thirds had been taken up. At least 25 of the early purchasers were Cheltenham tradesmen, buying properties not in order to build houses for themselves, but as investments and maybe to secure the vote in parliamentary elections as freeholders. Their names duly appeared on the electoral roll. Ten of the early purchasers were resident in the High Street, others were scattered through Cheltenham's main streets. A wide variety of trades was represented among the new owners: there was another house agent, an auctioneer, two solicitors, an architect, two booksellers and a stationer and librarian, three chemists, two linen drapers, and a house-master at Cheltenham College, all representatives of the higher-class services of the town. Among the older trades were a baker, butcher, currier and leather seller, candle manufacturer, tailor and hatter, builder, glazier and painter, boot- and shoemaker and printer. In the early years, plots changed hands quite frequently. Bain and Dangerfield both purchased lots, as did George James Engall, an estate and house agent whose firm became the manager of the estate. He later lived in Battledown House.

Building started in about 1863, through the initiative of Charles Andrews, one of the booksellers who showed an early interest in the estate and purchased several lots. He had lived for some time in Brighton, and was a successful investor in Brighton Villas, a row of houses off Hales Road on what became Battledown Approach. He started building three houses but did not personally live in any of them: Stanley Lodge (later called 'Avalon'), Battledown Tower and Simla Lodge (later 'The Leasowe' and then Charlton manor). This last was the first to be occupied, sold in 1864 to Commander Thomas Tickell RN, who in early life lived in India where his father was a general in the Bengal Engineers. Stanley Lodge was also sold quickly, but Battledown Tower was Andrews' undoing. It was a joint project with Ridge, and in 1867 had to be auctioned. There was little more activity for several years. Battledown View was built in 1870, and just six more houses by 1881. Like Pittville, it was some time before the estate was successful.

There were already two houses on Battledown Hill before the land for the new estate was purchased by the three entrepreneurs. Battledown House was possibly built before the end of the eighteenth century, and occupied plot 8; the other was Battledown Knoll, later called 'The Knowle', and finally 'Battledown Manor', and it had been built about 1800. Including these two, twelve houses were visited by the census enumerator when in 1881 he walked up the hill

The mock-Tudor style of the houses in Park Lane, Prestbury, built by a private developer just before the Second World War, is a pleasant reference to the historic nature of the site on the edge of the old moated Prestbury manor house, and adjacent to Prestbury Park. The proposal to build led to an excavation which established the outlines of the medieval manor house, with its two moated enclosures. Park Lane is at present outside Prestbury Conservation area.
PHOTOGRAPH: AUTHOR, 2009

and along the diagonal road (later Stanley Road). Households were generally rather large; the average was over seven people. The largest was the household of Frederick S. Johnston at 'Benvennie' (or 'Ben Venue', later 'Greenacre'). He was a supervisor in the Inland Revenue, aged 65; there was a resident governess for his six daughters, a 'pupil scholar', a general servant and a nurse. This speaks of affluence but not wealth. Two households contained eleven people – those of George Edwin Hewett at 'The Leasowe' and Donald McNeale at 'Charlecote'. Hewett gave his occupation as 'silk mercer, merchant, cabinet manufacturer etc employing about 300 hands'; his domestic staff were an under-nurse, upper-nurse, housemaid and cook. McNeale, born in Ireland, and his wife, daughter and sister were annuitants. He had the largest domestic staff, with three resident servants, and a coachman with his wife and 18-month old child.

The range of occupations is wider than might have been expected. Not all heads of households were professionals and only one, Sir Brook Kay, baronet, was from among the gentry. He had a small household of only three (the others being his wife and one female servant). Kay had served in India, though this was not revealed in the census in which his occupation was simply 'baronet', and was active in public life in Cheltenham and Gloucestershire over a long period. Three men were professionals: one was the supervisor in the Inland Revenue, one a barrister, and one a retired Unitarian Minister. There were two other industrialists (a 'cabinet manufacturer' born in Cheltenham, and a china merchant born in Pendleton, Lancashire), a retired builder, and a stock- and shareholder.

Occupations, 1881–1921

There was a different society at the bottom of the Approach Road and in Hales Road. There the average household size was 4.5 persons, the same as for the county but a little below the national figure of 4.7.[37] There were only sixteen servants among the 88 households. Although the area was on the edge of Cheltenham, just one man was an agricultural labourer and one a market gardener. All the others followed distinctively urban trades. A large cemetery had been opened in Bouncers Lane, Prestbury, in 1864,[38] which explains the presence at Beechworth Villas of a sculptor employing sixteen men and three boys. Another sculptor lived in Rosehill. A plumber lived at the reservoir at Hewletts, and a labourer to the Water Works Company in Rosehill Street. An unusual occupation was returned by one man – architectural modeller for artists.

The military connection in Cheltenham in 1881 was, in relation to the total population, small.[39] Some 261 people entered a military or naval occupation on their census form, of whom 68 specified the Indian service. Not all were heads of households; some were sons, lodgers or visitors, and a few were women apparently drawing pensions from the Indian service. For example, a father, three sons and a daughter living in 9 Oxford Street were all pensioners

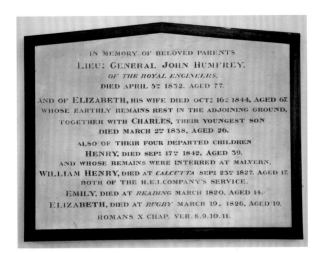

Much is made of the Indian connection in Cheltenham, with servants of the Honourable East India Company or army officers retiring to the town, and Cheltenham College founded with this career particularly in mind. But there were also connections with the West Indies, first evident in the presence of Lady Frances Stapleton at the Great House. Trinity church, Portland Street, built in 1819–20 and originally known as Holy Trinity, contains an astonishing array of plaques on its walls, some of which record these connections. Two hundred and forty-eight people have been listed, with dates of death between 1818 and 1876, and one of 1802; of these, 27 were servants of the East India Company. These memorials are to Lt Gen. John Humfrey, who had two sons in the Company's service, one aged 30, and one aged 17 who died in Calcutta; Henry Adams Mayers, of the island of Barbados; and Henry John Ross, solicitor to the crown at Jamaica.

PHOTOGRAPHS: CARNEGIE, 2009

This view of the High Street shows fashionable society driving along the road and visiting the shops there, while the bicycle suggests there were also more modest visitors to the street. There is a considerable contrast between the crowded buildings along the street and the spacious houses of the Promenade. The photograph was taken before the introduction of the motor car, but from the 1880s 'safety' bicycles such as the one seen here had begun to replace the older penny farthing machines, so this photograph probably dates from the last decade of the nineteenth century.

© CHELTENHAM ART GALLERY AND MUSEUM

of the Madras Military Fund – or was this a mistake by the enumerator? Thirty-one of the military were in Lansdown and seven in Clarence Square.

It is easy to overstate the affluence of the Cheltenham population. More than three-quarters of the town's households did not have a resident domestic servant (though perhaps some employed the almost 2,000 domestic servants who were *not* living-in). Ten per cent of households had more than three resident servants. Nine-tenths of the servants were female. There were also a few households where apprentices and business assistants were resident, most notably, as in 1851, in some of the draper's establishments. At 61 and 62 Regent Street, William J. Smith, silk mercer, had seventeen servants altogether, but only two were domestics, three were 'drapery apprentices', and ten were draper's assistants. Similarly Walter Dicks at 173 High Street was a draper with two domestic servants, one apprentice and seven drapers' assistants. A third draper's establishment, at 135 and 136 High Street, involved a master draper, J. Downing, employing four men and thirteen women, nine of whom lived on the premises with a housekeeper but not the master himself, who was elsewhere in Cheltenham. A second master draper, E. Dunn, employed two men and eleven women, seven of whom lived in.

Domestic service continued to be important in Cheltenham until the First World War. Almost two in every five households in the town had resident servants in 1911. Nearly half of the more than 4,000 women who stated an occupation in Cheltenham were described as servants, compared with one-third in Gloucester. The other important occupations of the women of the town were still supplying the domestic needs of wealthier households, as laundresses, seamstresses and cleaners. Forty per cent of the women in Cheltenham were in employment, but in Gloucester only 29 per cent. The 1911 census also confirms that Cheltenham continued to attract the retired. There were significantly more people over 65 in Cheltenham than in Gloucester.

The elderly in Cheltenham and Gloucester in 1911 (percentages)

| | Age groups 65 and above | | |
	M	F	Total
Cheltenham	7.4	9.2	16.6
Gloucester	5.2	6.5	11.7

But it is the female population which shows clearly the different social structures of the two towns. There was still an extraordinary preponderance of women in Cheltenham in the early twentieth century. In Gloucester in 1901 there were eleven women for every ten men, but in Cheltenham no fewer than sixteen. The ratio in the next thirty years remained stable in Gloucester, while it fell only a little in Cheltenham, where there were fifteen women to every ten men in 1911 and fourteen in 1921 and 1931.

INDUSTRY

Richard Beamish, in his paper to the British Association for the Advancement of Science, which met in Cheltenham in August 1856, said then of the town that 'Devoid of the manufacturing industry that distinguishes Manchester, unsupported by the commercial resources which impart so great an impetus to Liverpool and Cardiff, Cheltenham has nevertheless far outstripped these towns in the race of increase'. Manchester and Liverpool each had more than 300,000 people in 1851, but Beamish was making a very important point. It was indeed the case, as is frequently said, that Cheltenham lacked any industry, but it was also true that its population had grown at a remarkable rate.[40] The situation regarding industry did not materially change until the 1930s.

One successful business that started in Cheltenham in the 1880s was Barnby Bendall & Co. Ltd. 'Furniture removals and storage' is boldly proclaimed on the side of their wagons. The firm appears to have organised a container-type system of transport, hauled by a traction engine. This photograph was taken in London about 1910, but the headquarters and extensive storage facilities of the firm were in Cheltenham; removals between London and Cheltenham were common, and men in the colonial service and the church were frequent and appreciative customers. As the last member of the family approached retirement, he sold the business to Cantay in 1976. The large brick 'Depository' which remains in St George's Place, was built in 1898–99.

© CHELTENHAM ART GALLERY AND MUSEUM

There was a notable firm engaged in metalworking, William Letheren & Sons at the Vulcan Iron Works, but they were 'art metal' workers. In 1867 Letheren had won a Society of Arts competition for a wrought-iron screen, and this marked the beginning of a successful career in this field. *Kelly's* 1894 *Directory of the Engineers, Iron and Metal Trade* classified the firm under 'medieval metal workers' and also under 'mechanical engineers'. Two other mechanical engineers were listed in 1894, and there were also the gasworks and waterworks, but 'industry' in the sense more generally understood, of producing or using machinery for producing textiles, ship-building or coal mining, simply did not exist. Cheltenham's skills and employment opportunities were in supplying the requirements of wealthier individual clients in their houses or churches, or in consumer goods.

At the time William Letheren was producing fine ironwork, Herbert Henry Martyn was starting out in the same field, catering to the Victorian passion for decoration, and the firm he founded became notably successful. He was born in Worcester, and as a young teenager studied at the School of Art, but had a struggle to earn enough in a succession of jobs. Once employed as a wood and stone carver, however, he made rapid progress. He came with his employer, R. L. Boulton, when he moved to a studio in Cheltenham, attracted by the 'considerable church building in progress'.[41] In 1874 Martyn set up on his own, with a stonecarver, E. A. Emms, who was able to put a little money into the enterprise. Ten years later Martyn's son, Alfred Willie, joined the business, and it became a limited company in 1900. H. H. Martyn & Co. Ltd took over Letheren's premises in Lansdown in 1908, renaming it 'Sunningend' after the premises which the company had occupied in High Street. The company later expanded into cabinet-making and ship furnishing, known worldwide, and was an important Cheltenham employer.[42] But despite these examples of modest industrial activity, the 1901 census shows that Cheltenham remained largely unindustrialised, as it had been throughout the nineteenth century.

Percentages of men, 10 years and over, in the larger sectors of employment in 1901

	Number employed	Percentage of employed in					
		Transport	Engineering	Building	Chemicals	Food	Dress
Cheltenham	12,170	13.2	2.9	15.5	0.7	11.2	6.2
Gloucester	14,759	20.0	11.4	13.1	13.5	9.2	3.5

Gloucester was a largely urban area, whereas the more generously drawn boundaries of Cheltenham borough included some farmland. Consequently, nearly 800 men were in agricultural employment, almost the same number as were employed in the dress trades. The food sector included those employed in catering and in brewing. Cheltenham Original Brewery, formerly owned by Agg-Gardner, was a large concern, and brewing had been a prominent Cheltenham industry for centuries. The construction of the Gloucester and Berkeley canal and the docks had encouraged large-scale flour milling in Gloucester, and railway development there had led to the founding of the Railway and Carriage and Wagon Company in 1860. That in turn stimulated the growth of foundry work and engineering;[43] so ten years later 1,285 men in Gloucester were said to be employed 'on railways'. No comparable industry existed in Cheltenham.

When *Industrial Gloucestershire* was published by Chance & Bland in 1904, whole page advertisements were placed by the town councils of Gloucester and Tewkesbury, drawing attention to the advantages of locating industry in their towns, but nothing was included from Cheltenham. Only one Cheltenham firm featured, Cheltine Foods Ltd, the 'only food specialist in Gloucestershire', described as 'among the more notable of our new industries'. The firm was founded in 1899 by N.J. Bloodworth, who was described as 'a practical and scientific baker'. He pioneered the production of special foods, breads and biscuits for 'diabetics, invalids, infants, dyspeptics, and anaemics' and also the packaging of these products. It will be observed that the business was tailored to the health-seeking residents of Cheltenham. Popular lines were said to be Cheltine Malted Milk Chocolate and Cheltine Soluble Milk Food for babies. A new factory was built, 'entirely isolated from any other factory of any kind, and therefore removed from the smoke and dust inseparable from manufacturing districts', with seven ovens and steam mixing and kneading machines. There was great emphasis on cleanliness and on scientific consultation. The firm's head office, in Chester Walk, survived until the 1970s when the premises were demolished to make way for the new children's library.[44]

With its lack of heavy industry of any sort, the decline in the major staple industries of nineteenth-century Britain, which had perhaps started before 1900 and gathered pace rapidly after the First World War, did not directly affect the working men of Cheltenham. But in common with other towns it experienced rising unemployment in the early twentieth century.[45] Between 1905 and 1908 a Distress Committee tried to find ways of alleviating the hardship.[46] The council promised the spectacularly small sum of £50 towards their schemes, and the Queen's Fund supplied £115 in January 1906, but the committee relied on public appeals for funds, requesting free use of the Town Hall for a concert to raise money. The range of jobs offered to the unemployed was limited: wood-chopping, stone-breaking, ash-sifting and road-making, all reminiscent of the work required by nineteenth century overseers of the poor. The ground of Naunton Park was levelled in preparation for its landscaping. As well as paying a minimal wage, contributions had to be made to the Workmen's Compensation scheme under the 1906 Act. These men were clearly unskilled. In May 1906 two families on the unemployment register were helped to emigrate to Canada, a very small step towards solving the problem. In 1908 the government set up Labour Exchanges.

The First World War was not a watershed as far as the economy of Cheltenham was concerned; neither Cheltenham nor Gloucester in 1921 had changed in essentials since 1911. The 1921 census tables of occupations were published for those aged 12 years and above in the large municipal boroughs with a population greater than 20,000.[47] These showed that in Cheltenham over 1,000 men worked in agriculture, but one small sign of the differing social structure of that town and Gloucester was the importance of the motor car in Cheltenham: 216 men described themselves as 'motor mechanic', but in Gloucester only 97. On the other hand, some 2,487 men in Gloucester, 15 per cent of the employed, were foundry workers, machine tool workers, millwrights, mechanical engineers, or in other metal trades, but in Cheltenham only half as many, 932 men and most of them probably employed by H.H. Martyn. That firm had diversified during the First World War, using its established woodworking skills to make aircraft propellers, wings and fuselages. In 1917 A.W. Martyn founded the Gloucestershire Aircraft Company, but once the war was over the firm reverted to ornamental work. The Gloucestershire Aircraft Company was separated from Martyns in 1925, and established a new factory at Hucclecote, where there was a runway on which the aeroplanes had been tested; in 1926 it was renamed Gloster Aircraft Company.[48]

The roll-call of names of Cheltonians who lost their lives on active service in the First World War is long: here the war memorial on The Promenade lists 467 men of the Gloucestershire Regiment who fell. War memorials were a subject of debate after 1918; the mayor of Cheltenham, J. D. Bendall, formed a committee in December 1919 to find a suitable site and design. A number of grandiose schemes were considered, but there was a disappointing response to an appeal, and eventually a more modest cenotaph was constructed by R. L. Boulton & Sons, though placed in a prominent position.

PHOTOGRAPH: CARNEGIE, 2009

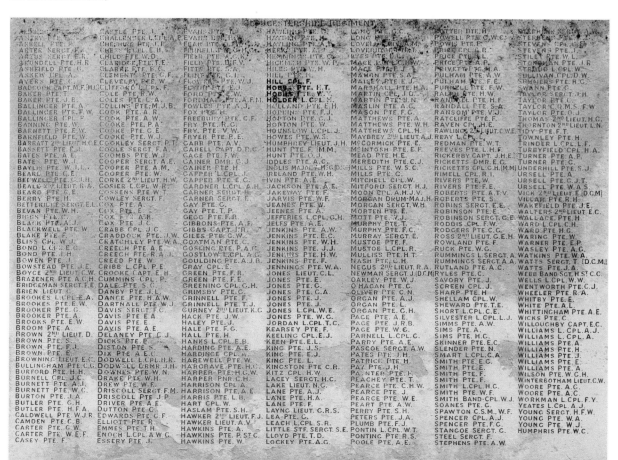

The end of the First World War caused a big downturn in economic prosperity, and returning soldiers wanted work. Attempts were made to provide them with smallholdings so that they could be self-sufficient; nearly 12,000 acres were made available for the purpose in Gloucestershire in 1919 and 1920.[49] James Agg Gardner, MP for Cheltenham, who had already provided work for the unemployed in levelling some of his land, supported the idea of 'crofts'. In June 1926 the National Homecroft Association was formed. The date is significant, for it followed the General Strike of the previous month. A 10-acre site was purchased north-west of Cheltenham, off the Tewkesbury Road, and here ten crofts were built of concrete slabs, though the initial aim was to build 25 dwellings. Like the Chartist Land Company eighty years before, the ideal was difficult to realise; the heavy clay of the site made cultivation difficult and the crofters did not find co-operative cultivation acceptable. But the crofts survived, in Homecroft Drive, and the association was not wound up until 1956.

HOUSING AS A SOCIAL DUTY

It might be assumed that Cheltenham, with its many well-known squares and terraces of great affluence, had less poor housing than many towns. But even a cursory reading of the minutes of the Public Health Committee of the borough council shows that this is a misconception. Awareness of poor housing was largely the result of conscientious work by medical officers of health over many years. Their focus was on health hazards, but at the same time a social conscience was awakened. The first meeting of the Committee after the newly constituted borough council was elected in 1877 considered a report on scarlatina in the town.[50] It noted 'numerous complaints of the nuisance arising from the keeping of pigs'; one case was in a family 'living in the midst of pigstyes kept in a filthy state'.[51] At every fortnightly meeting of the committee, the medical officer of health presented several addresses where one or more public health problems was of concern: overcrowding, dilapidation, lack of sewers and water supply, nuisance from overflowing drains, and lack of ash boxes for each house, and action was resolved upon. Lack of ash boxes, indeed, constituted a very frequent complaint, a surprising item until the necessity for each house to have a fire throughout the year is recalled: the abatement of smoke nuisance was secondary to the need to dispose of ashes. As the procedures of the Committee became more formalised, and the minutes printed, a frequently repeated standard heading was 'houses unfit for human habitation'.

The Torrens Act, the first legislation dealing with housing problems, was passed in 1866. It allowed councils to compel the owners of insanitary houses to put them in proper condition. More effective legislation was introduced in 1875: the Artisans Dwelling Act gave councils the authority to use compulsory purchase orders on any slum property which landlords refused to improve. A few vigorous local councils, for example Birmingham under the leadership of Joseph Chamberlain, made good use of the Act, but it did not lead to widespread local action. There is no evidence that Cheltenham borough council took advantage of its powers to purchase, though it did issue landlords with orders to remedy glaring deficiencies in their properties – for example to make houses safe, relieve overcrowding and connect them to water mains. The 1884–85 Royal Commission on Housing marked an important stage in the recognition of the social duty of providing adequate housing. In 1890 parliament gave councils further powers to close insanitary houses and to build new properties with money raised from the rates. Cheltenham borough council made use of these powers to close houses but not itself to build new.

An example of the sort of battle which the committee faced relates to the owner of numbers 1 to 9 Barnard's Row. This row, the first three houses of which were built in 1819, was between Knapp Street and New Street. The row was a long-running problem to which the medical officer frequently drew attention and eventually, when the owner Mr Edward Steel refused to comply with requests for improvement, the committee decided on a closing order. Steel's offer to sell the property to the council for £500 was indignantly rejected.[52] The borough surveyor, who was important in the story of Cheltenham's poorer housing, considered that nothing less than rebuilding would do. After months of wrangling, Steel eventually agreed to demolish the three oldest and most dilapidated houses if the closing order were withdrawn. He also undertook to make the remaining six fit for human habitation under the supervision of the medical officer and the borough surveyor. The nine dwellings in 1881 were occupied by 44 people, 13 of whom were children aged 12 years and under. If, as is probable, the three oldest (and thus those shortly to be demolished) were nos 1–3, they were occupied by a charwoman living on her own, a general labourer and his wife who was a housekeeper in domestic service, and another general labourer with a wife and six children. Not surprisingly, four men in the row were general labourers and one was an agricultural labourer; and six of the women worked either as laundresses or in domestic service. Only one 14-year-old was at school; the other younger denizens of Barnard's Row were all earning, if only, as in the case of one 13-year-old, as an errand boy. The problems of 'slum' property were only partly the result of the original house design and construction; poverty was also responsible, particularly if tenants could not pay the higher rents which landlords claimed were needed if properties were to be improved.[53]

In 1909 a Town Planning Act gave local authorities further powers. Council officers had to consider the application of successive housing acts, and the subject became one of considerable technicality. Moves towards council house building were stopped by the First World War, and the 1915 Rent Act discouraged private investment in housing for letting, but before the end of the First World War the subject moved rapidly up the political agenda. After the war, Cheltenham Council hoped fervently that house-building would help to reduce the substantial unemployment in the town.

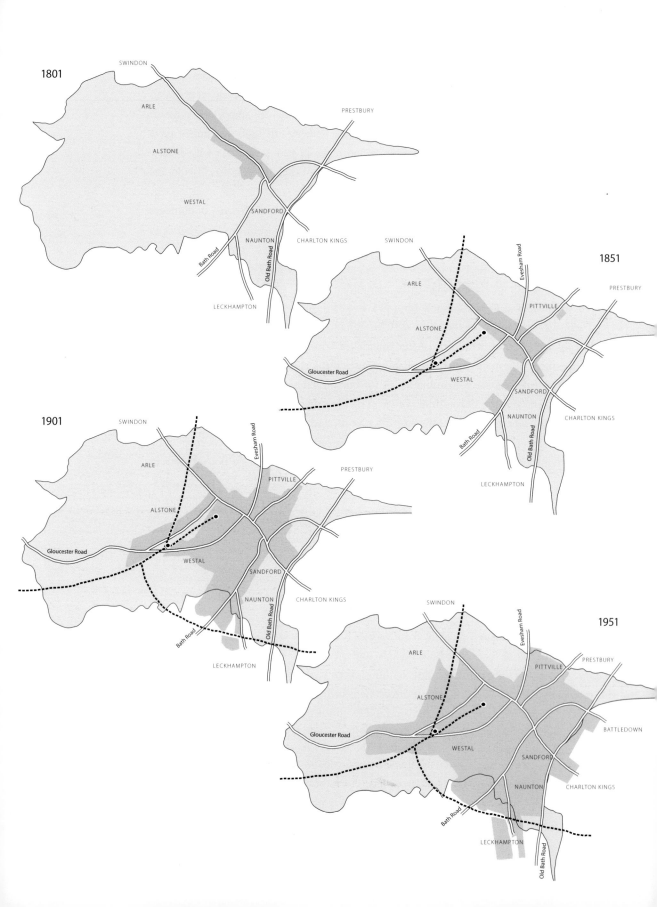

CHAPTER TEN

DIVERSIFICATION

THE MOST STRIKING FEATURE of Cheltenham in the twentieth century was the physical expansion of the town, which first filled the parish and borough with buildings, and then gradually expanded beyond the old boundaries, merging the surrounding parishes into a continuous urban district. Population grew with the changing industrial profile of the town. Regency period houses had given the town a strong identity and style; the twentieth-century residential suburbs, including significant areas of social housing, are less clearly focused, but in practice are of equal or even greater importance in the history of the town, and in indicating and controlling its social composition. 'Houses are principally interesting because people live in them.'[1]

Local government units were altered to make them match the actual growth of population. Cheltenham municipal borough and the civil parish were enlarged in 1935 to take in more of Charlton Kings and Leckhampton, and also parts of Prestbury and Up Hatherley. In 1963, despite the recommendation of the Local Government Commission, an application by Cheltenham for county borough status was refused by Gloucestershire County Council, a decision upheld by the minister of Housing and Local Government. Local government reform in 1974 created a new district council (still called Cheltenham Borough) with an area of 4,663 hectares. The formerly separate Charlton Kings Urban District Council disappeared, amalgamated with the municipal borough of Cheltenham, and this and other extensions added nearly 22,000 people to the old borough from surrounding parishes. Cirencester became the centre of Cotswold District. Cheltenham was further enlarged in 1991, taking some areas from Tewkesbury District; the civil parishes of Leckhampton, Swindon, Prestbury and Up Hatherley, as well as Charlton Kings, are now wholly within Cheltenham borough, which has five parish councils as lower tier authorities. There is an echo here of the geographical extent of the ancient Cheltenham hundred.

Substantial growth in Cheltenham's population, which echoed a period of extensive house-building, occurred during and after the Second World War. Recalculating the population figures to match the present Cheltenham district suggests that the town grew more slowly than the national average during the second half of the nineteenth century and first quarter of the twentieth century, but thereafter a little faster than the national average. However, more recently, expansion has been constrained by the designation of the Cotswold Area of Outstanding Natural Beauty in 1966, an area of 790 square miles including parts of Charlton Kings, Leckhampton, and Prestbury, and by the green belt which limits Cheltenham's growth to north and west, and, with Tewkesbury Borough Council's share, separates Cheltenham from Gloucester.

Population of Cheltenham, Cotswold, Gloucester and Tewkesbury Districts, 1931–2001

	Cheltenham	Cotswold	Gloucester	Tewkesbury
1931	55,508	50,776	59,735	25,657
1941	62,437	57,312	65,324	33,815
1951	70,273	64,703	71,455	44,631
1961	82,419	63,603	81,006	52,404
1971	96,745	62,530	91,835	61,549
1981	96,882	66,477	94,968	66,588
1991	106,883	74,416	105,076	72,901
2001	110,025	80,379	109,888	76,394

Population figures as recalculated for 'Vision of Britain' by the Department of Geography of the University of Portsmouth.

THE POETS' ESTATE

Cheltenham's experience of social housing was entirely typical. Action mirrored government initiatives, the borough council responding to them rather than acting independently. In 1917 Christopher Addison was made minister of reconstruction and in 1919 he became head of the newly amalgamated Department of Health and Local Government Board. The Local Government Board, constituted in 1871, had supervised local authorities and the Ministry of Health was created in the last year of the war. The latter became the sponsoring department for the great surge in council housing, urging local authorities to make use of enabling legislation. The result changed the topography of towns. Starting in 1918, Cheltenham Borough Council built over 7,000 homes before local authority house-building was brought to an end.

As minister of reconstruction Addison at once instituted a survey to establish how many new houses would be needed once the war was over. The first official estimate for the whole country was 300,000. The housing question began to assume large proportions and in the general election of November 1918 Lloyd George promised half a million 'homes for heroes'. The extension of the parliamentary franchise to all men aged 21 years and over, and to a limited number of women, was also relevant; this act changed dramatically the nature of politics. By 1919, though, the estimated number of houses required had doubled, because of the surge in young married couples as well as the growing realisation of the number of slum properties which needed replacement.

In 1917, in response to the first circular from the Local Government Board, Cheltenham's Medical Officer of Health recommended to the council's Public Health Committee that 100 houses would be required at the end of the war 'to provide the necessary accommodation for the persons of the working classes'. This was accepted, but the full council considered it an underestimate, and returned the figure of 500 houses.[2] The Public Health Committee decided to inspect the slum houses listed in the MOH's report, starting in Exmouth Street off the Bath Road; the lower High Street was an area of courts and alleys but the Bath Road was also bad from the point of view of public health. In June 1918 the committee requested Dr Garrett to report on 'houses so unfit for human habitation as to require immediate action with a view to closing orders being made'. By the end of the year, soon after the Armistice, the committee

This booklet about the St Mark's estate in the mid-1930s suggested that in Cheltenham there was an acute shortage of housing that might hinder economic development. It pointed out the primary characteristics of the estate: 'variety of design, abundance of open space, generous provision for gardens, and convenient placing'. Every house had electricity.

GLOUCESTERSHIRE LIBRARIES

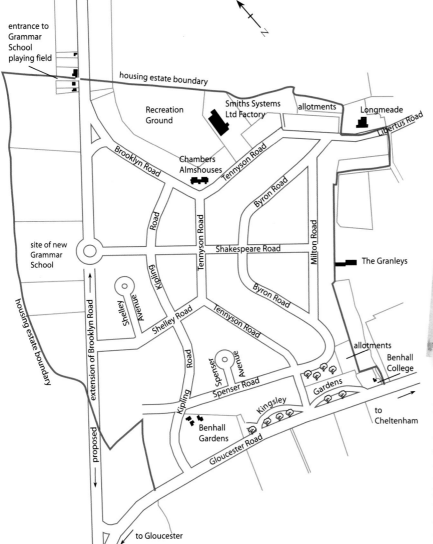

The Residential Amenities OF THE ST. MARK'S ESTATE CHELTENHAM SPA

In the mid-1930s, Cheltenham Borough Council made a considerable effort to advertise the possibilities of industrial sites in the town. The attractive booklet showed the layout of the St Mark's estate, now generally known as the 'Poets' estate' because the roads were all named after poets, and under this name it has been designated a conservation area.

ordered that the owners of five properties in St Paul's Street South should (under the Public Health Act of 1875) put them into habitable condition, while fourteen houses in Stanhope Street, off the Tewkesbury Road, three in Worcester Street and a scatter of others, should be closed until made fit for human habitation under the powers granted by the 1909 Town Planning Act. When in 1920 the council was discussing 'Improvement schemes' – that is, slum clearance – the Stanhope Street area was first to be considered.

A Local Government Board circular of March 1918, well in advance of the 1919 'Addison' Housing Act, offered councils financial inducements to spend the product of a penny rate on new housing, the Treasury agreeing to make up any shortfall. These were very favourable terms which councils were quick to accept, as the Exchequer and the taxpayer soon realised.[3] The aims were idealistic. A commission set up in 1918 under Sir John Tudor Walters and inspired by the pre-war garden cities movement, recommended low densities of twelve houses per acre, each 770 square feet with plenty of large windows, indoor bathrooms and WCs, separate kitchens, and two or more bedrooms.[4]

In Cheltenham a new Housing sub-committee was asked in November 1918 to prepare schemes, and the borough surveyor was to report on the number of houses to be demolished and new houses needed for those displaced.[5] The committee set energetically to work, purchasing 115¾ acres adjoining the Libertus estate from Herbert Unwin of Arle Court and 2¼ acres from T. Smith and approving plans for 400 houses. The committee also planned to purchase army huts at Brockworth as temporary accommodation. Smiths Systems Ltd bought 2¼ acres from the council for a joinery works; this firm supplied office equipment and continued in business on the new site in Tennyson Road until shortly after the Second World War, when the factory was purchased by Spirax Sarco.[6] Six types of house were designed, most with three bedrooms and a few with four, categorised as 'parlour' or 'non-parlour' type. At the Ministry's prompting, a Women's Advisory Committee was set up and offered suggestions, for example about the position of doors.

One factory, to be occupied by a firm making office furniture, Smiths Systems Ltd, was built in Tennyson Road. The front block was offices, and behind it were the industrial buildings. During the Second World War the firm produced wings for Mosquito fighters, but after the war was over, the site was bought by Spirax Sarco, and enlarged considerably. There will be another change when Spirax Sarco concentrate their Cheltenham factories on a site on Kingsditch Industrial Estate.

© SPIRAX SARCO

When Spirax and Sarco were combined, and separated from Walker Crosweller, in 1939, they took over premises in St George's Road previously occupied by a wholesale confectionary business, trading under the unexpected name of Dingley Dell Candles Ltd, manufacturers. The 5,000 ft² factory may therefore have been converted in 1935 to the confectionary business rather than being newly built at that date. The building is behind Alpha House, where Dr Jenner performed smallpox vaccinations, although he did not live there (as the blue plaque above the door states). His house, with extensive modern buildings, all form part of this Spirax-Sarco site.

PHOTOGRAPH: AUTHOR, 2010

In February 1920 there were 1,080 men registered unemployed in Cheltenham. A Special Distress Committee hoped that house-building would provide work; it also paid for men to plant potatoes on the council's new site. For the next three years the Housing Committee continued to find work for the unemployed, preparing roads, digging drains, and making shrubberies. The same policy was adopted in 1931, when unemployment again became a major problem. In April 1920 the mayor cut the first sod for Cheltenham council's first council housing, to be built by A. C. Billings. The roads were named after English poets.[7] Tennyson Road was first; Tennyson had lived in Cheltenham from 1843 to 1849, and had been poet laureate from 1850 until his death in 1892, so was an ideal figure – and his poetry was consonant with the idealistic aims of the housing programme. Milton and Byron soon followed. This was the beginning of the St Mark's estate. Later Shakespeare, Shelley, Spenser, Kingsley and Kipling Roads were built. The 'Poets' estate became a conservation area in 2001, a recognition of Cheltenham council's imaginative first experiment in social housing. The architectural style, especially the variety of rooflines and gables, illustrates the influence of the Arts and Crafts movement, and is testimony to a sense of civic consciousness.[8]

Nationally, a conflict of objectives in housing policy soon emerged. Local councils concentrated on replacing poor housing, but the government wanted to provide for industrial workers. Cheltenham gave preference to ex-servicemen with large families, perhaps helping to dissipate any revolutionary ideas returning soldiers might have, but the council initially refused to give priority to workers for Smiths Systems or Gloucestershire Aircraft Co. Some firms, such as W.H. Cole & Co. Ltd (which made hooks and eyes and, like Smiths Systems, occupied a site on the new estate in Milton Road) and H. H. Martyn & Co. Ltd, 'architectural decorators', sought accommodation for their workers. Martyns said they had fifteen sheet metal men in urgent need of housing. A year later the council changed its policy and agreed to give special consideration to 'key men' in these firms.

Government money inevitably brought bureaucratic controls, as civil servants altered schemes and prescribed the types of houses to be built and rents to be charged.[9] As the scale of the financial burden he had accepted became apparent, Addison was forced to resign in 1921. The Ministry received the Stanhope Street plans in February 1921, but two months later requested that the scheme be deferred. There were many problems: the 'Middle Classes Union' presented Cheltenham council with a resolution opposing any further expenditure on the housing scheme; the unduly enterprising tenant of 3 Tennyson Road advertised his empty house for rent – his tenancy was swiftly terminated – and the ceilings of four houses in the road had to be repaired soon after completion. In 1922 government grants were withdrawn, as were the subsidies for houses built by private builders (either for sale or for rent) which Cheltenham council had exploited.

Cheltenham had planned 120 'parlour' type houses and 40 'non-parlour' and by April 1921, 24 were occupied. In Tewkesbury, where the borough council had made a modest start before the First World War in what became known as Prior's Park, 122 houses were built, and in Gloucester the Corporation built 280.[10] Nationally about 200,000 council houses were built before the scheme came to an abrupt end. The first experiment to encourage council house building did not solve the housing problem, but it pushed it high up the political agenda and Cheltenham had acquired a large site for future development.

ATTRACTING INDUSTRY

The 1920s marked a watershed in Cheltenham's industrial history. The General Strike and, more seriously, the collapse in the stock market in 1929, directed particular attention to the economic structure of Cheltenham. The General Strike started on 4 May 1926. At first there were no trains, buses, trams or postal service. Martyn's men stopped work, and work on the Boots building ceased.[11] Volunteers gradually provided a minimum level of services; by 8 May there were 860 in Cheltenham including 74 men students from St Paul's Training College (compared with 1,600 in Gloucester). After the strike collapsed on 13 May, the deputy mayor congratulated the town on the lack of violence. Employees were successful in insisting that they be reinstated on the basis of their terms of employment before the strike, although the Cheltenham tram company at first resisted the men's unconditional return. H. H. Martyn and the Gloucestershire Aircraft Company, which negotiated jointly, appear to have been sympathetic employers. There were many different trades involved in their works, and the company required that all should return together and thereafter remain at work, but they made no other conditions and wages were to be as before the strike. There was a suggestion of a sympathetic strike if all local men were not reinstated. For Martyns, it was 'impossible to keep opening and shutting works where over 1,000 men and their dependants were involved'. After several meetings between delegations over two days, the men accepted the terms. Unions did have support, but there were not the bitter disputes which were seen in other parts of the country; the miners who had originally secured the general support of the trades unions were left to fight on alone.

In its 'professional and trades section' Kelly's *Directory of Cheltenham* of 1926 listed a limited number of small, specialist manufacturers employing skilled men. In addition to H. H. Martyn & Co, Smiths Systems and Wm. H. Cole & Co. Ltd, Dale, Forty manufactured pianos in Regent Street; Davis & Co. made invalid chairs in Sherborne Place; and A. J. Price & Sons were organ builders. Other specialised firms included Dowlings, chocolate manufacturers in Montpellier Avenue; United Chemists' Association Ltd, established in 1915, which evaporated and bottled Cheltenham water. There were two coach and carriage builders (W. G. Tibbles & Co. Ltd and Chas. J. Vince), and three motor-car body builders (Haines & Strange, A. Tombs and Williams & Bayliss), while the Cheltenham Motor & Cycle Co. made the 'famous Spa bicycle', and five other firms were in the same business. T. W. Smith & Sons made portable buildings; and Moody, Bell & Lamb Ltd and Gloucestershire Surgical Appliance Co. produced

In 1926 the official *Guide to Cheltenham Spa* carried, among others, an advertisement for Dale, Forty & Co Ltd, giving the address as Promenade; there was also a piano workshop behind the *Plough*. The firm had supplied the Ladies' College with pianos until Dale closed Leckhampton hill. The Queen's Hotel has always been one of the most prominent buildings in Cheltenham, both because of its design and its position at the top of The Promenade. This advertisement makes a point of its suitability for the new and well-to-do motoring tourist.

surgical appliances. The last-named had been set up in 1915 when A. W. Martyn backed John Chandler to produce his innovative metal splints for wounded soldiers.[12] Skilled workers in these businesses were those most likely to be tenants of Cheltenham Borough Council's first housing.

Faced with the problem of unemployment, Cheltenham Borough Council encouraged the expansion of industry, and between the General Strike and the beginning of the Second World War, significant employment opportunities started to open up, most notably in the formation of the first Dowty company. However, most of the new firms did not employ the many *unskilled* men in the town. The Chamber of Commerce was formed in 1928 and in 1951, referring to the 1920s, an introduction to the Chamber's *Report on Industry* observed that 'twenty-five years ago we had an army of unskilled men whose employment was a continual problem'.

Cheltenham Council had already made industrial sites available in St Marks, and the acquisition of Whaddon Farm in 1934 offered further opportunities. A 'Factories and Industries Committee' was set up in April 1931 and minutes of meetings of the next nine months have survived.[13] At first, potential sites were sought from property owners, and four were offered. London papers were examined for firms advertising for factory sites. The numerous advantages of Cheltenham were said to be its central position and excellent railway facilities, cheap electricity, the cleanliness and healthiness of the town, the plentiful supply of unskilled (and especially female) labour, together with its proximity to potential factory sites, little prospect of labour troubles, and 'every assistance to provide housing accommodation'. The Board of Trade assumed that local councils would be looking to relocate factories, but Cheltenham replied that it was seeking to attract industry. Ed. J. Burrow printed 5,000 brochures, which were distributed in the USA via the American Rotary Club and transatlantic shipping routes,

The *Cheltenham Guide* for 1935 advertised Reed & Paterson, suppliers of motor cars. The following year there was a splendid photograph of Cavendish House (*below*) as it was before the post-Second World War rebuilding.
GLOUCESTERSHIRE LIBRARIES

and in Europe via embassies and other outlets – 1,000 each were allocated to France and Germany, later increased to 2,000. Some replies from foreign firms were received, but the most notable success was in attracting Walker Crosweller.

About the same time the council showed entrepreneurial flair by joining with Gloucester Corporation in 1936 to buy an extensive tract of land in Staverton for the construction of an aerodrome. The development of Gloster Aircraft no doubt encouraged the initiative, together with the arrival of other firms engaged in aeroplane construction, such as Rotol Air Screws Ltd (a venture by Rolls-Royce and Bristol Engines to combine their production of airscrews, the name being based on those of the two sponsoring companies). During the Second World War Staverton was an RAF training base, but its post-war development was in general aviation, and in 1993 the two councils' venture became 'Gloucestershire Airport Ltd', an ALMO (arms-length management organisation) while the councils continued as share-holders, drawing rental and dividend income from the airport. Both councils have backed expansionary plans and there is now a small number of scheduled domestic flights.

The first jet propelled aircraft to fly successfully, the Gloster, flew from RAF Cranwell on 15 May 1941, piloted by P. E. G. Sayers, OBE. It was designed by Sir Frank Whittle, but the airframe was made by the Gloster Aircraft Company. Gloster's chief designer, George Carter, worked closely with Whittle, and the specification was issued by the Air Ministry in 1939, E.28/39, E standing for 'experimental'. Manufacture started at Hucclecote, but was moved to Regent Motors in the High Street, considered a safer location. Once its success had been demonstrated, the technology was shared with America, who financed the production of more jet engines.

INDUSTRIAL SUCCESSES

Ironically, at the time the council was trying to attract industry, it was frustrating George Dowty's wish to build a factory, on the grounds that the heavy engineering undertaken by Dowty was likely to cause smoke pollution. George Herbert Dowty (1901–75) came to Cheltenham in 1924, aged 23, to work for Gloucestershire Aircraft. When only a teenager he had gone to work for a general engineering firm in Worcester. He studied at evening classes and worked in a variety of engineering departments, becoming particularly interested in hydraulics, which was to be prominent in his subsequent career. In 1918 he moved to an aeronautical firm and his expertise was demonstrated in a number of papers which he read to the Institute of Aeronautical Engineers. In Cheltenham he investigated and patented innovative designs and in 1931 decided to go into production on his own, setting up the Aircraft Components Company working from modest premises in Montpellier. His first large order, from Kawasaki in Japan, encouraged him to leave Gloster Aircraft, and by 1934 his enterprise was flourishing. He needed to expand and when in 1935 the borough council refused permission for the erection of a new factory on the outskirts of the built-up area, A.W. Martyn, seeing Dowty's potential, helped to finance the purchase of Arle Court. This was George Dowty's home until 1972.[14] In 1936 Aircraft Components became a public company, with A. W. Martyn as its first chairman, a position he retained until his death in 1947.

At first there were just 45 men working for Dowty, but during the Second World War the business expanded greatly, with new factories in Canada, the USA, and elsewhere in Britain.

In 1935 A.W. Martyn purchased Arle Court, a house built in the middle of the previous century, and which had been empty for a number of years, for the benefit of George Dowty and his firm, Aircraft Components Ltd. It gave him a splendid home, and a large site which he could develop for his engineering business. The drawing office occupied the former ballroom, as Terry Elmes remembers, and the premises were shared with an army of frogs and houseflies.

© CHELTENHAM ART GALLERY AND MUSEUM

The Dowty enterprise was moved from Arle Court after it was taken over by Tube Investments. In 1998 the site was bought by Cheltenham Studios Ltd. Subsequently, in 2006, the industrial part of the site was sold to Cheltenham Film & Photo Studio, while the house itself became a venue for weddings and conferences under the name 'Manor by the Lake'; it also hosts the annual International Screenwriters Festival.
© THE MANOR BY THE LAKE

More than a million hydraulic units were supplied for RAF planes. After the war, the areas of expertise widened; in 1954 Rotol Propellers was acquired, in 1959 Boulton and Paul, and in 1964 Meco of Worcester. Rotol eventually merged with Dowty Equipment and British Messier in 1960. A factory was opened in Ashchurch, near the railway, and Northway housing estate in Tewkesbury was built to accommodate the workforce. Dowty's engineering brilliance and entrepreneurial flair and his contribution to the war effort were recognised when he was knighted in 1956. He received many other honours, and became a freeman of Cheltenham in 1955 and of Tewkesbury in 1966. By 1980 Dowty's consisted of 44 companies with 17,000 employees.

As soon as industrial sites on Whaddon Farm were offered by the council in 1934, Walker Crosweller and Co. Ltd (now Kohler Mira) applied, assuring the council there would not be a chimney. The firm wanted more space and better working conditions than their site in Bermondsey could offer, and manufacturing of thermostatic mixing valves started two years later, in November 1937. More land was purchased from the council,[15] and Walker Crosweller expanded internationally, using the trade name 'Mira' in the UK and 'Rada' abroad. In 1985 the firm became part of Caradon Ltd, changing its name to 'Caradon Mira Ltd' the following year. In 2000 it was sold to HSBC, who in turn sold it to Kohler, but it continues to occupy the Cromwell Road premises. In 2004 Kohler Mira funded a new borehole to tap into the spa waters at Pittville Pump Room, so 'saving the spa'.

When Walker Crosweller opened a factory in Cheltenham, it brought another industrial enterprise which became a world-wide business, Spirax-Sarco. The story behind the name and the location of the firm in Cheltenham is complicated.[16] Sarco, like Rotol, was based on letters from the names of the founders. Three men established a company in London in 1888 to import recording instruments from Germany, including thermostatic steam traps crucial in securing the efficient use of steam. Sarco was the American trade name. Walter Crosweller worked for Sarco, but in 1921 set up a partnership with James Walker to act as English agents for this and other firms. The American name Sarco could not be used in England, so 'Spirax' was christened, because of the spiral tubing used in the traps. Eventually the American products were manufactured in England, and in 1937 premises were leased from Walker Crosweller. It was said that Cheltenham was convenient because it was near Birmingham, the home of most of Spirax's suppliers.

The Cheltenham enterprise flourished, because it sold not just 'ironmongery' but 'knowledge

Walker Crosweller's front offices (*left*) faced towards Clyde Crescent, on the opposite side of the site to the present-day entrance in Cromwell Road, which was only very short with a few houses at the southern end. The first office block in front of the factory was an attractive Art Deco building in then fashionable style, which still exists embedded in the considerable expansion of the factory that has taken place since it was erected. The photograph was taken soon after it was erected. The aerial view of the Walker Crosweller factory (*below*) was taken about 1940, and shows the range of factory buildings behind the front office building. There has been further expansion since this date.

© KOHLER MIRA

Some of the work in the Walker Crosweller factory in 1939, when the photograph of the assembly shop was taken, was done by women. This is still a factory where brass work is polished and cut with threads, and the manufacture of showers is still largely done in Cheltenham; every shower is tested at the Cromwell Road site before being dispatched to a customer.

and service'. Walker Crosweller's agency for Sarco was eventually bought out, and new premises for Spirax were found in Dingley Dell in St George's Road, where a large sweet factory had been built in 1935. This remained the headquarters of an expanding business until after the Second World War, when Spirax bought Charlton House as the American army vacated it, and in 1946 took over a factory in St Mark's where Smiths, the office furniture manufacturer, had been making wings for Mosquito aeroplanes. It plans eventually to vacate the St Mark's factory. The two businesses, Spirax Manufacturing Co. and Sarco Thermostats, were sold in 1952 to the two British managing directors, and on 1 January the new hyphenated Spirax-Sarco Ltd was established. New premises have been built on Kingsditch Trading Estate, where the business is now being concentrated.

Burrow's *About and Around Cheltenham*, published in the late 1930s, included a sympathetic overview of growing industrial enterprises,[17] giving a list which started with R. L. Boulton & Sons, in business and still in competition with H. H. Martyn, also listed; two more art metal firms, Hancock & Sons and A. H. Isher & Son., were also mentioned. Burrow's modestly placed their own business after Boulton, rather than first in this list, 'one of the most important industrial assets of Cheltenham', employing 'close on 400 persons'. The firm was founded by Ed. J. Burrow FRGS 'who for many years played a prominent part in the public life of the town'. He came to Cheltenham as a chemist's assistant, took up etching, and then in 1900 established a printing firm. The business expanded after 1918, and from 1935, the year of Burrow's death, had London premises; the firm left Cheltenham in 1974 and moved to London.[18] Then came the Gloster Aircraft Co, strictly speaking not in Cheltenham but in Brockworth, though it had started in the town. Burrows noted two other firms recently established in Gloucester Road, Rotol Air Screws Ltd opposite the municipal airport, and Aircraft Components Ltd of Arle Court. Walker, Crosweller & Co. Ltd 'one of the most recent businesses to open works in Cheltenham', employed more than 110 people and about fifty salesmen. When the buildings were being erected, Burrow said, they were popularly supposed to be a munitions factory. He ended his review of Cheltenham industries with references to United Chemists Association Ltd, whose 'laboratories and works are very extensive', Cheltine Foods, the Cheltenham Original Brewery, and the first egg-testing, grading and packing station, established in Cheltenham by Gloucestershire Marketing Society Ltd, 'whose well-equipped model premises are situated conveniently in Market Street'.

Soon after *About and Around Cheltenham* was published, another firm which became as important as Dowty's came to the area. Recognising the probable approach of war with Germany, Smiths English Clocks Ltd prepared to move to Bishops Cleeve, in the rural district of Cheltenham but not the borough.[19] Samuel Smith had been a watchmaker in London in 1850; he had expanded into the production of clocks for motorcars and in 1904 into revolution counters for aeroplanes. In 1932 Smiths English Clocks Ltd was established, and in 1936 it amalgamated with a firm of marine instrument makers. The key specialist skills of the company were recognised and the government encouraged Smiths to relocate away from London. Ralph Gordon-Smith, knighted in 1939, was company secretary and also an estate agent. He found a 300-acre site at Keyte Farm in Bishops Cleeve, and in April 1939 the move was authorised. It may not be coincidence that he already had a house in Cheltenham and was rumoured to enjoy the races. He also bought the adjoining Cleeve Grange, making the whole site

SPECIMEN SCHOLASTIC POST-CARD.
Produced by EDWARD J. BURROW,
Scholastic Publisher,
CHELTENHAM.

500 for 21/-.
1000 ,, 32/-.

Edward John Burrow came to Cheltenham in 1889 to work as a qualified pharmacist, but three years later he abandoned this career to concentrate on his drawing and etching. So successful was he, that in 1900 he started a publishing business, producing a guide to Cheltenham. This type of work became a major business. His company was profit-sharing, and he was an astute business man who applied his recommended principle 'To be "off the Beaten Track" in the matter of your printing, the first step is to think'. A second business interest was the 'Scholastic Department', which not only produced brochures, but acted as an agency giving advice to parents. Both businesses reached far beyond the town.
COURTESY JOE STEVENS

500 acres. S. Smith & Sons (Cheltenham) Ltd was formed and the first factory was opened in May 1940, just in time – the main instrument repair department at Cricklewood was bombed in August. The following year there were three camouflaged factory buildings at Bishops Cleeve. In 1944 Smiths Aircraft Instruments Ltd was set up; in 1947 the total number of employees was over 10,000, some 2,500 of them in Bishops Cleeve.

Smiths Industries Ltd was formed in 1966, and Smiths Industries Aerospace and Defence Systems in 1979; Microcircuit Engineering was established in Ashchurch near Tewkesbury. Two firms operated at Bishops Cleeve in 1990: Smiths Industries plc, and Smiths Industries Aerospace and Defence Systems Ltd. In 2000 the merger of Smiths Industries Ltd with Tube Investments, who already controlled the Dowty Group, led to the reorganisation of the aerospace operations of both to form Smiths Aerospace. The 2000 reorganisation following the merger with TI was followed just seven years later by Smiths Aerospace becoming part of the General Electric Group.

In the early years housing in Bishops Cleeve for Smiths' workforce was a problem. The first technical staff lived in caravans in the grounds of the Grange. Priority was given to building 52 houses in Bishops Cleeve, the Meadoway estate. After the war, Cheltenham Rural District Council cooperated in building 478 houses for Smiths' employees. The staff looked to Cheltenham for general amenities, and in 1956 the company presented a tower clock to the town to mark the association. The town clock outside the former town offices in High Street was taken down two years later, according to John Hyett who maintained it.[20] Smiths' clock on its pillar in Royal Well Road has recently been added to Cheltenham Borough Council's list of buildings of local interest, which means the council will endeavour to preserve it, and it has been thoroughly renovated.[21]

SOCIAL HOUSING

With the waning of the initial enthusiasm for house-building after the First World War, more limited encouragement was offered by government, and progress was beset by many confusing changes of policy. Cheltenham Borough Council's stock of houses, however, steadily increased. In 1923 a government subsidy of £6 a year for twenty years was offered on houses built by local authorities or by private enterprise to an agreed specification (non-parlour type) and then sold for prices approved by the ministry. They were to accommodate the 'working classes', a recognition that rents for the first Addison houses had been beyond the means of many whose need was greatest. The hope that families in poorer accommodation would move into the better premises vacated by the new council tenants had not been realised. Nationally some half a million houses were built under this scheme before it was stopped in 1929. Part II of the 1923 Act also facilitated slum clearance. In Cheltenham, the St Paul's area was the first to be discussed by a sub-committee set up to consider a scheme. By March 1925 Cheltenham had built 25 pairs of houses and all were sold; five had been allocated to the Chief Constable

A photograph of the rear of numbers 59–60, Sun Street, off the Tewkesbury Road, was taken in 1936. One house was entered from the street and one from the rear. The derelict building on the left houses the toilet facilities for both houses. Some of the houses along this street were built in the early nineteenth century, but the road was not fully developed until later in the century. Four houses in the street were declared unfit for human habitation in 1926, and eight houses here were scheduled for slum clearance in 1936.
© CHELTENHAM ART GALLERY AND MUSEUM

for occupation by married police constables. Sales of council houses continued thereafter, and were not new when the policy was promoted on a much larger scale in 1980.

Conservative governments favoured private enterprise, while generally short-lived Labour governments favoured local authority housing and subsidised rents. The (Labour) Wheatley Act in 1924 offered a subsidy of £9 a year for forty years for houses built for controlled rents, and also attempted an expansion of trained building workers. Nationally another half-million houses were built on these terms before the subsidy was discontinued in 1932. Cheltenham continued to develop the 'Poets' estate under the provisions of this act, at a density of twelve houses per acre, which was only to be exceeded with specific permission from the ministry.

By March 1926, 304 houses had been built. At the same time the council continued to build under the 1923 act; no difficulties were encountered in selling these houses before they were finished.

There was a continuing battle to maintain standards, requiring many individual decisions at each housing committee meeting, which also had to deal with an endless list of minor repairs or requests from tenants: water penetrating door-cills, damp, a fallen ceiling, nuisances like the drum of liquid manure kept in one front garden, erection of sheds, a request for a telephone line. Starting in 1922, the council had encouraged pride in the large plots by offering prizes for front gardens; later, pigeon-keeping was excluded by new tenancy agreements,[22] but when the Second World War started, poultry-keeping was allowed provided the plots were thought large enough.

As the complexity of the legislation increased, the Borough Surveyor made returns of the numbers built under each particular act. In 1928 the total had reached 372 but unemployment was again rising. The ministry was asked to hurry the decision on houses in Kipling Road in order to provide work. New sites were purchased, in Folly Lane, Whaddon Farm, Pilley Lane, and Asquith Road, as the social housing policy gathered momentum. In January 1929, under the St Paul's Street South Improvement scheme, three blocks of tenements were planned, each to contain four units, one-third with one bedroom and two-thirds with two bedrooms. The council also bought a few houses and reconditioned them.

Two rows of mid-Victorian houses condemned as slums in the 1930s, Carlton Place and Brunswick Terrace, were probably photographed in anticipation of their demolition. Brunswick Terrace is slightly earlier, thirteen houses built about 1844, and numbers 1 to 6 were included in a slum-clearance scheme in 1936, whereas seven houses in Carlton Place, built about a decade later, and close to the Honeybourne line, were listed for clearance in 1934.

© CHELTENHAM ART GALLERY AND MUSEUM

This typical group of houses on the St Mark's estate (*left*) were built in the late 1920s. The designs were influenced by the Arts and Crafts movement, and variety of roof line, gables, dormer windows and decorative chimneys all made the estate attractive. The houses were built by the borough council to let, but have mainly become owner-occupied since tenants have been enabled to buy. The two mock-Tudor houses in Brooklyn Road (*right*), on the other hand, were built by a private developer in the later 1930s. The Alstone Spa building after it became a private house was named Brooklyn, and probably the name of the road came from this earlier house which is not far away.
PHOTOGRAPHS: AUTHOR, 2009

The Council's achievement to date was summarised in May 1930:

Area	Relevant act	No.	Sold	Let	Not yet completed
St Mark's	1919	160	8	152	
	1923	164	152	12	
	1924	130	26	79	25
	No subsidy	16	5	7	4
St Paul's	1924	215		215	
Cobham Road	1924	15		15	
Stanhope Street improvement scheme	Under scheme	52		52	
	1924	16			16
Old houses retained		9		9	
Malvern Street	1924	2		2	2
Whaddon Avenue	1924	91		29	62
Pilley Crescent	1924	102			102
Totals		972	191	587	194

At the end of the year the total had exceeded 1,000.

Slum clearance was given priority from 1930, under government instructions which required local authorities to submit five-year plans. Cheltenham planned to clear property in St Paul's Street south and Limekiln Row, with Swindon Passage, Swindon Place and Grove Street also being considered. By 1930 more than 1,200 men in Cheltenham were registered as unemployed, and some were again given work building roads for the new estates. The government asked for rents to be reduced, but the council noted that this would represent a cost to the ratepayers, a clear indication of how dependent the council's action was on government subsidies. The national financial crisis came to a head in 1931, and put a stop to slum clearance schemes for two years.

When the programme was restarted in 1933, the government aimed to clear a quarter of a million slum houses. The Swindon Place scheme was approved by the council in January 1933, displacing 134 people. Rutland Street was renamed as a continuation of Brunswick Street, where the modest terraces of stuccoed houses were a little more prosperous; most had been built between 1834 and 1840, and survive in the twenty-first century. The first slum clearance scheme listed 26 areas and 145 separate blocks of property scattered quite widely through the town; the second, in February 1935, affected 26 areas of the town and 129 addresses. Nineteenth-century builders had each developed small blocks of houses, which led to patches of poor housing rather than whole streets being demolished. The requirement for new houses steadily increased. On the site of the former Alstone Lawn 49 houses were built, developed as Pates Avenue, where the council was cooperating with the Cheltenham and Gloucestershire Building Society. An area of 12 acres at The Moors was purchased in 1934, and 130 houses planned, and in December a compulsory purchase order was granted for 81 acres of Whaddon Farm. Gradually, the peripheral farms in Cheltenham parish and in surrounding parishes were taken over.

Whaddon Farm became an estate as extensive as the 'Poets' and likewise had 'themed' road names, this time 'British rivers'. The first three were Colne Avenue, Thames Road and Wymans Road, filling a triangular site and leading off Whaddon Road. Thirteen more river names followed before 1939. Some non-subsidy houses were also being built, making for a socially wider population, and a church and playing field were provided. The following year a site for a Methodist church was agreed. Later plans for Whaddon Farm echoed earlier Cheltenham developments, with a large circular open space or recreation ground ringed by houses in Clyde Crescent. The styles are common to other estates of this period, part brick, part pebbledash, and with wide frontages.

In 1935 the government asked every local authority to undertake a survey of overcrowding, defined as the lack of a separate bedroom for each sex if aged 10 years or more (unless married), and by the number of rooms in the house. Cheltenham returned 287 families living in overcrowded conditions, another 169 borderline cases, and in 269 houses where there were sex segregation difficulties. Payne, in his *Survey of Gloucestershire* at the end of the Second World War, calculated that just under 3 per cent of the dwellings in Cheltenham Borough

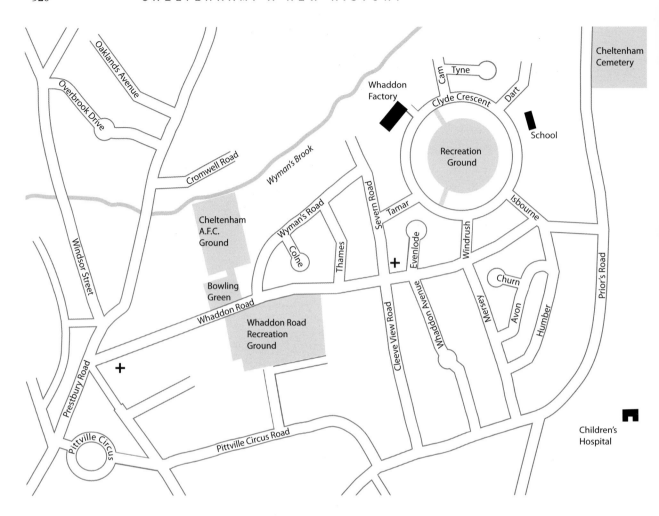

ABOVE

The Whaddon Farm estate was the second big development project undertaken by Cheltenham Borough Council, consisting mainly of houses to let, but also a factory site taken by Walker Crosweller in 1934.

LEFT

Cleeve View Road contains houses dating from several periods. The first houses were built in the early twentieth century, and then those shown in the picture, following the purchase of land in 1921 to extend the road. Beyond the junction with Whaddon Road is one of the river names, Severn Road, and the houses here were built by Cheltenham Borough Council about 1935.

PHOTOGRAPHS: AUTHOR, 2009

were overcrowded, closely comparable with Tewkesbury and Cirencester Urban Districts, so Cheltenham was not exceptional, but perhaps a lower than average ratio might have been expected. Charlton Kings Urban District had less over-crowding, 2 per cent, as also did Cheltenham Rural District.[23] It was hoped that some 'decrowding' would occur as new houses were built. Another 59 areas were being proposed for slum clearance; the ministry of health asked for the houses to be allocated both to slum clearance and relief of overcrowding.

Between 1919 and 1939, just over a million council houses nationally were built, making up approximately a tenth of the housing stock, though private rented accommodation still accounted for over half of all housing.[24] Ambitious council house programmes made it convenient to employ large firms of builders, so encouraged the trend towards the increasingly 'large-scale regional builders [which] emerged in the 1930s'.[25] For example, in 1938 a private developer of 200 houses was able to proceed when Cheltenham Borough Council guaranteed above-average mortgages for houses to be let at approved rents under the provisions of the 1936 Housing Act. It has been suggested that another significant effect, combined with the extension of the franchise, was to change the apparent overall identity of towns from predominantly 'middle class' to predominantly 'working class'.[26] But in Cheltenham the identity of 'spa town', with all its associations, remained, despite the construction of more than 2,000 council houses before 1939.[27]

THE GROWTH OF THE SUBURBS

Simultaneously with council house building during the 1930s, there was a boom in the private sector which created expansive suburbs round Cheltenham – and much more suburban development took place after the Second World War. The suburbs reached into Prestbury, Leckhampton and Charlton Kings. Burrow's Cheltenham guide of about 1938, under the heading 'The Residential Suburbs of Cheltenham', noted that Charlton Kings was 'technically ... a town, with its own Urban District Council, but so far as outward appearances go, it forms part of Cheltenham', and also listed in this category Leckhampton, Battledown, 'the very old village of Prestbury', and Cleeve Hill.[28]

A growing number of semi-detached houses characterised the suburbs. Speculative builders responded to demand, both in the number of houses built and in details of the accommodation, and often suffered bankruptcy when there was a downturn in the economy.[29] There was a major increase nationally in the proportion of owner-occupied houses, from approximately one-tenth before 1914 to a quarter in 1939 and two-fifths by 1961.[30] The boom helped to reduce unemployment;

Typically, private developers bought villas which had once been on the outskirts, and built on their large gardens. Wheeler and Mansell planned seventy houses on the site of Beech Hurst, off Hewlett Road, naming the roads Beechurst Avenue and Eldon Avenue. In Prestbury, the sale of Cleevemount estate allowed G. A. M. Hall to build Cakebridge Road, Cleevemount

Road, Overbrook Drive and Welland Lodge Road. The firm also built Chatsworth Drive off Leckhampton Road, and Southern Road and Trye's Road. The Hatherley Court estate was developed in 1937, and 40 new houses in New Barn Avenue, Prestbury, were built in the thirties. A local builder, Trigg Bros of Beauchamp Lodge in Whaddon Road, developed Whaddon Drive. J. Bendall & Sons, a builder based in Naunton Lane, built fifty semi-detached houses in Mead Road, Leckhampton. In Charlton Kings, A. E. Marshall & Sons Ltd, based in Lyfield Road, built thirty houses in Brookway Drive off Copt Elm Road and B. Gough secured planning permission for 28 houses in Greenway Lane.[31] Pye Brothers started to build in Cheltenham at this time. The firm was founded in Oxford in 1928, and quickly undertook work in Reading and in Cheltenham, where it has continued to be a significant developer. In 1938 and 1939 Pye began to build off the arterial road later named Princess Elizabeth Way, naming the roads Orchard Way and Orchard Avenue, Hawthorn Road and Tanners Road; the council had demurred at too many 'apple' names.

INDUSTRIAL EXPANSION AND DECLINE AFTER THE SECOND WORLD WAR

At the end of the Second World War, a former county planning officer, G. E. Payne, published a comprehensive survey of Gloucestershire to facilitate future planning. He drew on Dudley Stamp's *Land Utilisation Survey* of 1942 for his review of agriculture, a reminder not only of the importance of agriculture in wartime, but also of the small but highly rated market gardening sector in Cheltenham, evident at the beginning of the nineteenth century. The survey showed that three-quarters of the land in Cheltenham borough was under permanent grass, and there was little cereal growing. Stamp had emphasised that Cheltenham's light sandy soil was of 'the very highest horticultural value' from which it was possible to get three crops a year; he included Uckington with Cheltenham in this market gardening area 'of more than local importance'.[32] About fourteen per cent of the land was used in this way. The main crops were brussels sprouts, cabbages, peas and beans, but carrots, turnips, celery, and numerous other crops were also grown for the market. Cultivation was intensive, comparable with that of Mickleton. Apples and plums were also significant, as were poultry and egg production. Produce was disposed of through a very efficient market at Cheltenham, which had been reorganised in 1919 when the Gloucestershire Fruit and Vegetable Cooperative Marketing Society was established. It is fascinating to find that it pioneered non-returnable containers, and operated a registration scheme which raised standards of packing and marketing. Stamp said that as well as Cheltenham retailers, wholesalers from Birmingham, the Midlands, South Wales and Swindon attended the market. With mechanisation and housing development after the war, though, the numbers employed in agriculture in Cheltenham have inevitably declined.

In 1946 Payne commented that 'Those who think of Cheltenham only as a fashionable resort and residential centre, where the rich, the retired, and the tourist are the "raw materials" of local business, will be surprised to learn that about 6,000 working-class folk earn their living in the district apart from those who cater solely for visitors.'[33] He placed aircraft construction and manufacturing of components first in his survey of industry,[34] estimating that some 3,000 people might be employed in future in half a dozen firms; some smaller engineering firms employed around 100 each. Twelve firms in printing together employed 300, two confectionary firms 200, the brewery 250, woodworkers 400 and decorative crafts 400. The gasworks employed about 350. Laundries were important, staffed mainly by women. He recorded complaints by employers that the labour force was not sufficiently skilled, and that industry would not be attracted to the town unless labour of the right type and quantity were available, a viewpoint which counters the council's earlier optimistic assertion. Another complaint was a shortage of houses, which shows how the arrival of GCHQ, with its demand for council houses, could easily be resented.

It was decided in 1949 to relocate the consolidated Government Code and Cypher School (which had been known from 1946 as GCHQ) in Cheltenham.[35] It brought a significant expansion of employment, and an influx of professional people, though the famed discretion of those who work at GCHQ means that little is known in detail of their work. Cheltenham was considered a suitable site for government offices because it was sufficiently far from London and at that time had rail communication in all directions.[36] Also relevant, there were government-owned premises which were going to be vacated. In 1939 and 1940 the Ministry of Works had purchased half of Benhall Farm, to the west of Cheltenham, and Oakley Farm to the east, and erected single-storey office blocks to accommodate parts of the War Office and the Foreign Office, and the Duke of York's Royal Military School from Dover. In July 1941, the American Services of Supply took up residence at Benhall, setting up sophisticated

The exuberant brick buildings of the former gas works were built by local apprentices from the Mechanics' Training School. Although such a striking building, described as a combination of Gothic, French and Baronial styles, these buildings are outside Cheltenham's central conservation area, and are not locally listed, although they have been preserved by being used for a supermarket. Tesco opened here in 1990.

PHOTOGRAPH: AUTHOR, 2009

landline communications, which also influenced the decision to locate GCHQ in Cheltenham, and stayed until after D-Day when the Ministry of Pensions moved in.

Initially the staff at Bletchley Park moved to Eastcote in Middlesex, but this was considered too near London in the event of another war. The future of the Oakley and Benhall sites had been under discussion from the end of 1945 – the pensions department was due to vacate the Benhall buildings at the end of 1947, but the Oakley site was being used for shortened courses of teacher-training for those demobilised from the armed forces. Part of the site thus became available in 1948, but the whole site was not vacated until March 1951. GCHQ was split from the first, and remains so, despite the erection at Benhall of new accommodation, approved by the government in 2002, popularly known as 'the doughnut'. Some staff also remained at Eastcote. In September 1949 the ministry of health approached Cheltenham Borough Council, and in February 1950 the first advanced contingent of GCHQ staff arrived. The main move started in the summer of 1952 and was not completed for over a year, during which time nearly a thousand staff were recruited locally. Great efforts were made by GCHQ staff to integrate with Cheltenham's inhabitants and a number of activities, sporting and cultural, were started. Dudley Owen told the *Gloucestershire Echo* in June 1953 that 'the people of Cheltenham have accepted us wonderfully; shopping is a real pleasure … the friendliness makes it worthwhile',[37] so Cheltenham clearly was considered to have a communal identity.

Between 1950 and 1974 manufacturing in Cheltenham and its area rose to a peak. Its growth did not equal the national rate, though since then its decline has been entirely typical.[38] In the 1971 census, nearly three in every ten people in employment and resident in Cheltenham were engaged in manufacturing; in 2001, by contrast, the proportion had been almost halved, despite the success of Dowty, Smiths, Walker Crosweller and Spirax-Sarco. Gloucester, whose employed total was almost the same as Cheltenham's, had a larger number in industry in 1971 but a similar number in 2001. Meanwhile Tewkesbury had been building up both population and industry in Ashchurch and, though smaller, the picture here was similar.

Manufacturing and service sectors in Cheltenham, Gloucester and Tewkesbury, 1971 and 2001

	Cheltenham		Gloucester		Tewkesbury	
	1971	2001	1971	2001	1971	2001
Total no. in employment	43,710	50,610	40,290	50,320	26,600	36,420
percentage in manufacturing	29	16	34	17	34	19
percentage in services	60	71	48	65	49	65

Manufacturing declined partly because road and air transport and electricity were changing previous constraints on location. The 'Beeching axe' was a sign of changing times. Between 1962 and 1966 Cheltenham lost all but one of its five railway stations, with the closure of

St James's station in St James's Square, Malvern Road (now the site of Travis Perkins), Leckhampton, and Charlton Kings. The striking Dowdeswell viaduct was demolished in 1967.[39] Leckhampton and Charlton Kings stations provided sites for industrial estates; St James's Square was bought by Cheltenham Council and office development was planned. The collapse in shipbuilding (and especially the passenger liner business) caused the closure in 1971 of H. H. Martyn, which had been bought by Maples, the furniture manufacturer, before the Second World War; Martyns had fitted both the *Queen Elizabeth* and *QEII*. The rival firm, R. L. Boulton & Sons, closed the following year. UCAL suffered a bad fire in 1969, and was bought in 1972 by McCarthy's Pharmaceuticals and closed soon after.

The service sector, however, increasingly dominated the employment profile of Cheltenham – to an even greater degree than nationally – despite the almost total disappearance of resident domestic service. The term 'services' includes not only shops, hotels and catering, but also financial services and most government activity, including health care and defence. In this respect, Cheltenham was more than echoing national trends, but Gloucester and Tewkesbury were close to the national average. By 2001 three-quarters of those working in the service sector were women, so although their employment was no longer in the home, the nature of their work had changed less than might appear. Here, too, Cheltenham's experience emphasised national trends. In 1901 only one in eight of those in clerical employment was a woman, but in 1981 the proportion was almost three in four. At the same time, there were more professional and managerial people in Cheltenham than there had been thirty years before, and markedly more in Cheltenham than in Gloucester. This was because of the major expansion of large offices in Cheltenham after the Second World War, as well as the general growth of office employment.[40]

The relocation of government departments to Cheltenham during the war, and the consequent transfer of GCHQ, set the pattern for the post-war period. It has been calculated

Among the organisations coming to Cheltenham after the Second World War was the Universities Central Council on Admissions, UCCA, followed by PCAS, the Polytechnics' complementary body. They were amalgamated in 1993. A new office building, which merits the description 'prestigious', had been built in 1993 in New Barn Lane, opposite the racecourse, for Gulf Oil, designed by Anthony Burke of Fletcher Joseph Partnership. UCAS moved here in 1998. Previously a large Regency house called Rosehill had been on this site, which Gulf Oil demolished.

PHOTOGRAPH: AUTHOR, 2010

that in 1967 there was over a million square feet of office space and in 1974 1.8 million square feet; another half a million square feet had been approved.[41] Eagle Star is thus a significant landmark in several ways. When in 1968 an office block thirteen storeys high was built in Bath Road, it caused outrage both in the town and among a wider public interested in conserving 'historic towns'. The same year UCCA, the Universities Central Council on Admissions, moved from London to Cheltenham and PCAS, the Polytechnics Central Admissions System was likewise based there from 1985. The two amalgamated in 1993, and the successor body, UCAS, the Universities and Colleges Admissions Service, moved in 1998 into fine new premises which had been built for Gulf Oil on the outskirts of the town. Whitbread Flowers in 1963 bought West Country Brewery Holdings Ltd, which had grown from the Cheltenham Original Brewery, and a few years later built a major seven-storey headquarters in Monson Avenue. The Cheltenham and Gloucester Building Society had established its 'chief office' in Clarence Street in 1899, and between 1972 and 1975 built a new and interesting curved building in Clarence Street which was decorated on the outside with a sculpture by Barbara Hepworth titled 'Themes and Variations'; but fourteen years later it had again outgrown its headquarters and in 1989 moved to premises in Barnwood in Gloucester. The Clarence Street building was sold.[42] Although taken over by Lloyds TSB in 1997, the identity of the building society as yet survives.

The *Cheltenham Spa Official Guide* of 1977 highlighted the growing importance to the town of these developments. It not only had sections on tourism, shopping and festivals, but also a new section headed 'Commerce and Industry', and it records 'a change of mood in Cheltenham [which] besides being an elegant spa … has in the last few years become an important centre

Cheltenham and Gloucester Building Society has been an important employer in the town. Its headquarters were in Clarence Street from 1899, and this headquarters building was erected in 1972–75, but is not any longer occupied by the Society. It was enriched with some public art by Barbara Hepworth, 'Theme and Variations', probably an unappreciated piece of public art in the town (*right*).
PHOTOGRAPH: CARNEGIE, 2009

The former headquarters building of Cheltenham and Gloucester Building Society follows the curve of Clarence Street. This aerial photograph, taken in 2007, shows how the buildings all round turn their backs on St Mary's church and churchyard and shut it off; the effect is emphasised by the large trees that darken it. Entrances to the churchyard are also narrow, although it is a green space in the heart of the town.
WWW.WEBBAVIATION.CO.UK

for commerce and industry'. The *Guide* mentioned Dowty Group and Smiths Industries, the two largest industrial employers in the area, Eagle Star, Spirax-Sarco, Whitbread Flowers, Walker Crosweller, and subsidiaries of David Brown, Delapena Honing Equipment Co. and Rio Tinto Zinc. It also mentioned GCHQ. It went on to list recent newcomers: the UK branch of Kraft Cheese, which occupied St George's House, Bayshill; Gulf Oil (which in 1982 moved to new premises in Imperial Square, but ten years later to new headquarters in New Barn Lane); Mercantile and General Reinsurance Company, which occupied Ellenborough House in Wellington Street and soon moved to the first office development in the former St James's station area, but left again by 2000; and the Countryside Commission, now Natural England, which made a regional headquarters in Crescent Place in one of the oldest hotel buildings, John Dower House, until 1970 the police headquarters. The *Official Guide* noted that there were two motorways which gave Cheltenham a special advantage, thus exaggerating the proximity of at least one!

The *Guide* did not mention Chelsea Building Society, whose headquarters have been in Thirlestaine Hall since 1973, and which in 2008 was the fifth largest building society in the country. Since 1977 the headquarters of other large businesses have been located in Cheltenham. Endsleigh Insurance, the business founded by the National Union of Students, was acquired by Zurich in 2007. It had merged with Eagle Star ten years earlier and now occupies premises in Imperial Square and a large new building in Shurdington Road. In 2004 the racecourse developed a conference centre, the Centaur, which is a major venue for 'corporate events and activities', and adds to the business character of the town.

LEFT

The Town Clock in Royal Well Road is handily placed for catching trains and buses. It was given to Cheltenham in 1956 by Smiths of Bishops Cleeve, and, while recently restored, deserves more attractive immediate surroundings.

RIGHT

Surprisingly, the hub of Cheltenham was marked by a 'Centre Stone'. with its emphatic fullstop. On the corner of High Street and Bennington Street, where the 1823 market house was built, it has recently been repainted. It appears to have been installed in the nineteenth century, to facilitate the measurement of distances around and to the town.

PHOTOGRAPHS: AUTHOR, 2010

Redevelopment of St James's station site has taken many years, and was not yet complete in 2009. St James House was the first building on the station site. Waitrose's new store on much of St James's station land was opened on 20 October 2002. The architect has given the building a hint of the grander style of railway station buildings, and the River Chelt has been channelled to provide fountains outside the restaurant area. Nearby on the path along the course of the river there are six sections of the old track erected as supports for seats.
PHOTOGRAPH: AUTHOR, 2009

The first major new shopping centre was the Regent Arcade of 1984, which replaced the *Plough* and its once spacious coaching yard. A second mall, the Beechwood Centre off the upper High Street, was opened in 1991. Montpellier has been dramatically revived as a shopping and leisure area. At the end of the twentieth century the market was moved to a car park off the lower High Street, but continues its weekly function as it has done for centuries, even though the cattle and sheep are no longer herded down the High Street, while a farmers' market at intervals enlivens the Promenade, which has never lost its special character for smart shopping.

HOUSING AFTER THE SECOND WORLD WAR

During the Second World War all building was restricted, but evacuation, bomb damage and the relocation of government offices made housing a major concern once the war was over. It became an important aspect of the work of every council, and in Cheltenham the number of council houses, including maisonettes and flats, quadrupled in the following thirty years. Despite acute shortages of building materials (and strict regulation of their supply) the rate of council house building accelerated after 1947, reaching a peak in 1953 when more than 900 houses were completed.

The war itself had affected Cheltenham directly – in September 1939, 2,000 people were evacuated to the town,[43] and there was also enemy action. The most severe air raid occurred on 11 December 1940, when it was estimated that 1,600 properties were damaged and 600

Cheltenham did not experience many serious air raids during the Second World War, but nonetheless there was considerable damage to property on occasion. This picture of clearing up bomb damage to the rear of Dunally Parade is dated 27 July 1942. It is a street of mid-Victorian houses in the St Paul's area of Cheltenham.

© CHELTENHAM ART GALLERY AND MUSEUM

people were made homeless.[44] It was thought that more than half of the houses could be given 'first aid repairs', but labour was scarce, and only 50 to 60 men could be found for building work. The Ministry of Health suggested that houses condemned for slum clearance could perhaps be made fit to accommodate those whose homes had been bombed. From July 1941, building materials were rationed.

Vigorous planning for the post-war period started in September 1942, when it was suggested that 2,000 new council houses were required – and this was before the plans to bring GCHQ to Cheltenham had been formulated. The area being considered was provisionally named the Hester's Way estate, after a former farm. Private housing development there had been considered in the late 1860s, and some preliminary roads made, but no actual building was ever done. The Ministry of Health had to balance needs across the whole country, and required plans from Cheltenham for 450 houses for the first post-war year. At this time, too, the Ministry of Aircraft Production asked Cheltenham Borough Council to manage the new estate at Churchdown, which had been built for employees of Rotol Airscrews Ltd, as Gloucester

Corporation said it could not undertake the task. Cheltenham bargained with the Ministry for a larger percentage of the rents it would collect.

Housing assumed priority over agriculture. The Ministry of Agriculture in 1943 agreed to the council acquiring good agricultural land, including all the smallholdings in the area of the Hester's Way estate, and 60 acres at Lynworth Farm in Prestbury for an extension to the Whaddon Farm estate. Initially, the government would only sanction the purchase of half the farm,[45] and it was necessary to use compulsory purchase to acquire the land against the owner's wishes. In total, 1,000 houses were projected for Lynworth which the borough surveyor considered, correctly, would take three years to build. The owner of Arle House estate died in 1944 and the council also bought this property, allowing two tenants to stay temporarily in occupation. A short-term expedient to meet the urgent post-war housing need was prefabricated bungalows and in 1944 four sites were bought for these, in Selkirk Gardens, Prestbury Road (which became the Priors estate), Maida Vale and Alstone Croft; between 1945 and 1950, 493 pre-fabs were erected. Also in 1944, the social needs of the council estates were recognised; a youth club and community centre was started in St Mark's and Cheltenham College ran a youth club for Whaddon.

As the end of the war approached, circulars and regulations poured from the Ministry of Health. High priority was to be given to evacuees. Each three-bedroom house was to be 900 square feet, but to bring costs within the Ministry's requirements unfortunate economies were made: for example, thinner concrete slabs for the floors, and no insulating jackets for the hot water cylinders. Shortage of building materials, even of asphalt for floors, of wooden roof trusses, and of porcelain sanitary ware, handicapped the effort.[46] Concrete block construction was investigated. In 1947, when outlining the following year's programme, the borough surveyor regretted the inclusion of non-traditional houses in his plans – he had hoped 'that it would be possible to develop Hester's Way estate in a manner worthy of the town with good type traditional dwellings', but instead had to build as fast as the Ministry insisted.

Work on Hester's Way estate started in 1949 with the building of its main road, named Princess Elizabeth Way in 1952 in commemoration of her recent visit. Six roads were given names relating to the history of Arle; these included four earlier owners, Dormer, Grevil, Lygon and Welch, a field-name (Ashlands) and the misleading 'Redgrove'.[47] In 1953 five more roads were named after honorary freemen of the borough, including Miss Beale, the headmistress of Cheltenham Ladies' College, given the freedom in 1901. By 1959, Kelly's *Cheltenham Directory* recorded close to 500 households in nineteen blocks of flats in Princess Elizabeth Way. The Empire was a theme adopted for some of the blocks: with a nice sense of precedence Australia House and Canada House were the largest, New Zealand and South Africa, Ceylon, Rhodesia, Quebec and Montreal Houses had diminishing numbers of flats, and Auckland, Durban and Tasmania were the smallest. Two later blocks, India and Pakistan, did not stand the test of time and were demolished in 2006 but Cheltenham in general was not troubled with the severe problems of residential tower blocks.

The surge of completions in 1953 coincided with the arrival of GCHQ. It had been estimated that the move to Cheltenham would create a demand for 850 houses and 500 flats or hostel spaces for single persons. These figures, and the cost, dismayed the Ministry of Health, but costs were reduced, happily, by substituting copper pipes for lead. There were to be 326 'non-traditional' dwellings, 114 traditional, and 72 flats. Wimpeys started building in August 1951. Most of the flats were provided in Scott and Edward Wilson Houses in Princess Elizabeth Way. The first residents were said to be 'delighted' with the accommodation. Kelly's *Directory of Cheltenham* for 1959 listed 89 occupants in Scott House and 118 in Edward Wilson House. Thirty-two 'managerial' houses were built for GCHQ personnel in Ledmore Road in Charlton Kings, where the council had purchased The Knapp.[48] However, priority for Foreign Office staff caused some local ill-feeling. It was suggested that residents on the waiting list for

One of the first blocks of flats in Princess Elizabeth Way was named Edward Wilson House. It was designed by G. H. Ryland, who worked in a local architectural practice, L. W. Barnard & Partners. Ryland also designed Scott House. Both are brick. No fewer than 61 of the occupants of Edward Wilson House listed in *Kelly's Directory* for 1959 were women, an insight into the GCHQ staff who had recently arrived in Cheltenham, for whom the borough council was building both houses and flats. The names of the two blocks refer to the Antarctic expedition led by Scott, in which Dr Edward Wilson, who was born at 91 Montpellier Terrace, and grew up in the town, took part.

© CHELTENHAM ART GALLERY AND MUSEUM

council houses (nearly 3,500 names in 1952)[49] were not being given their due share. GCHQ had certainly added to the post-war housing shortage.

The years of intensive council building were over by the end of 1955. Remarkably, 3,500 houses had been completed in Cheltenham since the end of the war, and the council now had a stock of 5,500 houses and flats. But council building programmes throughout the country failed to solve the post-war housing shortage quickly enough. A new Conservative government policy from 1951 allowed more freedom to private developers, and government grants to councils were reduced. This change did not result in an acceleration of house-building in Cheltenham (if council and private developments are taken together) but it did shift the financial burden. In 1955, the private sector built 266 houses in Cheltenham, and over the next two decades built three times as many units as the council, completing between 250 and 500 a year. For example, George Wimpey & Co. saw opportunities for large-scale development, applying to build 1,000 houses on the 100 acres of Benhall Farm – after a long planning dispute, permission was gained for a reduced number. Council building continued at a slower pace, largely to meet slum clearance needs. Nearly two thousand more houses were built by 1972, when there was a fundamental change in government policy. The municipal stock was probably then at its maximum, at about 7,300 dwellings – out of a population of about 97,000, with an average of three persons per house,[50] a fifth lived in Cheltenham Borough Council houses.

As always, the council was responsive to government initiatives. The 1972 Housing Finance Act forced councils to charge 'fair rents', which were to be related to rents in the private sector. Cheltenham decided to offer council houses for sale, making use of section 104 of the Housing Act 1957; 'managerial houses' were already being sold as they became available. The minutes recorded that 'some tenants may prefer to buy rather than continuing to rent'. The Housing Committee divided 16 for and 12 against. Initially, those who had occupied their houses for five years could buy, but on implementation of the 'fair rents' requirements, three years was sufficient. Prices were discounted according to number of years of occupation, and a mortgage scheme was introduced; in the two years that the scheme was operated, 212 applications were received and 81 sales completed. Between 1974 and 1976 sales were discontinued while local government reorganisation was taking place. In 1976 the policy was resumed. Applications came in steadily and 223 houses were sold by the end of 1979.[51]

In 1980 a policy of 'right to buy' was introduced by the Conservative government. From this time, although houses and flats were still being built, the stock was steadily reduced. The response in Cheltenham was immediate. In January 1980 over a thousand applications were received. At the end of 1981 the town clerk reported that 612 council houses had been sold; more than half, 386, had been under the council's former scheme; and 151 were with the help of council mortgages. In 1991, 14 per cent of the total of Cheltenham's homes were council houses with another 3 per cent owned by 'registered social landlords;[52] 72 per cent were owner-occupied and 11 per cent rented. Nationally, the increase in the proportion of owner-occupiers is partly attributable to the sale of council houses, which may have accounted for more than a third of the increase. Since 1991, Cheltenham Borough Council has built no more houses, concentrating on 'affordable housing' provided by the private sector. After the initial surge, sales have continued steadily at a rate of about 100 a year into the twenty-first century, mostly of houses rather than flats. Nationally 1.5 million council houses were sold by 2003.[53] The general growth of owner occupation and the policy of council house sales have completely changed the concept of 'social housing'. Councils were no longer catering for a range of social groups, but for the most disadvantaged; the proportion of economically inactive council tenants rose significantly. Throughout, Cheltenham's experience has been surprisingly typical.[54]

In a drive to improve standards, councils were required by the 1988 Housing Act to offer tenants the choice of remaining as council tenants, or to have their houses transferred to a housing association which would have access to private finance. Most councils favoured the housing association route because modernising their stock was costly. Cheltenham tenants twice voted against a transfer.[55] There was another option available. Cheltenham was ranked as a 'high-performing council' and financially viable; this allowed the council to set up an arms-length management organisation, or ALMO, a not-for-profit company able to raise private finance but remaining in the ownership of the council. Cheltenham Borough Homes Ltd, launched in 2003, was one of the first twenty such organisations in the country. The company took over 5,025 houses, of which approximately half were flats; in addition 376 flats which had been sold on leasehold tenancies were to be managed.[56] Numbers under management have continued to fall, with some sales and some demolitions, so that in 2006 the number was 4,687; there are slightly more flats than houses.[57]

In 2005, in connection with the erection of a new building for GCHQ, largely completed the previous year, Hester's Way Park was rejuvenated. It had first been opened in 1957, and unusual trees were carefully enhanced. Gordon Long, sculptor, was commissioned to create a work of 'public art' for the Park. His solution for this site was to echo the theme of GCHQ's work. Nine glacial boulders were placed, six in a circle and three on the path leading directly to GCHQ. Each has a different form of communication worked into it: code, cipher, encrypted messages, mysterious symbols, languages or prayer.
PHOTOGRAPH: AUTHOR, 2009

The twenty-first century has started with a proliferation of organisations and funds intended to improve housing conditions. Hester's Way estate 'is the largest social housing estate in Gloucestershire', and was the first of three areas in Cheltenham to be identified in the mid-1990s for 'regeneration', covering a band of housing on either side of Princess Elizabeth Way. The other two areas were Whaddon, Lynworth and Priors, since 2004 known as 'Oakley',[58] and St Paul's, now combined in a regeneration partnership with Lower High Street and named 'West Central'. Hester's Way and Oakley were mainly built at a time when quality was compromised by post-war shortages and austerity, and the urgent need to build housing as quickly as possible. Densities here are relatively low, but St Paul's, on the other hand, with an average eighty persons per hectare, is by a long way the most densely populated area of the town. The roads and terraces, built for working people in the Victorian and Edwardian periods, are almost inevitably congested and crowded.

The Local Government Act of 2000 required cooperation between local authorities and other organisations to produce community plans, and this has led to a bewildering succession of sometimes ephemeral 'partnerships' which bid for money from a 'single regeneration budget'. Locally, an overall organisation, the Cheltenham Partnership, was set up in 2002. Two years later the Office of the Deputy Prime Minister produced a national index of deprivation, using 'Super Output Areas'. These are similar-sized geographical units which will remain unchanged and so provide comparability. The most important indicator of deprivation was mean household income. Measured on a national basis, five areas in Cheltenham were among the 20 per cent most deprived areas in England and Wales: three streets in St Paul's were among the worst 7 per cent, the other four being Hester's Way Road, Princess Elizabeth Way and Welch Road area, and the Mersey, Avon and Humber road areas of Whaddon.[59]

'Partnership' and 'community' are the most frequently used words – ironically, perhaps, in the context of attempts to reintroduce an ancient sense of locality which is simultaneously being rendered totally invisible by the growth of computerised sorting and mapping. Administrative convenience overrides comprehensibility; 'postal towns' and postcodes replace parishes and counties; Super Output Areas are identified by number. Not even ward identity remains.

Havana Walk, part of the redevelopment of the former GCHQ site, was built in 2006, and is typical of the whole estate in colouring and style. Pedestrians have more importance than motorists and Havana Walk is an attractive pedestrianised road between two rows of houses.
PHOTOGRAPH: AUTHOR, 2009

The Neptune fountain was placed in the Promenade by the Borough Council in 1893, in front of the former Sherborne Spa building, which had been moved from the top of the Promenade. The Spa was replaced by the Regal Cinema, and between 1985 and 1987 the cinema in turn has given way to a 'clever pastiche' by the Falconer Partnership which echoes the pillars of the Spa. Dominating both are the sixty-three bays of Harwards Buildings.

PHOTOGRAPH: CARNEGIE, 2010

CHAPTER ELEVEN

ETHOS

CHELTENHAM developed a much stronger sense of civic identity after the charter of incorporation in 1876 had created a borough council, with aldermen and a mayor. The earlier town commissioners had looked after specific areas of responsibility but offered little encouragement to civic awareness or sense of civic responsibility, even in terms of the purely practical. During the first half of the nineteenth century the market remained the traditional focus of the town, and spa buildings were on its periphery, but the phenomenal and continuing growth of the town demanded larger attitudes. Having a mayor and corporation allowed Cheltenham to rival the ancient boroughs of Gloucester and Tewkesbury, and also fostered a new civic ethos, expressed in the development of municipal buildings such as a council chamber and mayor's parlour, town hall, library, art gallery and museum. Later, there were large municipal housing schemes, and the provision of recreation grounds and sports facilities. The town's wider image is created by the environment of hills, white stucco Regency houses, trees and gardens and, more specifically, by famous schools, colleges and latterly a university campus, a hospital, theatres, concerts, horse-races, festivals and traffic congestion. Much is therefore also owed to private enterprise. The later twentieth and early twenty-first centuries have been characterised by town plans and conservation areas, as the protection of the heritage of the town and its style has assumed a greater importance.

A very early decision of the new council was to employ a part-time town meteorologist.[1] It was thought that the mild climate of Cheltenham was one of the attractions of the town – the publicity certainly suggested this – and that it could be more firmly established by regular rainfall and temperature readings. A weather station was therefore placed in Montpellier Gardens. A record high temperature for Great Britain, of 37.1°C (98.8°F) on 3 August 1990, is recorded on a plaque in the gardens ... a second plaque notes that the record was held by the town for just thirteen years, being superseded by Cambridge on 10 August 2003.

In 1887 the Corporation received a grant of arms and a crest, adding to its dignity. The arms display two pigeons, two books and an oak tree; the crest includes a fountain and another pigeon.[2] The motto shows what that group of men perceived as the distinctive features of the new borough: *salubritas et eruditio* or 'health and learning'. The arms were placed above the grandiose entrance of the library, which was the first public building erected by the new council. As Cheltenham's historian Gwen Hart observed, the market – for centuries the geographical centre of the town and its *raison d'être* – was not referred to at all. Indeed, in the year that Cheltenham obtained its charter of incorporation, the market was moved to the site of the Albion Brewery in Gloucester Road, which might have been advantageous to certain traders in the High Street, but showed how peripheral it had become.

MUNICIPAL ENTERPRISE

It was perhaps natural for a newly created council to build a council chamber and offices, but the 'Public Offices' in High Street, which had served the Improvement Commissioners, was where the new council met for some years (the rural district council met in the Workhouse).[3] Instead, the council gave visible expression to 'the municipal state' in the provision of 'parks, libraries, and art galleries'.[4] The public library, a stone building on the corner of Clarence Street and St George's Place, was opened in 1889; the free library had been in temporary accommodation for five years previously. On the upper floor were the Schools of Art and Science, which in 1905 were moved to St Margaret's Road – in 1907 a museum took their place. Adjacent to the library, and opened a year later, was the art gallery, built by the council but

The last nineteenth-century terrace to be completed in Cheltenham was the west side of Wellington Square; part was built in 1845–7 and part 1856–59. This terrace is rather different from the more usual 'Regency' style in the town, and has been described as Tudor Gothic. Like Lypiatt Terrace, which was built about the same time, it marks a move away from classical architecture. Two houses were occupied in 1851, one by a widow who was a fundholder, and her family, and one by a clergyman; twelve houses were occupied in 1881. The renowned actor William Charles Macready (1793–1873) lived in one of the central houses from 1860 until his death, and it is probably his statue (*right*) which adorns the niche above the doorways to numbers 6 and 7; a plaque marks his residence there.
PHOTOGRAPH: CARNEGIE, 2009

Both the Library (*left*) and the Town Hall are examples of municipal building style, which expressed the civic pride of elected town councils. The Library came first, built between 1887 and 1889, with its eccentric tower, and the Museum was later housed in part of the Library building. The electricity 'palazzo' on the corner of St George's Place (*right*) was built in 1900, and the same year also the Art Gallery, though it was rebuilt between 1987 and 1989 to a design by the borough architect advised by Sir Hugh Casson. In 2009 an imaginative extension to the Museum is in prospect.

PHOTOGRAPH: CARNEGIE, 2009

much encouraged by a large donation from Baron de Ferrières, who also gave a significant collection of Dutch art.[5] A hundred years later, in 1989, the old gallery was demolished and the Art Gallery and Museum was enlarged and opened by Princess Anne. A painted and stained glass window was incorporated, and two years later a steel, aluminium and bronze 'grille' was installed over the entrance, both features making reference to the Museum's important Arts and Crafts collection.

The charter gave the new borough council the status and authority to take initiatives in many more areas than the preceding town commissioners. Construction of the library had just begun when the opportunity arose to purchase Pittville Pump Room and gardens. This was therefore one of the first conservation projects of the new borough council. The County of Gloucester Bank still owned this property, as a result of the demand by Joseph Pitt, the grandson of the original projector of the estate, that the estate should be sold in order to pay his grandfather's debts. The Bank offered to sell it at a favourable price if the council would agree to preserve the pump room and gardens. Authority to raise the money was given by the 1889 Cheltenham Improvement Act, and in 1890 ownership of this part of the original Pittville estate passed to the council. Sir James Agg-Gardner presented the council with a recreation ground in Pittville in 1888, and with a further council purchase soon after of part of Marle Hill House grounds, Pittville park and gardens were established. The Pump Room is listed Grade I and the park Grade II by English Heritage. Responsibility for its upkeep has involved repair and renovation on several occasions.[6]

In 1937 the Parks Committee ordered major works, but they were no sooner completed than the Second World War started. The Pump Room was immediately requisitioned and used as a storage facility by the US army. There was damage done, and the lack of maintenance told seriously on the structure. After the war, a heated debate ensued about the cost of the necessary work, at a time of acute shortages, and it was seriously suggested by some that the building should be demolished. It was also uncertain how it should be used in the future. Courageously, in 1950 a large-scale restoration involving eradication of dry rot and complete redecoration was agreed, together with modernisation and a small extension. Private donations and fundraising helped to offset the costs, but the major share was borne by the council. The Pump Room was officially reopened on 4 July 1960. Redecoration has again been carried through in the early twenty-first century.[7] The question of appropriate uses for the building is still a matter of debate, but it is a valuable asset. With its excellent acoustic, it is a highly favoured venue for chamber music groups, small orchestras and soloists. Spa water may still be drunk there from the grandiose fountain, thanks to Kohler Mira. The old supply was cut off in 2003 after it became contaminated with groundwater and the mineral content was reduced so much that it no longer qualified as spa water. This was very unfortunate, as Cheltenham had restored the label 'Spa' to its name only three years before. A bore hole was sunk and a new source of mineral water found and a pump installed. Restoration work began in summer 2004, and was completed the following year.

In 1893, three years after the purchase of the Pump Room, the council purchased Montpellier Gardens, which had been laid out in 1830 as 'pleasure grounds'. In 1861 a private company purchased them and installed a bandstand and other facilities for public entertainment. After the council became the owner, the Broadwalk was extended northwards to Montpellier Walk; the Proscenium building was erected about 1900 as an outdoor theatre; and railings were installed. These, sacrificed in 1940 to aid the war effort, are being replaced some seventy years later. During the First World War the gardens were used as a drill ground and then to grow vegetables. Through all their vicissitudes they have remained in council ownership and in 2007 a major restoration scheme costing just over £1 million was undertaken. The unusual Proscenium building, designed as a stage and wings for outdoor performances, is now the smartly painted Gardens Gallery, a community art gallery, new planting has been carried out, the walk leading to the statue of William IV attractively resurfaced in a gravel colour, and the statue itself cleaned; the plinth has an inscription recording the coronation of the king, although the statue was erected by public subscription to celebrate Cheltenham becoming a parliamentary borough in 1832. Provision has been made in other areas of the gardens for children, sports facilities, amenities and refreshments as well as maintaining the pleasant grassland and borders.

Another council-owned public open space, Naunton Park, was opened in 1893, a year which seems to deserve the title of 'the green year'; the land had been bought in 1892 for a recreation ground. No wonder Cheltenham marketed itself as 'the garden town'. These purchases added to the justification for the title of guidebooks in the 1880s and 1890s, but as the Cotswolds acquired their special role as a tourist area, with their rolling upland landscapes and quiet villages, Cheltenham was marketed as 'the centre for the Cotswolds'.[8] At the end of the century the council sold a small area of Naunton Park to Mr and Mrs Hay, private benefactors, to provide the site for fourteen cottages for the poor. The attractive cottages, partly stone and partly timbered or tile-hung, face south across the garden. Naunton Park was replanned in 2004–05.[9]

In 1893, the same year that Naunton Park was opened, the Neptune Fountain was completed. The council may have been stimulated in this exhuberant piece of public art by the erection in 1887 of the elaborate 'Gordon Lamp' in Montpellier by public-spirited residents – General Gordon had died two years earlier. The borough engineer, Joseph Hall, was commissioned to design and construct the fountain as a public reminder and tribute to the crucial part which water had played in the development of Cheltenham.[10] It was placed in the Promenade in front of the former Sherborne or Imperial Spa building on the corner of St George's Road. A cinema replaced the Spa building in 1937 and recently an office block in the 'Regency' style.[11]

The unusual Proscenium Building was originally erected in Montpellier Gardens about 1900 to provide stage and wings for outdoor theatrical performances. It was restored in 2007 as the Gardens Gallery, a community art gallery, at the same time as the Bandstand and the gardens were restored.

PHOTOGRAPH: AUTHOR, 2009

'These Cottage Homes were founded by John Alexander Hay and Marianne Louise, his wife, AD 1899, as a memorial to their long residence in Cheltenham.' Naunton Park had been laid out in 1892–94, and the Borough Engineer, Joseph Hall, had designed a drinking fountain in a tower decorated with Doulton tiles, unfortunately demolished. When the Hays offered to fund twelve cottages for the aged poor, Joseph Hall designed the Arts and Crafts Tudor cottages. One was for a resident nurse.
PHOTOGRAPH: AUTHOR, 2009

Continuing its civic policies, in 1895 Cheltenham Council purchased Imperial Square and the Winter Garden.[12] The iron and glass crystal palace-like building, erected between 1876 and 1878 by a private company for a rink during a short-lived skating craze, was a hugely ambitious building. It served a number of functions, none of which proved financially successful, and for a short while during the First World War it had been used by Martyn's to build fighter planes. The council found the building unacceptably expensive to maintain. It was under threat for at least a decade and, shortly before the Second World War, the council planned a large and comprehensive sports, arts and social centre on the site.[13] The Winter Garden was finally closed in 1938 and, as it was deemed unsafe, was demolished in 1940. In its place, after the war, the Imperial Gardens were created.

The purchase of the building, and the availability of some land, did allow the council to use part of the Winter Garden site to erect a town hall. This compensated for the loss of the Assembly Rooms on the corner of Rodney Road, which had served as the social centre in Cheltenham until Lloyds Bank acquired the building in 1900 – internally the bank's new building seems to have been modelled on the previous Assembly Rooms. The Town Hall was opened at the end of 1903, and equipped in 1906 with a pump room for dispensing spa water.[14] It has fulfilled the social functions which it was designed for, but in the twenty-first century, with the success of the many festivals, concerts and other events, it is not large enough. Cheltenham needs a scheme of vision, similar to that abandoned at the outbreak of war.

The civic offices as yet remained in the High Street. An architectural competition was held in 1912 to design new offices, but all entries were considered too expensive. Instead the

From the 1870s, Cheltenham had a grandiose glass building called the Winter Garden (*above*). It featured in *The Illustrated London News* in November 1878, and was a good subject for pictures, but proved less successful as a practical recreational centre. The Borough Council erected the Town Hall (*below*) on part of the site after purchasing the Winter Garden in 1895, and continued to use it until the Second World War.

THE TOWN HALL AND WINTER GARDEN, CHELTENHAM.

council purchased five houses in the centre of Harwards Buildings, converted them using a loan from the Local Government Board, and in 1915 moved in. A showroom for the Electricity Department was included, as the council was the supplier. The former Town Offices became a shop and were demolished following a fire in 1969.[15] Subsequent purchases of more of Harwards Buildings enlarged the council offices, but in the twenty-first century they are now insufficiently spacious for the district council, and new offices are planned on what is currently a car park.

Another example of the borough council's enterprising attitude was the purchase in 1898 of the Montpellier Baths in the Bath Road, together with the former salt manufactory. The baths, built by Henry Thompson about 1806, consisted of fourteen warm baths and one cold swimming bath, steam rooms and showers, and were fitted with marble and Dutch tiles. Thompson set up the salts manufactory some years later, and it continued in operation for at least forty years. After purchasing the baths, the council converted part of the complex into a public swimming pool, retaining some medicinal baths which were used until 1984; then the tall chimney which supplied the draught for the furnaces was demolished.[16]

Before the end of the Second World War, the swimming bath was in need of much refurbishment, and surprisingly it was decided to convert it into a theatre which would be available to amateur societies; the swimming bath survives under the floor. The Borough Council funded the running of the theatre. The Civic Playhouse opened in 1945 (with a performance of Shaw's 'Arms and the Man') and the Civic Players Society was formed. Amateur societies also came from a wide area to put on performances. In 1957, when the council announced its impending withdrawal from active participation in the Playhouse, the Cheltenham Theatre and Arts Club was founded, and another resident company, the Playhouse Company, was formed. This achieved substantial improvements in the 1970s and 1980s. The remaining baths were closed and became rehearsal rooms and an adjacent blacksmiths' shop became a store for scenery. The building continues in council ownership, but in 2001 the Playhouse Theatre Cheltenham became a charity, supported by box office receipts. Modernisation and improvement has continued to be funded by voluntary contributions.[17]

The new council had moved quickly to take over the Cheltenham Water Works two years after it was instituted, but it was some years before it provided an electricity supply. Local government acts in 1882 and 1888 had encouraged municipal enterprise, and an abortive attempt by a private company to supply Cheltenham with electricity had been made in 1889. Gloucester started along the municipal route in 1896, though its first electricity generating station was not opened until 1900. Cheltenham Council resolved a year earlier, in 1895, to become a supplier. A power plant was erected near Arle Road, and an exuberant small 'palazzo' in stone and brick was built on the opposite side of St George's Place to the Library, from which the supply was to be distributed round the town. Several business premises had been connected before a switch was ceremoniously thrown in May the following year, and all present retired to the *Plough* for a celebratory dinner. Later in the year, the library was illuminated, and in 1897 two main streets, High Street and Clarence Street, were provided with electric streetlights.[18] The supply was extended to Charlton Kings in 1900 and to Leckhampton in 1912, but the surrounding rural areas were not supplied until the 1930s.

Two-thirds of electricity companies in Britain were in municipal ownership by 1900; the main function of an electricity supply was not considered to be the connection of domestic or even business consumers, but to provide street lighting.[19] Domestic use spread only slowly. There were 5,000 customers of the Cheltenham Electricity Department in 1928, and 10,000 in 1934. Before the Second World War started, and a blackout imposed, two-thirds of Cheltenham houses had electricity. After the war, in 1947, municipal and private companies alike were nationalised. The Midland Electricity Board took over the Cheltenham department in 1948.

Immediately the borough council's intention to supply electricity to Cheltenham was known, Thomas Nevins, an Irish-American entrepreneur, proposed an electric tramway for the town. He formed the Cheltenham and District Light Railway Co. in 1898; the tramway was authorised by the Board of Trade under the provisions of the 1896 Light Railway Act. The Borough Council formed a special committee which inspected the route: it was to link together the railway stations starting from Lansdown and going along the High Street and

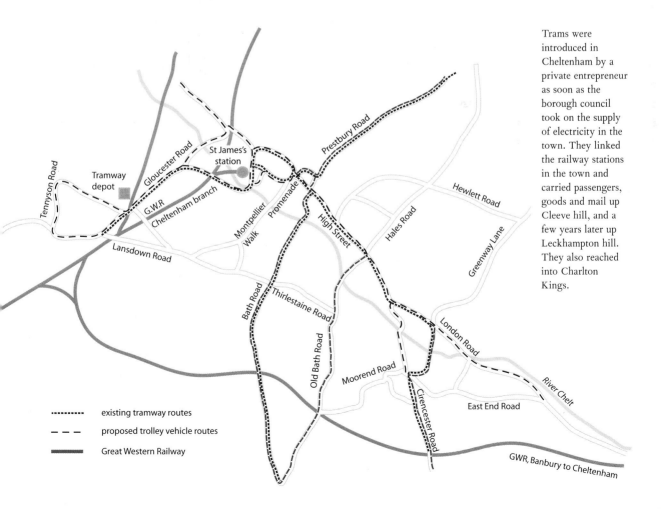

Trams were introduced in Cheltenham by a private entrepreneur as soon as the borough council took on the supply of electricity in the town. They linked the railway stations in the town and carried passengers, goods and mail up Cleeve hill, and a few years later up Leckhampton hill. They also reached into Charlton Kings.

The elegant standards that carried the electric wires for the trams along Prestbury Road have been utilised as very effective street lights. If trolley buses had been introduced, many more overhead wires would have been needed, which made the borough council decide instead to adopt a motor bus service.

PHOTOGRAPH: AUTHOR, 2009

A gas light in the churchyard of Holy Apostles is listed grade II by English Heritage. It was probably installed about 1871, and was later converted to electricity. It has been suggested that it was manufactured at Coalbrookdale.

PHOTOGRAPH: AUTHOR, 2009

out to Cleeve Hill. There were objections, but the project went ahead, and the Board of Trade inspection of the first lines took place in 1901. The service also ran to Charlton Kings and in 1905 the line to Leckhampton was opened. The trams had a short life. At their peak they carried three million passengers in a year, but their decline became marked in the 1920s, as passengers deserted them for motor buses, with their greater flexibility. Motor buses had been introduced in Cheltenham in 1913. The tram company wished to modernise its services by introducing trolley buses, but this would have required many more overhead wires, and there were vehement objections – the trams ran on a single overhead wire supported by an

This postcard was produced to celebrate the opening of the Leckhampton section of the tramway – it is postmarked 17 October 1905. The rural nature of Leckhampton Road is striking. The last tram to run up the hill was on 31 March 1930.

COURTESY OF JOE STEVENS

LECKHAMPTON HILL & THE TRAM TERMINUS, CHELTENHAM.

attractive gantry and a few still serve as street light standards. Council and company came to an agreement that the lines would be taken up and the streets reinstated by the company, which would thereafter operate a bus service. The last trams ran at the end of 1930.[20]

DEVELOPING THE GARDEN TOWN

One of Cheltenham Borough Council's most imaginative actions was the purchase in 1927 of 400 acres on Leckhampton Hill and Charlton Kings Common, including the quarries. For generations it seems that no one had disputed the public's right of access to the hill. The rough grassland and pasture had long been used for recreation by Cheltenham inhabitants as well as local parishioners, and there were well-established footpaths across the hill to Cowley and Coberley. The largest part of the hillside was already owned outright by Henry Norwood, lord of the manor of Leckhampton, when common rights over lands in Leckhampton were extinguished by Act of Parliament in 1778 and, indeed, common rights may never have existed on much of the hill.[21] An area of about 50 acres, called 'All hill' and 'The Common', were part of the common field system, and in the enclosure of 1778 were allotted to Henry Norwood. When he died in 1797 his property was inherited by Charles Brandon Trye. There had been quarrying on a small scale before this time, but Trye now began to exploit the stone more energetically, demand being fuelled by the house-building boom in the town below. Successive members of the Trye family tried for a hundred years to make money from the quarries, but in 1894 financial problems forced Henry Norwood Trye to sell the estate, which was divided into several lots.

The quarries were bought by John Henry Dale, of Daisybank House. He was not at all paternalistic or altruistic in his attitudes, asserting firmly that there were no public rights of access to the hill, either on the long-used footpaths or for recreation.[22] The principal of Cheltenham Ladies' College was incensed at the loss of the open space which was used by the pupils, and ordered all the pianos in the school (hired from the piano firm which Dale owned) to be sent back. Some local people took the law into their own hands, breaking down fences and destroying the cottage built in the former gravel pit. The legal case for access was, however, weak. Although a long legal battle was fought, the courts decided that only in the case of the footpaths over the fields which had been subject to enclosure could access rights be upheld. Despite much negotiation with Cheltenham Borough Council and the rural district council, Dale had effectively won. He proceeded to increase the scale of quarrying operations, building a railway and limekilns, and

Designed by Cecil Harry Birtwhistle, the poster produced just before the Second World War suggests that Cheltenham was in the heart of the Cotswolds. The claim appears to have been sponsored by the borough council.
SCIENCE AND SOCIETY PICTURE LIBRARY

blasting and drilling to the annoyance of local inhabitants. The Lilleybrook estate, including the golf course, was purchased by the quarry company, to enable the railway to be routed across the land. But the company over-reached itself, became bankrupt, and in 1925 was forced into receivership. The 1926 miners' strike gave the final *coup de grace*, and the company stopped work. The business could not be sold, and the equipment and land were auctioned at the *Plough* in August 1927.

At that point the opportunity to buy the hill was not taken up by Cheltenham Borough Council. However, as no other buyer came forward willing to pay the reserve price of £10,000, the council was at last persuaded to act, and the purchase was negotiated for £6,500. The hill would once again be available for leisure activities. On its formal opening in 1929 by

Trams had a short life in Cheltenham, as motor buses quickly made them look very inflexible. The last tram to run in Cheltenham and Charlton Kings was on 31 December 1930. But a body without wheels, apparently almost new, was transported in 1967 to Crich, seen here on its transporter in the High Street. A few years earlier, in 1959, a National Tramway Museum had been established at Crich in a derelict quarry, where the railway pioneer George Stephenson had built a railway to carry limestone to his lime kilns, a splendid link for the tramway museum. The Cheltenham tram was narrow gauge, and it proved almost impossible to restore its wheels. It has since travelled to Bournemouth and back to Cheltenham Museum.

© CHELTENHAM ART GALLERY AND MUSEUM

the mayor of Cheltenham, the *Echo* wrote that it was 'one of the great days in the history of Cheltenham'. Three areas of common land are now registered: 72 acres called Leckhampton Hill in Leckhampton parish; 76.5 acres called Charlton Kings Common in Charlton Kings; and a further 11.2 acres in Leckhampton, protecting the area from development. A small part of the common in Shurdington is in Tewkesbury District. The whole area now managed is 165 acres (67 ha). Rights of way have also been registered. That there are no common rights over the areas concerned is stated again and, apart from the footpaths, access was permissive until the right to roam legislation of 2000. In practice the borough council does not impose restrictions on public use unless for example an unauthorised attempt were made to graze animals, so in the end both Dale and the 'Leckhampton worthies' who protested at his closure of the paths won partial victories. Much of the area is now designated a site of special scientific interest (SSSI), and it comes within the AONB. A recent management scheme has introduced a 'sustained grazing project' by Dexter cattle, a pleasing development with historical resonance.

In the same year that Leckhampton Hill was purchased, Cheltenham Borough Council also bought Sandford Park, through which the Chelt runs.[23] When the *Guide* was written just before the Second World War, this was said to be the most popular of the town's public parks, but can now be described as 'one of Cheltenham's lesser known treasures'. The Borough Council provided a fine pair of iron gates at the Bath Road entrance, made locally in Bennington Street by Charles William Hancock.[24] Two years later, the drinking fountain from Westal Green was moved to the Keynsham Road entrance. The Sandford Park Lido was created in 1935. In 1993 'Friendship Circle' by Neville Gable was installed, an early example of 'public art' sponsored by the council.

Seven years after the purchase of Sandford Park, Pearson Thompson's Hatherley Court estate was put on the market, offering an opportunity to create a public park in the Hatherley area. Cheltenham Ladies' College bought the house, but the council acquired enough land for a park and recreation ground, as well as to provide 2½ acres for houses, and to build Hatherley Court Road. The developer of the adjacent housing established Hatherley Court Gardens in 2001. In the municipal tradition of

Now a private house, the former *Malvern Inn* was the site of gatherings to protest at the closure of Leckhampton Hill. It was also the terminus of the railway from the quarry for a number of years, after the rest of the line had been removed. Groceries for the inhabitants of Cowley and Coberley were loaded here and collected in the quarry up the hill. A plaque on the wall records meetings at the *Malvern Inn* between 1902 and 1906.

PHOTOGRAPHS: AUTHOR, 2009

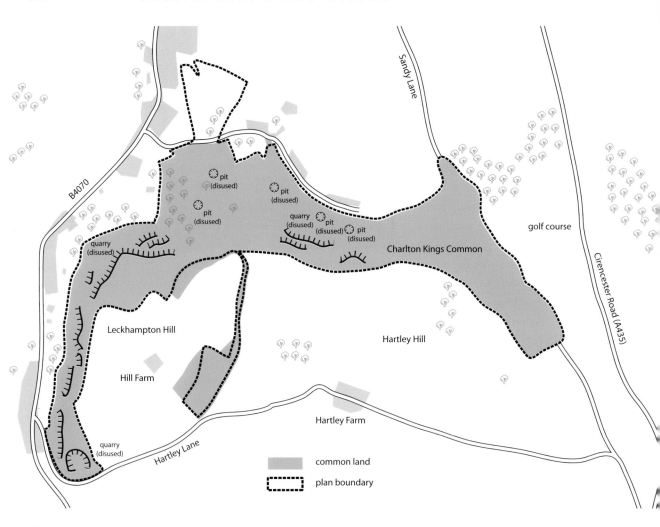

Cheltenham Borough Council manages a large area of land in Leckhampton and Charlton Kings, a certain amount of which has been designated 'common land'. A management plan for Leckhampton Hill and Charlton Kings Common was adopted in 2002.

providing open space in each housing area, the council has continued to provide smaller parks and green space, and 62 are now listed by the borough council, including recreation grounds and playing fields. Some of these are sites for public art, like 'The Friendship Circle', or 'Listening Stones', nine huge glacial boulders each inscribed in a different way and displaying a big variety of types of language, which were installed in Hesters Way Park in 2005 through an arrangement with the developer of the GCHQ doughnut.

The council takes the encouragement of 'public art' seriously enough to have produced a 'Strategy document' in 2004, its first aim being 'to increase the amount of high quality public art throughout the borough'. While recognising its desirability, public art is mainly dependent on the public for fund-raising, and in more recent times also on developers. The list of public art in Cheltenham includes 'The hare and the minotaur' by Cirencester-based sculptor Sophie Ryder. It may have been 'two and a half tonnes of controversy',[25] but enough people enjoyed

The sculpture by Sophie Ryder, 'The Hare and Minotaur', is placed in the Promenade in front of the former Imperial Hotel, now Waterstone's. It is an unusual piece of public art, which the public subscribed to buy.
PHOTOGRAPH: CARNEGIE, 2009

it when first exhibited to help raise the necessary money to keep it, and it adds greatly to the gaiety of the Promenade. Most 'public art' is very solemn. Other examples listed by the council include the Friendship Circle, Barbara Hepworth's 'Theme and Variations' on the former Cheltenham and Gloucester Building Society headquarters, Churchill Gardens cycle track, and the Drew Fountain with the statue of Edward VII, erected in Montpellier Gardens in 1914 by public subscription. Two pieces of sculpture were installed in 2005: the 'Golden Boy' in Beechwood Shopping Centre to record Cheltenham-born Rolling Stone Brian Jones, and the 'Listening Stones'.

An outstanding contribution to public art in 2008 was the fruit of cooperation between the Civic Society and the council, supported also by donations and fund-raising by the public. The Cheltenham Civic Society decided to use a generous bequest to commission Anthony Stones to create a life-size statue of Gustav Holst, who was born in Cheltenham in 1874. It seemed fitting to place it in Imperial Gardens, close to the Town Hall where in 1927 there was a festival of Holst's music, and it was agreed to site the sculpture in the middle of the fountain which then required considerable refurbishment. Holst stands on an octagonal plinth with plaques on seven sides representing the planets; he himself conducted the first Cheltenham performance of that celebrated work in the 1927 festival. Sculpture and plaques were both cast in Chalford. This piece of public art is without doubt an enhancement of the Gardens.

The Springbok Bar in Albion Street occupies a building with a varied history. The façade survives from Mr John Alder's 'Cabinet and Upholstery Warerooms', offering for sale, as Rowe suggests in his 1845 *Guide*, 'a recherche assortment of articles of usefulness and vertu'. In 1913 a music hall or theatre called The Hippodrome opened here; the warehouse was probably adapted, and the theatre interior designed by a local architect, Herbert Rainger. It seated nearly a thousand people. Its projector, Cecil Gill Smith, sold the building in 1919 and left Cheltenham; he was later convicted of theft and embezzlement. The Hippodrome was then renamed the Coliseum. It became a cinema in 1931. This closed in 1974. The building and its older façade survives, although without the grand Georgian pedimented central doorway of the original, and is a locally listed building.

PHOTOGRAPH: CARNEGIE, 2010

LEISURE AND CULTURAL ENTERPRISES

The numerous hotels and boarding houses, the style of the town, and the surroundings, all encouraged a variety of leisure or cultural enterprises. Traditions which contribute much to the town's modern ethos were established when it was still a fashionable spa. One of these, horse-racing, has brought Cheltenham international fame.

Cheltenham was not a holiday destination in the way that seaside
resorts were, but a line in humorous postcards was developed.
This card would seem to represent fashion in the town in the
1930s.
© CHELTENHAM ART GALLERY AND MUSEUM

JUST A FEW LINES FROM CHELTENHAM

THE RACES

Cheltenham races had a somewhat uncertain start, and
were not permanently established in their present location
at Prestbury Park until the end of the nineteenth century.
A report in *The Times* at the end of the eighteenth
century suggests that the 'ton' of Cheltenham then went
to Tewkesbury races, despite them being frequented by
pickpockets and other petty criminals.[26] Horse races had
been held since at least 1721 on Tewkesbury Ham, the
large meadow between the Severn, the Mill Avon and
the Swilgate rivers. There was good flat going on what
at certain times of the year was common land, a typical
venue for horse-racing. But between 1813 and 1824 races
did not take place and in 1829 they were cancelled because
of floods. There was a motive, therefore, to hold a meeting
somewhere else near Cheltenham, and in 1815 races were
run on Nottingham Hill in Bishop's Cleeve. They were
apparently not a success,[27] but three years later races were
successfully organised on the more extensive upland pasture
of Cleeve Common, and in the following year there was a three-day event, a grandstand
was built on West Down, and a Gold Cup was offered (though the continuous history of the
Cheltenham Gold Cup did not start until 1924). Horse-racing was an aristocratic pursuit.
The Duke and Duchess of Gloucester were patrons of the Cheltenham races, together with
Colonel Berkeley who gave generously and who regularly brought his hounds to Cheltenham.
Other patrons included Lord Sherborne, Lord Ducie, Craven Berkeley, a cousin of Colonel
Berkeley, and Fulwar Craven of Brockhampton.[28] Goding noted that in 1819 'a vast number
of the nobility and gentry attended; and during the race week the town was like a continental
carnival, owing to the crowds and gaiety which prevailed'.

For a few years the races were an annual event. The Revd Francis Close fulminated against
them, though it was not his ire but a fire in the grandstand in 1830 that brought Cleeve Hill
racing to an end. The following year a 'new course' in Prestbury Park was advertised for the
'Cheltenham' races, and they took place there until 1835. The bishop of Hereford's ancient
deer park had remained for centuries a clearly defined and roughly oval area, with boundaries

RIGHT

A painting of the races on Cleeve Hill in 1826 by an unknown artist is the first indication of the popularity that racing in Cheltenham would acquire. It suggests the nature of the hill top, open and expansive, its height perhaps suggested by the clouds. The course on the top of Cleeve Hill is still visible in part.

BRIDGEMAN ART LIBRARY

BELOW

Prestbury Park, once the larder or sporting facility of the Bishops of Hereford, replaced other hilltop venues in the area in the late nineteenth century. The racecourse now has facilities for year-round use to help to maintain the occasional use of the race course itself.

BY COURTESY OF CHELTENHAM RACECOURSE

(that can still be traced on the ground) circled by footpaths. Crucially, it had not been broken up through divided ownership.[29] There were already plans to move the races to Prestbury Park in 1823: the Craven family who owned it, and their tenant farmer, had agreed with 'John David Kelly, gentleman, secretary and agent … of the gentlemen forming the committee for the purpose of erecting a Grand Stand for the Cheltenham races', that for a rent of £35 a year, three pasture fields could be used for one week in June or July for the races and for erecting a grandstand, apparently therefore a temporary structure. The agreement was to run for the remaining nineteen years of the farmer's lease, and could be extended by the Craven family to 40 years, but would lapse if the races were discontinued. The Turf Club was to have the profits of booths erected, but the farmer could erect a booth and charge a shilling for admitting four-wheeled carriages or six pence for the two-wheeled.[30] The agreement was activated for a few years; however the races again returned to Cleeve Hill in 1835 and another grandstand was built. Cheltenham races gradually declined in popularity and were again discontinued in 1842.[31]

Racing resumed at Tewkesbury in 1841 and continued for a few years. According to James Bennett, publisher and historian of the town, 'an immense number of persons from Cheltenham were present' in 1843. He accounted for this by cheap railway excursions at a shilling each way, and said it was estimated that a thousand people travelled by train to Tewkesbury. The *Cheltenham Journal* lamented that there were no races locally, and some Cheltenham people decided to act. At a meeting at the *Plough* in 1844 it was decided to hold a steeplechase in various locations around Cheltenham. In 1847 Colonel Berkeley mapped an exciting course round Prestbury.[32] This was a different type of race, but it was held successfully for several years, until in 1853 Lord Craven sold Prestbury Park and the new owner put an end to it. In 1861 the Grand National Hunt and military races were held on the property of Lord Ellenborough of Southam. A grandstand was erected on Kayte Farm in Bishop's Cleeve, and steeplechasing took place until 1866, when the grandstand collapsed.

Cheltenham Racecourse station on the Honeybourne line was a modest building, opened in 1912 and closed in 1976 following closure of the Honeybourne line. It has been splendidly restored by enthusiasts and volunteers in the Gloucestershire–Warwickshire Railway, together with railway track from Toddington, but in 2010 a landslip near Gotherington has once again stopped steam trains reaching Cheltenham racecourse.

PHOTOGRAPH: AUTHOR, 2010

The modern history of the race course begins in 1881 when W. A. Baring Bingham bought Prestbury Park and announced that races there would be revived, a promise fulfilled in 1898. Four years later, Cheltenham Racecourse Company was formed and took over the course.[33] The first National Hunt Festival was held in Prestbury Park that year, and since 1911 has always been held there. A new grandstand was built in 1908 and a clubhouse. In 1912 the tiny Racecourse station was opened; the line closed in 1960, but the section between Toddington and the racecourse has been reopened by volunteers as a steam heritage railway. At the beginning of the First World War, the newly completed grandstand was taken over by the Red Cross, and at the start of the Second World War the facilities of the race course were once again requisitioned, first by the British and then by the American army, but races were only cancelled in two of the war-time years.

A serious threat to Cheltenham races was faced in 1964, with the possibility of the land being used for building. A Racecourse Holding Trust was formed, and took over ownership of Prestbury Park. Since then the racecourse has been developed with a diversity of social amenities and functions including corporate entertainment.[34] Although all green spaces are under threat from the remorseless requirement for more houses, the economic importance of the racecourse, and its important social role, seem for the moment to have assured its future.

THEATRE

The creation of the Playhouse repertory theatre by the borough council has already been described. Theatre had been a feature of Cheltenham's cultural life since the mid-eighteenth century through the enterprise of a number of private proprietors who erected theatres and organised entertainments. A small theatre was built in Grosvenor Terrace in 1782, and a larger one in Cambray in 1805, burned down in 1839. Cheltenham had other social halls, and after 1850 the Royal Wells Music Hall was used to stage plays, and was later renamed the Theatre

The Princess Hall. Ladies' College, Cheltenham.

The demolition of the old Royal Well Theatre by Cheltenham Ladies' College helped stimulate the borough council to build an alternative assembly rooms, the Town Hall. The new Ladies' College building on the old site was named the Princess Hall. It had a stage, with over it a painting called 'The Dream of Fair Women' by James Eadie Reid in the pre-Raphaelite manner, and very appropriately based on a Tennyson poem, since with his mother and sisters he lived for a while at 10, St James's Square. The hall was clearly a multi-purpose room, with gymnastic equipment evident. This postcard was produced about 1905.

© CHELTENHAM ART GALLERY AND MUSEUM

Royal, but Cheltenham Ladies' College acquired the hall in 1890 and it was no longer available to the general public; the College had already bought a large part of the Old Well Walk. A most ambitious building was then planned for the town by a group of enterprising local people who formed a limited company.[35] They commissioned the well-known theatre architect Frank Matcham, and the New Theatre and Opera House is the oldest surviving example of more than 150 theatres which he designed; it is noted for its elaborate decoration which has survived largely intact, for the uninterrupted view of the stage from most seats, and for the innovative crash bars for the speedy opening of the doors, an idea subsequently taken up by all theatre designers. The New Theatre opened in 1891, with, among other attractions, a performance by Lily Langtry. The old Royal Theatre building was demolished by the Ladies' College in 1895, and replaced by the Princess Hall, completed in 1897.

It did not prove easy to make the theatre self-supporting, and after a change of owner in 1925, the range of entertainments staged was widened to include ballet and comedy.[36] The viability of the New Theatre was again threatened after the end of the Second World War, particularly by the growing popularity of the cinema. At this stage Cheltenham Borough Council, showing a commendable appreciation of the value of the building, bought it – and still owns it. But the experiment in direct entrepreneurship was not successful, and neither was a consortium of businessmen. In 1959 the theatre was expected to close. The civic pride of a group of local people, Noel Newman, Sir George Dowty, Richard Walker of Walker Crosweller, and Lionel Northcroft of Spirax-Sarco, resulted in vigorous campaigning to save both the theatre and Pittville Pump Room. As a result the Cheltenham Theatre Organisation was formed, which secured the council's acceptance of their offer to take over its running. A very necessary refurbishment was carried out, heavily supported by the developers of the Regent Arcade, and in 1960 the theatre opened again as the 'Everyman', signalling that it would cater for a wide range of interests. The cold winter three years later nearly defeated the Everyman, as potential audience could not reach the town, but Noel Newman worked tirelessly to enable it to survive. In 1964 the Everyman became a charity. For some thirty years until the mid-1980s, it supported its own repertory company and a major repair and refurbishment was carried out in 1983. Another is projected in 2010. The promise of the name is today being fulfilled with a wide range of activities. The theatre, listed grade II by English Heritage, is one of Cheltenham's valued and unique buildings, and justifiably has a project to make its history widely known.

MUSIC

The Cheltenham Music Festival has become as famous as the Cheltenham Gold Cup race. Music was a typical feature of the entertainments in any spa town and in mid-eighteenth century Cheltenham a band played in the morning while company was taking the waters.[37] In the early nineteenth century the leisured inhabitants and visitors attended concerts in ballrooms, spa buildings and Assembly Rooms. Ruff in his *History of Cheltenham* (1803) described the

LEFT

The house in
which the Holst
family lived at
one time was in
a terrace built in
1832–33 called
Pittville Terrace but
renamed Clarence
Road. Professional
working people
lived in these
houses. The house
is a museum
dedicated to
Holst's life, and
has been furnished
in Victorian style.
The portrait over
the fireplace, by
Bernard Munns and
painted in 1923, was
presented to Holst
on the occasion
of Cheltenham's
festival of his
music in 1927.
When the Holst
Birthplace Museum
was opened, both
portrait and the
composer's piano
were lent to the
museum.

PHOTOGRAPH: CARNEGIE,
2009, WITH THE MUSEUM'S
PERMISSION

recently opened 'musical warehouse and library' where 'ancient and modern productions of the most eminent composers are to be hired', and noted that pianofortes could be hired from three places. In the course of the season, Ruff said, there were three or four concerts in the Lower Ball Room which was in High Street; 'they make an interesting morning lounge … attended by the first fashion of the place'.[38] All this reveals an active musical scene, though Ruff's own tastes were surprising – he wrote a much longer section on the joys of hearing the hand-organ. 'Organ grinders, hurdy-gurdy players, and fiddlers, frequently parade the streets of Cheltenham; the tambourine is also touched by some female hand'. Charitable listeners sometimes threw a shilling or 2s. 6d. into their hats.

Among the well-known musicians who played in Cheltenham was the virtuoso violinist Paganini, who on his first visit in 1831 was engaged to play three times, twice at the Assembly Rooms and once to a less distinguished audience at the Theatre Royal. His initial refusal to perform there for a smaller fee than he expected nearly led to a riot, and he defused the situation by playing in the *Plough*.[39] The recital by Jenny Lind in 1848 was given at Montpellier Rotunda, the first of her three appearances in the town. Eight years later she sang in the Assembly Rooms. When the Old Well Long Room was rebuilt in 1850 and named the Old Wells Music Hall and Pump Room, it was opened with a grand concert. Other well-known musicians who agreed to play in Cheltenham included Johann Strauss, Franz Liszt and Paderewski. By the end of the nineteenth century, there was a Triennial Music Festival. In the twentieth century the Chamber of Commerce sponsored a competitive festival, which started in 1926 and continues. The last *Guide* before the war said that there was a concert or recital every week in the autumn and winter, and gave a roll call of famous musicians.

Of musicians who have lived in Cheltenham, Holst is notable as a composer. He was born and went to school in the town. His father's family was of Scandinavian origin, but had settled in London. Holst's grandfather, a pianist and composer, lived in Cheltenham. His father, Adolph von Holst, was a skilled pianist, and married one of his pupils, the daughter

The association of Gustav Holst with Cheltenham is celebrated with the creation of the Holst Museum in the house where he was born, and in 2008 with the erection of a fine statue of him by Anthony Stones in Imperial Gardens. It was funded by a legacy to the Civic Society, much fund-raising by the Society, and by the borough council. The Eagle Tower, formerly Eagle Star Insurance company's headquarters, is a backdrop to many views in central Cheltenham. Imperial Gardens are a well-used recreational open space in the centre of Cheltenham, and the place where marquees are erected to supplement the facilities of the Town Hall at Festival times.

PHOTOGRAPHS: AUTHOR, 2009

of a Cirencester solicitor. The couple came to live at 4 Pittville Terrace, now named Clarence Road, and their son was born there in 1874. It was a small terrace of seven houses built in 1832, and inhabited in 1881 by several professional people, including another professor of music. All the households were small, but had one or two resident servants; the von Holsts had one young woman living in. Holst later dropped the 'von' in front of his surname, and also called himself Gustav — not Gustavus, as his parents had named him.

In 1881, some 145 people connected with music were living in Cheltenham, mainly teachers, though 30 were engaged in selling music, including Henry Dale, of 13, Pittville Parade, who employed 28 men and 8 boys, a piano tuner and a man who made musical strings. A group of five musicians from Germany and two from Italy were living in a lodging house at 20 & 21 Stanhope Street, off the Swindon Road, along with 31 other lodgers of varied but unskilled occupations; this was a notoriously poor area, later condemned as a slum. The group might have been a small orchestra playing in the town, or entertaining in Cheltenham's public houses. Other musicians were the publican at the *Bath Inn*, Bath Road, and two musicians lodging at *The Grapes* in Gloucester Place. The description 'musician' obviously had a wide range of meaning as far as social status was concerned.

Gustav Holst's musical interests took him to London, where he became a close friend of another Gloucestershire musician, Ralph Vaughan Williams. The two often walked on the Cotswolds. Holst said that three things were important in his life: 'music, friendship, and the Cotswold hills'. On the occasion of the 1927 Holst festival, he was presented with a fine portrait of himself now hanging in the Holst Birthplace Museum. In 1949, The Planets was again played in the town Hall at the Cheltenham festival, and Vaughan Williams unveiled the blue plaque on the house where Holst once lived. The owner of the house, who often had callers interested in seeing his home, offered in 1974 to sell the house to the council, and this was accomplished after an appeal for funds. It was envisaged not only for Holst memorabilia, but also as a Regency period museum. The acquisition coincided with an exhibition celebrating Holst at Cheltenham Art Gallery, in support of the Cheltenham Music Festival. Imogen Holst donated some furniture which had belonged to her father, and the house was furnished with items drawn from the Cheltenham Museum collections. It has not proved easy to finance, and in 1999 the borough council closed it. Associated Newspapers, owners of the *Echo*, gave enough money to keep it open for one more year, and in 2000 an independent trust was formed, the council offering a tapering annual grant. An appeal for an endowment fund was launched in 2003. The museum is still insecure financially, and relies on volunteers, but is an important cultural attraction in the town

FESTIVALS

While the winter concerts had been primarily for residents of the town, Cheltenham's First Annual Music Festival in 1945 was in the spa tradition of entertaining — and encouraging — summer visitors. It was building on a tradition, but it was also innovating in its focus on contemporary music and most important, it was an expression of the idealism generated by the war, of hopes for peace, and a vote of confidence in the future of music in the town. The Festival was the inspiration of one man, George Wilkinson, Cheltenham Corporation Entertainments Manager, who particularly deserves to be remembered. Even before the war ended he convinced the borough council that a music festival would be good for Cheltenham. He assembled a committee of interested musicians, which included the editor of the *Gloucestershire Echo*, and in June 1945, during three days of live music, three eminent British composers, Arthur Bliss, Benjamin Britten and William Walton, conducted their own music. The Arts Council of Great Britain was established that same year.[40]

The second Annual Cheltenham Festival of British Contemporary Music reflected the focus which had emerged in the first, and this was the name used for the next eighteen years. The Hallé Orchestra under Sir John Barbirolli came in 1947, the year the Edinburgh Festival was inaugurated, and continued to come every year for fifteen years. In 1948 the Arts Council of Great Britain helped to expand the programme to nearly two weeks, after the Cheltenham Arts Festivals Ltd was established as a non-profit making company, a step made necessary in order to qualify for help not available to local authorities. Nonetheless, the borough council supplied a majority of the directors, and continued to provide the administration. Many new works were given their first performance in the Cheltenham festivals, and it was one of the major Festival of Britain sites in 1951, showing how quickly its importance had become established. In 1963 it rechristened itself simply the 'Cheltenham Festival'. There was another change of name in 1974 to 'Cheltenham International Festival of Music' and this has stuck. Sponsorship contributed to its success; the 1975 programme listed among others Boots, Cavendish House, Dowty, Eagle Star and Spirax-Sarco, and the funds raised in this way become ever more important, the support of the BBC particularly so. The music festival continued to grow in size and scope, and in 2001 gained the Royal Philharmonic Society award for the best festival and concert series in the year. Important employers in the town have continued to give support; major sponsors in 2007 were Messier-Dowty, HSBC, Mitsubishi Motors and UCAS, and the Cheltenham Festival Society was also significant.

Meantime, George Wilkinson had approached John Moore about another first, a 'Literary' festival. Before the war Moore had organised a series of mystery plays in Tewkesbury abbey to raise money for the preservation of the great Norman tower. He agreed to put together a three-day Festival of Contemporary Literature in Cheltenham which was accounted a success, and he led the Literary Festival in many of the succeeding years. But it was rather less assured than its musical companion, although less expensive to run and more humorous and light-hearted. There were no festivals in 1961 and 1964. It was also on a smaller scale. Alan Hancox, who became director in 1965, 'made the festival what it is today', while Gordon Parsons introduced significant sponsorship from 1983. The great leap forward, however, was sponsorship by newspapers, first the *Daily Telegraph* in 1991, then *The Independent* and most recently *The Times;* this has hugely increased the range of the Literary Festival. Both festivals have wanted to widen audiences and draw in schoolchildren, while taking events to other buildings outside the traditional halls, to other places, and indeed 'outside' to streets and Pittville Park.

Two more festivals have started: the Jazz Festival in 1996 and the Science Festival in 2001. The annual Folk Festival Weekend is run separately from the other four festivals. But in 2006 the festivals made an overall loss of over £100,000, the largest part attributable to the Music Festival. The loss made by the Jazz Festival was significantly offset by the profit of the Literary Festival, and the Science Festival also made a small profit. A little under a third of the income of the festivals came from the Box Office; nearly half from sponsors, grants and donations. Altogether, 120,000 tickets were sold in 2006.

In 2005 the borough council commissioned a 'Cultural Review' from David Pratley Associates, which reported in February 2006. It suggested that 'Cheltenham borough council already occupied an almost unique role in cultural provision among second-tier authorities in the UK': 'Cheltenham has built a remarkable portfolio of cultural assets, including a full-time professional theatre, four nationally regarded Festivals, the Art Gallery and Museum, one of the few surviving year-round amateur theatres, and a high-class year-round arts and entertainments programme. It also maintains two heritage buildings primarily for cultural purposes. The borough council has been the significant direct provider in this development. For a town of 110,000 population, this is an impressive achievement'.

The report urged that the separation of the festivals from the council be accelerated. It also recommended an extension to the art gallery and museum, refurbishment of the town hall, and a commercial partner to help bear the costs of the Pittville Pump Room. The option of setting up an independent Cultural Foundation in the town, which would have been another 'first', was rejected, but in line with the twenty-first-century policy of 'externalising' council functions (and in accordance with the recommendation of the Cultural Review) all the festivals were taken out of house and registered as a charity in 2006. Several considerations prompted the move, foremost being the shrinking resources of the council and its expanding social service obligations. This has meant a large increase in the costs of organising the festivals, as both the direct grant and the hidden subsidy of council administrative services are lost. HSBC has given important support by providing office accommodation for five years. If Cheltenham became the centre of a larger, unitary authority, its focus would have to be education and social services. In the twenty-first century, Cheltenham's inheritance of nineteenth-century spa development may cease to be the most important aspect of the town.

CONSERVATION

CONSERVATION AREAS

Conservation became a major concern in the second half of the twentieth century, as it became clear how rapid and total was the demolition possible with modern building equipment.

RIGHT
The elegant church of St James's, Suffolk Square, is one of several in Cheltenham which have been closed, and in this case converted very well into a restaurant. It was designed by Edward Jenkins, a local architect, begun in 1825 and completed five years later. It was one of three churches built at this time, with Trinity (1823), designed by George Underwood, and St Paul's (1831), designed by John Forbes, the original Pittville architect. Jenkins had a technical problem with the ambitious single span of the roof covering both nave and aisles, and John Buonarotti Papworth was called in to advise. Serving the affluent development of Suffolk Square, it was largely proprietary, with just 350 free seats out of the total of 1750, the rest being individually owned. Average attendance at morning service, it was claimed in 1851, was 1400.
PHOTOGRAPH: CARNEGIE, 2009

Lypiatt Terrace
has been described
recently as 'the
last flourish of
Cheltenham's
glamour years'.
There was a large
field called the
Lypiates in 1765;
the land belonged
to Mr Delabere.
The first eleven
houses were built in
1847 and occupied
in 1851; James
Gardner the brewer
lived in number 2
with his wife, two
young children and
five servants. Six
were not built until
1857. If it were not
for Cheltenham's
social journal,
The Looker-On,
Samuel Whitfield
Daukes would
not be identified
as the architect,
although the towers
are typical, for
example in the
former St Paul's
Training College
and possibly in
Cornerways in The
Park, and in the
very large Horsted
Place, East Sussex
and Colney Hatch
Lunatic Asylum,
Barnet. Lypiatt
Terrace was built
to a high standard,
with party walls
rising through to
the roof, and with
overhanging eaves
both back and front.
In 1964 number
13 was gifted to
Cheltenham Civic
Society.

PHOTOGRAPH: AUTHOR,
2009

The damaging scale of redevelopment in Gloucester and Worcester led to heightened public awareness of the value of conserving old town centres while improving roads, providing housing and erecting exciting new buildings. There had been various Cheltenham civic societies since 1925, but a Cheltenham Civic Society sprang into new life in 1958, as the national Civic Society was formed, and was strong in its protests at the county council's plans for the town. After amalgamation with the Regency Society the present Cheltenham Society was formed in 1962; 'Civic' was later again added to its title. Its aims are 'to bring together all who are interested in the town and environment of Cheltenham and its immediate surroundings' in order to stimulate public interest; to preserve the best architectural and historical features of the town; and to promote high standards of design. Lord Parmoor gave the society his house in Lypiatt Terrace in 1964 to help it as far as possible to preserve the character and enhance the beauty of Cheltenham. That year the Council for British Archaeology published a memorandum drawing attention to the implications of the Buchanan Report *Traffic in Towns*. The following year a list of 324 towns in England, Scotland and Wales was drawn up, of which 51 were considered 'splendid' and 'precious'. Cheltenham was included on the list because of the number of Georgian and Regency buildings and the well-preserved Georgian town plan, though it was not in the 'precious' category.

Although the Town and Country Planning Act of 1947 had required development plans to be prepared, and had given councils powers to prevent major alterations to buildings, when the new district council took office in 1974 Cheltenham had not yet agreed one. Two had been prepared jointly with the county council and rejected, the second after a six-week enquiry in 1967. Following the failure of the first plan, an interim policy guide on redevelopment

was prepared in 1964, which proposed a new shopping precinct on the *Plough Hotel* and Regent Street carpark site.[41] In 1973 Gloucestershire County Council designated a central conservation area. It might be said that this was bolting the stable door after some of the horses had gone. In 1975, European Architectural Heritage Year, Cheltenham was one of thirty English towns described as 'scenes of rape'.[42] Hereford and Gloucester were also on the list. Two new buildings were particularly castigated as being out of scale: the Eagle Star building (1968) and the Cheltenham and Gloucester Building Society headquarters (1972), but there was also condemnation of the neglect of decaying 'villas' and the substitution in 1969 of a car park for Edward Jenner's house – though restitution for this particular demolition was made in 1994 when the house was rebuilt as a replica.

The borough council and town opinion generally had been divided on what should be major objectives – conservation or commerce – and that conflict continued to hamper planning. Central shopping facilities, rather than new out-of-town ones, were favoured by the advocates of commerce, and car parks rather than pedestrian precincts. The Conservative-dominated council was reluctant to spend ratepayers' money on conservation, and together with the lack of a town plan, the consequence was that organisations with the capital to carry out refurbishments and adaptations to the large nineteenth-century villa residences were usually given permission.[43] Furthermore, organisations were encouraged to locate their offices in Cheltenham in order to meet the need for employment. There are numerous examples, but particularly notable was the purchase by Lloyds Bank of the Montpellier Rotunda in 1961. Beautifully repaired and adapted, the bank continues to maintain this example of early nineteenth-century spa development. The stone lion, a symbol not usually associated with the bank, is an authentic part of the restoration; it was originally commissioned for the Pump Room in 1817.

Another notable example is the location of a regional headquarters of the Countryside Commission in the former hotel in Crescent Place, which had been the police headquarters for over a hundred years.[44] The royal coat of arms over the entrance was placed there after the visit of Adelaide, Duchess of Clarence, who consented to Liddell's Boarding House being renamed Clarence Hotel; the arms are those of her husband, later William IV.[45] The Countryside Commission restored the building and occupied it in 1974, renaming it John Dower House after the architect and civil servant who produced the first report on National Parks in England and Wales in 1945. The Commission has now become Natural England, comprising the former English Nature and parts of two other relevant organisations.

There is really nothing new in this. At earlier periods, houses and hotels had been converted to commercial use, or demolished to make way for newer, larger buildings. The Imperial Hotel in the Promenade became a club and then in 1874 the post office; the borough council took over Harwards Buildings; and all the other houses in the Promenade were gradually put to commercial use. Cavendish House, which had occupied several houses for well over a century, demolished them in 1964 to create what it was hoped would be more practical and attractive modern premises, a hope which is not usually thought to have been fulfilled. Some major office blocks were new, like the Eagle Star or the Cheltenham and Gloucester Building Society, as was more permanent accommodation for GCHQ, all subsequently given up by those organisations.

Four years after the new Cheltenham District Council took office, a town plan was finally agreed. It suggested that in future fewer office developments should be encouraged. After publication of the plan, the council's policy shifted towards rehabilitating 'Regency' housing (this being a somewhat loose term distinguishing early nineteenth-century buildings from more elaborate 'Victorian' architecture). It was claimed in 1988 that among local authorities Cheltenham was one of the ten highest spenders on historic buildings.[46] Local ratepayers and national taxpayers both contributed to subsidise renovation.

The Cheltenham conservation area was extended by the borough council in 1987 to cover an area of 600 hectares, reputedly the largest in Europe. Because of its size, it is subdivided into nineteen 'character areas', for example the High Street, Montpellier and Bayshill; these three areas alone contain several hundred listed buildings, and in Cheltenham there were in total at that date over 2,000.[47] But perhaps the most interesting development in the conservation approach has been the designation in 2001 of 'The Poets', the post-First World War estate developed by the council itself.

While Cheltenham did not have an extensive medieval plan, Charlton Kings, by contrast, contained several centres of settlement, a complex and ancient road pattern, and several large and significant houses.[48] The Borough Council was responsible in 1989 for designating three areas of Charlton Kings for conservation: round St Mary's church, Cudnall Street, and Bafford. The centre of Prestbury had been made a conservation area in 1979; in 1991 Prestbury was transferred to the reorganised Cheltenham District and the council in 2002 extended that conservation area. The Council's new boundaries also include Swindon where the conservation area had been designated by Tewkesbury Borough Council.

In his Introduction to the passionate appeal in *The Rape of Britain*, John Betjeman wrote of the 'importance of the modest old buildings which act as foils to greater ones ... and the little streets which had a life of their own'. There are many 'little streets' of stucco-fronted, terraced artisan houses in Cheltenham which, though less publicised than the villas, nonetheless contribute much to the overall style of the town There is now a register of 'locally listed buildings' which recognises the value of such buildings in the ambience of Cheltenham – while individually they may not contain striking and original features warranting statutory protection, collectively they contribute greatly to streetscapes, townscapes and the sense of place.

CONVERSION

If old and spacious houses were not to be converted into offices, how was their preservation to be financed? The treatment of Lansdown Crescent was one answer. Little of the Crescent was owner-occupied, and it had contained a number of lodging houses occupied by short-term residents; several blocks were owned by a single landlord.[49] As lodging declined, the houses were divided into single-room letting units or flats. The houses were already in poor condition in the early twentieth century, and after the Second World War deteriorated further so that in terms of amenities the area was in the worst 10 per cent of housing in the country. In 1971 nearly half the houses were occupied by single person households. To renovate and revitalise Lansdown Crescent would obviously need a large amount of capital.

In the early 1970s the philanthropic Guinness Trust was offering to convert buildings to student accommodation. Cheltenham Borough Council started negotiations with the Trust, but found the problem of displacing tenants and finding alternative housing difficult to solve, so the Trust started to negotiate with owners individually. Of the 46 houses, all listed grade

Harwards Buildings and Royal Crescent are in one sense the heart of Cheltenham – not the ancient core of the market town, but the core of successful early nineteenth-century development. Royal Crescent is on the site of Church Meadow, which in Thomas Robins' picture was grazed by sheep, and the path to the Royal Well passed through it. The garden in front now serves as a bus station. This recent aerial view, taken in 2007, shows the improvements that have been made to the area, but the quiet of a real garden here with the great trees which survive would be another asset to the 'Garden Town'. Internal features of Harwards Buildings have largely been removed in the process of creating municipal offices, but the borough council is planning eventually to vacate them, and return the magnificent terrace to domestic use.
WWW.WEBBAVIATION.CO.UK

II*, the trust finally purchased 26 in total. While waiting for conversion work to start, little maintenance was done, squatters moved in, and social problems multiplied. However, eventually the upgrading and restoration of Lansdown Crescent was a success, and the striking terrace provides many flats in attractive and unusually characterful buildings – more like London terraces than provincial ones. The Guinness Trust continues to work with the council as a 'partner' social landlord for affordable housing.

Conversions of large houses to flats is an important answer to both housing shortage and conservation, even if the resulting units are highly priced. For example, Hatherley Court, Pearson Thompson's house, was converted to flats in 1973, and the two grand houses along the south side of Suffolk Square were converted in 1986, each costing over a £1 million. If the council succeeds in its plans to build a new office block in North Place or Portland Street, what will happen to the row of Harwards Buildings in the Promenade? Could they once again become people's homes, as well as a hotel, shops and cafés?

As planning authorities become more aware of the requirement and advantage of 'consultation', the Civic Society is perhaps less significant, although commenting on planning matters is still regarded as its major function. It also takes the initiative in some projects, for example creating the Chelt Walk and the Jenner Gardens. It raised a considerable sum of money to restore the bandstand in Montpellier Gardens, and to place a statue of Holst in Imperial Gardens. Since 1982 it has undertaken the work of placing round blue plaques to mark where notable people were born, lived or worked, and rectangular green plaques commemorating sites or events. The first plaque was placed on 10, St James's Square, in 1926 by the Public Libraries Committee to commemorate Alfred Lord Tennyson's residence there. By 2008 another 38 had been added to the ten which already existed in Cheltenham, and one in Charlton Kings to mark the house where Cecil Day Lewis lived. They cover a wide range of reasons for fame and celebrity: actors and actresses, engineers, two poets laureate, Day Lewis and Tennyson, explorers and modern pop stars among others. The visit of George III has been marked with two green plaques.[50] The Civic Society and the borough council also cooperate annually in a civic awards scheme 'for the encouragement of standards of excellence in the restoration of historic buildings and other works in the field of improvement in Cheltenham's built environment'. Nominations are made by members of the public, and are a way of encouraging sensitivity to surroundings.

CIVIC PRIDE

It is appropriate that recent improvement schemes in Cheltenham are the result of the initiative named 'Civic Pride'. The guiding authority is the South West Regional Development Agency (SWRDA), which was established in 1999 with the overall aim of 'improving the urban environment to support economic renewal' within its large and diverse area. In this connection, the Agency has categorised as 'Civic Pride' a set of possible initiatives which promote the renaissance of the largest urban areas and improve the way the South West is perceived by investors, businesses, potential workers and visitors. A relatively small scheme was undertaken in Cheltenham under this banner between 2005 and 2007, the £1.25 million restoration of Montpellier Gardens, 3½ hectares, completed in July 2007.

Design consultants were appointed in 2006 for a much larger project, the product of a joint Urban Design initiative by the borough council, Gloucestershire County Council and SWRDA, supported by £250,000 from SWRDA. A scheme was published in 2007. Every Cheltenham resident will recognise the many awkward spots in Cheltenham's road system, and the unfortunate corners and areas which do not please aesthetically: Boots' corner, the Royal Well bus station and car park where over a hectare is in public ownership; and the backs of Harwards Buildings which display unattractive extensions; Albion Street, North Place and Portland Street car parks, covering 2 hectares; the remaining half-hectare portion of the St James's Square site; and North Place, earmarked for the new council offices. The problem of how to allow traffic to flow while not demolishing or blighting residential areas is as intractable in Cheltenham as in any town. The first phase of the improvements is to be completed by 2010. Boots Corner will be pedestrianised, but buses and taxis will still be able to use the road, and more 'shared space' introduced. The aim 'is to preserve our Regency heritage whilst at the same time revitalising our street scene, including the buildings, roads and open spaces'. It is apparently a simple and laudable aim, but the history of the town prompts the thought that civic consciousness should have a wider focus and a more generous confidence in recent periods in the town's development and in giving expression to contemporary design.

NOTES AND REFERENCES

NOTES TO CHAPTER 1: TERRITORY

1. P. H. Sawyer, *From Roman Britain to Norman England* (1998), pp. 197–9; F. Stenton, *Anglo-Saxon England* (1950), pp. 294–7; J. Campbell, *The Anglo-Saxon State* (2000), pp. 2–7.

2. See for example D. Hooke, 'Pre-Conquest estates in the west Midlands: preliminary thoughts', *Journal of Historical Geography* viii, 3 (1982), p. 228. The 30 hide estate might have been based upon a quarter of a 'long hundred' 120 hides (ten times the duodecimal unit 12).

3. A. Jones, *A Thousand Years of the English Parish* (Moreton-in-Marsh, 2000), pp. 54–7.

4. P. Sims-Williams, *Religion and Literature in Western England, 600–800* (Cambridge University Press, 1990), 138–9; he followed Finberg in raising the query as to whether the Bishop of Hereford's church at Cheltenham was the Prestbury estate.

5. *VCH Glos.*, viii, p. 72.

6. Jones, *The English Parish*, pp. 93, 128.

7. P. Sawyer, 'The royal TUN in Pre-conquest England', in P. Wormald (ed.), *Ideal and Reality in Frankish and Anglo-Saxon Society* (1983), pp. 277–8.

8. *VCH Glos.*, viii, p. 27.

9. Sawyer, *Roman Britain to Norman England*, pp. 197–200; W. A. Morris, *The Frankpledge System* (1910), pp. 3–4, 69, 87.

10. J. Barlow, 'Cheltenham manor court rolls, 1527–29', *CLHSJ*, xx (2004), p. 19; Glos. Arch., D855/M3.

11. A. M. Welch 'Old Arle Court', *TBGAS*, xxxvi (1913), p. 295; tithings ceased to be used in the administration of the poor law in 1851. J. Goding, *Norman's History of Cheltenham* (revised edn, 1868), p. 50.

12. G. E. Payne, *A Physical, Social and Economic Survey and Plan [of Gloucestershire]* (Gloucester, n.d, [1946]), pp. 93, 100; D. Stamp, *The Land of Britain* (1942), p. 348. T. Catchpole, 'Excavations at West Drive, Cheltenham, Gloucestershire', *TBGAS*, cxx (2002), pp. 89, 92, 100, shows Romano-British cultivation of some of the Cheltenham sands but no evidence of a settlement.

13. *VCH Glos.*, iv, pp. 13, 18.

14. Sawyer, 'The royal *TUN*', p. 292.

15. P. A. Stafford, 'The "Farm of One Night" and the organization of King Edward's estates in Domesday', *Economic History Review*, xxxiii, no. 4 (1980), pp. 491–502.

16. P. D. A. Harvey, 'The manorial reeve in twelfth-century England', in R. Evans (ed.), *Lordship and Learning: Studies in Memory of Trevor Aston* (2004), pp. 125–38.

17. Campbell, *The Anglo-Saxon State*, pp. 207–11.

18. C. Dyer, 'Towns and cottages in eleventh-century England', in H. Mayr-Harting and R. I. Moore (eds), *Studies in Medieval History Presented to R. H. C. Davis* (1985), pp. 91–106.

19. H. P. R. Finberg ed., *Gloucestershire Studies* (1957), pp. 60–1.

20. J. S. Moore, 'The Gloucestershire section of Domesday Book', *TBGAS*, cv (1987), p. 127, and cviii (1990) p. 106.

21. T. Moore-Scott, 'The manorial estates of Leckhampton', *Gloucestershire History* (2002); Moore-Scott wished to allocate *Lechetone* to Leckhampton, but ignored the strength of Moore's arguments concerning its identification.

22. T. H. Aston, 'The origins of the manor in England', in W. E. Minchinton (ed.), *Essays in Agrarian History* (1968), p. 26.

23. H. P. R. Finberg, 'Charltons and Carltons', *Lucerna* (1964), p. 144–60.

24. A. Mawer (ed.), *The Chief Elements used in English Place-Names* (English Place-Name Society, i, pt 2 (1930), p. 44.

25. D. Hooke, *The Anglo-Saxon Landscape* (Manchester, 1985), pp. 12–20; S. Bassett, 'In search of the origins of Anglo-Saxon kingdoms', in S. Bassett (ed.), *The Origins of Anglo-Saxon Kingdoms* (Leicester, 1989), pp. 6–17.

26. H. P. R. Finberg, *The Early Charters of the West Midlands* (1972), no. 88.

27. Sir R. Atkyns, *Ancient and Present State of Gloucestershire* (1712), p. 372.

28. Glos. Arch., D184/P1, a plan of Lord Craven's estate in Prestbury shows that Hyde Farm was then 170 acres including meadows; the arable lands with the name 'Hyde' were 94 acres.

29. J. Campbell, *Essays in Anglo-Saxon History* (1986), pp. 149–50; F. E. Harmer, *Anglo-Saxon Writs* (1989), pp. 160, 212, 214;

F. Barlow, *The English Church, 1000 to 1066* (1979), p. 129.

30. See the repetition of Henry I's charter by Edward III in K.J. Beecham, *The History of Cirencester* (1887; reprinted 1978), pp. 84–6, and C.D. Ross (ed.), *The Cartulary of Cirencester Abbey*, i (1964), no. 8; 'secular' canons served the church but did not lead ordered lives in a residential community; 'regular' canons lived according to a rule formulated by Augustine, the early fifth-century bishop of Hippo on the Mediterranean coast of Africa.

31. A. K. B. Evans, 'The collegiate church at Cirencester: a critical examination of the historical evidence', *Studies in the Archaeology and History of Cirencester* (British Archaeological Reports 30, 1976).

32. *Cirencester Cartulary*, no. 28.

33. *Cirencester Cartulary*, nos 8, 412, 416, 438, 484.

34. T. Moore-Scott, 'Beating the bounds: the 1823 perambulation of Cheltenham', *CLHSJ*, xviii (2002). See map 4 and point 11.

35. Ross, Introduction to *Cirencester Cartulary*, i, note 4, p. xxvii.

36. *Cirencester Cartulary*, iii, nos 407, 708, 417.

37. Finberg, *Early Charters*, p. 67.

38. *Cirencester Cartulary*, iii, nos 419, 425, 426.

39. J. Fendley (ed.), *Notes on the Diocese of Gloucester by Chancellor Richard Parsons, c.1700* (BGAS, 2005), p. 363.

40. B. Rawes, 'The hundred of Cheltenham and its boundaries', *CLHSJ*, ii (1984), pp. 1–9.

41. A. H. Smith, *The Place-Names of Gloucestershire*, i (1961) p. 13.

42. M. Paget, 'Our oldest place-name', *CKRB*, xxiii (1990), p. 29.

43. H. P. R. Finberg, 'Roman and Saxon Withington', *Lucerna* (Leicester, 1964), p. 22 note 4.

44. Finberg, 'Some early Gloucestershire estates', *Gloucestershire Studies*, pp. 12–13; Rawes, 'The hundred of Cheltenham', p. 7.

45. Moore-Scott, 'The 1823 perambulation', has made a splendid copy of the maps, and the following paragraphs are based on his article.

46. M. Paget, 'Beating the bounds', *CKRB*, xvi (1986), p. 55; E. Miller, 'Beating the bounds', *CKRB*, xxv (1991), p. 28.

47. W. E. Tate, *The Parish Chest* (1969), p. 28.

NOTES TO CHAPTER 2: STRUCTURES

1. B. Rawes, 'The fields and field names of the Hundred of Cheltenham (with some notes on the early topography), *CLHSJ*, vi, pt 1 (1988), pp. 1–27; vii, pt 2 (1989), pp. 1–7.

2. Place name evidence is drawn from Smith, *Place-Names of Gloucestershire*, ii, pp. 96–113.

3. It was published by Finberg in *The Early Charters* in 1961.

4. P. Sawyer (ed.), *Anglo-Saxon Charters* (1968), no. 1782.

5. J. Sale, 'Southfield Farm', *CKRB*, xlviii (2002), p. 3.

6. M. Paget (ed.), *A History of Charlton Kings* (1988), p. 36.

7. Paget, *Charlton Kings*, p. 38.

8. Glos. Arch., D9125 Austin 6107.

9. Glos. Arch., D8244/1.

10. M. Paget, 'Charlton tenants in 1557 and 1564', *CKRB*, xxx (1993), p. 16.

11. Goding, *History of Cheltenham*, p. 59.

12. T. H. Aston, 'The origins of the manor in England', in W. E. Minchinton (ed.), *Essays in Agrarian History*, i (1968), pp. 11–35.

13. G. Hart, *History of Cheltenham* (Leicester University Press, 1965), p. 28.

14. M. Chibnall, *The Empress Matilda* (1991), pp. 82–4.

15. A. L. Poole, *From Domesday Book to Magna Carta* (1951), pp. 133–48 and note 3.

16. *VCH Glos.*, v, p. 354.

17. D. Walker, 'The charters of the Earldom of Hereford', *Camden Miscellany*, xxii (1964), pp. 1–11.

18. *Rotuli Chartarum in Turri Londinensi asservati i ab anno 1199 to 1216* (Record Commission, 1837), i, pp. 53, 61.

19. R. S. Hoyt, *The Royal Demesne in English Constitutional History* (New York, 1950), pp. 230, 232.

20. D. Matthew, *The Norman Monasteries and their English Possessions* (1962), p. 5. The account of the alien priories is based on Matthew and on M. M. Morgan, 'The suppression of the alien priories', *History*, xxvi (1941), pp. 204–12.

21. Glos. Arch., Hockaday Abstracts/D3439/Cheltenham.

22. Paget, *Charlton Kings*, p. 6.

23. Glos. Arch., Hockaday Abstracts/D3439/Cheltenham.

24. Paragraphs on Syon based on *VCH Mddx*, i, pp. 182–91; iii, pp. 96–100.

25. It was specifically excepted from the pope's ruling against double houses.

26. D. Knowles and R. N. Hadcock, *Medieval Religious Houses, England and Wales* (1953), p. 178.

27. G. J. Aungier, *The History and Antiquities of Syon Monastery* (1840), p. 76.

28. *The Complete Peerage*, p.114.

29. E. F. Jacob, *The Fifteenth Century* (1985), p.114.

30. L. Toulmin Smith (ed.), *The Itinerary of John Leland* (1964), i, p. 102; iv, p. 44; v, p. 8.

31. Hart, *History of Cheltenham*, pp. 39–40.

32. Hart, *History of Cheltenham*, pp. 21–2.

33. *Cirencester Cartulary*, nos 158, 163, 409–10, 420–4 and Introduction, xxxi. These documents were referred to by Hart in her *History of Cheltenham* but not explored further.

34. Jones, *The English Parish*, pp. 110–14, 118.

35. *Cirencester Cartulary*, no. 418.

36. These two paragraphs are based on J. M. Hall, 'Sevenhampton', *TBGAS*, xiv (1889–90), pp. 349–50; *VCH Glos.*, viii, pp. 71, 75, 78.

37. Walker, 'Charters of the Earldom of Hereford', p46; following his practice, the priory is Llanthony Secunda, but the place-name is written Lanthony.

38. The information on 'Ashley' manor is drawn from F. B. Welch, 'The manor of Charlton Kings, later Ashley', *TBGAS*, liv (1932), pp. 145–65; *Book of Fees, Testa de Nevill sive Liber feodorum in curia Scaccarii. Temp. Hen. III & Edw. I* (1807), p. 51.

39. Paget, *Charlton Kings*, p. 77.

40. This account amplifies and amends that of Rawes, 'Fields and field names', pp. 19–21, and P. White, 'The Grovefield Estate and its houses', *CLHSJ*, xv (1999), pp. 25–32.

41. *VCH Glos.*, iv, pp. 353–4.

42. Rawes, 'Fields and field-names', pp. 19–20.

43. *Pope Nicholas Taxation*, p. 232.

44. The National Archives, Lands of the dissolved religious houses/ S.C.6/Hen VIII/1224.

45. Smith, *Place-names of Gloucestershire*; B. Rawes, 'The hundred of Cheltenham', p. 5.

46. J. R. Maddicott, 'The English peasantry and the demands of the crown', in T. H. Aston (ed.), *Landlords, Peasants and Politics in Medieval England* (1987), pp. 323–34.

47. *Inquisitions and Assessments relating to Feudal Aids*, ii (1900), pp. 264, 268, 273.

48. Aston, 'The origins of the manor', p. 22.

49. M. K. McIntosh, 'The privileged villeins of the English ancient demesne', *Viator*, vii (1976), especially pp. 295–9, 320–6.

50. M. Paget, 'Cheltenham (and most of Charlton Kings) in 1294 – an extent of the manor', *CKRB*, xiii (1987), p. 7.

51. *Cirencester Cartulary*, ii nos 425 and 426, 427 and 429, 428 (in order of reference).

52. M.Greet, 'Aspects of medieval Cheltenham', *CLHSJ*, xvii (2001), pp. 42–9 sets out aspects of these documents and the place-names to which they refer.

53. *Cirencester Cartulary*, iii nos 469, 470 and 475.

54. R. H. Hilton, *A Medieval Society* (1983), p. 129.

55. *Cirencester Cartulary*, ii nos 427, 428, 429, 430; iii, 473, 474, 477, 480.

56. *VCH Glos.*, viii, p. 74.

57. M. Paget, 'Cheltenham (and most of Charlton Kings)', p. 7.

58. *VCH Glos.*, viii, p. 74.

NOTES TO CHAPTER 3: GROWTH

1. A. Everitt, 'The primary towns of England', in A. Everitt (ed.), *Landscape and Community in England* (1985), pp. 94–107.

2. H. P. R. Finberg, 'The genesis of the Gloucestershire towns', *Gloucestershire Studies* (Leicester, 1957), pp. 80–1.

3. Goding, *History of Cheltenham*, p. 47.

4. C. Dyer, *An Age of Transition?* (2005), p. 193.

5. R. H. Britnell, 'English markets and royal administration before 1200', *Economic History Review*, xxxi, pt 2 (1978), pp. 183–9.

6. R. H. Britnell, 'The proliferation of markets in England, 1200–1349', *Economic History Review*, xxxiv, pt 2 (1978), pp. 210–11.

7. *Calendar of Patent Rolls of the reign of Henry III: preserved in the Public Record Office* (HMSO, 1901–13), i, p. 63.

8. Finberg, 'Some early Gloucestershire estates', p. 64; Britnell, 'English markets', p. 210.

9. *Cirencester Cartulary*, ii no. 430, p. 385.

10. Glos. Arch., D855/M68.

11. Hilton, *Medieval Society*, p. 170.

12. A. Jones, *The Cotswolds* (Chichester, 1994), p. 70.

13. *VCH Glos.*, viii, pp. 68, 74; S. Rudder, *A New History of Gloucestershire* (1779; reprinted Gloucester, 1977) p. 604.

14. Britnell, 'The proliferation of markets', p. 219.

15. *The Itinerary of John Leland*, iv, p. 134.

16. Hilton, *Medieval Society*, p. 78.

17. J. K. Griffith, *A General Cheltenham Guide* (Cheltenham, n.d. [1818]), p. 36, describes how the Paving Commissioners defined the area of the town.

18. *VCH Glos.*, viii, p. 110; *VCH Glos.*, iv, p. 13.

19. Glos. Arch., D855/M68

20. *VCH Glos.*, viii, p. 74.

21. Paget, 'Cheltenham (and most of Charlton Kings)', pp. 7–10.

22. C. Dyer, *Lords and Peasants in a Changing Society* (1980), pp. 72–3.

23. Paget, 'Cheltenham (and most of Charlton Kings)', pp. 6–10.

24. The sum entered for 'gardens and curtileges' at 12*d.* per person gives 52¾.

25. P. Franklin (ed.), *The Taxpayers of Medieval Gloucestershire* (Stroud, 1993), pp. 4–5.

26. C. C. Fenwick (ed.), Introduction to *The Poll Taxes of 1377, 1379 and 1381*, Part 1 (British Academy 1998), p. xiii.

27. J. F. Willard, 'Taxation boroughs and parliamentary boroughs, 1294–1336', *Historical Essays in Honour of James Tait* (Manchester, 1933), p. 420.

28. Finberg 'Some early Gloucestershire estates', p. 81; J. F. Willard, 'Taxation boroughs', pp. 417–31.

29. M. McKisack, *The Fourteenth Century* (1985), pp. 187–91.

30. Franklin, *Taxpayers of Medieval Gloucestershire*, pp. 37–8, 98, 116.

31. J. R.Maddicott, 'The English peasantry and the demands of the crown', in T. H. Aston (ed.), *Landlords, Peasants and Politics in Medieval England* (1987), pp. 291–3.

32. Tewkesbury parish contained Southwick, Mythe Hook and Walton Cardiff; Winchcombe parish contained Coates, Frampton and Naunton (divided into two vills), Greet, Gretton, and Postlip.

33. *VCH Glos.*, iv, p. 32; Dyer, *Lords and Peasants*, p. 379.

34. Goding, *History of Cheltenham*, pp. 77–82.

35. *VCH Glos.*, iv, pp. 13, 18; W. G. Hoskins, *Local History in England* (1959), p. 176; C. C. Fenwick (ed.), *The poll taxes of 1377, 1879 and 1381* (British Academy, 1998), pt 1, p. xxiii.

36. R. Schofield, 'The geographical distribution of wealth in England, 1334–1649', in R. Floud (ed.), *Essays in Quantitative Economic History* (1971), pp. 82, 88, 89; *The Lay Subsidy of 1334*, pp. 91–2, 100, 104.

37. P. Nightingale, 'The lay subsidies and the distribution of wealth in medieval England, 1275–1334', *Economic History Society*, 2nd series, lvii, 1 (2004), p. 8.

38. Maddicott, 'English peasantry', pp. 287, 354; Schofield, 'The geographical distribution of wealth', p. 97; Hart, *History of Cheltenham*, p. 71.

39. *VCH Glos.*, iv, p. 30.

40. Hart, *History of Cheltenham*, pp. 25–33; Jane Sale very generously made available her transcripts of the later fourteenth-century set of court rolls.

41. Dyer, *Lords and Peasants*, p. 346.

42. J. H. Baker, *An Introduction to English Legal History* (1979), pp. 64–5.

43. Dyer, *Lords and Peasants*, p. 228.

44. Glos. Arch., TRS 115/8; Hart, *History of Cheltenham*, pp. 36–7.

45. Glos. Arch., D855/M68.

46. Dyer, *Lords and Peasants*, p. 241.

47. M. J. Greet, 'Was there an "oratory" in Charlton in 1339–40?' and note by M.P., *CKRB*, xiii (1985), p. 8.

48. H. M. C. Bennett and M. Paget, 'The manor of Ham and Ham Court', *CKRB*, iii (1980), p. 5.

49. A. M. Welch, 'Old Arle Court', *TBGAS*, xxxvi (1913), p. 298; F. B. Welch, 'The manor of Charlton Kings, later Ashley', *TGBAS*, liv (1932), p. 156. The name Grevill is spelt variously with one 'l' or two and with or without a final 'e'.

50. C. T. Davis, *The Monumental Brasses of Gloucestershire* (1969), pp. 113–15.

51. J. H. Baker, *English Legal History*, pp. 135–6.

52. Glos. Arch., Hockaday Abstracts D3439/Cheltenham.

53. E. Duffy, *The Stripping of the Altars* (1992), p. 125.

54. Jones, *The Cotswolds*, p. 95.

55. D. E. Williams, *The Lygons of Madresfield Court* (Logaston Press, 2001), p. 7.

56. R. W. Hoyle (ed.), *The Military Survey of Gloucestershire, 1522* (BGAS 1993); J. Cornwall (ed.), *The County Community under Henry VIII* (Rutland Record Society, 1980), pp. 3–5.

57. G. J. Aungier, *The History and Antiquities of Syon Monastery* (1840) p. 451; Hart, *History of Cheltenham*, p. 50.

58. A. Savine, 'English Monasteries on the eve of the Dissolution', *Oxford Studies in Social and Legal History* (1909), Appendix.

59. A. Jones, 'Tewkesbury in 1540', *Tewkesbury Historical Society Bulletin*, iii (1994), p. 44.

60. See, for example, A. Jones, 'The parish of Tewkesbury after the Reformation', in R. K. Morris and R. Shoesmith (eds), *Tewkesbury Abbey* (Logaston 2003), pp. 75–88.

61. R. H. Hilton, 'Medieval market towns and simple commodity production', *Past and Present*, cix (1985), pp. 17–19.

62. J. Maclean, 'Chantry certificates, Gloucestershire', *TBGAS*, viii (1883–84), pp. 229–308.

63. J. H. Middleton, 'Notes on the manor and parish church of Cheltenham', *TBGAS*, iv (1879–80), p. 66.

64. *DNB*; J. Barlow, 'Cheltenham's manor court rolls, 1527–29', *CLHSJ*, xx (2004), p. 21.

65. A. Platts and G. H. Hainton, *Education in Gloucestershire* (1953), pp. 9, 10.

66. J. Hodsdon, 'A map of Cheltenham' *CLHSJ*, xv (1999), pp. 33–41.

67. Hart, *History of Cheltenham*, pp. 54–5.

68. J. S. Moore, 'Episcopal visitations and the demography of Tudor Gloucestershire', *Southern History*, xxii (2000), pp. 91–3.

69. Moore, 'Episcopal visitations', pp. 74, 123. My calculations do no agree perfectly with Moore's.

70. Moore, 'Episcopal visitations', pp. 75, 80, 88.

NOTES TO CHAPTER 4: TRANSITION

1. Glos. Arch., Hockaday Abstracts/D3439/Cheltenham.

2. Glos. Arch., Hockaday Abstracts/D3439/Cheltenham.

3. J. Mulvagh, *Madresfield* (Doubleday, 2008), p. 61.

4. P. White, 'The Grovefield Estate', p. 25.

5. *VCH Glos.*, ii, p. 87; iv pp. 353–4.

6. Glos. Arch., D855/M7.

7. Glos. Arch., Photocopy, 934.

8. Smith, *The Place Names of Gloucestershire*, ii, pp. 76, 84.

9. *Notes on the Diocee of Gloucester*, p. 372.

10. *VCH Glos.*, viii, pp. 73, 78.

11. That is, from 1539 until 1638.

12. Glos. Arch., Hockaday Abstracts/D3439/Cheltenham.

13. Glos. Arch., D855/M68; Goding, *History of Cheltenham*, pp. 189–206; Hart, *History of Cheltenham*, pp. 94–101; Paget, *Charlton Kings*, pp. 100–9.

14. Jones, *English Parish*, p. 142.

15. See below, Chapter 5, p. 128.

16. M. A. E. Green (ed.), *Calendar of the Proceedings of the Committee for Compounding* (1889–92), ii, pp. 109–10.

17. C. R. Elrington, 'The survey of church livings in Gloucestershire, 1650', *TBGAS*, lxxxiii (1964) pp. 85–98.

18. J. Barlow, 'Cheltenham Manor Court Rolls, 1527–29', pp. 19–23.

19. Glos. Arch., D855/M68; M. Paget, 'Charlton tenants in 1557 and 1564', *CKRB*, xxx (1993), pp. 16–24, gives a transcript of the

two surveys concerning enclosure; Hart, *History of Cheltenham*, pp. 66–8, 80–3.

20. Paget, *Charlton Kings*, pp. 29, 37; Glos. Arch., D855/M68.

21. Glos. Arch., D855/M3.

22. Glos. Arch., D855/M3.

23. Glos. Arch., D855/M2.

24. *Dictionary of National Biography* (Oxford 2004–9).

25. Glos. Arch., D855/M7.

26. This figure includes 32 acres of 'marsh' pertaining to the burgages. Glos. Arch., D9125.

27. Glos. Arch., D855/M51.

28. Hart, *History of Cheltenham*, p. 87.

29. Lord Sherborne had no common land when Cheltenham was enclosed in 1800.

30. My analysis does not entirely agree with that of Hart: see Hart, *History of Cheltenham*, pp. 84–91.

31. 35 out of 61, or 57 per cent.

32. Goding, *History of Cheltenham*, p. 47; C. M. Gray, *Copyhold, Equity and the Common Law* (1963), p. 65.

33. Hart, *History of Cheltenham*, p. 54.

34. Gray, *Copyhold*, chapter II.

35. Baker, *English Legal History*, pp. 215–19.

36. Glos. Arch., D855/M68.

37. A. J. H. Sale (ed.), *Cheltenham Probate Records*, Gloucestershire Record Series, xii (BGAS, 1999), nos 332, 339, 400.

38. Goding, *History of Cheltenham*, pp. 55–6; Hart, *History of Cheltenham*, pp. 329–38.

39. D. Verey and A Brooke, 'The Vale and the Forest of Dean', *The Buildings of England* (3rd edn, 2002); N. Kingsley, *The Country Houses of Gloucestershire*, i (Cheltenham, 1989), pp. 133–5.

40. Atkyns, *Glostershire*, p. 531.

41. L. Hall, 'New Court – an architectural report'; M. Paget, 'New court – an historical interpretation', *CKRB*, ix (1983), pp. 11–32.

42. It appears from the history of the manor recited by William Norwood that the original grant to the abbess of Syon gave her the authority to exchange or in any other way exploit the abbey property. See Goding, *History of Cheltenham*, p. 70.

43. M. Greet, 'Sir William Compton and Cheltenham', *CKRB*, xlviii (2002), p. 23; T. D. Fopsbrooke, *Abstracts of Records and Manuscripts Respecting the County of Gloucester*, i, 2 (Gloucester,

1807), p. 373.

44. Paget, 'New Court – an historical interpretation', p. 18.

45. J. Sale, 'The Court House – some extra information', *CKRB*, l (2004), p. 37.

46. Glos. Arch., D855/M2.

47. T. D. Fosbrooke, *Abstracts of Records and Manuscripts Respecting the County of Gloucester* (Gloucester, 1807), ii, p. 374.

48. Glos. Arch., D245/iv 1–7.

49. *Cheltenham Probate Records*, 14 (1986).

50. Welch, 'The manor of Charlton Kings', p. 160.

51. R. Beacham, 'Cheltenham's Assembly Rooms, 1734–1900', *CLHS*, v pp. 4–11.

52. M. Paget, 'Ham Court – the story continued', *CKRB*, xx (1988), p. 27.

53. Glos. Arch., D444/T6, 12; Bennett and Paget, 'The manor of Ham and Ham Court', p. 5.

54. D. S. Packer, *On Footings from the Past: the Packers in England* (Boyd K. Packer Family Society, 1988), from whom some interesting details of the Cheltenham and London families have been drawn.

55. *Valor Ecclesiasticus temp. Henry VIII auctoritate regia institutus* (Record Commission, 1810–34), ii.

56. Glos. Arch., Hockaday Abstracts/D3439/Cheltenham.

57. *Gloucestershire Inquisitiones Post Mortem* (BGAS, 1899), pp. 119–20.

58. *Charlton Kings Probate Records*.

59. Bennett and Paget, 'The manor of Ham and Ham Court', pp. 3–10; L. Hall, 'Ham Court – photographs and architectural description', *CRKB*, xx (1988), pp. 15–16.

60. The sketches are by A. D. Welch accompanying the article by A. M. Welch, 'Old Arle Court'.

61. Glos. Arch., GDR/Wills/1665/44.

62. J. Sale 'The manor of Ashley alias Charlton Kings', *CKRB*, liv (2008), p. 45.

63. Paget, *Charlton Kings*, p. 9. M. Paget, 'A court house for Ashley manor', *CKRB*, xiii (1985), pp. 9–13.

64. M. Paget, 'The Forden or Forden House (now Charlton Park) and Forden Bank road', *CKRB*, viii (1982), pp. 20–46; this provides a very full description of the development of the house and the park.

Notes to Chapter 5: Commerce

1. A. Dyer and D. M. Palliser (eds), *The Diocesan Population Returns for 1563 and 1603* (2005), pp. liv–lxxxv.

2. Elrington, 'Survey of church livings', pp. 85–98.

3. J. Smith,
Men and Armour for Gloucestershire in 1608 (1902; reprinted Gloucester, 1980); A. J. and R. H. Tawney, 'An occupational census of the seventeenth century', *Economic History Review*, v

(1934), pp. 25–64; I. Wyatt, 'Trades and occupations in Gloucester, Tewkesbury and Cirencester in 1608', *Gloucestershire Historical Studies*, vii (1976), pp. 2–34.

4. Reference 102/1st drawer; a transcript is in Glos. Arch., TRS 189.

5. Dyer and Palliser, *The Diocesan Population Returns*.

6. Tawney, 'An occupational census', p. 36.

7. Glos. Arch., D855/M8/1611.

8. E. A. Wrigley, *Poverty, Progress and Population* (Cambridge, 2004), pp. 129–37.

9. *VCH Glos.*, viii, pp. 68, 77.

10. A. Whiteman (ed.), *The Compton Census of 1676* (Oxford, 1986), pp. lxxvi, lxxix; P. Jackson, 'Nonconformity in Devon', in K. Schurer and T. Arkell, *Surveying the People*, Local Population Studies Supplement (Oxford, 1992), p. 124.

11. Whiteman, *The Compton Census*, pp. 537, 538, 541; Jones, 'The parish of Tewkesbury', pp. 75–88.

12. Whiteman, *The Compton Census*, p. lxvii, suggests the Compton census figures of 1676 usually need inflating by a third; Gregory King calculated that 40 per cent were under 16 years of age, but some younger than this may have been communicants.

13. Goding, *History of Cheltenham*, p. 281.

14. C. R. Elrington, 'Assessments of Gloucestershire: fiscal records in local history', *TBGAS*, ciii (1985), p. 7; there are a few returns for 1662 and 1664.

15. T. Arkell, 'Printed instructions for administering the Hearth Tax', in Schurer and Arkell, *Surveying the People*, pp. 38–64, and idem, 'Identifying regional variations from the Hearth Tax', *The Local Historian*, August 2003, pp. 148–74; his plea for comparability in analysis has led to the adoption of his categories here.

16. P. Pumpfrey and M. Paget, 'The 1672 Hearth Tax exemption list', *CKRB*, xli (1999), p. 18.

17. P. Slack, 'Measuring the national wealth in seventeenth-century England', *Economic History Review*, lvii, 4 (2004), pp. 617, 631–2.

18. P. Laslett, 'Natural and political observations on the population of late seventeenth-century England', in Schurer and Arkell, *Surveying the People*, pp. 6–30; D. V. Glass, 'Two papers on Gregory King', in D. V. Glass and D. E. C. Eversley (eds), *Population in History* (1969), pp. 159–220.

19. Glass, 'Two papers on Gregory King', pp. 177–8; P. L. Dickinson, 'The Heralds' Visitation of Gloucestershire, 1682–83', *TBGAS*, cxvii (1999), pp. 13, 26.

20. Goding, *History of Cheltenham*, p. 278.

21. Cheltenham town 48.6%; Cheltenham parish 51.2%; Charlton Kings 72%; Leckhampton 51.5%; Swindon 46.7%; Prestbury 45.3%.

22. Goding, *History of Cheltenham*, p. 280 quotes Fosbrooke, writing in *Abstracts* in 1798; Edward Cresy in 1849 in his report *Report to the General Board of Health on a preliminary inquiry into the sewerage, drainage and supply of water, and the sanitary condition of the inhabitants of the town of Cheltenham, in the county of Gloucester* (1849) wrote that about 1800 Cheltenham had 'many thatched houses, like cottages', and his source may have been local knowledge.

23. H. Chitting, *The Visitation of Gloucestershire taken in the year 1623 by Henry Chitty and John Philpot as deputies to William Camden, Clarenceux king of armes*, Harleian Society, xxi (1885).

24. J. Maclean, 'On feudal and compulsory knighthood', *TBGAS*, ix (1884–85), pp. 351–3.

25. Dickinson, 'The Heralds' Visitation', pp. 11–33.

26. J. Bedels, 'The gentry of Huntingdonshire', *Local Population Studies*, xliv (1990), p. 36.

27. S. Rowbotham and J. Walker, *Cheltenham, A History* (Chichester, 2004), p. 17.

28. A. J. H. Sale (ed.), *Cheltenham Probate Records, 1660–1740*, Gloucestershire Record Series, xii (1999). (Six wills were proved in the Prerogative Court of Canterbury and the rest in the bishop of Gloucester's Consistory Court.) References are given paragraph by paragraph to the numbers of the documents in *Cheltenham Probate Records*; inventory valuations have been rounded to the nearest pound.

29. Neither the exempt nor most of the women probably made wills.

30. *Cheltenham Probate Records*, nos 177 and 178; 133 and 134.

31. *Cheltenham Probate Records*, 50 (1676), 204, 205 (1699); 179 (1695); 91, 92 (1684); 213, 214 (1700); 163, 164 (1693); 53, 54 (1677).

32. *Cheltenham Probate Records*, 97, 98 (1684); 120, 121 (1686)..

33. *Cheltenham Probate Records*, 118, 119 (1686).

34. Goding, *History of Cheltenham*, p. 260.

35. *Cheltenham Probate Records*, 93, 94 (1684).

36. *Cheltenham Probate Records*, 131, 132 (1689); 124, 125 (1689); 187, 188 (1696).

37. *Cheltenham Probate Records*, 56 (1679); 196, 197 (1697); 129 (1688); 143, 144 (1690).

38. *Cheltenham Probate Records*, 87, 88 (1683).

39. *Cheltenham Probate Records*, 207, 208 (1699).

40. *Cheltenham Probate Records*, 89, 90 (1684); 58, 59 (1679); 135, 136 (1689).

41. *Cheltenham Probate Records*, 158, 159 (1692); 193, 194 (1697).

42. *Cheltenham Probate Records*, 71, 72 (1682); 152, 153 (1690).

43. Dickinson, 'The Heralds' Visitation', p. 18; *Cheltenham Probate Records*, 1682/81 and 1689/126, 127.

44. *Cheltenham Probate Records*, 81 (1682); 126, 127 (1688).

45. *Cheltenham Probate Records*, 115, 116 (1686); 150, 151 (1690); 64 (1681).

46. *Notes on the diocese of Gloucester*, p. 363.

47. *Cheltenham Probate Records*, 536 (1696); *Dictionary of National Biography*; G. Lipscombe, *The History and Antiquities of the County of Buckingham*, i (1831), pp. 415, 430.

48. *Cheltenham Probate Records*, 202, 203 (1698); 31 (1671).

49. P. Ripley, 'Village and town: occupations and wealth in the hinterland of Gloucester, 1660–1700', *Agricultural History Review*, xxxii (1984), pp. 174–7.

50. *Cheltenham Probate Records*, 25, 26 (1670).

51. *Gloucestershire Notes and Queries*, i, pp. 347–52; Thomas Mason issued another halfpenny token in 1669.

52. *Cheltenham Probate Records*, 113, 114 (1686).

53. *Cheltenham Probate Records*, 277, 278 (1710).

54. *Cheltenham Probate Records*, 320, 321, 322 (1715).

55. P. Hembry, *The English Spa, 1560–1815* (1990), p. 180.

56. A. Everitt, 'The English urban inn', *Landscape and Community in England* (1985), pp. 155–200.

57. *Cheltenham Probate Records*, 43 (1674); 487 (1733).

58. *Cheltenham Probate Records*, 537 (1677).

59. *Cheltenham Probate Records*, 217, 218 (1701).

60. *Cheltenham Probate Records*, 185, 186 (1696).

61. *Cheltenham Probate Records*, 1 (1660); 151 (1690); 84 (1683); 279,

280 (1710); 367, 368 (1720).

62. *Cheltenham Probate Records*, 238, 239 (1686); Hart, *History of Cheltenham*, p. 127; Everitt, 'English urban inn', p. 165; Goding, *History of Cheltenham*, p. 263.

NOTES TO CHAPTER 6: MYTH

1. P. Hembry calls Cheltenham at this period 'The village spa': see *The English Spa, 1560–1815* (1990), p. 179.

2. P. Borsay, *The English Urban Renaissance* (Oxford, 2002).

3. Jones, *Tewkesbury* (2nd edn, 2003), p. 123.

4. *Universal British Directory* (query 1792, King's Lynn, 1993).

5. Glos. Arch., D5130/82. The date of this small manuscript is not stated, but can be deduced from the candidates who were elected in 1741 and the names of some of the voters, which included Henry Skillicorne, William and Thomas Robins and John Prinn (the son) who may have secured the list; it was annotated 'Prynne MSS No 4'.

6. Goding, *History of Cheltenham*, pp. 258–60.

7. Rudder, *New History of Gloucestershire*, pp. 331, 337.

8. Hart, *History of Cheltenham*, p. 127, S. Blake and R. Beacham, *The Book of Cheltenham* (Buckingham, 1982), p. 61, Rowbotham and Walker, *Cheltenham*, pp. 47–8.

9. W. Butler the elder, *The Cheltenham Guide or Useful Companion* (1781), p. 28.

10. H. Ruff, *The History of Cheltenham* (1803), p. 23, gives the breakdown between town and rural tithings.

11. Rowbotham and Walker, *Cheltenham*, p. 19; Butler, *Guide*, p. 41; Goding, *History of Cheltenham*, p. 251. Goding said he used two manuscript accounts of the finding of the spring, dated 1749 and 1763, and gives the date 1716 for the purchase of all the Bayshill land.

12. Payne, *Physical, Social and Economic Survey [of Gloucestershire]*, pp. 26, 208.

13. Goding, *History of Cheltenham*, pp. 254, 256–7.

14. Hembry, *The English Spa*, pp. 43, 64.

15. D. A. Defoe, *A Tour Through the Whole Island of Great Britain* (1724–26; reprinted 1968), p. 434.

16. Goding, *History of Cheltenham*, p. 251.

17. Goding, *History of Cheltenham*, pp. 258–60 (poor relief payments were levied at the rate of 3*d*. per £ rateable value).

18. In the minutes of the Quaker men's monthly meeting in February 1725 William Mason's name was annotated 'deceased'. B. Little, 'Gloucestershire Spas', in P. McGrath and J. Cannon (eds), *Essays in Bristol and Gloucestershire History* (1976), p. 182.

19. A. W. Moore, *Manx Worthies* (Douglas, 1901), pp. 161–2, 181.

20. Hembry, *The English Spa*, p. 97.

21. Little, 'Gloucestershire Spas', p. 183.

22. See the discussion of Robins' paintings which follows.

23. Ruff, *History of Cheltenham*, p. 66.

24. Hembry, *The English Spa*, p. 180.

25. Goding, *History of Cheltenham*, pp. 249–50.

26. The National Archives, PROB 11/954, 1393.

27. 'Some history of Quakers in Cheltenham', website http://www.cheltenhamquaker.org.uk. This first meeting house was in Grove Street, the second in Clarence Street, the third in Portland Street, and the present meeting house is in the former garden of this last house.

28. I am grateful to James Hodsdon for giving me his summaries of entries in the Cheltenham manor court books relating to the Stapleton family (to be published in 2010 in the BGAS Record Series), and for other comments on this section.

29. Hart, *History of Cheltenham*, p. 81, suggested that the house was built about 1736; Hembry, *The English Spa*, p. 181, 'about 1739'.

30. Ruff, *History of Cheltenham*, p. 66; Hembry, *The English Spa*, pp. 184, 238; Goding, *History of Cheltenham*, p. 268.

31. Goding, *History of Cheltenham*, pp. 261–2.

32. University of North Wales Bangor/Introduction to Stapleton-Cotton manuscripts; J. R. V. Johnston, 'The Stapleton sugar plantations in the Leeward Islands', *Bulletin of the John Rylands Library*, xlviii, 1 (1965), pp. 175–206.

33. Goding, *History of Cheltenham*, pp. 261–2.

34. Butler, *Guide*, p. 39.

35. Glos. Arch., Q/REL/1/Cheltenham.

36. Butler, *Guide*, p. 31; Hembry, *The English Spa*, p. 185.

37. Hart, *History of Cheltenham*, p. 126; Blake and Beacham, *The Book of Cheltenham*, pp. 32, 60; J. Harris, *Garden of Delight. The Rococo English Landscape of Thomas Robins the Elder* (1978), i, no. 53.

38. Glos. Arch., GDR will 1745/36, inventory 1745/1; Paget, *Charlton Kings*, pp. 189–91.

39. C. Spence and D. Brown, *Thomas Robins the Elder, 1716–1770* (Bath, 2006).

40. M. Paget, 'Thomas Robins "The Limner of Bath" and his Charlton background', *CKRB*, ii (1979), p. 11.

41. Harris, *Gardens of Delight*, ii, nos 73 and 92.

42. Goding, *History of Cheltenham*, p. 250.

43. Butler, *Guide*, pp. 37–8.

44. Stephen Blake suggested this identification.

45. R. & W. p. 22; E. B. Challinor, *The Story of St Mary's College, Cheltenham* (n.d. [1978]), p. 19.

46. Harris, *Gardens of Delight*, i, pp. 22–3; nos 36, 38, 39.

47. R. Beacham, 'Cheltenham's Assembly Rooms, 1734–1900', *CLHS*, v pp. 4–11.

48. Hart, *History of Cheltenham*, pp. 134–5; Hembry, *The English Spa*, pp. 181–2, 185, 187.

49. G. F. Barwick, 'Some early guide-books', *Transactions of the Bibliographical Society*, vii (1904), pp. 192, 197–9.

50. *Dictionary of National Biography*.

51. Hembry, *The English Spa*, pp. 185, 187.

52. John Vaughan, *The English Guide Book c.1780–1870* (1974), pp. 104–5.

53. Little, 'Gloucestershire Spas', p. 186.

54. Glos. Arch., P78/1 VE 2/1.

55. Glos. Arch., ROL/G4: A. Cossons, 'Schedule of turnpike Acts relating to Gloucestershire'.

56. *The Gentleman's Magazine*, lviii (1788), p. 757.

57. Hembry, *The English Spa*, p. 191.

58. *The Gentleman's Magazine*, lviii (1788), p. 649.

59. F. Fraser, *Princesses* (2004), p. 114.

60. J. Brooke, *King George III* (1998), pp. 322–3, 336–41.

61. Extracts relating to the king's visit to Tewkesbury were reproduced in Jones, *Tewkesbury*, and relating to Cheltenham in A. Jones, *A Short History of the First Cheltenham Spa in Bayshill* (1988). Mary Yorke's letters are deposited in Bedfordshire and Luton Archives and Records Service, Wrest Park (Lucas) archive; those to Marchioness Grey are referenced L30/9/111 and to Amabel, Lady Polwarth L30/11/339. Abbreviations have been expanded, but some capital letters retained to give the flavour of the letters. The catalogue numbers of the letters are the order quoted 153, 108, 157, 164, 116, 165.

62. *The Gentleman's Magazine*, lviii (1788) p. 884.

63. Hembry, *The English Spa*, pp. 155, 193.

64. Goding, *History of Cheltenham*, p. 250.

65. P. Hembry, *British Spas from 1815 to the Present: A Social History*, edited by L. W. Cowie and E. E. Cowie (1997), pp. 133, 189, 254.

66. C. Wilkins-Jones, Foreword to *The Universal British Directory* (King's Lynn, 1993).

67. Bailey's *Directories* appeared at this time for other areas.

68. Based on the population actually in the town in 1801, and assuming a household size of four or five.

69. Hembry, *The English Spa*, p. 193.

70. E. A. Wrigley, 'The occupational structure of England', pp. 129–37.

71. *VCH Glos.*, viii, p. 124.

72. Borsay, *Urban Renaissance*, p. 32.

73. C. Fiennes, *The Illustrated Journeys of Celia Fiennes, 1685–c.1712*, edited by C. Morris (1982), p. 32.

74. Borsay, *Urban Renaissance*, pp. 222, 297. There was a steady increase in the number of Londoners purchasing Cheltenham copyholds from the 1770s; James Hodsdon, Cheltenham manor court books (BGAS, forthcoming), kindly made this material available to me.

75. Ruff, *History of Cheltenham*, pp. 51–2.

76. Hembry, *The English Spa*, p. 186.

77. Borsay, *Urban Renaissance*, p. 220.

78. Hembry, *The English Spa*, p. 191.

NOTES TO CHAPTER 7: POWER

1. B. E. V. Savine, *A History of Income Tax* (1966), p. 16.

2. G. J. Wilson, 'The Land Tax problem', *Economic History Review*, 2nd series, xxxv (3) (1982), pp. 422–6; Glos. Arch., Q/REL/1/1780, 1783..

3. Hart, *History of Cheltenham*, pp. 280–1, 346.

4. Glos. Arch., P78/1 VE 2/1; Hart, *History of Cheltenham*, pp. 275–9, 285.

5. J. K. Griffith, *A General Cheltenham Guide* (1818), p. 124.

6. Hart, *History of Cheltenham*, pp. 286–7.

7. Hart, *History of Cheltenham*, p. 282.

8. *VCH Glos.*, iv, pp. 104, 128–9.

9. The account of the turnpikes is based on A. Cossons, 'Schedule of turnpike Acts relating to Gloucestershire', Glos. Arch., ROL/G4.

10. *VCH Glos.*, iv, p. 137.

11. W. Marshall, *The Rural Economy of Glocestershire* (1796; reprinted Gloucester, 1979), pp. 14–15.

12. 26 George III, cap. 116.

13. Glos. Arch., CBR/A1/1/1.

14. Hart, *History of Cheltenham*, p. 302.

15. 46 George III, cap. 117.

16. J. Hodsdon, *An Historical Gazetteer of Cheltenham*, Gloucestershire Record Series, ix (BGAS, 1997) records that Suffolk House is shown on the 1806 *Plan of Cheltenham*.

17. Jones, *English Parish*, pp. 202–5.

18. Hembry, *The English Spa*, p. 258.

19. Glos. Arch., CBR/A1/1/2.

20. A. Hann, 'Modernity and the marketplace' in S. Pinches, M. Whalley and D. Postles (eds), *The Market Place and the Place of the Market* (Friends of the Centre for English Local History, 2004), pp. 67–88.

21. Hart, *History of Cheltenham*, pp. 264, 269, 298–9; Cheltenham Local Society Newsletters 61 and 62 (2008).

22. Total acreage 3,054; 1,355 acres tithable in 1732.

23. *VCH Glos.*, viii, p. 76.

24. B. Elliott, 'Squire Delabere and the enclosure of Prestbury', *CLHSJ*, iv (1986), p. 6.

25. Glos. Arch., Q/RI 88.

26. Identified by comparing the enclosure map and the details of Cheltenham parish boundary in the 1823 perambulation.

27. Hart, *History of Cheltenham*, p. 100.

28. Goding, *History of Cheltenham*, pp. 100–10.

29. Possibly Naunton Meese had been the manor demesne, but in 1632 the Rector 'enjoyed' it. It was then 23 acres.

30. Glos. Arch., D5809/1/1

31. Glos. Arch., D9125/PF21.18 GS.

32. Hembry, *The English Spa*, p. 181; Ruff, *History of Cheltenham*, p. 68; Glos. Arch., D855/E9, Cheltenham enclosure award.

33. G. E. Mingay, *Parliamentary Enclosure in England, 1750–1850* (1997), pp. 412–44.

34. M. Turner, *Enclosures in Britain, 1750–1830* (The Economic History Society, 1984), p. 64.

35. J. Sawyer, *Cheltenham Parish Church* (Cheltenham, 1902), p. 105, said it rested on an estate in Arle.

36. The records of copyhold transactions in the manor court show a significant surge between 1800 and 1803. James Hodsdon, *Cheltenham Manor Court Books* (BGAS, forthcoming); material kindly made available to me by James Hodsdon.

37. P. White, 'The Grovefield Estate and its houses', *CLHSJ*, xv (1999), pp. 25–32.

38. Glos. Arch., P78/SD 2.

39. Glos. Arch., GDR/T1/49.

40. Paget, *Charlton Kings*, pp. 36, 43–5.

NOTES TO CHAPTER 8: REALITY

1. R. Sweet, *Antiquaries: The Discovery of the Past in Eighteenth-century Britain* (2004).

2. Ruff, *History of Cheltenham*, p. 15.

3. *William Cobbett's Illustrated Rural Rides, 1821–1832*, compiled by C. Morris (Exeter, 1984), pp. 33–4.

4. J. Hodsdon, *An Historical Gazetteer of Cheltenham* (BGAS, 1997); the chronology of development of Cheltenham's streets is drawn from this very valuable compendium of information.

5. W. E. Minchinton, 'Agriculture in Gloucestershire during the Napoleonic Wars', *TBGAS*, lxviii (1968), pp. 175, 180.

6. Glos. Arch., P78/1 MI 1, 2 and 3.

7. D. A. Gatley, 'Urban and rural England and Wales in the 1831 Census', *Local Population Studies Society Newsletter* (2004), pp. 9–11.

8. *Pigot's Directory, 1830*.

9. S. Blake, *Pittville, 1824–1860* (Cheltenham Art Gallery and Museums, 1988), p. 9.

10. The total excludes 67 names living in neighbouring parishes but listed under Cheltenham.

11. A. Everitt, 'Kentish Family Portraits', *Landscape and Community in England* (1985), p. 248.

12. The catalogue is undated, but Williams opened his library in 1815 and moved to the premises by the new Assembly Rooms in 1818 (Blake and Beacham, *The Book of Cheltenham*, p. 49); in 1818 he published *An autumn in Cheltenham, or Mysteries in high life, a fashionable novel in 3 vols*, and in 1823 *Three tracts by a Gloucestershire gentleman*. Jane Austen to Cassandra, 6–7 November 1813.

13. M. Blake, 'A passage in time: The story of Swindon Passage and its back-to-back houses', *CLHSJ*, vii (1989), pp. 28–42.

14. *Cheltenham Directory* (Cheltenham, 1800).

15. R. Howes, 'The rise and fall of Joseph Pitt', *Gloucestershire Studies*, viii (1979), pp. 62–72.

16. A. Courtenay, 'Cheltenham Spa and the Berkeleys, 1832–1848: pocket borough and patron?', *Midland History* xvii (1992) p. 98.

17. E. J. Evans, *The Forging of the Modern State* (1996), pp. 399–400.

18. Statues of William IV, one of the least memorable of English kings,

19. Glos. Arch., Q/REr 1832/33; H. Davies, *The Stranger's Guide through Cheltenham* (Cheltenham, 2nd edn, 1834) p. 8: 849 assessed at less than £10; 1,939 at £10–£19; 1,225 at £20 and over; Glos. Arch., Q/REr; W. R. Williams, *The Parliamentary History of the County of Gloucester* (Hereford, 1898), p. 145, gives 919 registered voters for 1832, but this is not the same number as on the first electoral register.

are by no means common!

20. A. Courtenay, 'Beer, breakfasts and bribery: electoral corruption in Cheltenham during the elections of 1847 and 1848', *CLHSJ*, iv (1986), p. 45.

21. Courtenay, 'Cheltenham Spa and the Berkeleys', p. 94.

22. Courtenay, 'Beer, breakfasts and bribery', pp. 46–52.

23. Hart, *History of Cheltenham*, p. 282.

24. Hart, *History of Cheltenham*, p. 184.

25. O. R. Ashton, 'Chartism in Gloucestershire: the contribution of the Chartist Land Plan, 1843–1850', *TBGAS*, civ (1986), pp. 206–7.

26. O. Ashton, 'Clerical control and radical responses in Cheltenham Spa, 1838–1848;, *Midland History*, viii (1983) p. 130; idem, 'The Mechanics' Institute and radical politics in Cheltenham 1834–40' *CLHSJ*, ii (1984), pp. 25–30.

27. R. Homan, 'The early development of the building society movement in the Cheltenham region', *TBGAS*, ci (1983), pp. 163–5.

28. R. Beamish, *Statistical Notice of the Town and Parish of Cheltenham* (Cheltenham, 1856), p. 2.

29. Goding, *History of Cheltenham*, p. 370; Williams, *Parliamentary History*, p. 145.

30. Borsay, *Urban Renaissance*, pp. 45, 62.

31. Sir R. Atkyns, *Glostershire*; the Kip engraving of 'Cirencester the seat of Allen Bathurst Esq', shows the manor house and town.

32. *George Rowe's Illustrated Cheltenham Guide* (Gloucester, 1981), Introduction, p. 83.

33. A. Clifton-Taylor, *The Pattern of English Building* (1972) pp. 366–9.

34. S. Blake, *Pittville*, p. 14.

35. Glos. Arch., P78/1/OV1/1.

36. D. E. Bick, *Old Leckhampton* (Cheltenham, 1971), pp. 5–8, 35–6.

37. Hart, *History of Cheltenham*, pp. 299–300.

38. J. Hodsdon, 'Thomas Morhall's legacy: building survey certificates, 1824–48', *CLHSJ*, xii (1995), pp. 8–18.

39. M. Grindley, 'The Portland Square and Albert Place district: land, houses and early occupants', *CLHSJ*, xxi (2005), pp. 12–23.

40. These houses were called Beaufort Buildings and Beaufort Place, now Portland Square. Two of the terraces have been renamed Albert Place, and some houses called Portland Parade have been renamed Prestbury Road.

41. W. C. Baer, 'Is speculative building unappreciated in urban history?' *Urban History*, xxxiv, 2 (2007), in particular p. 309.

42. TNA, PROB 11/1504..

43. Hart, *History of Cheltenham*, p. 177.

44. The renaming followed the purchase of the Spa in 1825. Hembry, *The English Spa*, p. 258.

45. Hart, *History of Cheltenham*, p. 149.

46. Hembry, *British Spas*, pp. 35, 45.

47. Various dates are given for this transaction: Goding said 1801; Davies said several good mineral springs were discovered in 1806.

48. D. Verey and A. Brooke, *Gloucestershire The Vale and the Forest*.

49. G. A. Williams, *A New Guide to Cheltenham* (Cheltenham, 1825), pp. 65–6.

50. A. B. Granville, *Spas of England* (1841) pp. 289–90.

51. Glos. Arch., D3755.

52. Hart, *History of Cheltenham*, p. 148.

53. TNA, Prob.11/1637.

54. Turnpike Act, 1813.

55. Glos. Arch., D5809/1/1.

56. Hart, *History of Cheltenham*, p. 282.

57. B. Torode, *Cheltenham The story of Tivoli 'near this town'* (1998), p. 16.

58. *Dictionary of National Biography*; G. Brandwood and A. Davison, *Licensed to Sell. The History and Heritage of the Public House* (2004), pp. 23–4.

59. Hembry, *British Spas*, pp. 44–5.

60. Blake, 'The building of the Montpellier shops: an outline chronology', *CLHSJ*, ii (1984), pp. 15–20; D. Verey and A. Brooke, *The Vale and the Forest*, says three were by Rossi.

61. Granville, *Spas of England*, p. 288.

62. *Cheltenham Chronicle*, 1828.

63. D. Verey and A. Brooke, 'The Vale and the Forest'.

64. See discussion in R. J. Morris, 'Structure, culture and society in British towns', *Cambridge Urban History*, iii, particularly pp. 403–4.

65. F. G. Hilton Price, *A Handbook of London Bankers* (1890–91), p. 19.

66. R. Howes, 'Joseph Pitt, Landowner', *Gloucestershire History*, viii (1976), p. 22.

67. Hart, *History of Cheltenham*, pp. 100, 157.

68. Blake, *Pittville*, p. 8; the following two paragraphs are based on this thorough examination of the estate.

69. Granville, *Spas of England*, p. 305.

70. S. Blake, 'The unfortunate Mr Forbes: the rise and fall of a Cheltenham architect', *CLHSJ*, vii (1989), pp. 7–27.

71. Hart, *History of Cheltenham*, p. 326; Goding, *History of Cheltenham*, p. 198.

72. A. B. Granvills, *Spas of England*, pp. 284–324.

73. Bailey's *Directory* (1784), pp. 49–51; B. Little, 'Calcuta in the Cotswolds', *TBGAS*, lxxxviii (1980), p. 9.

74. Blake, *Pictorial History*, p. 105.

75. E. Bailey, 'Cheltenham and the Indian Connection', *CLHSJ*, xiv (1998), p. 8.

76. Little, 'Calcuta in the Cotswolds', pp. 9–10.

NOTES TO CHAPTER 9: IMPROVEMENT

1. Hart, *History of Cheltenham*, p. 353.

2. Material drawn from Glos. Arch., CBR A1/2/2, CBR B2/9/3/6 and CBR D1/1/2/1.

3. F. B. Smith, *The People's Health, 1830–1910* (London, 1990), p. 233.

4. *Parliamentary Papers*, 1847 (21).

5. Evans, *The Forging of the Modern State*, p. 245.

6. Cresy, *Report*, pp. 12, 18, 45–6.

7. Cresy, *Report*, p. 13.

8. S. Pruen, *The Cheltenham Improvement Act 1852* (Cheltenham, 1853).

9. E. Heasman, 'The Cheltenham town survey of 1855–57', *CLHSJ*, xviii (2002), pp. 2–12.

10. Jones, *Tewkesbury*, p. 159.

11. *Parliamentary Papers*, 1847 (21).

12. M. Kippin, 'Under water: flooding in Cheltenham, 1731–1985', *CLHSJ*, xxiii (2007), particularly p. 12.

13. Glos. Arch., CBR C2/3/24/1 (1894).

14. Information on the Waterworks Company and its successors is from the pamphlet by J. Henderson and J. D. Bradley, *Sabrina – praeter spem fons aquae* (Severn Trent, 1969) and information published by Severn Trent.

15. C. G. Maggs, *The Swindon to Gloucester Line* (Stroud, 1991), pp. 2–3.

16. D. E. Bick, *The Gloucester and Cheltenham Railway* (Locomotion Papers, 43, 1968).

17. P. J. Long and Revd W. V. Awdry, *The Birmingham and Gloucester Railway* (Gloucester, 1987).

18. M. Oakley, *Gloucestershire Railway Stations* (Wimborne, 2003), pp. 37–46.

19. Bick, *The Gloucester and Cheltenham Railway*, pp. 18, 22, 25, 28, 51; Long and Awdry, *The Birmingham and Gloucester Railway*, pp. 222–3.

20. J. Shorey Duckworth, 'The Cheltenham Female Orphan Asylum', *TBGAS*, cxvii (1999), pp. 141–9.

21. J. Hamblett, 'The condition of milliners and dressmakers in Cheltenham, 1865', *CLHSJ*, v (1987), pp. 41–3; A. Jones, 'Some milliners and dressmakers in Cheltenham in 1851', *CLHSJ*, xxiii (2007), pp. 68–71.

22. B. I. Coleman, *The Church of England in the Mid-nineteenth Century* (The Historical Association, 1980).

23. Glos. Arch., GDR V5/73a T.

24. Gloucestershire County Council (2008) wishes to use a car park next to the churchyard for high-density residential development.

25. A. Munden, 'The proposed enlargement of Cheltenham parish church, 1841', *CLHSJ*, iv (1986), pp. 41–5; 'This convenient edifice', *CLHSJ*, xix (2003), pp. 40–3; *Wearing the Giant's Armour* (Cheltenham Local History Society, 2003).

26. A. Platts and G. H. Hainton, *Education in Gloucestershire* (Gloucestershire County Council, 1955), p. 54.

27. B. I. Coleman, 'The incidence of education in mid-century', in E. A. Wrigley (ed.), *Nineteenth-century Society* (Cambridge, 1972), p. 399.

28. Paget, *Charlton Kings*, p. 165.

29. Platts and Hainton, *Education in Gloucestershire*, pp. 85, 108.

30. Rowbotham and Walker, *Cheltenham*, p. 53.

31. This account is based on Hart, *History of Cheltenham*, pp. 339, 349–55.

32. Paget, *Charlton Kings*, p. 176.

33. Boundary changes from 'Vision of Britain', http://www.visionofbritain.org.uk/index.jsp/, and from F. Youngs, *Local Administrative Units* (1979).

34. *VCH Glos.*, iv, p. 171.

35. The paragraphs on Battledown are based largely on D. A. O'Connor, *Battledown The story of a Victorian Estate* (Stroud, 1992); other sources are indicated where appropriate.

36. Glos. Arch., D855/M68 ff21–23; D9125/Austin 6107.

37. Calculated from a 5 per cent sample.

38. Rowbotham and Walker, *Cheltenham*, p. 44.

39. Based on 1881 census enumerators' returns, computerised in the University of Essex UK Data Archive.

40. For example, J. E. Hurley, 'Capital, state and housing conflict', Ph.D. thesis, Warwick University, 1979, p. 116. Rowbotham and Waller, *Cheltenham*, p. 109, suggest that there was 'heavy industry', but they concentrate on the art metal businesses.

41. J. Whitaker, *The Best* (Cheltenham, 2nd edn, 1998), pp. 3, 8–18. H. H. Martyn wrote an account of his early life which was later found in the house once owned by a secretary of the company.

42. Whitaker, *The Best*, p. 21.

43. *VCH Glos.*, iv pp. 172, 178–9.

44. ex. inf. Roger Beacham, to whom grateful thanks for help on this and other questions.

45. M. Daunton, *Wealth and Welfare* (Oxford, 2007), pp. 175, 181.

46. Glos. Arch., CBR C2/3/5/2.

47. The categories used were not the same as in 1911.

48. Whitaker, *The Best*, pp. 164, 170.

49. R. Homan, 'J. W. Scott and Cheltenham's Homecrofts', *Gloucestershire History*, Spring 1982, pp. 10–12.

50. Glos. Arch., CBR C2/3/24/1.

51. In January 1917 the Inspector of Nuisances was instructed to allow pig-keeping, at the height of the German U-boat campaign which was causing acute food shortages; the order was rescinded in 1921.

52. Glos. Arch., CBR/C2/3/24/1.

53. W. C. Baer, 'Is speculative building unappreciated in urban history', *Urban History*, xxxiv 2 (2007), p. 313.

NOTES TO CHAPTER 10: DIVERSIFICATION

1. P. Borsay, 'Why are houses interesting?', *Urban History* 34, ii (2007), pp. 338–46.

2. Glos. Arch., CBR C2/3/24/3.

3. See for example A. Martin, 'Shattered hopes and unfulfilled dreams: council housing in rural Norfolk in the early 1920s', *The Local Historian* (2005), pp. 107–19.

4. L. Hanley, *Estates: An Intimate History* (2007), pp. 65–66.

5. An enormous archive of Cheltenham Borough Council minutes relating to housing is deposited in Gloucestershire Archives. Two principal sources have been used here: Housing Committee minutes, 1919–74, Glos. Arch., CBR C2/3/18 and Public Health Committee, CBR C2/3/24. Unless otherwise specified, the material here is drawn from this source.

6. In some accounts of Cheltenham, this firm has been wrongly identified with Smiths Industries at Bishops Cleeve, which was so named in 1966; H. Cowen, 'Regency icons: marketing Cheltenham's built environment', in M. Harloe, C. G. Pickvance and J. Urry (eds), *Place, Policy and Politics* (1990), p. 130.

7. Resolution November 1920.

8. N. Hayes, 'Civic perceptions: housing and local decision-making in English cities in the 1920s', *Urban History*, 27, i (2000), pp. 211–33.

9. A. Martin, 'Shattered hopes and unfulfilled dreams', pp. 107–18, describes a very similar struggle with bureaucracy.

10. Jones, *Tewkesbury*, p. 190; *VCH Glos.*, iv (1988), p. 202.

11. Whitaker, *The Best*, pp. 195–201; A. R. Williams, 'The General Strike in Gloucestershire', *TBGAS*, xci (1972), pp. 207–13.

12. Whitaker, *The Best*, p. 21.

13. Glos. Arch., CBR C2/4/8/1.

14. Whitaker, *The Best*,, pp. 31–3.

15. Glos. Arch., CBR/C2/3/18/2; Mira website: http://www.mirashowers.com/

16. N. Watson, *When the Question is Steam. The Story of Spirax-Sarco* (2000).

17. *About and Around Cheltenham The Guide for Visitors* (ed. J. Burrow & Co. Ltd, Cheltenham, n.d.), pp. 49–50 (his guidebooks, published in Cheltenham, were not dated).

18. P. J. Pearce, 'Edward John Burrow – man of many parts', *CKRB*, liv (2008), pp. 30–41; Rowbotham and Walker, *Cheltenham*, p. 123.

19. *Smiths Industries at Cheltenham. The Story of 50 Years at Bishops Cleeve, 1940–1990* (Smiths Industries Aerospace and Defence Systems, 1990); http://www.geaviationsystems.com/

20. The date has been mistakenly given as 1969. Rowbotham and Walker, *Cheltenham*, p. 106. See S. Blake, 'Memories of the town clock', *CLHS Newsletter*, 61 (July 2008).

21. See Council minutes, 28 June 2007. Grant Brown of Cheltenham Borough Council Property Maintenance Dept. says that the clock was made by Smiths' apprentices. In July 2007 it was given a major refurbishment including replacement plinth in stainless steel and brighter lights behind the face.

22. 1933.

23. Payne, *A physical, social and economic survey*, p. 299.

24. Pooley, 'Patterns on the Ground', pp. 445–6.

25. New Ideal Homesteads Ltd claimed to have been erecting 10,000 houses in 1933, and in 1935 Costain had an estate planned for 7,500 houses. J. A. T. Yelling, 'Land, property and planning', *CUH*, iii, p. 487, comments on this as particularly marked in outer London.

26. Morris, 'Structure, culture and society', p. 418.

27. Hurley, *Capital, State and Housing Conflict*, p. 128. The 1931 population of the borough was a little over 50,000.

28. *About and Around Cheltenham* pp. 51–3.

29. Baer,, 'Is speculative building unappreciated?', pp. 296–315.

30. Pooley, 'Patterns on the Ground', pp. 445–6.

31. Based on J. Hodsdon, *Cheltenham Gazetteer*.

32. L. Dudley Stamp, *The Land of Britain: Gloucestershire* (1942), pp. 348, 386–7.

33. Payne, *A Physical, Social and Economic Survey*, p. 93.

34. Payne, *A Physical, Social and Economic Survey*, pp. 139–42.

35. The information on GCHQ is drawn from P. Freeman, *How GCHQ Came to Cheltenham* (Cheltenham, 2002), with thanks to GCHQ for giving me a copy.

36. Freeman, *How GCHQ Came to Cheltenham*, pp. 3, 6, 7.

37. Quoted by Freeman, *How GCHQ Came to Cheltenham*, pp. 33–4.

38. These statistics are drawn from 'A Vision of Britain'

39. Brooks, *The Story of Cheltenham*, p. 170.

40. P. Scott, 'The evolution of Britain's urban built environment', *CUH*, iii, pp. 519, 619.

41. Hurley, *Capital, State and Housing Conflict*, p. 153.

42. J. Mantle, *C & G: The story of Cheltenham and Gloucester Building Society* (James & James, 1991).

43. Brooks, *The Story of Cheltenham*, p. 131.

44. Glos. Arch., CBR C2/3/18/2 (memo. November 1941).

45. 1943.

46. Glos. Arch., CBR C2/3/18/2 & 3.

47. See Chapter 2 and page 95.

48. Hodsdon, *Cheltenham Gazetteer*.

49. Hurley, *Capital, State and Housing Conflict*, pp. 179–80.

50. Glos. Arch., CBR C2/3/18/7.

51. Glos. Arch., DC 11/5, council minutes, 24 January 1979.

52. After the boundary changes of that year the number is stated to be 46,141. Review in 1997 of local structure plan: see http://www.cheltenham.gov.uk/

53. Based on Housing Committee reports to the council and *The Times* database.

54. I. Cole and R. Furbey, *The Eclipse of Council Housing* (1994), provides a survey of the whole period.

55. Hanley, *Estates*, p. 195. Audit Commission report 2004: see http://www.cheltenham.gov.uk/

56. Statement of accounts 2006/07 records 4,687 dwellings owned by the council at 31 March 2007; half are flats, half bungalows: see http://www.cheltenham.gov.uk/

57. Cheltenham Borough Council Annual statements of accounts.

58. To reflect ward changes.

59. Information presented by the Cheltenham Partnership, http://www.cheltenham.gov.uk/

NOTES TO CHAPTER 11: ETHOS

1. Glos. Arch., CBR/C6 & 7 contains meteorological reports.

2. Hart, *History of Cheltenham*, pp. 353–4.

3. *Kelly's Directory* (1890).

4. Morris, 'Structure, culture and society', p. 414.

5. S. Blake, *Cheltenham: A Pictorial History* (Chichester, 1996), nos 47 and 48; Blake and Beacham, *The Book of Cheltenham*, p. 105.

6. A. Rossiter, 'Renovation of Pittville Pump Room and its reopening', *Gloucestershire History* (2003), pp. 16–20.

7. Blake, *Pittville*, p. 47, and information from Cheltenham Entertainment Manager.

8. *The Guide to Cheltenham and the Cotswolds* (Ward Locke, n.d. [in or post 1951]), p.71, noted: 'To its fame as a spa and as a residential and educational centre, Cheltenham has in recent years added a reputation as a centre for exploring the Cotswolds.'

9. Information from Cheltenham Borough Council.

10. Its commemorative purpose has not been generally recognised. See

for example Brooks, *The Story of Cheltenham*, p. 63.

11. Blake, *A Pictorial History*, nos 21 and 28.

12. Hart, *History of Cheltenham*, p. 359.

13. *About and Around Cheltenham*, c.1939, p. 27.

14. S. Osmond, *A Chronology of Cheltenham, 200 BC–2,000 AD* (Cheltenham, n.d. [2001]); Blake and Beacham, *The Book of Cheltenham*, p.36.

15. Brooks, *The Story of Cheltenham*, pp. 71–2; Rowbotham and Walker, *Cheltenham*, p. 106.

16. Blake, *A Pictorial History*, no. 141.

17. Information from the Playhouse Theatre.

18. R. Beacham, 'The Clarence Street Palazzo', *CLHSJ*, i (1983), p. 14.

19. M. Pugh, *State and Society* (2004), p. 65.

20. C. Martin, *Cheltenham's Trams and Early Buses* (Stroud, 2001).

21. Glos. Arch., Q/RI 88.

22. This account of the dispute is based largely upon D. E. Bick, *Old Leckhampton* (Cheltenham, 1972).

23. Cheltenham Borough Council 'Parks and green spaces', http://www.cheltenham.gov.uk/

24. Rowbotham and Walker, *Cheltenham*, p. 110.

25. Brooks, *The Story of Cheltenham*, pp. 206–7.

26. D. Benson, 'The Tewkesbury races', *Tewkesbury Bulletin* (2005), pp. 19–24.

27. Much of this account is based upon P. Gill, *Cheltenham Races* (Stroud, 1997), pp. 10–12, 38–9, 90–1.

28. Hart, *History of Cheltenham*, pp. 193, 203.

29. B. Elliott, 'The deer park at Prestbury: traces in the landscape', *CLHSJ*, xvi (2000), pp. 48–50.

30. Glos. Arch., D184/T79; B. Elliott, 'Prestbury Park Farm', *CLHSJ*, iii (1984), p. 2.

31. Goding, *History of Cheltenham*, p. 546, gives a reliable account of the early history of Cheltenham races.

32. Hart, *History of Cheltenham*, p. 227.

33. *VCH Glos.*, 8 p. 71.

34. See page 334.

35. This account is based on the interestingly illustrated booklet published by the Everyman Theatre (2004). The assistance of Jackie McKenzie is gratefully acknowledged.

36. Brooks, *The Story of Cheltenham*, pp. 42–4.

37. Goding, *History of Cheltenham*, pp. 268–9.

38. Ruff, *History of Cheltenham*, pp. 58–60.

39. Rowbotham and Walker, *Cheltenham*, pp. 66–7.

40. The account of the Festivals is based on the 2004 Programme for the Cheltenham International Festival of Music and N. Bennett, *Speaking Volumes* (Stroud, 1999), for both of which and the 2006 Annual Report I am indebted to Donna Renney, Chief Executive of 'Cheltenham Festivals'.

41. Brooks, *The Story of Cheltenham*, p. 184.

42. C. Amery and D. Cruikshank, *The Rape of Britain* (1975).

43. Hurley, *Capital, State and Housing Conflict*, pp. 167, 187–8.

44. (1858–1970). Rowbotham and Walker, *Cheltenham*, p. 94.

45. Blake and Beacham, *The Book of Cheltenham*, p. 59.

46. Cowen, 'Regency icons: marketing Cheltenham's built environment', in Harloe, Pickvance & Urry, *Place, Policy and Politics*, p. 138, quoting English Heritage's Monitor survey.

47. Cowen, 'Regency icons', p. 138.

48. Paget, *Charlton Kings*, pp. 75–8.

49. This section is based on the study by J. E. Hurley, *Capital, State and Housing Conflict*.

50. P. Smith and S. Rowbotham, *Commemorative Plaques of Cheltenham* (Cheltenham Civic Society, 2009).

BIBLIOGRAPHY

ABBREVIATIONS

BGAS	Bristol and Gloucestershire Archaeological Society
CKRB	*Charlton Kings Local History Society Research Bulletin*
CLHSJ	*Cheltenham Local History Society Journal*
Glos. Arch.	Gloucestershire Archives
TBGAS	Transactions of the Bristol and Gloucestershire Archaeological Society
VCH Glos.	*Victoria History of the County of Gloucester*

Place of publication London unless otherwise specified.

PUBLISHED PRIMARY SOURCES AND GENERAL REFERENCE BOOKS

Alumni Oxonienses: The Members of the University of Oxford, edited by J. Foster (1891–92)

Anglo-Saxon Charters, edited by P. Sawyer (1968)

Bishop Benson's Survey of the Diocese of Gloucestershire 1735–1750, edited by J. Fendley, Gloucestershire Record Series, xiii (BGAS, 2000).

Calendar of Patent Rolls of the Reign of Henry III: Preserved in the Public Record Office (HMSO, 1901–13)

Calendar of the Proceedings of the committee for compounding etc. 1643–1660, ii, edited by M. A. E. Green (1889–92)

Charlton Kings Probate Records 1600–1800, edited by J. Paget and T. Sale (Charlton Kings Local History Society, 2003)

Cheltenham Probate Records, 1660–1740 edited by A. J. H. Sale, Gloucestershire Record Series, xii (BGAS, 1999)

Dictionary of National Biography (Oxford, 2004–09)

Inquisitions and Assessments Relating to Feudal Aids, AD 1284–1431 (HMSO, 1899–1920)

Gloucestershire Inquisitiones Post Mortem (BGAS, 1899)

Men and Armour for Gloucestershire in 1608, compiled by J. Smith (Gloucester, 1980)

Notes on the Diocese of Gloucester by Chancellor Richard Parsons c.1700, edited by J. Fendley, Gloucestershire Record Series, xix (BGAS, 2005)

Patent Rolls of the Reign of Henry III: Preserved in the Public Record Office (HMSO, 1901–13)

Rotuli Chartarum in Turri Londinensi Asservati i ab anno 1199 to 1216 (Record Commission, 1837)

Rowe's Illustrated Cheltenham Guide (Cheltenham, 1850; reprinted Wakefield, 1969)

Taxatio Ecclesiastica Angliae et Walliae, Auctoritate P. Nicholai IV. Circa AD 1291 (Pope Nicholas Taxation) Record Commission (1802)

Testa de Nevill sive Liber feodorum in curia Scaccarii. Temp. Hen. III & Edw. I (1807)

The Buildings of England: The Vale and the Forest of Dean, edited by D. Verey and A. Brooke (3rd edn, 2002)

The Cartulary of Cirencester Abbey, edited by C. D. Ross, i (1964), ii (1977)

The Complete Peerage of England, Scotland, Ireland, Great Britain, and the United Kingdom, extant, extinct, or dormant, G. E. Cokayne (Gloucester, 1982–98)

The Compton Census of 1676, edited by A. Whiteman (Oxford, 1986)

The County Community under Henry VIII, edited by J. Cornwall (Rutland Record Society, 1980)

The Diocesan Population Returns for 1563 and 1603, edited by A. Dyer and D. M. Palliser (2005)

The Early Charters of the West Midlands, H. P. R. Finberg (Leicester, 1972)

The Itinerary of John Leland, edited by L. Toulmin Smith (1964)

The Lay Subsidy of 1334, edited by R. E. Glasscock (Oxford, 1975)

The Military Survey of Gloucestershire, 1522, edited by R. W. Hoyle, Gloucestershire Record Series, vi (BGAS, 1993)

The Poll Taxes of 1377, 1379 and 1381 Part 1, edited by C. C. Fenwick (British Academy 1998)

Return of the name of every member of the lower house of parliament of England, Scotland, and Ireland, with name of constituency represented, and date of return, from 1213 to 1874 (1878)

The Taxpayers of Medieval Gloucestershire edited by P. Franklin (Stroud, 1993)

The Universal British Directory (Kings Lynn, 1993)

Valor Ecclesiasticus temp. Henry VIII auctoritate regia institutus (Record Commission, 1810–34)

Visitation of the County of Gloucester, taken in the year 1623, by Henry Chitty and John

Phillipot as deputies to William Camden, Clarenceux king of armes London (Harleian Society xxi, 1885)

Youngs, F. A., *Guide to the Local Administrative Units of England*, i, *Southern England* (1979)

BOOKS, PAMPHLETS, ARTICLES AND THESES

Atkyns, Sir R., *The Ancient and Present State of Glostershire* (1712)

About and Around Cheltenham, edited by J. Burrow (n.d. [1938/1939])

Amery, C. and D. Cruickshank, *The Rape of Britain* (1975)

Arkell, T. 'Printed instructions for administering the Hearth Tax', in K. Schurer and T. Arkell (eds), *Surveying the People*, Local Population Studies supplement (Oxford, 1992), pp. 38–64

——, 'Identifying regional variations from the Hearth Tax', *The Local Historian*, August 2003

Ashton, O. R., 'Chartism in Gloucestershire: the contribution of the Chartist Land Plan, 1843–1850', *TBGAS*, civ (1986)

——, 'Clerical control and radical responses in Cheltenham Spa, 1838–1848', *Midland History*, viii (1983)

——, 'The Mechanics' Institute and radical politics in Cheltenham, 1834–40', *CLHSJ*, ii (1984).

Aston, T. H., 'The origins of the manor in England', in W. E. Minchinton (ed.), *Essays in Agrarian History* (1968)

Aungier, G. J., *The History and Antiquities of Syon Monastery* (1840)

Baer, W. C., 'Is speculative building unappreciated in urban history?', *Urban History*, xxxiv 2 (2007)

Bailey, E., 'Cheltenham and the Indian connection', *CLHSJ*, xiv (1998)

Baker, J. H., *An Introduction to English Legal History* (1979)

Barlow, F., *The English Church, 1000 to 1066* (1979)

Barlow, J. 'Cheltenham manor court rolls, 1527–29', *CLHSJ*, xx (2004)

Barwick, G. F., 'Some early guide-books', *Transactions of the Bibliographical Society*, viii (1904)

Bassett, S., *The Origins of Anglo-Saxon Kingdoms* (Leicester, 1989)

Beacham, R., 'The Clarence Street Palazzo', *CLHSJ*, i (1983)

——, 'Cheltenham's Assembly Rooms, 1734–1900', *CLHS*, v (1987)

Beamish, R., *Statistical Notice of the Town and Parish of Cheltenham* (Cheltenham, 1856)

Bedels, J., 'The gentry of Huntingdonshire', *Local Population Studies*, xliv (1990)

Beecham, K. J., *The History of Cirencester* (1887; reprinted 1978)

Bennett, H. M. C. and M. Paget, 'The manor of Ham and Ham Court', *CKRB*, iii (Spring 1980), pp. 3–10

Bennett, N., *Speaking Volumes* (Stroud, 1999)

Benson, D., 'The Tewkesbury Races', *Tewkesbury Bulletin* (2005)

Bick, D. E., *Old Leckhampton* (Cheltenham, 1971)

Blake, M., 'A passage in time: the story of Swindon Passage and its back to back houses', *CLHSJ*, vii (1989)

Blake, S. and R. Beacham, *The Book of Cheltenham* (Buckingham, 1982)

Blake, S., 'The building of the Montpellier shops: an outline chronology', *CLHSJ*, ii (1984)

——, *Pittville 1824–1860: A Scene of Gorgeous Magnificence* (Cheltenham: Art Gallery and Museums, 1988)

——, 'The unfortunate Mr Forbes: the rise and fall of a Cheltenham architect', *CLHSJ*, vii (1989)

——, *Cheltenham A Pictorial History* (Chichester, 1996)

Borsay, P., *The English Urban Renaissance* (Oxford, 2002)

——, 'Why are houses interesting?', *Urban History* xxxiv pt. 2 (2007)

Brandwood, G. and A. Davison, *Licensed to Sell. The History and Heritage of the Public House* (2004)

Britnell, R. H., 'English markets and royal administration before 1200', *Economic History Review* xxxi, pt. 2 (1978)

——, 'The proliferation of markets in England, 1200–1349', *Economic History Review*, xxxiv, pt 2 (1978)

Brooke, J., *King George III* (1998)

Brooks, R., *The Story of Cheltenham* (Stroud, 2003)

Campbell, J., *Essays in Anglo-Saxon History* (1986)

——, *The Anglo-Saxon State* (2000)

Catchpole, T., 'Excavations at West Drive, Cheltenham, Gloucestershire', *TBGAS*, cxx (2002)

Challinor, E. B., *The Story of St Mary's College, Cheltenham* (n.d. [1978])

Cheltenham Directory (J. Shenton, Cheltenham, 1800)

Cheltenham Guide or Useful Companion in a Journey of Health and Pleasure to the Cheltenham Spa [Butler, W. the Elder], (1781)

Chibnall, M., *The Empress Matilda* (1991)

Chitting, H., *Visitation of the County of Gloucester, taken in the year 1623, by Henry Chitty and John Phillipot as deputies to William Camden, Clarenceux king of armes*, Harleian Society, xxi (1855)

Clifton-Taylor, A., *The Pattern of English Building* (1972)

Cole, J. and Furbey, R., *The Eclipse of Council Housing* (1994)

Coleman, B. I., 'The incidence of education in mid-century', in E. A. Wrigley (ed.), *Nineteenth Century Society* (Cambridge, 1972)

——, *The Church of England in the Mid-nineteenth Century* (The Historical Association, 1980)

Courtenay, A., 'Beer, breakfasts and bribery: electoral corruption in Cheltenham during the elections of 1847 and 1848', *CLHSJ*, iv (1986)

Courtenay, A., 'Cheltenham Spa and the Berkeleys, 1832–1848: pocket borough and patron?', *Midland History*, xvii (1992)

Cowen, H., 'Regency icons: marketing Cheltenham's built environment', in M. Harloe, C. Pickvance and J. Urry, *Place, Policy and Politics* (1990)

Cresy, E., *Report to the General Board of Health on a preliminary inquiry into the sewerage, drainage, and supply of water, and the sanitary condition of the inhabitants of the town of Cheltenham, in the county of Gloucester* (1849)

Daunton, M. (ed.), *The Cambridge Urban History of Britain* (2000)

——, *Wealth and Welfare* (Oxford, 2007)

Davies, H. *The Stranger's Guide through Cheltenham* (1834)

Davis, C. T., *The Monumental Brasses of Gloucestershire* (1969)

Defoe, D. A., *A Tour thorough the whole island of Great Britain* (1724–26; reprinted 1968)

Dickinson, P. L., 'The Heralds' Visitation of Gloucestershire, 1682–83', *TBGAS*, cxvii (1999)

Duffy, E., *The Stripping of the Altars* (1992)

Dyer, C., *Lords and Peasants in a Changing Society* (1980)

——, 'Towns and cottages in eleventh-century England', in H. Mayr-Harting and R. I. Moore (eds), *Studies in Medieval History Presented to R.H.C. Davis* (1985)

——, *An Age of Transition?* (2005)

Elliott, B., 'Prestbury Park Farm', *CLHSJ*, iii (1984)

——, 'Squire Delabere and the enclosure of Prestbury', *CLHSJ*, iv (1986)

——, 'The deer park at Prestbury: traces in the landscape', *CLHSJ*, xvi (2000)

Elrington, C. R., 'The survey of church livings in Gloucestershire, 1650', *TBGAS*, lxxxiii (1964)

——, 'Assessments of Gloucestershire: fiscal records in local history', *TBGAS*, ciii (1985)

Evans, A. K. B., 'The collegiate church at Cirencester: a critical examination of the historical evidence', *Studies in the Archaeology and History of Cirencester*, British Archaeological Reports, 30 (1976)

——, 'Cirencester Abbey: the first hundred years', *TBGAS*, cix (1991)

Evans, E. J., *The Forging of the Modern State* (1996)

Evans, R. (ed.), *Lordship and Learning: Studies in Memory of Trevor Aston* (2004)

Everitt, A., 'The English urban inn', *Landscape and Community in England* (1985)

——, 'Kentish family portraits', *Landscape and Community in England* (1985)

——, 'The primary towns of England', *Landscape and Community in England* (1985)

Finberg, H. P. R., *Gloucestershire Studies* (Leicester, 1957)

——, 'Some early Gloucestershire estates', *Gloucestershire Studies* (Leicester, 1957)

——, 'The genesis of the Gloucestershire towns', *Gloucestershire Studies* (Leicester, 1957)

——, 'Charltons and Carltons', *Lucerna* (Leicester, 1964)

——, *Lucerna* (Leicester, 1964)

Fosbrooke, T. D., *Abstracts of Records and Manuscripts Respecting the County of Gloucester* (Gloucester, 1807)

Fraser, F., *Princesses* (2004)

Freeman, P., *How GCHQ Came to Cheltenham* (GCHQ, 2002)

Gatley, D. A., 'Urban and rural England and Wales in the 1831 Census', *Local Population Studies Society Newsletter* (2004)

Gill, P., *Cheltenham Races* (Stroud, 1997)

Glass, D. V., 'Two papers on Gregory King', in D. V. Glass and D. E. C. Eversley (eds), *Population in History* (1969)

Gloucestershire Notes and Queries, i (1881)

Goding, J., *Norman's History of Cheltenham* (revised edition, 1868)

Granville, A. B., *Spas of England and Principal Sea-bathing Places* (1841; reprinted Bath, 1971)

Gray, C. M., *Copyhold, Equity and the Common Law* (1963)

Greet, M. J., 'Was there an "oratory" in Charlton in 1339–40?', and note by M.P., *CKRB*, xiii (1985)

——, 'Aspects of medieval Cheltenham', *CLHSJ*, xvii (2001)

——, 'Sir William Compton and Cheltenham', *CKRB*, xlviii (2002)

Griffith, J. K., *A General Cheltenham Guide* (1818)

Grindley, M., 'The Portland Square and Albert Place district: land, houses and early occupants', *CLHSJ*, xxi (2005)

H. Ruff, *The History of Cheltenham* (1803)

Hall, J. M., 'Sevenhampton', *TBGAS*, xiv (1889–90)

Hall, L., 'New Court – an architectural report', *CKRB*, ix (1983)

Hamblett, J., 'The condition of milliners and dressmakers in Cheltenham, 1865', *CLHSJ*, v (1987)

Hanley, L., *Estates: An Intimate History* (2007)

Hann, A., 'Modernity and the marketplace', in S. Pinches, M. Whalley and D. Postles (eds), *The Market Place and the Place of the Market* (Friends of the Centre for English Local History, 2004)

Harloe, M., C. G. Pickvance and J. Urry, *Place, Policy and Politics* (1990)

Harmer, F. E., *Anglo-Saxon Writs* (1989)

Harris, J., *Gardens of Delight: The Rococo English landscape of Thomas Robins the Elder* (Basilisk Press, 1978)

Hart G., *A History of Cheltenham* (Leicester, 1965)

Harvey, P. D. A., 'The manorial reeve in twelfth-century England', in R. Evans (ed.), *Lordship and Learning: Studies in Memory of Ttrevor Aston* (2004)

Hayes, N., 'Civic perceptions: housing and local decision-making in English cities in the 1920s', *Urban History*, xxvii, 1 (2000)

Heasman, E., 'The Cheltenham town survey of 1855–57', *CLHSJ*, xviii (2002)

Hembry, P., *The English Spa, 1560–1815* (1990)

——, *British Spas From 1815 to the Present: A social history*, edited by L. W. Cowie and E. E. Cowie (1997)

Henderson, J., and J. D. Bradley, *Sabrina – praeter spem fons aquae* (Severn Trent, 1969)

Hilton Price, F. G., *A Handbook of London Bankers* (1890–91)

Hilton, R. H., *A Medieval Society* (1966)

——, 'Medieval market towns and simple commodity production', *Past and Present*, cix (1985)

Hodsdon, J., *An Historical Gazetteer of Cheltenham*, Gloucestershire Record Series, ix (BGAS, 1997)

——, 'Thomas Morhall's legacy: building survey certificates, 1824–48', *CLHSJ*, xii (1995)

——, 'A map of Cheltenham', *CLHSJ*, xv (1999)

Homan, R., 'J. W. Scott and Cheltenham's Homecrofts', *Gloucestershire History*, Spring 1982

——, 'The early development of the building society movement in the Cheltenham region', *TBGAS*, ci (1983)

Hooke, D., 'Pre-Conquest estates in the west Midlands: preliminary thoughts', *Journal of Historical Geography*, viii, 3 (1982)

——, *The Anglo-Saxon Landscape* (Manchester, 1985)

Hoskins, W. G., *Local History in England* (1959)

Howes, R., 'Joseph Pitt, Landowner', *Gloucestershire History* viii (1976)

——, 'The rise and fall of Joseph Pitt', *Gloucestershire Studies*, viii (1979)

Hoyt, R. S., *The Royal Demesne in English Constitutional History* (New York, 1950)

Hurley, J. E., 'Capital, state and housing conflict', Ph.D. thesis, Warwick University (1979)

Mantle, J., *C. and G.: The Story of Cheltenham and Gloucester Building Society* (James and James, 1991)

Jackson, P., 'Nonconformity in Devon', in K. Schurer and T. Arkell (eds), *Surveying the People* (Oxford, 1992)

Jacob, E. F., *The Fifteenth Century* (1985)

Jones, A., *The Cotswolds* (Chichester, 1994)

——, *A Thousand Years of the English Parish* (Moreton in Marsh, 2002)

——, *Tewkesbury* (1987; 2nd edn 2003)

——, 'The parish of Tewkesbury after the Reformation', *Tewkesbury Abbey* (Logaston, 2003)

——, 'Some milliners and dressmakers in Cheltenham in 1851', *CLHSJ*, xxiii (2007)

Kingsley, N., *The Country Houses of Gloucestershire*, i (Cheltenham, 1989)

Kippin, M., 'Under water: flooding in Cheltenham, 1731–1985', *CLHSJ*, xxiii (2007)

Knowles D. and R. N. Hadcock, *Medieval Religious Houses, England and Wales* (1953)

Laslett, P., 'Natural and political observations on the population of late seventeenth-century England', in K. Schurer and T. Arkell (eds), *Surveying the People* (Local Population Studies 1992)

Lipscombe, G., *The History and Antiquities of the County of Buckingham* (1831)

Little, B., 'Gloucestershire Spas', in P. McGrath and J. Cannon (eds), *Essays in Bristol and Gloucestershire History* (1976)

——, 'Calcutta in the Cotswolds', *TBGAS*,

lxxxviii (1980)

Long, P. J. and Revd W. V. Awdry, *The Birmingham and Gloucester Railway* (Gloucester, 1987)

Maclean, J., 'Chantry certificates, Gloucestershire', *TBGAS*, viii (1883–84)

Maddicott, J. R., 'The English peasantry and the demands of the crown', in T. H. Aston (ed.), *Landlords, Peasants and Politics in Medieval England* (1987)

Maggs, C. G., *The Swindon to Gloucester Line* (Stroud, 1991)

Marshall, W., *The Rural Economy of Gloucestershire* (reprinted Gloucester, 1979)

Martin, A., 'Shattered hopes and unfulfilled dreams: council housing in rural Norfolk in the early 1920s', *The Local Historian* (2005)

Martin, C., *Cheltenham's Trams and Early Buses* (Stroud, 2001)

Matthew, D. *The Norman Monasteries and their English Possessions* (1962)

Mawer A. (ed.), *The Chief Elements used in English Place-Names*, English Place-Name Society, I, pt 2 (1930)

Mayr-Harting, H. and R. I. Moore (eds), *Studies in Medieval History Presented to R.H.C. Davis* (1985)

McIntosh, M. K., 'The privileged villeins of the English ancient demesne', *Viator*, vii (1976)

McKisack, M., *The Fourteenth Century* (1985)

Middleton, J. H., 'Notes on the manor and parish church of Cheltenham', *TBGAS*, iv (1879–80)

Miller, E. 'Beating the bounds', *CKRB*, xxv (1991)

Minchinton, W. E., 'Agriculture in Gloucestershire during the Napoleonic Wars', *TBGAS*, lxviii (1968)

Mingay, G. E. *Parliamentary Enclosure in England: An Introduction to its Causes, Incidence and Impact, 1750–1850* (1997)

Moore, A. W., *Manx Worthies* (Douglas, 1901)

Moore, J.S. 'The Gloucestershire section of Domesday Book', *Transactions of the Bristol and Gloucestershire Archaeological Society*, part 1 (105, 1987) 127; part 4 (108, 1990)

——, 'Episcopal visitations and the demography of Tudor Gloucestershire', *Southern History*, xxii (2000)

Moore-Scott, T., 'Beating the bounds: the

1823 perambulation of Cheltenham', *CLHSJ*, xviii (2002)

——, 'The Manorial Estates of Leckhampton', *Gloucestershire History* (2002)

Moreau, S., *A Tour to Cheltenham Spa* (1783)

Morgan, M. M., 'The suppression of the alien priories', *History*, xxvi (1941)

Morris, R. J., 'Structure, culture and society in British towns', *CUH*

Morris, R. K. and R. Shoesmith (eds), *Tewkesbury Abbey* (Logaston, 2003)

Morris, W. A., *The Frankpledge System* (1910)

Munden, A., 'The proposed enlargement of Cheltenham parish church, 1841', *CLHSJ*, iv (1986)

Nightingale, P., 'The lay subsidies and the distribution of wealth in medieval England, 1275–1334', *Economic History Review*, 2nd series, lvii, 1 (2004)

Oakley, M., *Gloucestershire Railway Stations* (Wimborne, 2003)

O'Connor, D. A., *Battledown: The Story of a Victorian Estate* (Stroud, 1992)

Oosthuizen, S. 'The Anglo-Saxon kingdom of Mercia and the origins and distribution of common fields', *Agricultural History Review*, lv (ii) (2007)

Osmond S. E., *A Chronology of Cheltenham 200 BC–2000 AD* (Cheltenham, n.d. [2001])

Packer, D. S., *On Footings from the Past: The Packers in England* (Boyd K. Packer Family Society, 1988)

Paget, M., 'Cheltenham (and most of Charlton Kings) in 1294 – an extent of the manor', *CKRB*, xiii (1981)

——, 'The Greville pedigree', *CKRB*, viii (Autumn 1982)

——, 'New court – an historical interpretation', *CKRB*, ix (1983)

——, 'Beating the bounds', *CKRB*, xvi (Autumn, 1986)

——, *A History of Charlton Kings* (revised edn, Charlton Kings History Society, 1989)

——, 'Our oldest place-name', *CKRB*, xxiii (1990)

——, 'Charlton tenants in 1557 and 1564', *CKRB*, xxx (1993)

Payne, G. E., *A physical, social and economic survey and plan [of Gloucestershire]* (Gloucester, n.d [1946])

Pearce, P. J., 'Edward John Burrow – man of

many parts', *CKRB*, liv (2008)

Place-names of Gloucestershire, 4 vols, edited by A. H. Smith (1964–65)

Platts A. and G. H. Hainton, *Education in Gloucestershire* (Gloucestershire County Council, 1955)

Poole, A. L., *From Domesday Book to Magna Carta* (1951)

Pooley, C. G., 'Patterns on the ground', in M. Daunton (ed.), *The Cambridge Urban History*, iii (2000)

Price, F. G. H., *A Handbook of London Bankers, with some account of their predecessors, the early goldsmiths. Together with lists of bankers from the earliest one printed in 1677* (1890–91)

Pruen, S., *The Cheltenham Improvement Act, 1852* (Cheltenham, 1853)

Pumpfrey, P. and M. Paget, 'The 1672 Hearth Tax exemption list', *CKRB*, xli (1999)

Rawes, B., 'The fields and field names of the Hundred of Cheltenham (with some notes on the early topography), *CLHSJ*, pt 1 (1988); pt 2 (1989)

Rawes, B., 'The hundred of Cheltenham and its boundaries', *CLHSJ*, ii (1984)

Ripley, P., 'Village and town: occupations and wealth in the hinterland of Gloucester, 1660–1700', *Agricultural History Review*, xxxii (1984)

Rossiter, A., 'Renovation of Pittville Pump Room and its reopening', *Gloucestershire History* (2003)

Rowbotham, S. and Walker, J., *Cheltenham: A History* (Chichester, 2004)

Rudder, S., *A New History of Gloucestershire* (1779; reprinted Gloucester 1977)

Rudge, Rev T., *A History of the County of Gloucestershire*, 2 vols (1803)

Ruff, H., *The History of Cheltenham* (Cheltenham, 1803)

Sale, J., 'Southfield Farm', *CKRB*, xlviii (2002)

——, 'The court house – some extra information', *CKRB*, l (2004)

Savine, A. 'English monasteries on the eve of the Dissolution', *Oxford Studies in Social and Legal History* (1909)

Sawyer, J., *Cheltenham Parish Church* (Cheltenham, 1902)

Sawyer, P., *From Roman Britain to Norman England* (1998)

——, 'The royal TUN in Pre-conquest England', in P. Wormald (ed.), *Ideal and Reality in Frankish and Anglo-Saxon Society* (1983)

Schofield, R., 'The geographical distribution of wealth in England, 1334–1649', in R. Floud (ed.), *Essays in Quantitative Economic History* (1971)

Schurer, K. and T. Arkell, *Surveying the People* (Oxford, 1992)

Scott, P., 'The evolution of Britain's urban built environment', *CUH*, iii (2000)

Shorey Duckworth, J., 'The Cheltenham Female Orphan Asylum', *TBGAS*, cxvii (1999)

Sims-Williams, P., *Religion and Literature in Western England, 600–800* (CUP, 1990)

Slack, P., 'Measuring the national wealth in seventeenth-century England', *Economic History Review*, lvii, 4, (2004)

Smith, A. H. (ed.), *Place-names of Gloucestershire* (4 vols, 1964 and 1965) *(PNG)*

Smith, F. B., *The People's Health, 1830–1910* (1990)

Smith, P. and Rowbotham, S., *Commemorative Plaques of Cheltenham* (Cheltenham Civic Society, 2009)

Smiths Industries at Cheltenham. The story of 50 years at Bishops Cleeve, 1940–1990 (Smiths Industries Aerospace and Defence Systems, 1990)

Spence, C. and Brown, F., *Thomas Robins the Elder, 1716–1770* (Bath, 2006)

Stafford, P. A., 'The "Farm of one night" and the organisation of King Edward's estates in Domesday', *Economic History Review*, xxxiii, no. 4 (1980)

Stamp, D., *The Land of Britain* (1942)

Stenton, F., *Anglo-Saxon England* (1950)

Sweet, R., *Antiquaries: The Discovery of the Past in Eighteenth-century Britain* (2004)

Tate, W. E., *The Parish Chest* (1969)

Tawney, A. J. and R. H., 'An occupational census of the seventeenth century', *Economic History Review*, v (1934)

The Chief Elements used in English Place-Names, edited by A. Mawer English Place-Name Society, i, pt 2 (1930)

The Universal British Directory, ii (?1792, reprinted King's Lynn, 1993)

Torode, B., *Cheltenham: The Story of Tivoli 'near this town'* (1998)

Turner, M., *Enclosures in Britain, 1750–1830* (The Economic History Society, 1984)

Vaughan, J., *The English Guide Book, c.1780–1870* (1974)

Venn, J. and J. A., *Alumni Cantabrigienses: a biographical list of all known students, graduates, and holders of office at the University of Cambridge, from the earliest times to 1900* (1974–78)

Walker, D., 'The Charters of the Earldom of Hereford', *Camden Miscellany*, xxii (1964)

Watson, N., *When the Question is Steam: The Story of Spirax-Sarco* (Spirax-Sarco, 2000)

Welch, A. M., 'Old Arle Court', *TBGAS*, xxxvi (1913)

Welch, F. B. 'The manor of Charlton Kings, later Ashley', *TGBAS*, liv (1932)

Whitaker, J., *The Best* (Cheltenham, 1998)

White, P., 'The Grovefield Estate and its houses', *CLSHJ*, xv (1999)

Willard, J. F., 'Taxation boroughs and parliamentary boroughs', 1294–1336', in *Historical Essays in Honour of James Tait* (Manchester, 1933)

William Cobbett's Illustrated Rural Rides, 1821–1832, compiled by C. Morris (Exeter, 1984)

Williams, A. R., 'The General Strike in Gloucestershire', *TBGAS*, xci (1972)

Williams, D. E., *The Lygons of Madresfield Court* (Logaston Press, 2001)

Williams, G. A., *A New Guide to Cheltenham* (1825)

Williams, W. R., *The Parliamentary History of the county of Gloucester (1212–1898)* (Hereford, 1898)

Wilson, G. J., 'The Land-tax problem', *Economic History Review*, 2nd series, xxxv (1982)

Wormald, P. edited by *Ideal and Reality in Frankish and Anglo-Saxon Society* (1983)

Wrigley, E. A.,*Nineteenth-century Society* (Cambridge, 1972)

——, 'The occupational structure of England in the mid-nineteenth century', *Poverty, Progress and Population* (Cambridge, 2004)

——, *Poverty, Progress and Population* (Cambridge, 2004)

Wyatt, I., 'Trades and occupations in Gloucester, Tewkesbury and Cirencester in 1608', *Gloucestershire Historical Studies*, vii (1976), 2–34

Yelling, J. A., 'Land, property and planning', in M. Daunton (ed.), *The Cambridge Urban History*, iii (2000)

INDEX

Index entries in *italic* type refer to illustrations or, more usually, to the text of their accompanying captions.

ACKNOWLEDGEMENTS

My thanks first to all in Cheltenham Borough Council for help while writing this book. The Council had an excellent website, http://www.cheltenham.gov.uk, which included information on recent decisions, on development plans, and on the amenities owned by the council, although this has since been redeveloped. Staff working in the council's offices have cheerfully and speedily answered questions and traced relevant departments and people, and include John Steed, Head of Service Development (Customer Access and Service Transformation Division), who searched for a missing item, Karen Radford, Heritage, Derek Aldridge, Town Hall & Entertainment Manager and Susan Sullivan, Press and Marketing Office at Pittville Pump Room. Helen Brown, Collections Manager, and Ann-Rachael Harwood, Curator of Human History at Cheltenham Art Gallery and Museum, have been most helpful. A particular debt is owed to Steven Blake, who is unfailingly generous in sharing his wide knowledge of Cheltenham's history and of the museum's resources, and has prevented some errors being made, though all the inevitable errors through mis-reading, mis-understanding and mis-interpretaion are the author's. The librarians of Cheltenham Reference Library have willingly responded to requests. Thanks are extended to Donna Renney, Chief Executive, Cheltenham Festivals, who provided published material on the music and literary festivals, and to Jackie McKenzie, Press and Marketing Officer of the Everyman Theatre. The Holst Birthplace Museum helpfully gave me copies of material they hold.

Information has been given by some long-established firms in the town: Mrs J. S. Husband, secretary to the chief executive of Spirax-Sarco sent me a copy of their substantial history, and Mick Fereday secured illustrations of the St Mark's factory; Andrew Read, Marketing Assistant, Kohler Mira, provided a copy of their history and John Makuch and David Pixton provided some excellent early photographs. Alan Thompson of the Public Affairs and Corporate Communications Unit, GCHQ, sent books about that organisation coming to Cheltenham. Mike Spittle and Rebecca West gave help on the UCAS building.

A research project of this kind relies very much on the resources of Gloucestershire Archives, and on the staff, all of whom are thanked. I should particularly like to mention Vicky Thorpe, Customer Services Manager, who has a deep knowledge of Cheltenham Borough records, and has answered many questions, and Shaun Carroll who scanned illustrations on several different occasions. Caro McIntosh at the University of Gloucestershire also provided a scan for the book. Ray Wilson helped to make available articles in the annual *Transactions of the Bristol and Gloucestershire Archaeological Society*, and Geoffrey North of Cheltenham History Society supplied back numbers of the journal and has also answered questions. Jane Sale and James Hodsdon generously shared information.

Many people have allowed me to photograph their houses and often, too, lent me helpful material. My thanks go to Mr and Mrs P. Ball, Mr and Mrs P. Grainger, Mr and Mrs L. Bailey, Mr and Mrs B. Morris, Mr and Mrs M. Neal, Mr C. Rayward, Mr D. Rees, Mr M. Williams, Mr and Mrs J. Wright. I am glad to mention also permissions from Anjna Patel-Holtham, Manor House coordinator, Cheltenham College, Cheltenham Ladies' College, Claire Minett, manager, Waterstones of Cheltenham, Inlingua, St Edward's school, Sue Ryder Care and Zizzi. Monica Maiman early provided splendid encouragement and scans of the beautiful fan which is in her possession. Joe Stevens and Mary Nelson have made several illustrations available to me. Eric Miller's fine collection of prints and lithographs have made an outstanding contribution to the illustration of *Cheltenham: A New History* and I am glad to offer him my sincere thanks.

It is a pleasure to thank John Yorke once more for permission to publish extracts from the letters of his ancestor Mary Yorke. Eve Andrew, Mary Ralphs and Margaret Brearley lent me books and offered personal support, and Tom Jones is thanked for urging me to return to writing after the death of my husband. My son, Peter, created two databases and later repaired them, too. Judith Franks, while at Carnegie Publishing, contributed much practical effort to the book, and Alistair Hodge first stimulated the project, and encouraged and supported it through not one but two periods of inactivity. Working with him and with his editor, Dr Alan Crosby, has been a pleasure. Alan's lovely sense of humour and sharp eye for detail, accuracy and irrelevance made the editing fun and the book a much better one.

To all who have offered help and observations this is a sincere thank you.